CHILDREN'S WORLD ATLAS

Consultant

Dr Kathleen Baker

Senior Lecturer in Geography, King's College London (retired)
Senior Visiting Fellow, London South Bank University

Written by

Simon Adams • Mary Atkinson • Sarah Phillips • John Woodward

A Dorling Kindersley Book

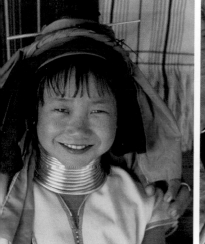

**LONDON, NEW YORK,
MUNICH, MELBOURNE, AND DELHI**

Project editors Lucy Hurst, Sadie Smith,
Shaila Awan, Amber Tokeley
Art editors Joe Conneally, Sheila Collins,
Rebecca Johns, Simon Oon, Andrew Nash
Senior editor Fran Jones
Senior art editor Floyd Sayers
Managing editor Andrew Macintyre
Managing art editor Jane Thomas
Picture research Carolyn Clerkin, Brenda Clynch
DK Pictures Sarah Mills
Production Jenny Jacoby
DTP designer Siu Yin Ho
Senior cartographic editor Simon Mumford
Cartographer Ed Merritt
Digital Cartography Encompass Graphics Limited
Satellite images Rob Stokes
3D globes Planetary Visions Ltd., London

THIS EDITION
Editor Jessamy Wood
Art editors Mark Lloyd, Katie Knutton
Senior editor Rob Houston
Senior art editor Carol Davis
Managing editor Linda Esposito
Managing art editor Jim Green
Picture research Myriam Megharbi
Production editor Marc Staples
Print production Charlotte Oliver
Senior cartographic editor Simon Mumford
Satellite images Ed Merritt
3D Globes Planetary Visions Ltd., London

First published in Great Britain in 2003
This revised edition first published in 2011 by
Dorling Kindersley Limited, 80 Strand, London WC2R 0RL

Copyright © 2003, 2008, 2011 Dorling Kindersley Limited
A Penguin Company

10 9 8 7 6 5 4 3 2 1
001 – 179338 – Jun/11

ISBN: 978-1-40536-391-4

Colour reproduction by Colourscan, Singapore, and MDP, UK
Printed and bound by Star Standard Industries Ltd, Singapore

Discover more at
www.dk.com

Contents

Active Planet

EARTH IS A DYNAMIC PLANET that is always changing its form. Heat generated by nuclear reactions deep below the surface creates hugely powerful currents that keep Earth's rocks on the move, triggering earthquakes and volcanic eruptions. Meanwhile, solar energy striking the planet in different ways creates currents in the air, driving the atmospheric turmoil of the weather. This changes with the seasons and from place to place, creating an enormous range of climates and habitats for the most dynamic element of all – life.

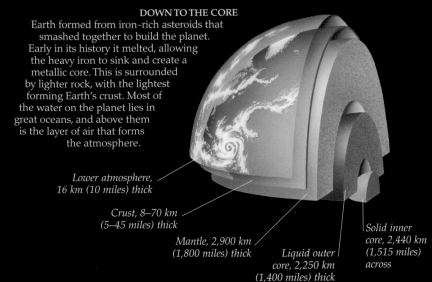

DOWN TO THE CORE
Earth formed from iron-rich asteroids that smashed together to build the planet. Early in its history it melted, allowing the heavy iron to sink and create a metallic core. This is surrounded by lighter rock, with the lightest forming Earth's crust. Most of the water on the planet lies in great oceans, and above them is the layer of air that forms the atmosphere.

Lower atmosphere, 16 km (10 miles) thick

Crust, 8–70 km (5–45 miles) thick

Mantle, 2,900 km (1,800 miles) thick

Liquid outer core, 2,250 km (1,400 miles) thick

Solid inner core, 2,440 km (1,515 miles) across

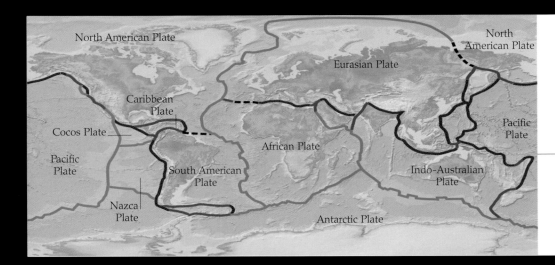

North American Plate

Caribbean Plate

Cocos Plate

Pacific Plate

South American Plate

Nazca Plate

Eurasian Plate

African Plate

North American Plate

Pacific Plate

Indo-Australian Plate

Antarctic Plate

THE PLATES OF EARTH'S CRUST
Heat generated deep within the planet creates currents in the mobile mantle rock beneath the crust. These currents drag some sections of the cool, brittle crust apart while pushing other parts together, fracturing the crust into separate plates. The biggest of these span oceans and continents, but there are many smaller plates. At their boundaries the plates may be diverging (pulling apart), converging (pushing together), or sliding past each other at transform faults.

Key to map

———— Transform fault

– – – – Uncertain boundary

———— Divergent boundary

———— Convergent boundary

WHERE MOVING PLATES MEET
The boundaries between the plates are volcanic earthquake zones. The plates move very slowly, pulling apart at divergent boundaries. This allows hot rock below to melt, erupt, and cool to form new crust – especially at the spreading rifts that form mid-ocean ridges. Meanwhile at convergent boundaries, one plate slides beneath another, pushing up mountain ranges and making volcanoes erupt. Other volcanoes erupt over hot spots in the mantle below the crust.

1 Continental crust, much thicker than oceanic crust

2 Broad basin formed near uplifted area

3 Ancient converging boundary, now inactive

4 Mountains created when plate boundary was active

5 Oceanic crust formed from heavy basalt rock

6 Upper mantle, mainly solid but very hot

7 Mantle, solid but mobile owing to heat currents

8 Spreading rift forming a mid-ocean ridge

9 Hot-spot volcano erupting over mantle plume

10 Ocean trench marking convergent plate boundary

11 Volcano erupting over convergent boundary

12 Earthquake zone – one plate grinding under another

13 Plates pulling apart, creating a rift valley

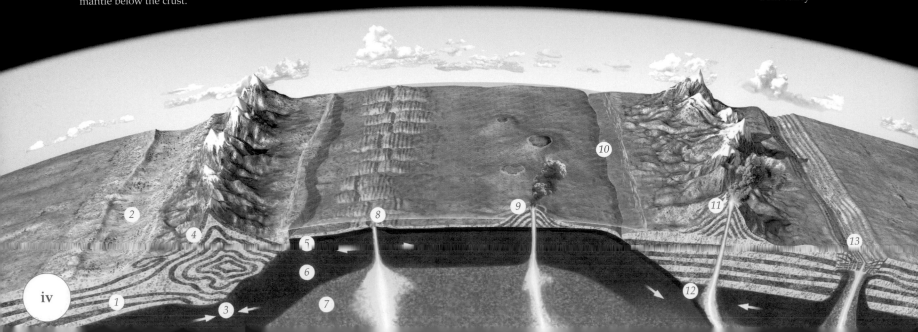

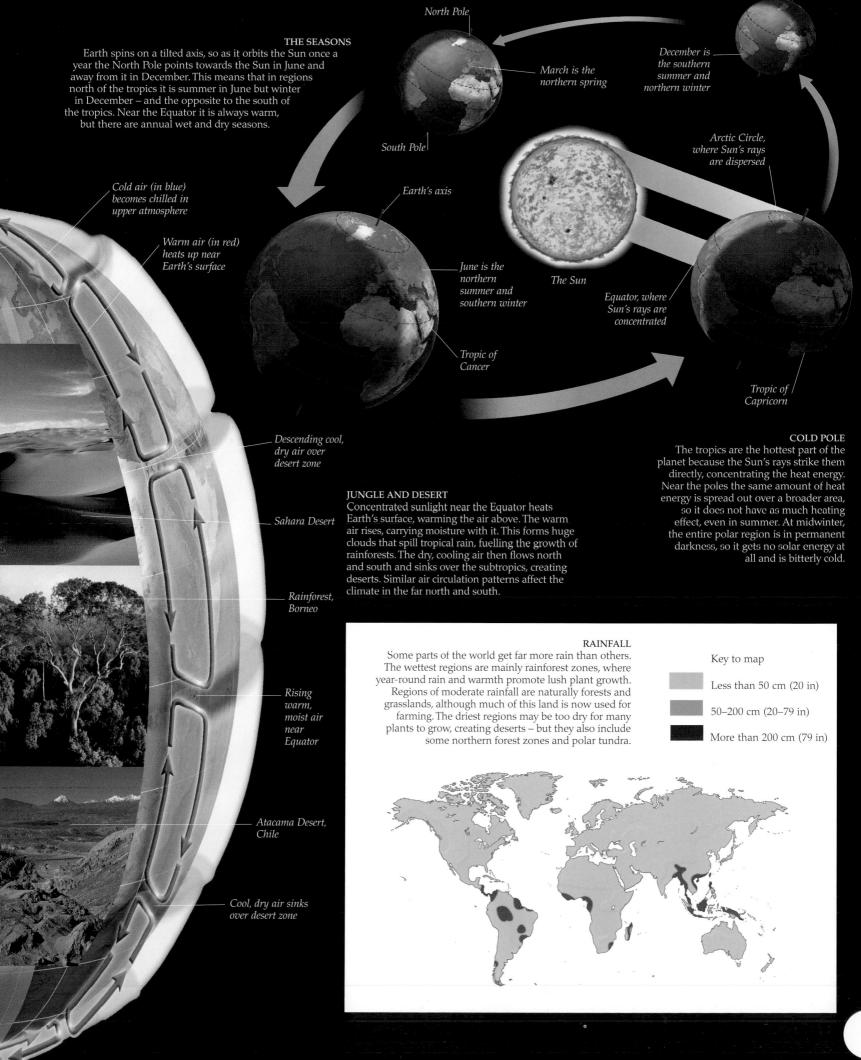

THE SEASONS

Earth spins on a tilted axis, so as it orbits the Sun once a year the North Pole points towards the Sun in June and away from it in December. This means that in regions north of the tropics it is summer in June but winter in December – and the opposite to the south of the tropics. Near the Equator it is always warm, but there are annual wet and dry seasons.

North Pole

South Pole

March is the northern spring

December is the southern summer and northern winter

Cold air (in blue) becomes chilled in upper atmosphere

Warm air (in red) heats up near Earth's surface

Earth's axis

The Sun

Arctic Circle, where Sun's rays are dispersed

June is the northern summer and southern winter

Equator, where Sun's rays are concentrated

Tropic of Cancer

Tropic of Capricorn

Descending cool, dry air over desert zone

Sahara Desert

Rainforest, Borneo

Rising warm, moist air near Equator

Atacama Desert, Chile

Cool, dry air sinks over desert zone

JUNGLE AND DESERT

Concentrated sunlight near the Equator heats Earth's surface, warming the air above. The warm air rises, carrying moisture with it. This forms huge clouds that spill tropical rain, fuelling the growth of rainforests. The dry, cooling air then flows north and south and sinks over the subtropics, creating deserts. Similar air circulation patterns affect the climate in the far north and south.

COLD POLE

The tropics are the hottest part of the planet because the Sun's rays strike them directly, concentrating the heat energy. Near the poles the same amount of heat energy is spread out over a broader area, so it does not have as much heating effect, even in summer. At midwinter, the entire polar region is in permanent darkness, so it gets no solar energy at all and is bitterly cold.

RAINFALL

Some parts of the world get far more rain than others. The wettest regions are mainly rainforest zones, where year-round rain and warmth promote lush plant growth. Regions of moderate rainfall are naturally forests and grasslands, although much of this land is now used for farming. The driest regions may be too dry for many plants to grow, creating deserts – but they also include some northern forest zones and polar tundra.

Key to map

Less than 50 cm (20 in)

50–200 cm (20–79 in)

More than 200 cm (79 in)

Planet People

THE NUMBER OF PEOPLE ON THE PLANET has quadrupled since 1900. Much of this growth has taken place in the developing world, which is now home to more than 80 per cent of the population. Many of these people are very poor and do not enjoy the living conditions that most citizens of the developed world take for granted. This is changing, however, especially in nations such as China, India, and Brazil. Here, new technology and international trade are fuelling rapid economic growth that is transforming how people live. But as more of the planet's people demand more of its scarce resources, there may be some difficult challenges ahead.

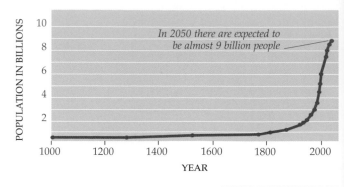

In 2050 there are expected to be almost 9 billion people

POPULATION INCREASE
For centuries, the number of people on the planet stayed the same, at roughly 300 million. But since the 1750s, better living conditions and healthcare have allowed more babies to survive, causing a population explosion. In just 60 years from 1950, the population soared from 2.5 billion to 6.8 billion. It will keep growing, but probably not quite so fast.

POPULATION DENSITY
On this map the area of each part of the world is adjusted to reflect the number of people who live there. For example, Japan's population of 128 million is far bigger than that of Australia, with 22 million, so it is shown much larger here despite being a smaller country. More people live in Nigeria – 153 million – than in the whole of Russia. But the nations with the biggest populations by far are India and China, each with far more than 1 billion citizens.

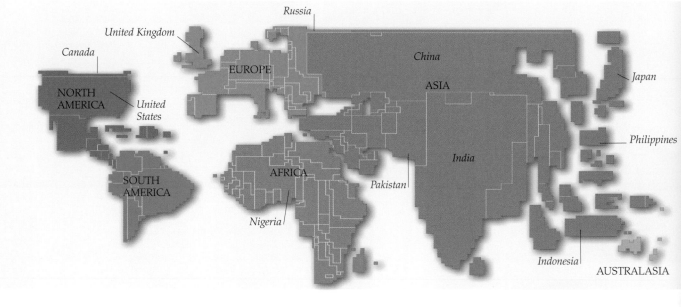

FAMILY SIZE
All over the world, some women have more children than others, but the average varies from continent to continent. European women have 1.5 children on average, so two families may have three children between them. This is far fewer than in Africa, where the population is growing faster despite higher death rates among children. Worldwide the average is 2.6 – more than enough to replace both parents.

AFRICA	ASIA	SOUTH AMERICA	NORTH AMERICA	AUSTRALASIA	EUROPE

4.6 children per woman	*2.3 children per woman*	*2.2 children per woman*	*2 children per woman*	*1.8 children per woman*	*1.5 children per woman*

BIRTH AND DEATH RATES
If the birth rate is the same as the death rate, the population stays the same. But in most countries, the birth rate is higher. In Niger, west Africa, there are 50.6 births but only 13.1 deaths per 1,000 people, and the population is growing at 4 per cent a year. Brazil's population is also growing, with 14.2 births against 6.5 deaths. By contrast, Lithuania has a shrinking population, with 9.9 births outweighed by 13.8 deaths.

A country with few young people is said to have an ageing population. But these school children in Burundi, east Africa, are part of a youthful population, with fewer old people. Both situations can cause problems.

NIGER

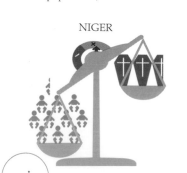

BRAZIL

LITHUANIA

CITY POPULATIONS

As populations grow, people tend to move from the country to a city to find work. Today, one-third of the world's people live in cities, which grow bigger every year. Some are colossal, like Tokyo – the largest city in Asia. The other cities shown here are the most populous on each continent. They are vibrant centres of civilization, but some cities are fringed by sprawling shantytowns, where poor people live in makeshift shacks with no proper services such as clean water.

34,000,000
23,400,000
22,200,000
20,900,000
15,200,000
12,400,000
4,475,000

TOKYO   MEXICO CITY   NEW YORK   SÃO PAULO   CAIRO   LONDON   SYDNEY

LANGUAGES

These are the 10 most common languages worldwide, sized in proportion to the number of native speakers. Chinese outstrips the others because China has such a huge population. But Spanish comes next because it is the main language of many Latin American countries, such as Mexico. English is almost as common, thanks mainly to being the language of the United States. It is also used as an international language for trade.

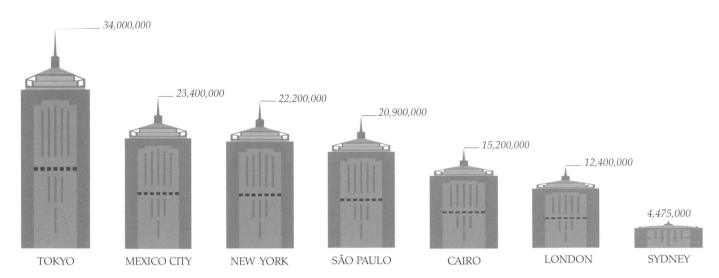

HINDI ARABIC SPANISH
CHINESE
ENGLISH PORTUGUESE RUSSIAN
JAPANESE BENGALI GERMAN

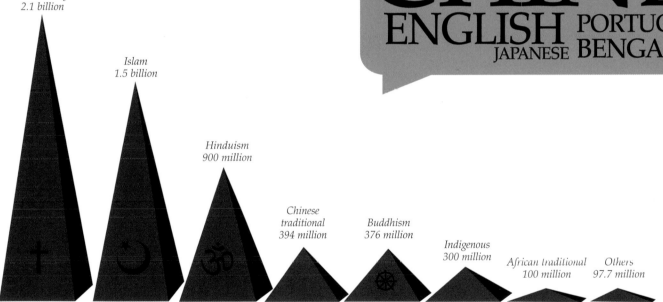

Christianity
2.1 billion

Islam
1.5 billion

Hinduism
900 million

Chinese
traditional
394 million

Buddhism
376 million

Indigenous
300 million

African traditional
100 million

Others
97.7 million

Others	
Sikhism	*23 million*
Juche	*19 million*
Spiritism	*15 million*
Judaism	*14 million*
Baha'i	*7 million*
Jainism	*4.2 million*
Shinto	*4 million*
Cao Đài	*4 million*
Zoroastrianism	*2.6 million*
Tenrikyo	*2 million*
Neo-Paganism	*1 million*
Unitarian Universalism	*800,000*
Rastafarianism	*600,000*
Scientology	*500,000*

RELIGIONS AND BELIEFS

Almost three-quarters of the world's population are followers of Christianity, Islam, Hinduism, or Buddhism. But many people follow other faiths, particularly in China where the traditional folk religion, Shenism, is practised by nearly one-third of the huge population. The "indigenous" and "African traditional religions" data points are both groupings of different, but similar, religions. Others are listed at far right, in order of popularity.

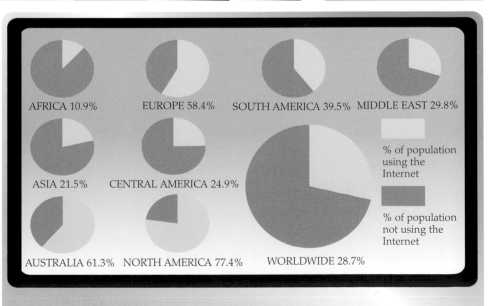

AFRICA 10.9%   EUROPE 58.4%   SOUTH AMERICA 39.5%   MIDDLE EAST 29.8%

ASIA 21.5%   CENTRAL AMERICA 24.9%

% of population using the Internet

% of population not using the Internet

AUSTRALIA 61.3%   NORTH AMERICA 77.4%   WORLDWIDE 28.7%

ONLINE ACCESS

Over the last decade, the Internet has become a vital tool for global business, education, and politics, so the more people who can use it, the better. These charts show the percentage of people with Internet access both worldwide and in particular regions. North America, Australia, and Europe lead the field, but the number of Internet users is growing fastest in the Middle East and Africa.

PLANET PEOPLE

WEALTH

A country's wealth is usually measured in terms of the money it earns divided by the number of its citizens. This is called its Gross National Product (GNP) per capita. Qatar in the Middle East has huge wealth generated by exports of oil and natural gas, and since it has a small population, its GNP per capita is very high. Burundi in east Africa has only one-thirtieth of the income of Qatar divided between seven times as many people, so its GNP per capita is very low.

Burundi	Bolivia	Lithuania	Japan	Canada	Norway	Qatar
$135	$1,457	$11,871	$38,207	$41,729	$87,068	$93,201

BUSIEST AIRPORTS

Air travel has expanded hugely since the 1950s, when international air travel was a luxury enjoyed by a few wealthy people known as the "jet set". Today, flying is often the most economical way to travel, as well as the quickest. This is reflected in the vast number of passengers who pass through the world's airports as they travel for business or pleasure. The busiest airport is Hartsfield-Jackson International Airport in Atlanta, USA, with more than 90 million people arriving and departing each year.

AIRBUS A380

The growth in air travel has led to the development of giant airliners such as the Airbus A380. When it entered service in 2007, this was the world's largest passenger plane, capable of carrying up to 853 people. The first commercial jet airliner, the Comet 1, had seats for only 44 passengers at most.

HARTSFIELD-JACKSON, ATLANTA, USA
90,039,280

HEATHROW, LONDON, UK
67,056,379

TOKYO, JAPAN
66,754,829

KINGSFORD SMITH, SYDNEY, AUSTRALIA

GUARULHOS, SÃO PAULO, BRAZIL
32,900,000

TAMBO, JO'BURG, RSA

20,400,304

18,400,000

TRADE

Although air freight is an important element of international trade, about 80 per cent of cargoes by weight are transported by sea. Altogether, this adds up to around 8 billion tonnes of freight. Much of this is transported in containers, carried by more than 4,700 container ships. The busiest shipping routes link Europe and North America with the Middle East and Far East, with ports such as Singapore, Shanghai, Dubai, and Rotterdam handling most of the trade.

Traffic in millions of tonnes

400+
300–400
200–300
100–200
20–100
10–20
5–10

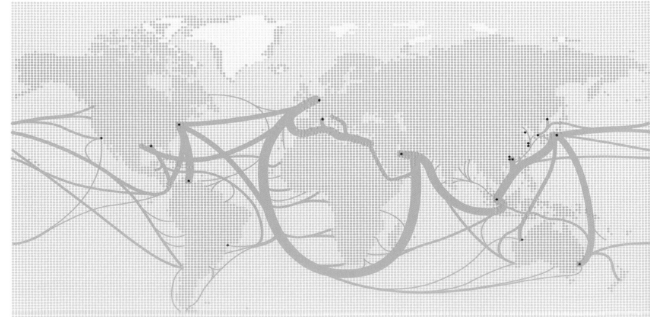

Mapping the World

ABOUT THE ATLAS
This atlas is divided into six continental sections – North America, South America, Africa, Europe, Asia, and Australasia and Oceania. Each country, or group of countries, then has its own map that shows cities, towns, and main geographical features such as rivers, lakes, and mountain ranges. Photographs and text provide detailed information about life in that country – its people, traditions, politics, and economy. Each continental section has a different colour border to help you locate that section. There is also a gazetteer and an index to help you access information.

FOREIGN NAMES
Features on the maps are generally labelled in the language of that country. For example, it would be:

Lake on English-speaking countries
Lago on Spanish-speaking countries
Lac on French-speaking countries

However, if a feature is well-known or mentioned in the main text on the page, it will appear there in English so that readers can find it easily.

MAP LOCATER
This map shows, in red, the location of each country, part of a country, or group of countries in relation to the whole planet. There is a locater for each map in the book.

MAP COLOURS
The colours shown on the maps are built up from numerous satellite photographs and reflect the true colours of the land, averaged over the seasons. Certain colours give clues to what the land is like – whether it is forested or farmland, mountains or desert.

Land appearing sandy tends to be desert, semi-desert, or scrub

Mountainous desert looks like this, with shadows on the sandy background colour

Pale green is usually grassland or crop land

Darker greens usually indicate wooded land or pasture

White shows land under permanent cover by snow and ice

USING THE GRID REFERENCES
The letters and numbers around the outside of the page form a grid to help you find places on the map. For example, to find Kabul, look up its name in the gazetteer (pp 112–133), and you'll find the reference 85 J7. The first number is the page, the letter and number refer to the square made by following up or down from J and across from 7 to form J7.

SCALE
Each map features a scale that shows how distances on the map relate to kilometres and miles. The scale guide can be used to see how big a country is. Not all maps in the book are drawn to the same scale.

KEY TO MAP SYMBOLS

BORDERS

International border: Border between countries which is mutually recognized.

State border: Border used in some large countries to show internal divisions.

Disputed border: Border used in practice, but not mutually agreed between two countries.

Claimed border: Border which is not mutually recognized – where territory belonging to one country is claimed by another.

Ceasefire line

Undefined boundary

PHYSICAL FEATURES

△ Mountain

▽ Depression

◮ Volcano

⤬ Pass/Tunnel

DRAINAGE FEATURES

Major river

Minor river

Seasonal river

Dam

Canal

Waterfall

Seasonal lake

MISCELLANEOUS FEATURES

◇ Site of interest

〰 Ancient wall

COMMUNICATIONS

Highway

Major road

Minor road

Rail

✈ Airport

TOWNS & CITIES

◉ More than 500,000

◉ 100,000 – 500,000

○ 50,000 – 100,000

○ Less than 50,000

● National capital

● Internal administrative capital

● Polar research station

LATITUDE & LONGITUDE

Equator

Tropics/Circles

NAMES

REGIONS

FRANCE Country

JERSEY (to UK) Dependent territory

KANSAS Administrative region

Dordogne Cultural region

TOWNS & CITIES

PARIS National capital

SAN JUAN Dependent territory capital city

Seattle
Limón
Genk
San José
Other towns & cities

NAMES *continued*

PHYSICAL

Andes | Landscape features
Ardennes

Balearic Islands | Island group

Majorca | Island

Lake Baikal | Lake/River /Canal

PACIFIC OCEAN
Gulf of Mexico | Sea features

Bay of Campeche

Chile Rise | Undersea feature

OTHER FEATURES

Tropic of Cancer | Graticule text

NORTH AMERICA

The North American continent extends from the frozen wastes of Arctic Canada to the Caribbean islands and the tropical jungles of Panama. It is dominated politically by the United States, the richest nation on Earth, yet life in countries such as Mexico and Nicaragua is still a struggle. The data below is arranged in order of each nation's size.

Canada
- 9,984,670 sq km
  3,855,103 sq miles
- 33,600,000
- Ottawa
- English, French, Chinese, Italian, German, Ukrainian, Portuguese, Inuktitut, Cree

Mexico
- 1,964,375 sq km
  758,449 sq miles
- 110,000,000
- Mexico City
- Spanish, Nahuatl, Mayan, Zapotec, Mixtec, Otomi, Totonac, Tzotzil, Tzeltal

Honduras
- 112,090 sq km
  43,278 sq miles
- 7,470,000
- Tegucigalpa
- Spanish, Garífuna (Carib), English Creole

United States of America
- 9,826,675 sq km
  3,794,100 sq miles
- 315,000,000
- Washington, DC
- English, Spanish, Chinese, French, German, Tagalog, Vietnamese, Italian, Korean, Russian, Polish

Nicaragua
- 130,370 sq km
  50,336 sq miles
- 5,740,000
- Managua
- Spanish, English Creole, Miskito

The warm seas and glorious beaches of the Caribbean make islands like St Lucia magnets for tourists. The wealth they bring is vital to the local economy.

Cuba
- 110,860 sq km
  42,803 sq miles
- 11,200,000
- Havana
- Spanish

Panama
- 75,420 sq km
  29,120 sq miles
- 3,450,000
- Panama City
- English Creole, Spanish, Amerindian languages, Chibchan languages

Dominican Republic
- 48,670 sq km
  18,792 sq miles
- 10,100,000
- Santo Domingo
- Spanish, French Creole

Guatemala
- 108,889 sq km
  42,042 sq miles
- 14,000,000
- Guatemala City
- Quiché, Mam, Kakchiquel, Kekchí, Spanish

Haiti
- 27,750 sq km
  10,714 sq miles
- 10,000,000
- Port-au-Prince
- French Creole, French

The Statue of Liberty in New York Harbour is a potent symbol of freedom, especially for political refugees to the United States who arrived by ship.

Costa Rica
- 51,100 sq km
  19,730 sq miles
- 4,580,000
- San José
- Spanish, English Creole, Bribri, Cabecar

Belize
- 22,966 sq km
  8,867 sq miles
- 306,800
- Belmopan
- English Creole, Spanish, English, Mayan, Garifuna (Carib)

El Salvador

- 21,041 sq km
  8,124 sq miles
- 6,160,000
- San Salvador City
- Spanish

Dominica

- 751 sq km
  290 sq miles
- 70,400
- Roseau
- French Creole, English

Bahamas

- 13,880 sq km
  5,359 sq miles
- 341,700
- Nassau
- English, English Creole, French Creole

St Lucia

- 616 sq km
  238 sq miles
- 172,200
- Castries
- English, French Creole

Antigua and Barbuda

- 443 sq km
  171 sq miles
- 82,800
- St John's
- English, English Patois

Jamaica

- 10,991 sq km
  4,244 sq miles
- 2,720,000
- Kingston
- English Creole, English

Grenada

- 344 sq km
  133 sq miles
- 103,900
- St George's
- English, English Creole

Much of Canada is still untamed wilderness – a land of huge, dramatic landscapes like this lake high in the rugged, frost-shattered Rocky Mountains.

Trinidad and Tobago

- 5,128 sq km
  1,980 sq miles
- 1,340,000
- Port-of-Spain
- English Creole, English, Hindi, French, Spanish

Barbados

- 430 sq km
  166 sq miles
- 255,900
- Bridgetown
- Bajan (Barbadian English), English

St Vincent and the Grenadines

- 389 sq km
  150 sq miles
- 109,200
- Kingstown
- English, English Creole

St Kitts and Nevis

- 261 sq km
  101 sq miles
- 46,100
- Basseterre
- English, English Creole

Western Canada and Alaska

CANADA IS A HUGE COUNTRY and its western half stretches from the flat prairies in the east to the towering Rocky Mountains in the west, and from the relatively mild south to the permanently frozen area north of the Arctic Circle. Harsh conditions over much of the region mean that most of the population is concentrated in cities in the south, such as Vancouver, Calgary, and Winnipeg. The Prairies – once a vast expanse of grassland – are now used mainly for growing wheat on huge mechanized farms. Oil and natural gas are found there as well. These natural resources are also important in Alaska, a part of the United States. The majority of Alaska's people moved there to work in these lucrative industries.

FORESTRY
Large parts of western Canada are covered in forests and lumbering is a major part of the local economy. The trees are used to make buildings, furniture, and paper. In the past, whole areas of trees were cleared but now sustainable methods, such as selective cutting and replanting, are practised.

Felled trees transported down a river near Vancouver

TOTEM POLES
The native peoples of British Columbia use totem poles to record their clan history. Each carved and painted totem describes a real or mythical event and often features animals that the clan has a close connection with, such as the eagle (left).

DOGSLED RACING
The state sport of Alaska is dogsled racing. Here, competitors take part in the annual Iditarod Trail Sled Dog Race, a gruelling run across the rugged landscape for drivers and their teams of dogs.

VANCOUVER
This city's vibrant cultural mix is typical of Canada's diversity. Many South Asian, Chinese, as well as other ethnic groups live here and reflect Vancouver's historic role as a destination for migrants. Hosting the 2010 Winter Olympics raised its profile and its bustling economy, mild climate, and cultural links make it an attractive place to live.

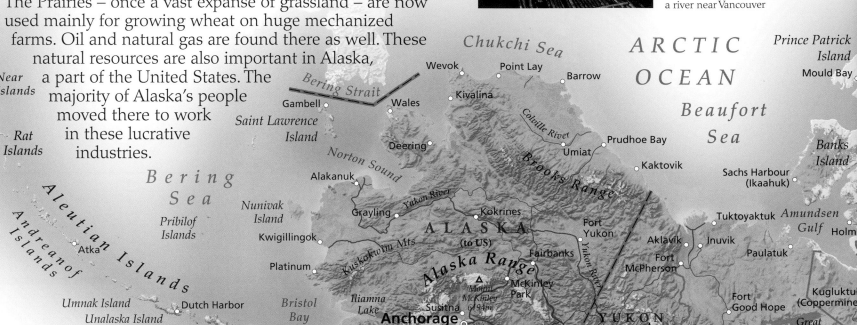

Near Islands

Rat Islands

Andreanof Islands

Aleutian Islands

Atka

Umnak Island
Unalaska Island
Unimak Island

Dutch Harbor

Belkofsky

Chukchi Sea

Bering Strait

Gambell

Wevok
Point Lay
Barrow

Wales
Kivalina

Saint Lawrence Island

Deering

Norton Sound

Bering Sea

Pribilof Islands

Nunivak Island

Alakanuk

Grayling
Yukon River
Kokrines

ALASKA
(to US)

Kwigillingok

Platinum

Kuskokwim Mts

Iliamna Lake

Bristol Bay

Susitna

Alaska Peninsula

Shumagin Islands

Kodiak

Kodiak Island

Katalla

Mount McKinley 6194m

Anchorage

Hope

Valdez

Cordova

Gulkana

Chitina

ARCTIC OCEAN

Prince Patrick Island

Mould Bay

Beaufort Sea

Banks Island

Prudhoe Bay
Umiat
Kaktovik

Brooks Range

Sachs Harbour (Ikaahuk)

Fort Yukon

Fairbanks

McKinley Park

Alaska Range

Aklavik
Fort McPherson

Tuktoyaktuk

Inuvik

Paulatuk

Amundsen Gulf

Holma

Fort Good Hope

Mackenzie

Kugluktuk (Coppermine

Great Bear Lake

Echo

YUKON TERRITORY

Mount Logan 5959m

Whitehorse

Yakutat

Gulf of Alaska

Haines
Gustavus

Atlin

Juneau

Kake

Port Alexander

Ketchikan

Alexander Archipelago

Prince Rupert

Queen Charlotte Islands

Kitimat

Ocean Falls

Queen Charlotte Sound

Port Hardy

Campbell River

Vancouver Island

Nanaimo

Victoria

PACIFIC OCEAN

Tungsten
Fort Simpson

Fort Providence

Fort Liard

Rocky Mountains

BRITISH COLUMBIA

Ware

Prince George

Mount Waddington 4019m

Mount Robson

NORTHWES TERRITORI

Edzo
Yellowknife

Great La

Fort Nelson

Fort St. John

Fort Vermil

Ri

Grande Prairie

Athabas

Athabasca

Edmonton

Red Deer

Calg

ALBERT

Kamloops

Kelowna

Lethbridge

Cranbrook

Milk

UNIT

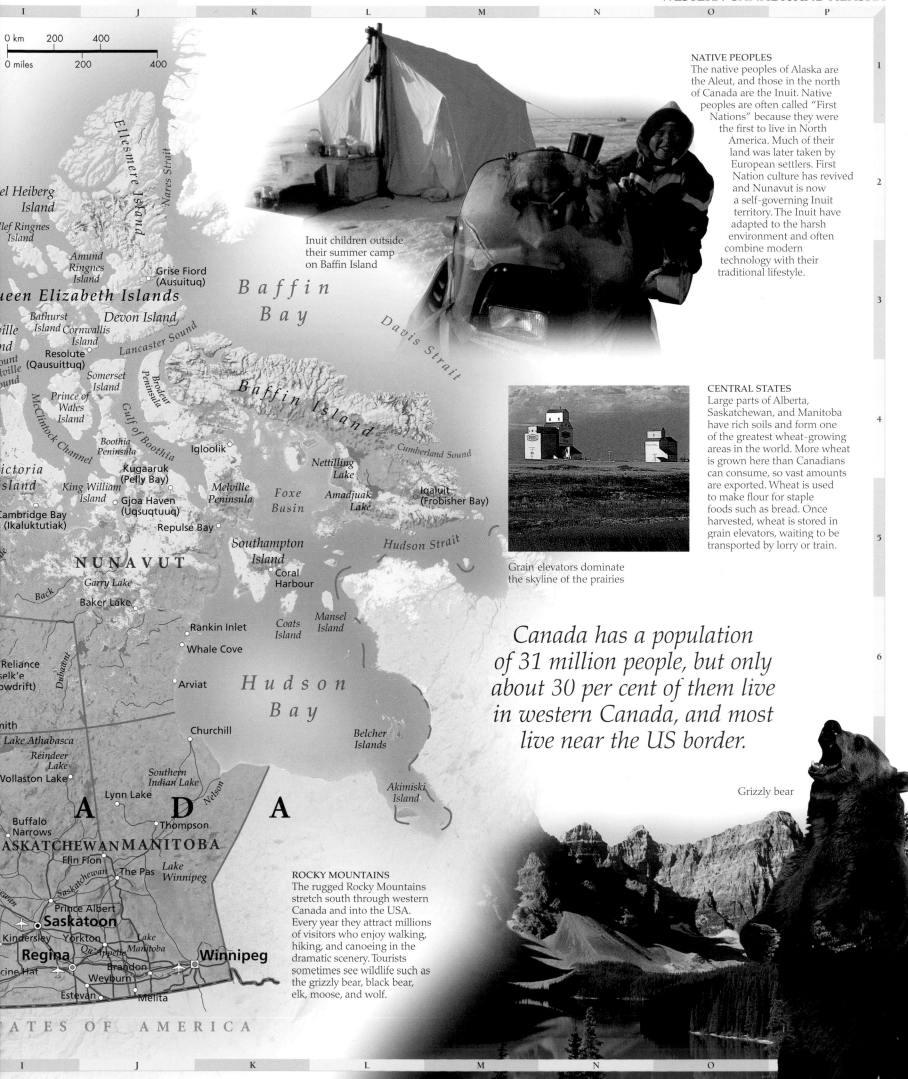

0 km   200   400

0 miles   200   400

Ellesmere Island

el Heiberg
Island

Nares Strait

llef Ringnes
Island

Amund
Ringnes
Island

Grise Fiord
(Ausuittuq)

ueen Elizabeth Islands

Bathurst
Island   Cornwallis
Island

Devon Island

ville
nd

Lancaster Sound

Baffin
Bay

Davis Strait

Resolute
(Qausuittuq)

ount
ville
ound

Somerset
Island

Prince of
Wales
Island

Brodeur
Peninsula

McClintock Channel

Boothia
Peninsula

Gulf of Boothia

Igloolik

Baffin Island

Cumberland Sound

ictoria
land

Kugaaruk
(Pelly Bay)

King William
Island

Melville
Peninsula

Nettilling
Lake

Cambridge Bay
(Ikaluktutiak)

Gjoa Haven
(Uqsuqtuuq)

Foxe
Basin

Amadjuak
Lake

Iqaluit
(Frobisher Bay)

Repulse Bay

NUNAVUT

Southampton
Island

Hudson Strait

Back

Garry Lake

Coral
Harbour

Baker Lake

Reliance
selk'e
owdrift)

Dubawnt

Rankin Inlet

Coats
Island

Mansel
Island

Whale Cove

Arviat

Hudson
Bay

nith

Lake Athabasca

Churchill

Belcher
Islands

Reindeer
Lake

Southern
Indian Lake

Nelson

Akimiski
Island

Vollaston Lake

Lynn Lake

A   D   A

Buffalo
Narrows

Thompson

ASKATCHEWAN   MANITOBA

Elin Flon

Saskatchewan

Lake
Winnipeg

The Pas

Prince Albert

Saskatoon

Lake
Winnipeg

Kindersley   Yorkton

Lake
Manitoba

Regina   Qu'Appelle

Winnipeg

cine Hat

Brandon

Weyburn

Estevan

Melita

ATES   OF   AMERICA

NATIVE PEOPLES

The native peoples of Alaska are the Aleut, and those in the north of Canada are the Inuit. Native peoples are often called "First Nations" because they were the first to live in North America. Much of their land was later taken by European settlers. First Nation culture has revived and Nunavut is now a self-governing Inuit territory. The Inuit have adapted to the harsh environment and often combine modern technology with their traditional lifestyle.

Inuit children outside their summer camp on Baffin Island

CENTRAL STATES

Large parts of Alberta, Saskatchewan, and Manitoba have rich soils and form one of the greatest wheat-growing areas in the world. More wheat is grown here than Canadians can consume, so vast amounts are exported. Wheat is used to make flour for staple foods such as bread. Once harvested, wheat is stored in grain elevators, waiting to be transported by lorry or train.

Grain elevators dominate the skyline of the prairies

Canada has a population of 31 million people, but only about 30 per cent of them live in western Canada, and most live near the US border.

Grizzly bear

ROCKY MOUNTAINS

The rugged Rocky Mountains stretch south through western Canada and into the USA. Every year they attract millions of visitors who enjoy walking, hiking, and canoeing in the dramatic scenery. Tourists sometimes see wildlife such as the grizzly bear, black bear, elk, moose, and wolf.

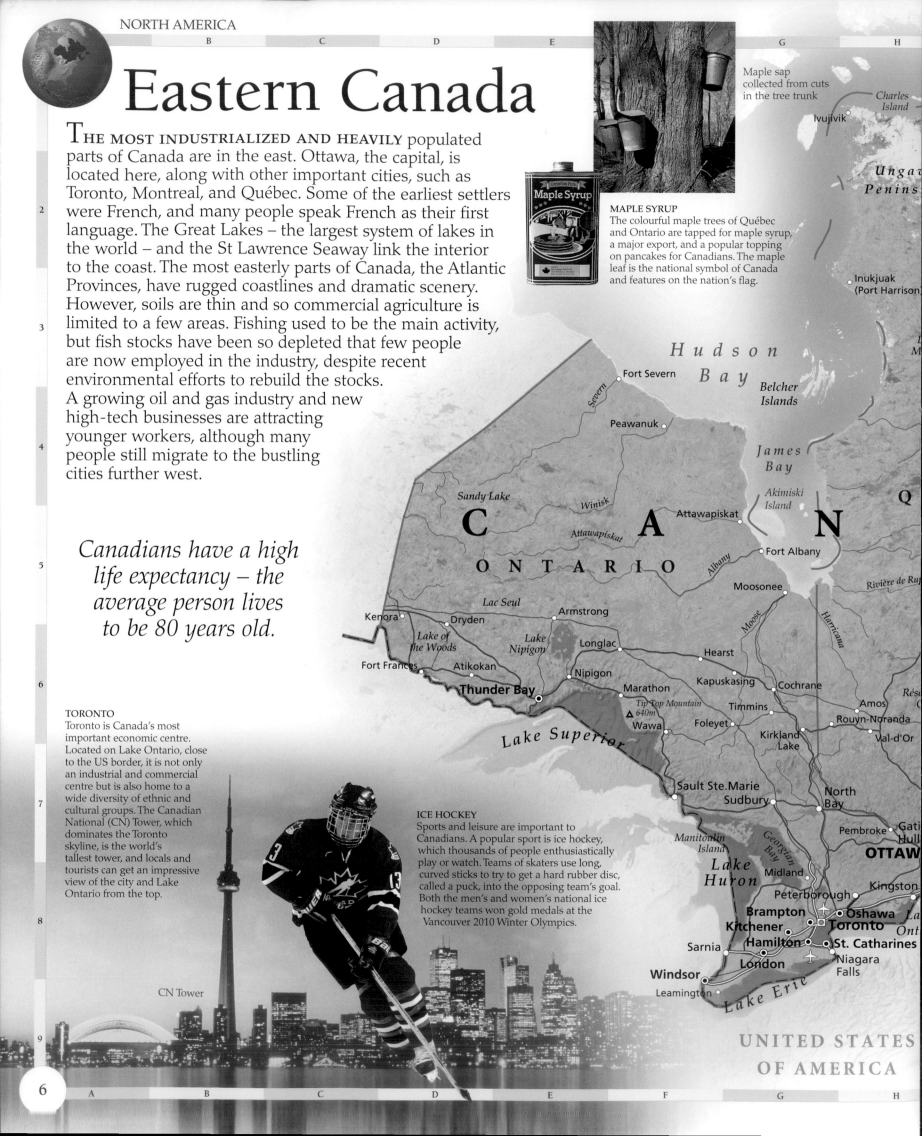

Eastern Canada

THE MOST INDUSTRIALIZED AND HEAVILY populated parts of Canada are in the east. Ottawa, the capital, is located here, along with other important cities, such as Toronto, Montreal, and Québec. Some of the earliest settlers were French, and many people speak French as their first language. The Great Lakes – the largest system of lakes in the world – and the St Lawrence Seaway link the interior to the coast. The most easterly parts of Canada, the Atlantic Provinces, have rugged coastlines and dramatic scenery. However, soils are thin and so commercial agriculture is limited to a few areas. Fishing used to be the main activity, but fish stocks have been so depleted that few people are now employed in the industry, despite recent environmental efforts to rebuild the stocks. A growing oil and gas industry and new high-tech businesses are attracting younger workers, although many people still migrate to the bustling cities further west.

Canadians have a high life expectancy – the average person lives to be 80 years old.

Maple sap collected from cuts in the tree trunk

MAPLE SYRUP
The colourful maple trees of Québec and Ontario are tapped for maple syrup, a major export, and a popular topping on pancakes for Canadians. The maple leaf is the national symbol of Canada and features on the nation's flag.

TORONTO
Toronto is Canada's most important economic centre. Located on Lake Ontario, close to the US border, it is not only an industrial and commercial centre but is also home to a wide diversity of ethnic and cultural groups. The Canadian National (CN) Tower, which dominates the Toronto skyline, is the world's tallest tower, and locals and tourists can get an impressive view of the city and Lake Ontario from the top.

CN Tower

ICE HOCKEY
Sports and leisure are important to Canadians. A popular sport is ice hockey, which thousands of people enthusiastically play or watch. Teams of skaters use long, curved sticks to try to get a hard rubber disc, called a puck, into the opposing team's goal. Both the men's and women's national ice hockey teams won gold medals at the Vancouver 2010 Winter Olympics.

Hudson Bay

Charles Island

Ivujivik

Ungava Peninsula

Inukjuak (Port Harrison)

Fort Severn

Belcher Islands

Peawanuk

James Bay

Akimiski Island

Sandy Lake

Winisk

Attawapiskat

C A N

Attawapiskat

Fort Albany

O N T A R I O

Albany

Moosonee

Rivière de Rup

Lac Seul

Armstrong

Moose

Harricana

Kenora

Dryden

Lake of the Woods

Lake Nipigon

Longlac

Hearst

Kapuskasing

Cochrane

Amos

Rés

Fort Frances

Atikokan

Nipigon

Marathon

Tip Top Mountain ▲ 640m

Timmins

Foleyet

Rouyn-Noranda

Val-d'Or

Thunder Bay

Wawa

Kirkland Lake

Lake Superior

Sault Ste.Marie

Sudbury

North Bay

Manitoulin Island

Georgian Bay

Pembroke

Gati Hull

OTTAW

Lake Huron

Midland

Peterborough

Kingston

Brampton

Kitchener

Oshawa

Toronto

La Ont

Sarnia

Hamilton

St. Catharines

London

Niagara Falls

Windsor

Leamington

Lake Erie

UNITED STATES OF AMERICA

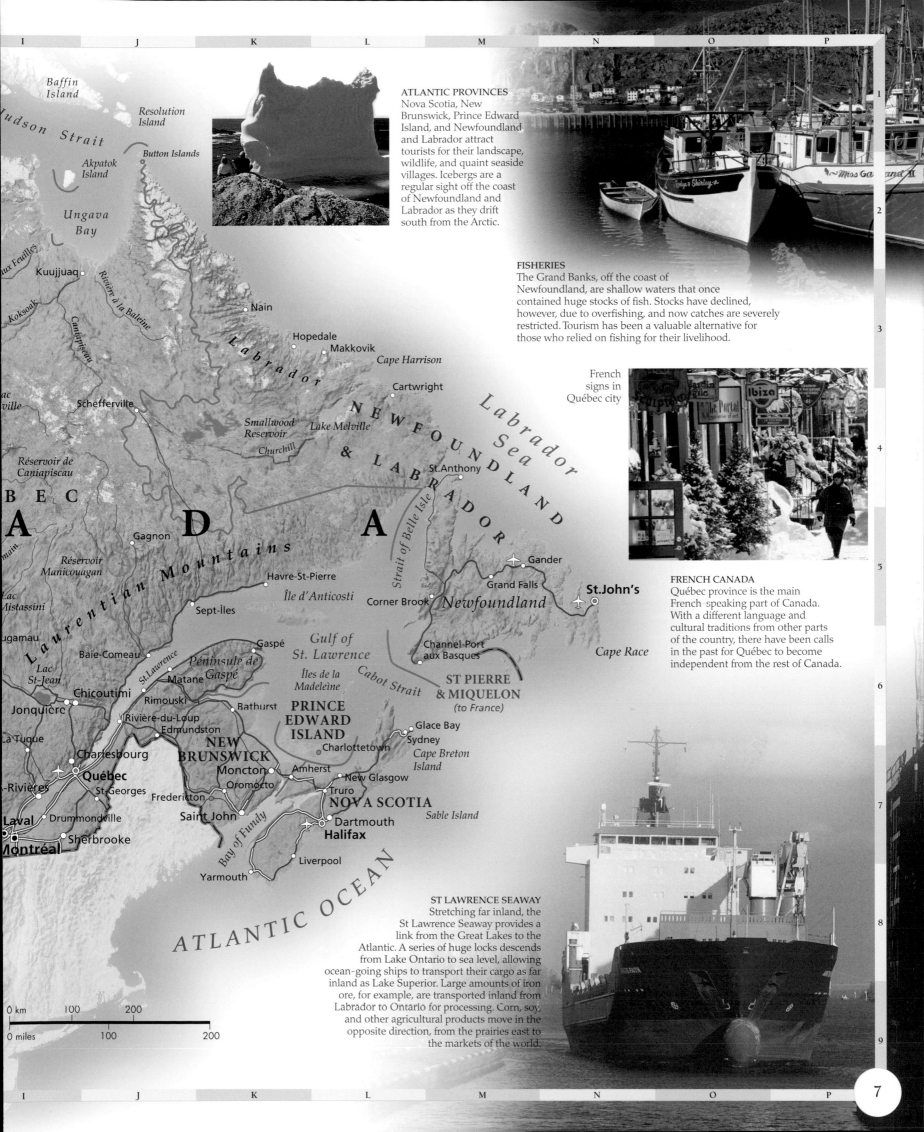

ATLANTIC PROVINCES
Nova Scotia, New Brunswick, Prince Edward Island, and Newfoundland and Labrador attract tourists for their landscape, wildlife, and quaint seaside villages. Icebergs are a regular sight off the coast of Newfoundland and Labrador as they drift south from the Arctic.

FISHERIES
The Grand Banks, off the coast of Newfoundland, are shallow waters that once contained huge stocks of fish. Stocks have declined, however, due to overfishing, and now catches are severely restricted. Tourism has been a valuable alternative for those who relied on fishing for their livelihood.

French signs in Québec city

FRENCH CANADA
Québec province is the main French-speaking part of Canada. With a different language and cultural traditions from other parts of the country, there have been calls in the past for Québec to become independent from the rest of Canada.

ST LAWRENCE SEAWAY
Stretching far inland, the St Lawrence Seaway provides a link from the Great Lakes to the Atlantic. A series of huge locks descends from Lake Ontario to sea level, allowing ocean-going ships to transport their cargo as far inland as Lake Superior. Large amounts of iron ore, for example, are transported inland from Labrador to Ontario for processing. Corn, soy, and other agricultural products move in the opposite direction, from the prairies east to the markets of the world.

Baffin Island
Resolution Island
Hudson Strait
Button Islands
Akpatok Island
Ungava Bay
aux Feuilles
Kuujjuaq
Koksoak
Rivière à la Baleine
Caniapiscau
Nain
Hopedale
Makkovik
Cape Harrison
Cartwright
ville
Scheffervillle
Labrador
NEWFOUNDLAND & LABRADOR
Labrador Sea
Réservoir de Caniapiscau
Smallwood Reservoir
Lake Melville
Churchill
St.Anthony
QUEBEC
CANADA
Gagnon
Laurentian Mountains
Strait of Belle Isle
Gander
Grand Falls
St.John's
Réservoir Manicouagan
Havre-St-Pierre
Île d'Anticosti
Corner Brook
Newfoundland
Lac Mistassini
Sept-Îles
Cape Race
ugamau
Baie-Comeau
Gaspé
Gulf of St. Lawrence
Cabot Strait
Channel-Port aux Basques
ST PIERRE & MIQUELON
(to France)
Péninsule de Gaspé
Îles de la Madeleine
Lac St-Jean
Chicoutimi
Matane
St.Lawrence
Jonquière
Rimouski
Rivière-du-Loup
Bathurst
PRINCE EDWARD ISLAND
Glace Bay
Sydney
Cape Breton Island
La Tuque
Edmundston
NEW BRUNSWICK
Charlottetown
Charlesbourg
St-Georges
Moncton
Amherst
New Glasgow
Québec
Oromocto
Truro
NOVA SCOTIA
Fredericton
Sable Island
Rivières
Saint John
Dartmouth
Laval
Drummondville
Bay of Fundy
Halifax
Montréal
Sherbrooke
Liverpool
Yarmouth

ATLANTIC OCEAN

0 km   100   200
0 miles   100   200

USA: Northeast

THE NORTHEASTERN UNITED STATES is a heavily populated area that is steeped in history. This is traditionally the main immigration point into the States, with the Statue of Liberty lighting the way for those arriving into New York by boat. People from all over the world have settled in this region to live and work, creating a "melting pot" of cultures and ethnic groups. Important historical events, such as the signing of the Declaration of Independence and the Constitution, took place in Philadelphia. These documents set the foundations for American life today. It is also here that the capital and centre of government were established. Today, while industry and agriculture are still important, finance and commerce are the driving forces of the economy.

THRIVING CITY
New York is the largest city in the USA. Historically it grew because it has a good harbour and sits at the mouth of the Hudson River. Immigrants from overseas flooded into the city in the 19th and 20th centuries, boosting its population and economy. Today, it is the main financial centre, not just of the USA, but of the world.

Lake Ontario
Hudson River
New York City
Appalachian Mountains

The White House in Washington, D.C. has been home to every president except George Washington, whom the city is named after.

PITTSBURGH
Once a major steel-manufacturing centre with a polluted environment, Pittsburgh is now a thriving financial centre with a large number of corporate headquarters. Bridges span the three rivers that run through the city, connecting the core downtown area (above) to the suburbs.

CENTRE OF GOVERNMENT
All three branches of the federal government, the executive, legislative, and judicial, reside in Washington D.C. The United States Congress (the legislative branch) meets here in the Capitol building. Many of the city's residents work for the government.

Capitol building, the seat of government

Map labels

CANADA

ONTARIO

St. Lawrence
Ogdensbur

Lake Ontario

Adironda
Mountai

Watertown
Boonville

Oswego

Niagara Falls
Lockport
Rochester
Newark
Syracuse
Utica
A P
Mohawk

Niagara Falls
Avon
NEW YORK

Buffalo
Hamburg
Dansville
Oneonta

Ithaca

Lake Erie
Binghamton
Cats
Moun

Dunkirk

Erie
Jamestown
Allegheny Plateau
Elmira
Sayre

Warren
Mansfield

Meadville
Wilcox
Scranton
Wilkes Barre
Middlet
Milford

Mercer
PENNSYLVANIA

Allegheny River
Du Bois
Lock Haven
Milton
Stroudsberg

OHIO
Butler
State College
Allentow

Indiana
Reading
Trento

Aliquippa
Pittsburgh
Altoona
Appalachian Mountains
Harrisburg
Philadelphia

Washington
Bedford
Carlisle
Lancaster
Cherr
Hill

York
Wilmington

Uniontown
Hagerstown
Aberdeen
Vineland

Cumberland
Towson
Dover

WEST VIRGINIA
Oakland
Baltimore
Columbia

Annapolis
DELAWA

WASHINGTON D.C

VIRGINIA
Cambridge
Ocean City

MARYLAND
Salisbu

Chesapeake Bay

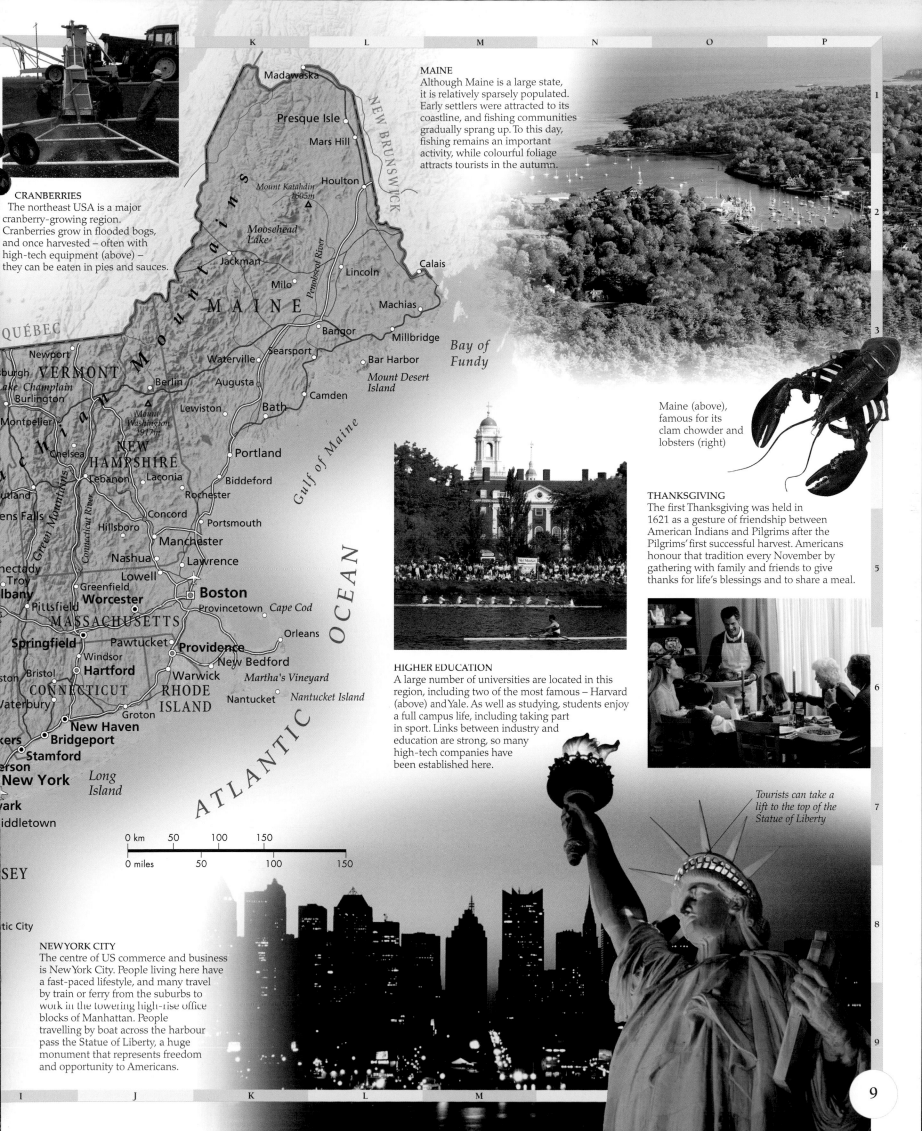

CRANBERRIES
The northeast USA is a major cranberry-growing region. Cranberries grow in flooded bogs, and once harvested – often with high-tech equipment (above) – they can be eaten in pies and sauces.

MAINE
Although Maine is a large state, it is relatively sparsely populated. Early settlers were attracted to its coastline, and fishing communities gradually sprang up. To this day, fishing remains an important activity, while colourful foliage attracts tourists in the autumn.

Maine (above), famous for its clam chowder and lobsters (right)

THANKSGIVING
The first Thanksgiving was held in 1621 as a gesture of friendship between American Indians and Pilgrims after the Pilgrims' first successful harvest. Americans honour that tradition every November by gathering with family and friends to give thanks for life's blessings and to share a meal.

HIGHER EDUCATION
A large number of universities are located in this region, including two of the most famous – Harvard (above) and Yale. As well as studying, students enjoy a full campus life, including taking part in sport. Links between industry and education are strong, so many high-tech companies have been established here.

Tourists can take a lift to the top of the Statue of Liberty

NEW YORK CITY
The centre of US commerce and business is New York City. People living here have a fast-paced lifestyle, and many travel by train or ferry from the suburbs to work in the towering high-rise office blocks of Manhattan. People travelling by boat across the harbour pass the Statue of Liberty, a huge monument that represents freedom and opportunity to Americans.

Map labels: Madawaska, Presque Isle, Mars Hill, Houlton, Mount Katahdin 1605m, Moosehead Lake, Jackman, Milo, Lincoln, Calais, Machias, Bangor, Millbridge, Searsport, Bar Harbor, Mount Desert Island, Bay of Fundy, Camden, Bath, Waterville, Augusta, Lewiston, Penobscot River, MAINE, NEW BRUNSWICK, QUÉBEC, Newport, VERMONT, Lake Champlain, Burlington, Berlin, Montpelier, Mount Washington 1917m, NEW HAMPSHIRE, Chelsea, Portland, Gulf of Maine, Rutland, Lebanon, Laconia, Biddeford, Rochester, Connecticut River, Green Mountains, Hillsboro, Concord, Portsmouth, Manchester, Nashua, Lawrence, Lowell, Greenfield, Worcester, Boston, Provincetown, Cape Cod, Albany, Troy, Pittsfield, MASSACHUSETTS, Springfield, Pawtucket, Providence, Orleans, Windsor, New Bedford, Hartford, Warwick, Martha's Vineyard, CONNECTICUT, RHODE ISLAND, Nantucket, Nantucket Island, Waterbury, Bristol, Groton, New Haven, Bridgeport, Stamford, Yonkers, New York, Long Island, Newark, Middletown, ATLANTIC OCEAN, Atlantic City, NEW JERSEY

Scale: 0 km 50 100 150 / 0 miles 50 100 150

USA: South

THE SOUTHERN STATES of the USA have a varied landscape and an interesting mix of people, both culturally and economically. Some areas of the region are poor, especially the Appalachian Mountain communities, while other parts, such as the Florida coast, are wealthy and attract many people from other states and countries. The cultural mix includes people of Latin American origin, African-Americans, Cajuns (French-Canadians), and European Americans, giving rise to diverse music styles, dialects, pastimes, and food. While coal mining in the Appalachian Mountains has declined in recent years, agriculture is still important, as are tourism and industry. Tourism is particularly important in Florida and in New Orleans near the mouth of the mighty Mississippi River.

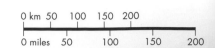

COTTON CROPS
Cotton was once the mainstay crop of the south and was grown by African-American slaves. Today, cotton is still important for the economy of the region and is grown in large fields and harvested with huge machinery. Cotton has many uses, primarily as the raw material for textiles.

Cotton pod, or boll

The Mississippi is the largest river in North America and the third largest in the world.

Jazz musician on Bourbon Street, New Orleans

MUSICAL ORIGINS
The southern USA is famous for its music, much of which reflects the cultural mix of the region. New Orleans and other parts of Louisiana are the birthplaces of jazz and Cajun music, while bluegrass and country have origins in Nashville and Memphis. These music styles started here, but quickly spread throughout the country and developed even further in the cities.

Chef holding a skillet of jambalaya, a Cajun dish

CAJUN CULTURE
The Cajuns in this region are French-speaking people who were expelled from Canada in the 18th century. They mixed with other cultures in Louisiana, but their French influence can be seen in the music, food, and place names, such as Lafayette.

FLORIDA EVERGLADES
The increasing population of Florida means that the Everglades, swampy plains inhabited by alligators and other wildlife, are under threat as land is needed for houses and farms. However, the Everglades National Park protects part of this important ecosystem.

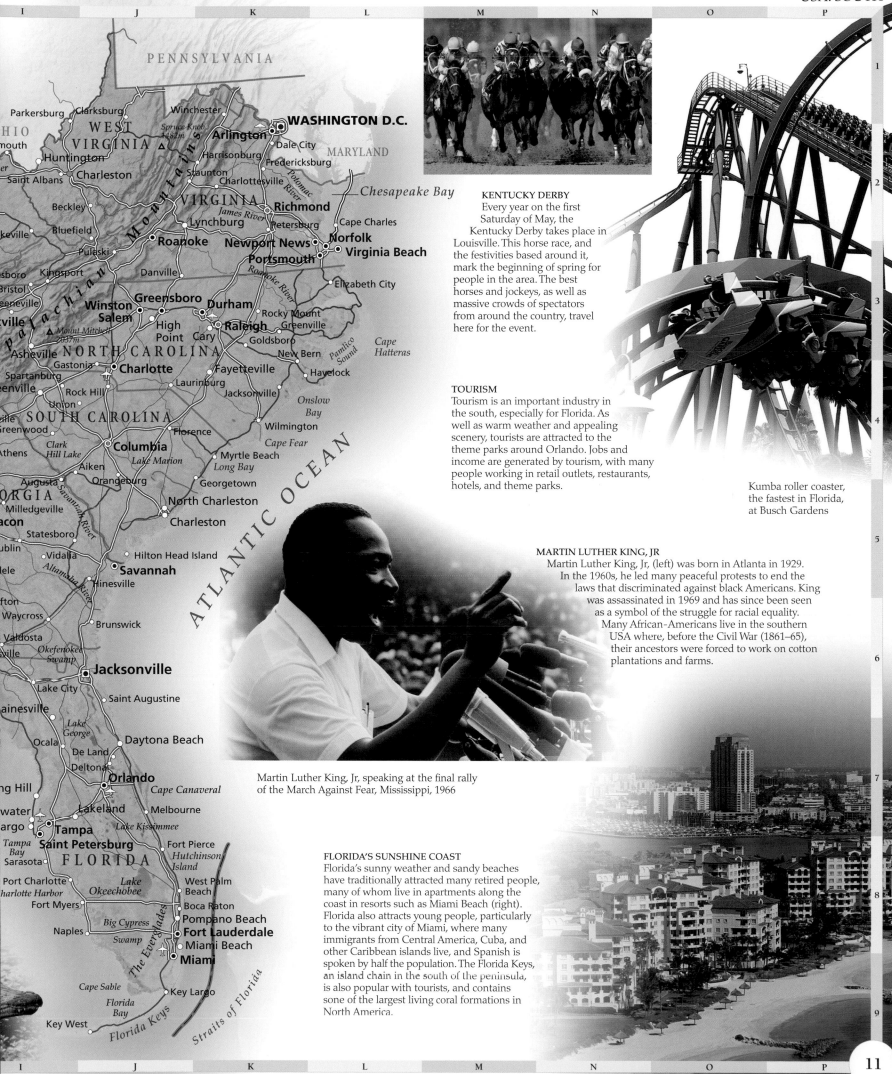

PENNSYLVANIA

Parkersburg
Clarksburg
Winchester
WASHINGTON D.C.
Arlington
Dale City
MARYLAND
Huntington
Harrisonburg
Fredericksburg
Saint Albans
Charleston
Staunton
Charlottesville
WEST
VIRGINIA
Spruce Knob
4482m △

James River
VIRGINIA
Richmond
Beckley
Lynchburg
Petersburg
Cape Charles
Bluefield
Puleski
Roanoke
Roanoke River
Danville
Roanoke
Newport News
Norfolk
Portsmouth
Virginia Beach
Bristol
Kingsport
Chesapeake Bay
Elizabeth City

Winston
Salem
Greensboro
Durham
High
Point
Cary
Raleigh
Rocky Mount
Greenville
△ *Mount Mitchell*
2037m
Asheville
NORTH CAROLINA
Goldsboro
New Bern
Pamlico Sound
Cape Hatteras
Spartanburg
Gastonia
Charlotte
Fayetteville
Rock Hill
Laurinburg
Jacksonville
Onslow Bay
Union
SOUTH CAROLINA
Florence
Wilmington
Greenwood
Clark Hill Lake
Columbia
Lake Marion
Myrtle Beach
Long Bay
Cape Fear
Athens
Aiken
Orangeburg
Georgetown
Augusta
Savannah River
North Charleston
Milledgeville
Statesboro
Charleston
Dublin
Vidalia
Hilton Head Island
Altamaha River
Savannah
Hinesville
Brunswick
Waycross
Valdosta
Okefenokee Swamp
Jacksonville
Lake City
Saint Augustine
Gainesville
Lake George
Ocala
Daytona Beach
De Land
Deltona
Orlando
Cape Canaveral
Hill
Lakeland
Melbourne
water
Lake Kissimmee
argo
Tampa
Fort Pierce
Tampa Bay
Saint Petersburg
Hutchinson Island
Sarasota
FLORIDA
Port Charlotte
Lake Okeechobee
West Palm Beach
Charlotte Harbor
Fort Myers
Boca Raton
Big Cypress Swamp
Pompano Beach
Naples
Fort Lauderdale
Miami Beach
Miami
Cape Sable
Key Largo
Florida Bay
Key West
Florida Keys
Straits of Florida

ATLANTIC OCEAN

KENTUCKY DERBY
Every year on the first Saturday of May, the Kentucky Derby takes place in Louisville. This horse race, and the festivities based around it, mark the beginning of spring for people in the area. The best horses and jockeys, as well as massive crowds of spectators from around the country, travel here for the event.

TOURISM
Tourism is an important industry in the south, especially for Florida. As well as warm weather and appealing scenery, tourists are attracted to the theme parks around Orlando. Jobs and income are generated by tourism, with many people working in retail outlets, restaurants, hotels, and theme parks.

Kumba roller coaster, the fastest in Florida, at Busch Gardens

MARTIN LUTHER KING, JR
Martin Luther King, Jr, (left) was born in Atlanta in 1929. In the 1960s, he led many peaceful protests to end the laws that discriminated against black Americans. King was assassinated in 1969 and has since been seen as a symbol of the struggle for racial equality. Many African-Americans live in the southern USA where, before the Civil War (1861–65), their ancestors were forced to work on cotton plantations and farms.

Martin Luther King, Jr, speaking at the final rally of the March Against Fear, Mississippi, 1966

FLORIDA'S SUNSHINE COAST
Florida's sunny weather and sandy beaches have traditionally attracted many retired people, many of whom live in apartments along the coast in resorts such as Miami Beach (right). Florida also attracts young people, particularly to the vibrant city of Miami, where many immigrants from Central America, Cuba, and other Caribbean islands live, and Spanish is spoken by half the population. The Florida Keys, an island chain in the south of the peninsula, is also popular with tourists, and contains sone of the largest living coral formations in North America.

USA: Midwest

THE AMERICAN MIDWEST is dominated by the Great Plains, once the home of cattle ranches, cowboys, and American Indian peoples. However, the discovery of gold in South Dakota brought a rush of settlers to the area. This, combined with a decline in bison numbers, led to the eventual displacement of the American Indians from the Plains. The area is prone to dramatic weather – tornadoes, freezing blizzards, and blazing hot summers. To the west, vast areas of farmland generate more wheat and maize than anywhere else in the world. East of the Mississippi the landscape varies and, although farming is still important, this is the industrial centre of the country. Big cities, such as Chicago, Detroit, and Cleveland, form the major manufacturing centres.

BUFFALO ON THE PLAINS
Up to 100 million bison once grazed on the Great Plains. They provided local American Indians with food for the family, and skin for clothes and tepees. The Dakota people used bison bones to make shields and tools, and the animal's bladder into a bag for carrying water. But over-hunting and the destruction of the bison's habitat by early European settlers drastically reduced the number of animals. The bison is now a protected species and lives in reserves.

Bison herd on a reserve, South Dakota

MOUNT RUSHMORE NATIONAL MEMORIAL
Mount Rushmore, in the Black Hills of South Dakota, was created as a tribute to the American presidency. Four of the United States' greatest presidents – (left to right) Washington, Jefferson, Roosevelt, and Lincoln – were carved into the granite cliff between 1927 and 1941. Teams of workers hung from saddles anchored to the mountain to complete the work, often enduring harsh winds or blazing sun. Today, it is a popular tourist attraction.

Each carved face is about 18 m (60 ft) high

TORNADO ALLEY
Dramatic tornadoes, or "twisters", regularly tear through the states of Kansas and Missouri, along a path known as Tornado Alley. Tornadoes occur when warm and cold air masses meet. As the warm air rises, it cools, and under the right conditions, it can suck in more and more air until a whirling twister develops. The more air that is drawn in, the greater the power of the tornado.

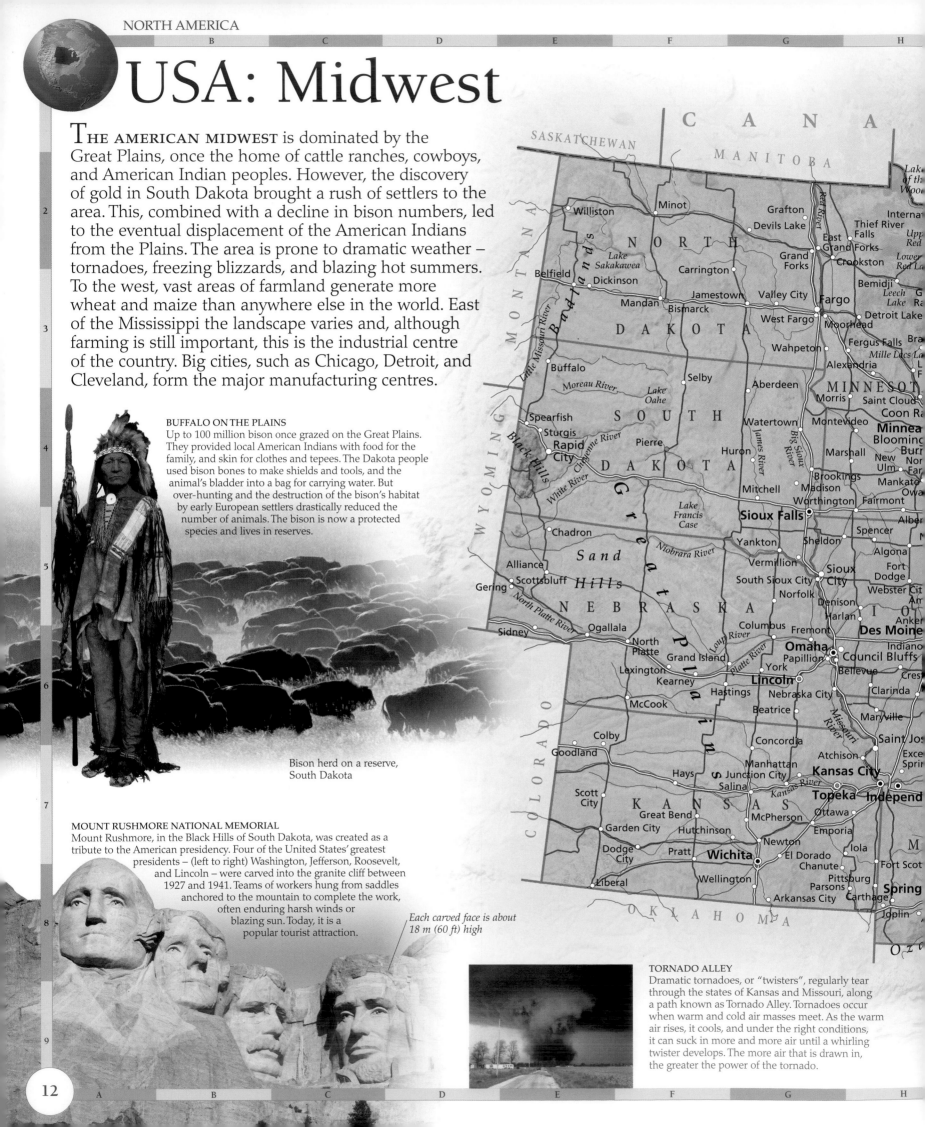

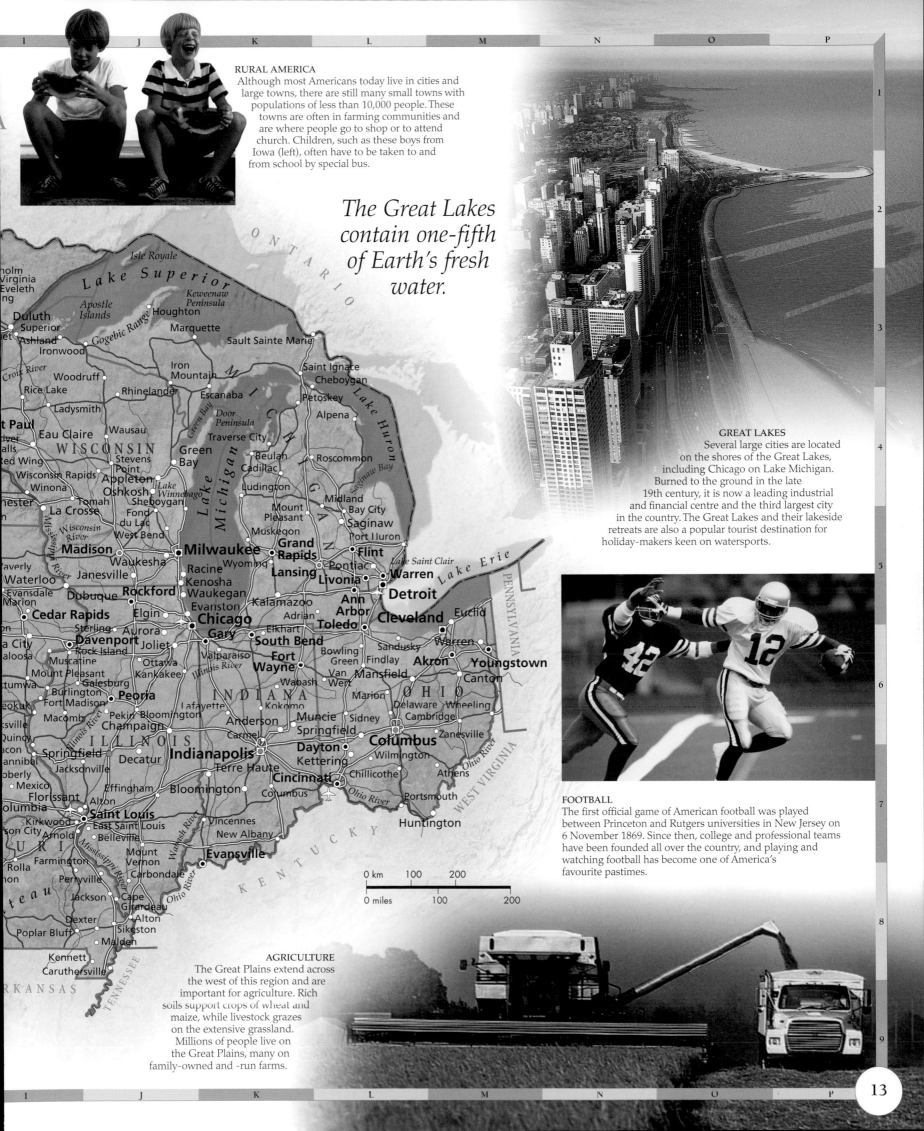

RURAL AMERICA
Although most Americans today live in cities and large towns, there are still many small towns with populations of less than 10,000 people. These towns are often in farming communities and are where people go to shop or to attend church. Children, such as these boys from Iowa (left), often have to be taken to and from school by special bus.

The Great Lakes contain one-fifth of Earth's fresh water.

GREAT LAKES
Several large cities are located on the shores of the Great Lakes, including Chicago on Lake Michigan. Burned to the ground in the late 19th century, it is now a leading industrial and financial centre and the third largest city in the country. The Great Lakes and their lakeside retreats are also a popular tourist destination for holiday-makers keen on watersports.

FOOTBALL
The first official game of American football was played between Princeton and Rutgers universities in New Jersey on 6 November 1869. Since then, college and professional teams have been founded all over the country, and playing and watching football has become one of America's favourite pastimes.

AGRICULTURE
The Great Plains extend across the west of this region and are important for agriculture. Rich soils support crops of wheat and maize, while livestock grazes on the extensive grassland. Millions of people live on the Great Plains, many on family-owned and -run farms.

0 km 100 200
0 miles 100 200

USA: West

THE ROCKY MOUNTAINS separate the coastal region from the drier inland states. Large and fast-growing cities, such as San Francisco, Los Angeles, and San Diego, hug the Pacific coast, and have attracted many migrants because of good job opportunities. Inland, blazing desert and towering mountains provide some of the most dramatic landscapes in the country. National parks, such as Yellowstone in northwestern Wyoming and Montana, and Yosemite in central California, protect some of these wilderness areas. Further east, the foothills of the Rockies give way to vast plains grazed by large herds of cattle.

NORTHERN FORESTS
The coastal areas of Oregon and Washington contain large forests. These produce economically important timber, but much land is also left in its natural state and is popular with hikers. Most people here live in large cities like Seattle, and in the fertile inland valleys.

CALIFORNIA AGRICULTURE
California is warm, fertile, and, with irrigation, ideal for agriculture. Grapes are an important crop north of San Francisco in the Napa Valley. Further south, citrus crops such as oranges also flourish. Premium farming land is under threat, however, as the population expands.

The American Indian name for Death Valley is Tomesha, which means "land where the ground is on fire".

LOS ANGELES
This sprawling city – the second largest in the USA – is home to migrants from all over the world, as well as from other states in the country. Sandwiched between the coast and the mountains, the city has massive air pollution problems. This mostly arises from the exhaust fumes from the high number of cars used by commuters on the city's highways.

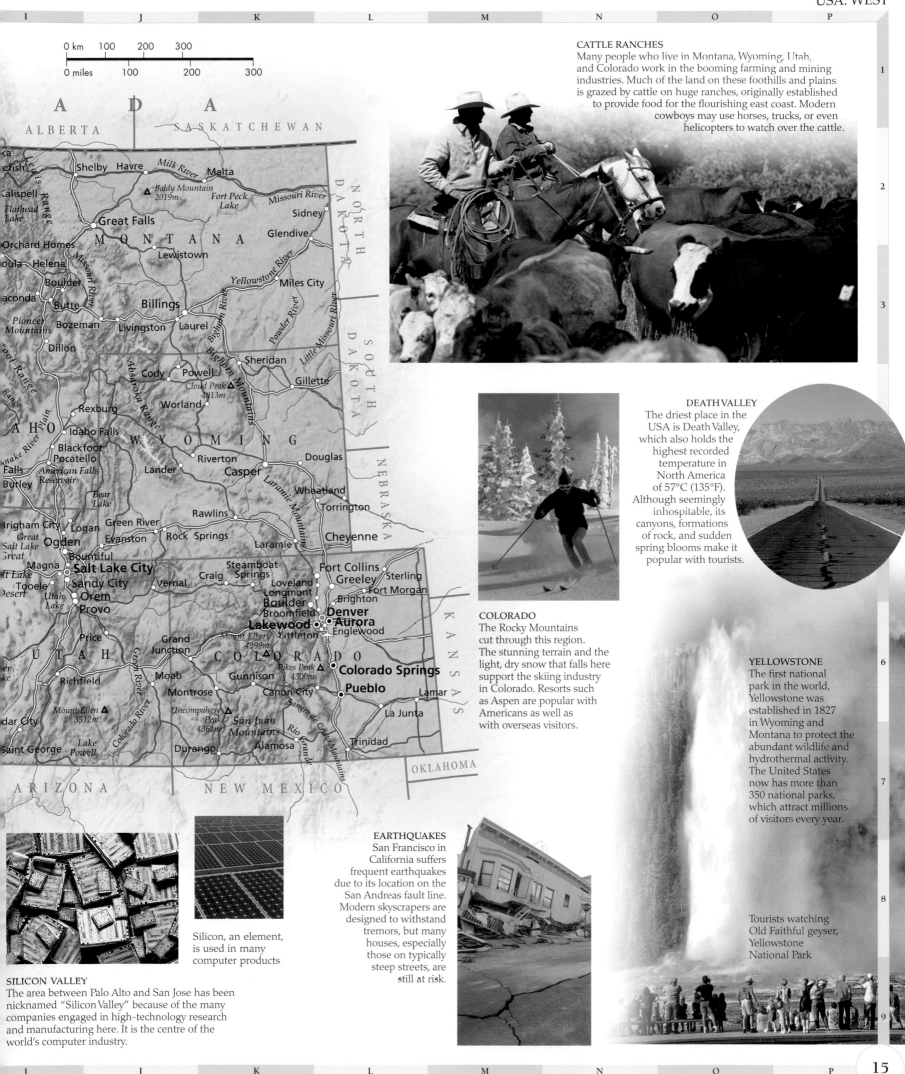

0 km 100 200 300

0 miles 100 200 300

Map labels

ALBERTA · **SASKATCHEWAN** · **NORTH DAKOTA** · **SOUTH DAKOTA** · **NEBRASKA** · **KANSAS** · **OKLAHOMA** · **NEW MEXICO** · **ARIZONA**

MONTANA · **WYOMING** · **UTAH** · **COLORADO** · **IDAHO**

Shelby · Havre · Milk River · Malta · Baldy Mountain 2019m · Fort Peck Lake · Missouri River · Sidney · Glendive · Great Falls · Lewistown · Orchard Homes · Helena · Boulder · anaconda · Butte · Bozeman · Livingston · Laurel · Billings · Miles City · Yellowstone River · Sheridan · Little Missouri River · Gillette · Bighorn River · Powder River · Pioneer Mountains · Dillon · Cody · Powell · Worland · Cloud Peak 4013m · Bighorn Mountains · Absaroka Range · Rexburg · Idaho Falls · Blackfoot · Pocatello · American Falls Reservoir · Lander · Riverton · Douglas · Casper · Laramie Mountains · Wheatland · Torrington · Bear Lake · Rawlins · Green River · Rock Springs · Laramie · Cheyenne · Brigham City · Logan · Evanston · Ogden · Great Salt Lake · Bountiful · Magna · Salt Lake City · Sandy City · Orem · Provo · Tooele · Utah Lake · Vernal · Craig · Steamboat Springs · Fort Collins · Greeley · Sterling · Loveland · Longmont · Fort Morgan · Boulder · Brighton · Broomfield · Denver · Aurora · Lakewood · Littleton · Englewood · Price · Grand Junction · Mount Elbert 4399m · COLORADO · Moab · Gunnison · Pikes Peak 4300m · Colorado Springs · Montrose · Canon City · Pueblo · Lamar · Mount Ellen 3512m · Uncompahgre Peak 4361m · San Juan Mountains · Rio Grande · La Junta · Richfield · Green River · Colorado River · Sangre de Cristo Mountains · Durango · Alamosa · Trinidad · Saint George · Lake Powell · dar City · Missouri River · Lewis Range · Flathead Lake · Kalispell · Kalispell

CATTLE RANCHES

Many people who live in Montana, Wyoming, Utah, and Colorado work in the booming farming and mining industries. Much of the land on these foothills and plains is grazed by cattle on huge ranches, originally established to provide food for the flourishing east coast. Modern cowboys may use horses, trucks, or even helicopters to watch over the cattle.

DEATH VALLEY

The driest place in the USA is Death Valley, which also holds the highest recorded temperature in North America of 57°C (135°F). Although seemingly inhospitable, its canyons, formations of rock, and sudden spring blooms make it popular with tourists.

COLORADO

The Rocky Mountains cut through this region. The stunning terrain and the light, dry snow that falls here support the skiing industry in Colorado. Resorts such as Aspen are popular with Americans as well as with overseas visitors.

YELLOWSTONE

The first national park in the world, Yellowstone was established in 1827 in Wyoming and Montana to protect the abundant wildlife and hydrothermal activity. The United States now has more than 350 national parks, which attract millions of visitors every year.

Tourists watching Old Faithful geyser, Yellowstone National Park

Silicon, an element, is used in many computer products

EARTHQUAKES

San Francisco in California suffers frequent earthquakes due to its location on the San Andreas fault line. Modern skyscrapers are designed to withstand tremors, but many houses, especially those on typically steep streets, are still at risk.

SILICON VALLEY

The area between Palo Alto and San Jose has been nicknamed "Silicon Valley" because of the many companies engaged in high-technology research and manufacturing here. It is the centre of the world's computer industry.

USA: Southwest

THE SOUTHWEST is an area of great contrasts. Much of Oklahoma and Texas consists of flat, rolling grasslands and huge farms, while both Arizona and New Mexico are hot, arid, and mountainous, with vast canyons and river valleys carving their way through the land. Since the discovery of oil in 1901, Texas has become the country's top oil producer with Houston as the centre of the billion-dollar industry. Tourism is also important to the southwest, as visitors flock to see the Grand Canyon, the Painted Desert, and other natural wonders. Buildings here reflect the mix of Hispanic, American Indian, European American, and modern American cultures.

HOT PLACE TO LIVE
The climate across much of the southwest is hot and dry, with summer temperatures often reaching 38°C (100°F). Although water can be scarce, many people have a swimming pool in their garden so they can cool off.

Suburbs of Phoenix, Arizona

DESERT LIFE
The saguaro cactus can reach up to 15 m (50 ft) tall, grow as many as 40 branches, and live for 200 years. Cacti, yucca, and other plants have all adapted to the hot, dry desert conditions found in the southwest. So, too, have many animals, including the deadly rattlesnake.

Saguaro cacti in the Sonoran Desert

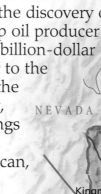

0 km 50 100 150 200
0 miles 50 100 150 200

THE GRAND CANYON
The Grand Canyon in northern Arizona is one of the natural wonders of the world. This incredibly deep gorge was slowly cut out of the rock, beginning 6 million years ago, by the Colorado River. People can hike around its edge or venture down into the canyon to camp for the night.

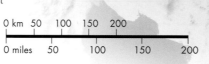

AMERICAN-INDIAN CULTURES
American Indians, including Navajo, Hopi, and Apache, used to live across the southwest but are now concentrated in reservations set up by the US government. The largest of these is in Arizona and New Mexico, and is home to the Navajo people. The Navajo farm the land and produce crafts, like the woven blanket wrapped around these Navajo children.

Kachina doll made by the Hopi

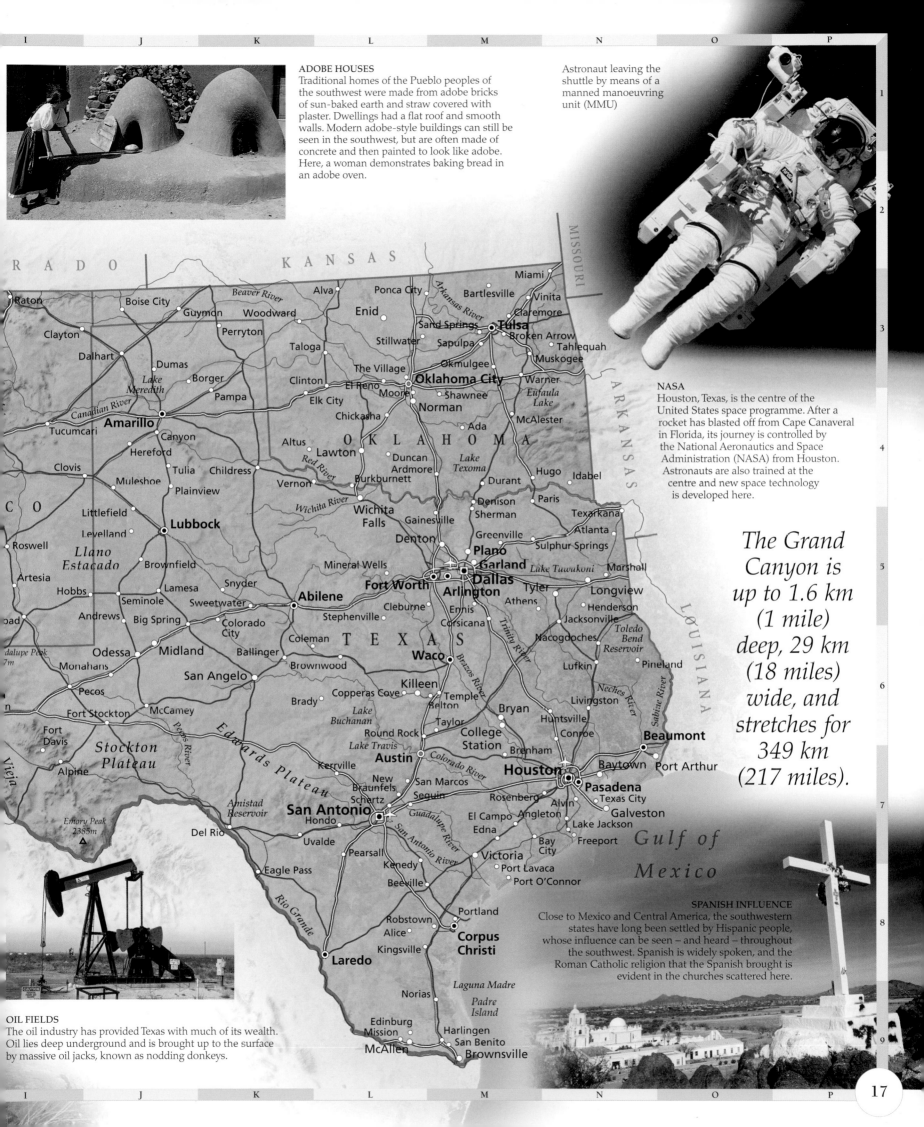

ADOBE HOUSES
Traditional homes of the Pueblo peoples of the southwest were made from adobe bricks of sun-baked earth and straw covered with plaster. Dwellings had a flat roof and smooth walls. Modern adobe-style buildings can still be seen in the southwest, but are often made of concrete and then painted to look like adobe. Here, a woman demonstrates baking bread in an adobe oven.

Astronaut leaving the shuttle by means of a manned manoeuvring unit (MMU)

NASA
Houston, Texas, is the centre of the United States space programme. After a rocket has blasted off from Cape Canaveral in Florida, its journey is controlled by the National Aeronautics and Space Administration (NASA) from Houston. Astronauts are also trained at the centre and new space technology is developed here.

The Grand Canyon is up to 1.6 km (1 mile) deep, 29 km (18 miles) wide, and stretches for 349 km (217 miles).

SPANISH INFLUENCE
Close to Mexico and Central America, the southwestern states have long been settled by Hispanic people, whose influence can be seen – and heard – throughout the southwest. Spanish is widely spoken, and the Roman Catholic religion that the Spanish brought is evident in the churches scattered here.

OIL FIELDS
The oil industry has provided Texas with much of its wealth. Oil lies deep underground and is brought up to the surface by massive oil jacks, known as nodding donkeys.

COLORADO · KANSAS · MISSOURI · ARKANSAS · LOUISIANA · OKLAHOMA · TEXAS · NEW MEXICO

Raton, Boise City, Clayton, Dalhart, Guymon, Woodward, Perryton, Alva, Enid, Ponca City, Bartlesville, Miami, Vinita, Claremore, Sand Springs, Tulsa, Broken Arrow, Tahlequah, Muskogee, Warner, Dumas, Borger, Pampa, Taloga, Stillwater, Sapulpa, Okmulgee, Lake Meredith, Canadian River, Tucumcari, Amarillo, Canyon, Hereford, Clovis, Muleshoe, Tulia, Childress, Plainview, The Village, Clinton, El Reno, Oklahoma City, Moore, Shawnee, Norman, Elk City, Chickasha, Ada, McAlester, Eufaula Lake, Altus, Lawton, Duncan, Ardmore, Lake Texoma, Hugo, Idabel, Red River, Burkburnett, Vernon, Durant, Paris, Wichita River, Wichita Falls, Gainesville, Denison, Sherman, Texarkana, Littlefield, Levelland, Lubbock, Denton, Greenville, Atlanta, Sulphur Springs, Marshall, Roswell, Llano Estacado, Brownfield, Mineral Wells, Plano, Garland, Lake Tawakoni, Artesia, Hobbs, Lamesa, Snyder, Abilene, Fort Worth, Dallas, Arlington, Tyler, Longview, Andrews, Seminole, Sweetwater, Cleburne, Ennis, Athens, Henderson, Jacksonville, Big Spring, Colorado City, Stephenville, Corsicana, Nacogdoches, Odessa, Midland, Ballinger, Coleman, TEXAS, Toledo Bend Reservoir, Monahans, San Angelo, Brownwood, Waco, Brazos River, Trinity River, Lufkin, Pineland, Pecos, Fort Stockton, McCamey, Brady, Copperas Cove, Killeen, Temple, Bryan, Livingston, Neches River, Sabine River, Fort Davis, Stockton Plateau, Lake Buchanan, Belton, Taylor, Round Rock, College Station, Huntsville, Conroe, Beaumont, Alpine, Pecos River, Lake Travis, Brenham, Baytown, Port Arthur, Emory Peak 2385m, Edwards Plateau, Kerrville, Austin, Colorado River, Houston, Pasadena, Texas City, Del Rio, New Braunfels, San Marcos, Seguin, Rosenberg, Alvin, Galveston, Amistad Reservoir, Schertz, San Antonio, Hondo, Guadalupe River, El Campo, Angleton, Lake Jackson, Uvalde, Edna, Bay City, Freeport, Gulf of Mexico, Pearsall, Kenedy, Victoria, Port Lavaca, Port O'Connor, Eagle Pass, Beeville, San Antonio River, Portland, Rio Grande, Robstown, Alice, Corpus Christi, Kingsville, Laredo, Laguna Madre, Padre Island, Norias, Edinburg, Mission, Harlingen, San Benito, McAllen, Brownsville

| A | B | C | D | E | F | G | H |

Mexico

ONCE HOME TO THE GREAT Aztec and Mayan civilizations and then the focus of Spanish conquistadors who came in search of wealth, Mexico today reflects its colourful past through its culture and architecture. The majority of Mexicans is mestizo (mixed race), of Spanish and native Indian descent. Mexico City, site of the ancient Aztec capital, is today one of the largest cities in the world, with a population of more than 16 million. Despite oil and natural gas reserves, and a plentiful supply of labour, large numbers of Mexicans are still poor, especially in the rural areas and the urban slums.

ALONG THE BORDER
In 1994, Mexico signed the North American Free Trade Agreement (NAFTA), which effectively bound its economy to that of the USA. A large industrial area has developed along the Mexican border with the USA, and many American companies have relocated south of the border to benefit from the lower labour costs.

DAY OF THE DEAD
One of the biggest festivals in Mexico is the Day of the Dead. It is believed that once a year the souls of the dead can come back and visit their loved ones. In celebration of this, special food is prepared to welcome the souls, and offerings of flowers, candles, and incense are made at the gravesides.

LIFE IN THE CITY
Mexico City is the political, economic, and cultural hub of the country, and is home to some 16 million people. Its site, in a basin surrounded by mountains, means that expansion is difficult. Air pollution from factories and cars cannot escape, so on most days a thick layer of smog builds up over the city. Attempts to deal with the pollution, including banning cars from some parts, have had limited success.

The volcano Popocatépetl is the highest peak around the city

Mexico City is contained within a ring of mountains

WORKING ON THE LAND
Agriculture employs 6.5 million people – about one-eighth of Mexico's work force. However, only 12 per cent of the land is suitable for farming because it is so mountainous and dry. The peasant communities of the south rely on farming for their food, while communities in the north are more industrialized. Here, the agave plant is being harvested near the town of Tequila.

Map labels

UNITED STATES O

Mexicali
Tijuana
Rosarito
Ensenada
San Luis
Colorado River
Desierto de Altar
Sierra San Pedro Mártir
Baja California
Ciudad Juárez
Río Grande
Río Bravo del Norte
Nogales
Agua Prieta
Samalayuca
Cananea
Caborca
Magdalena
Cumpas
Nuevo Casas Grandes
El Sueco
Ojin
Río Bavispe
San Pedro de la Cueva
El Sáuz
Río Conchos
Isla Ángel de la Guarda
Hermosillo
Chihuahua
Cuauhtémoc
Delicias
Isla Tiburón
Ciudad Camargo
Empalme
Guaymas
Esperanza
San Francisco del Oro
Jimén
Hidalgo del Parral
Santa Barbara
Ciudad Obregón
Navojoa
Huatabampo
Gómez Pa
Bahía Sebastián Vizcaíno
Isla Guadalupe
Isla Cedros
Guerrero Negro
San Ignacio
San Blas
Los Mochis
Guasave
Guamúchil
Culiacán
M
Loreto
Sierra de la Giganta
Navolato
Durang
Bahía de La Paz
El Dorado
Isla Magdalena
Isla Santa Margarita
La Paz
Sierra Madre Occidental
Gulf of California
PACIFIC OCEAN
Tropic of Cancer
Miraflores
Mazatlán
Santa Genoveva 2406m
Escuinapa
Acaponeta
Tú
Islas Marías
Tepic
Puerto Vallarta
Manz

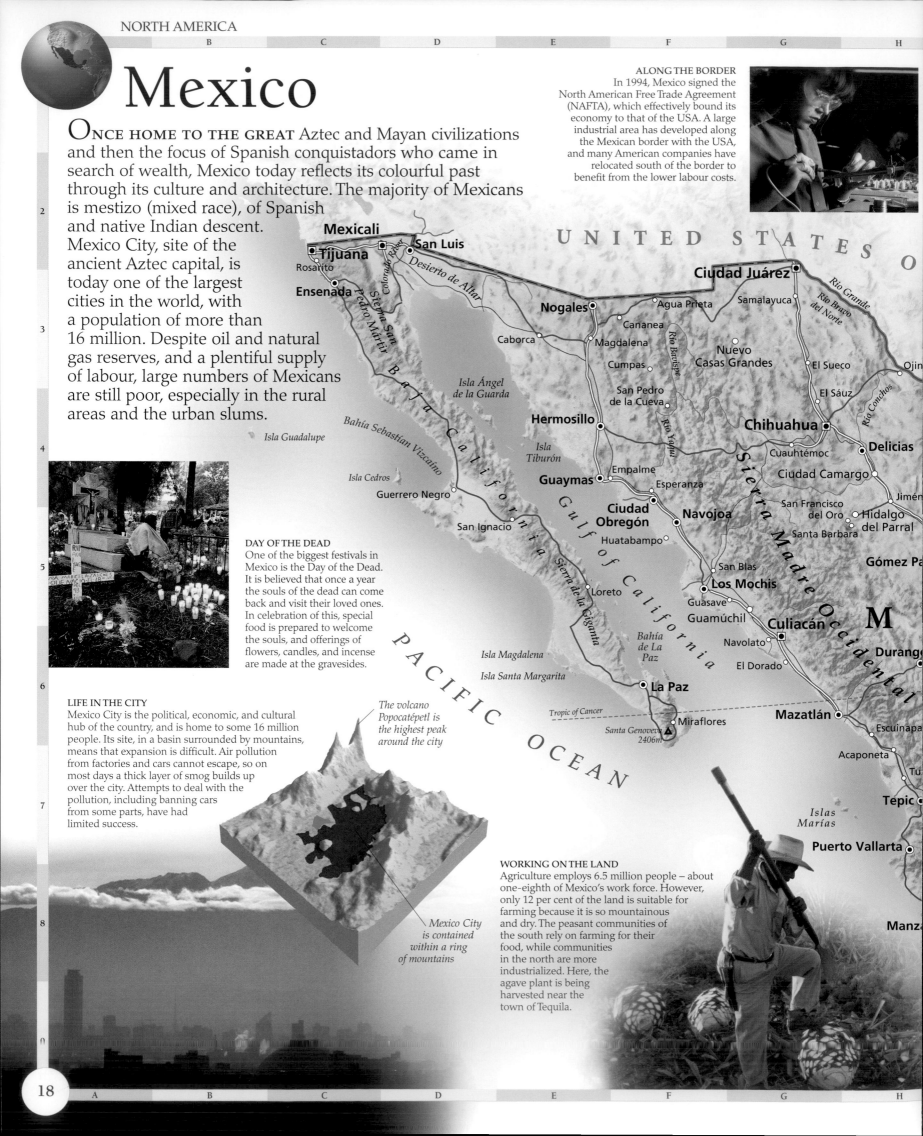

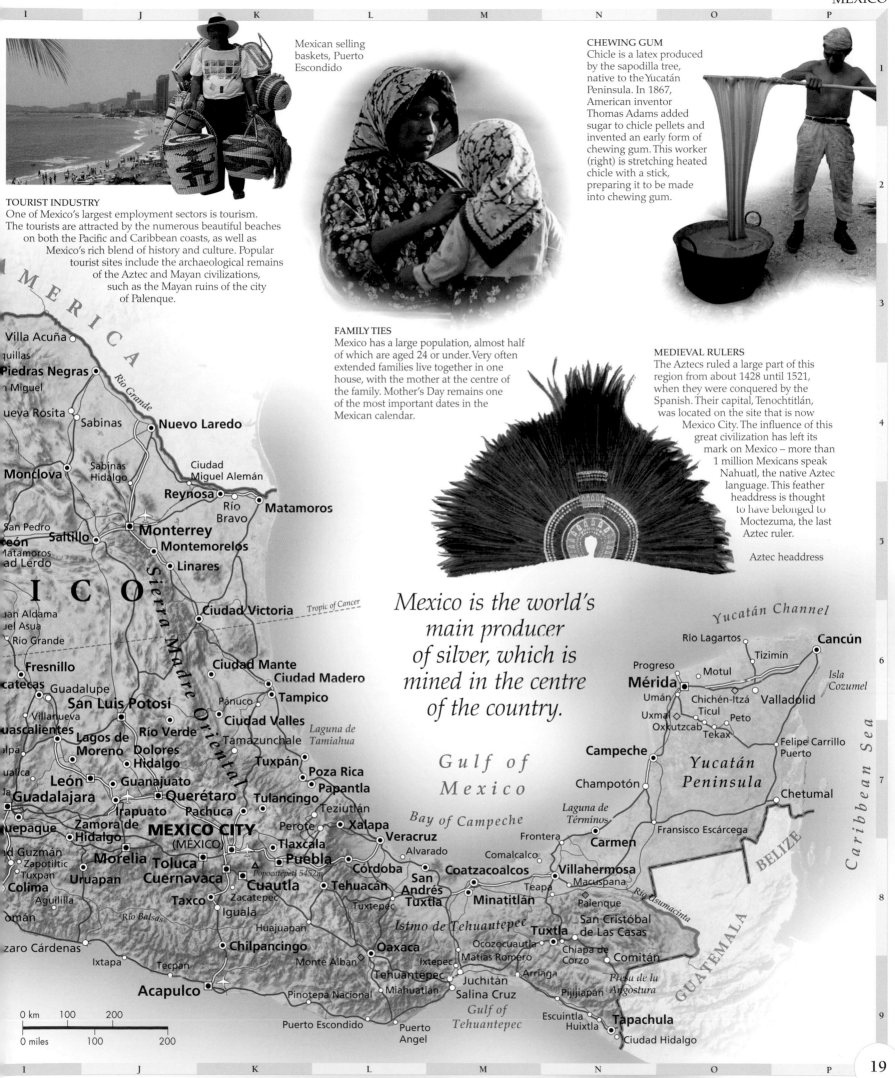

Mexican selling
baskets, Puerto
Escondido

TOURIST INDUSTRY

One of Mexico's largest employment sectors is tourism. The tourists are attracted by the numerous beautiful beaches on both the Pacific and Caribbean coasts, as well as Mexico's rich blend of history and culture. Popular tourist sites include the archaeological remains of the Aztec and Mayan civilizations, such as the Mayan ruins of the city of Palenque.

CHEWING GUM

Chicle is a latex produced by the sapodilla tree, native to the Yucatán Peninsula. In 1867, American inventor Thomas Adams added sugar to chicle pellets and invented an early form of chewing gum. This worker (right) is stretching heated chicle with a stick, preparing it to be made into chewing gum.

FAMILY TIES

Mexico has a large population, almost half of which are aged 24 or under. Very often extended families live together in one house, with the mother at the centre of the family. Mother's Day remains one of the most important dates in the Mexican calendar.

MEDIEVAL RULERS

The Aztecs ruled a large part of this region from about 1428 until 1521, when they were conquered by the Spanish. Their capital, Tenochtitlán, was located on the site that is now Mexico City. The influence of this great civilization has left its mark on Mexico – more than 1 million Mexicans speak Nahuatl, the native Aztec language. This feather headdress is thought to have belonged to Moctezuma, the last Aztec ruler.

Aztec headdress

Mexico is the world's main producer of silver, which is mined in the centre of the country.

Map labels

AMERICA
MEXICO
Sierra Madre Oriental

Villa Acuña
quillas
Piedras Negras
n Miguel
ueva Rosita
Sabinas
Nuevo Laredo
Sabinas Hidalgo
Ciudad Miguel Alemán
Monclova
Reynosa
Río Bravo
Matamoros
San Pedro
Saltillo
eón
Monterrey
Matamoros
ad Lerdo
Montemorelos
Linares
uan Aldama
uel Asua
Ciudad Victoria
Tropic of Cancer
Río Grande
Fresnillo
catecas
Guadalupe
Ciudad Mante
Ciudad Madero
San Luis Potosí
Pánuco
Tampico
Villanueva
Río Verde
Ciudad Valles
uascalientes
Lagos de Moreno
Dolores Hidalgo
Tamazunchale
Laguna de Tamiahua
alpa
León
Guanajuato
Tuxpán
ualica
Guadalajara
Querétaro
Tulancingo
Poza Rica
Papantla
uepaque
Zamora de Hidalgo
Irapuato
Pachuca
Teziutlán
MEXICO CITY (MÉXICO)
Perote
Xalapa
Bay of Campeche
d Guzmán
Zapotiltic
Morelia
Toluca
Tlaxcala
Veracruz
Alvarado
Tuxpan
Cuernavaca
Popocatepetl 5452m
Puebla
Córdoba
Colima
Cuautla
Tehuacán
San Andrés Tuxtla
Coatzacoalcos
Aguililla
Taxco
Zacatepec
Tuxtepec
Comalcalco
omán
Uruapan
Iguala
Huajuapan
Istmo de Tehuantepec
Teapa
Villahermosa
Macuspana
Río Balsas
Minatitlán
Palenque
Río Usumacinta
aro Cárdenas
Chilpancingo
Oaxaca
Ocozocuautla
Tuxtla
San Cristóbal de Las Casas
Ixtapa
Monte Alban
Ixtepec
Matías Romero
Chiapa de Corzo
Comitán
Tecpan
Tehuantepec
Juchitán
Arriaga
Presa de la Angostura
Pinotepa Nacional
Miahuatlán
Salina Cruz
Pijijiapán
Puerto Escondido
Puerto Angel
Gulf of Tehuantepec
Escuintla
Huixtla
Tapachula
Ciudad Hidalgo

Gulf of Mexico

Yucatán Channel
Río Lagartos
Cancún
Tizimín
Progreso
Motul
Isla Cozumel
Mérida
Umán
Chichén-Itzá
Valladolid
Uxmal
Ticul
Peto
Oxkutzcab
Tekax
Felipe Carrillo Puerto
Campeche
Yucatán Peninsula
Champotón
Chetumal
Laguna de Términos
Frontera
Fransisco Escárcega
Carmen
BELIZE
GUATEMALA
Caribbean Sea

Río Grande
San Miguel

0 km   100   200
0 miles   100   200

Central America

VOLCANOES, EARTHQUAKES, and hurricanes threaten the livelihoods of people in the seven countries of Central America. People here have also struggled with poverty and civil war. In more recent years, however, peace and economic recovery have offered hope, and education is now free in all countries. Remains of the ancient Mayan civilization that flourished until the 16th century, when the Spanish invaded, can be seen throughout the region. Large numbers of the native population died after the invasion, mostly from disease. Today, Spanish is the main language of the region.

Lake Nicaragua is the only freshwater lake in the world that contains sharks.

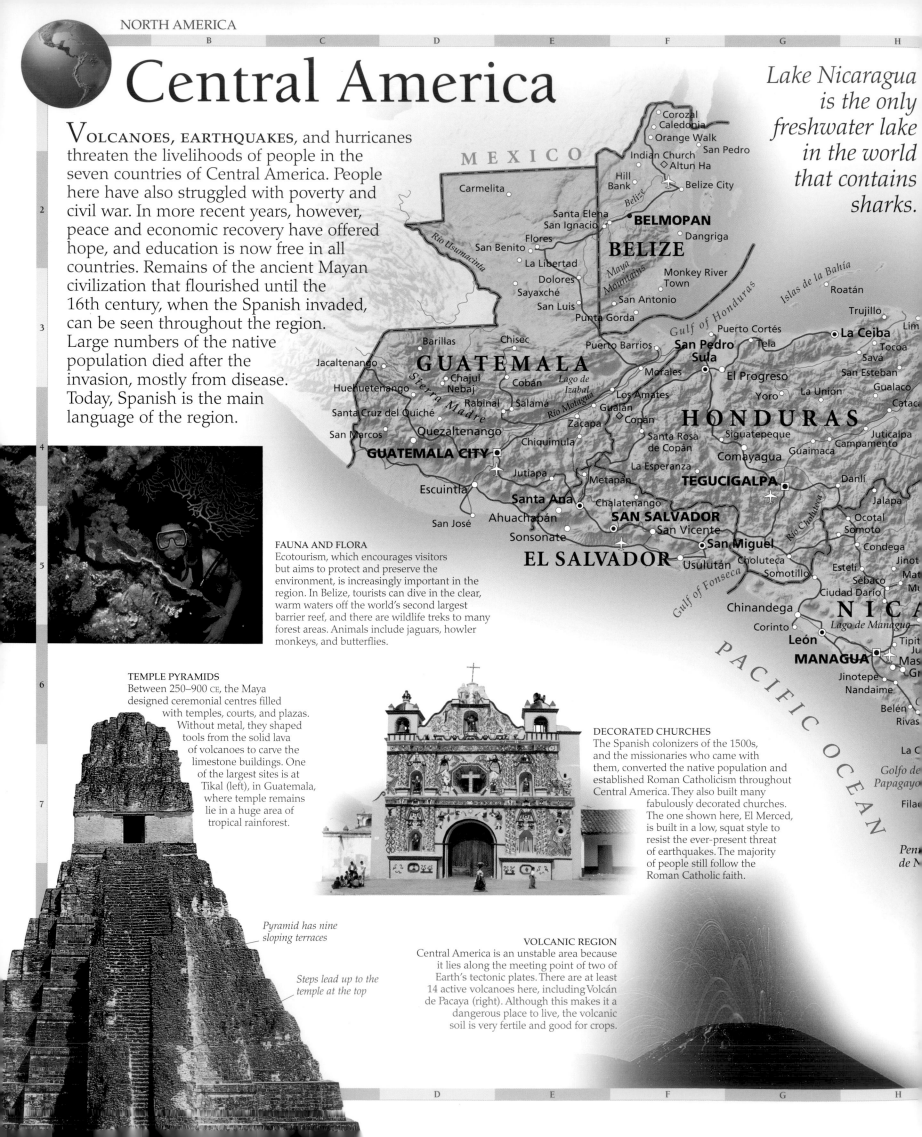

FAUNA AND FLORA
Ecotourism, which encourages visitors but aims to protect and preserve the environment, is increasingly important in the region. In Belize, tourists can dive in the clear, warm waters off the world's second largest barrier reef, and there are wildlife treks to many forest areas. Animals include jaguars, howler monkeys, and butterflies.

TEMPLE PYRAMIDS
Between 250–900 CE, the Maya designed ceremonial centres filled with temples, courts, and plazas. Without metal, they shaped tools from the solid lava of volcanoes to carve the limestone buildings. One of the largest sites is at Tikal (left), in Guatemala, where temple remains lie in a huge area of tropical rainforest.

Pyramid has nine sloping terraces

Steps lead up to the temple at the top

DECORATED CHURCHES
The Spanish colonizers of the 1500s, and the missionaries who came with them, converted the native population and established Roman Catholicism throughout Central America. They also built many fabulously decorated churches. The one shown here, El Merced, is built in a low, squat style to resist the ever-present threat of earthquakes. The majority of people still follow the Roman Catholic faith.

VOLCANIC REGION
Central America is an unstable area because it lies along the meeting point of two of Earth's tectonic plates. There are at least 14 active volcanoes here, including Volcán de Pacaya (right). Although this makes it a dangerous place to live, the volcanic soil is very fertile and good for crops.

Map labels:

MEXICO

Corozal
Caledonia
Orange Walk
Indian Church
San Pedro
Altun Ha
Hill Bank
Belize City
Carmelita
Santa Elena
San Ignacio
BELMOPAN
Dangriga
BELIZE
Flores
San Benito
La Libertad
Maya Mountains
Monkey River Town
Dolores
Sayaxché
San Antonio
San Luis
Punta Gorda
Gulf of Honduras
Islas de la Bahía
Roatán
Trujillo
Barillas
Chisec
Puerto Barrios
Puerto Cortés
La Ceiba
Lim
Jacaltenango
GUATEMALA
Chajul
Nebaj
Cobán
San Pedro Sula
Tela
Tocoa
Savá
Huehuetenango
Rabinal
Salamá
Lago de Izabal
Los Amates
Morales
El Progreso
San Esteban
Gualaco
Santa Cruz del Quiché
Sierra Madre
Río Motagua
Gualán
Copán
HONDURAS
Yoro
La Unión
Cataca
San Marcos
Quezaltenango
Zacapa
Santa Rosa de Copán
Siguatepeque
Juticalpa
Campamento
GUATEMALA CITY
Chiquimula
Comayagua
Guaimaca
Jutiapa
La Esperanza
TEGUCIGALPA
Danlí
Escuintla
Metapán
Chalatenango
Jalapa
Santa Ana
Ocotal
Somoto
San José
Ahuachapán
SAN SALVADOR
San Vicente
Condega
Esteli
Jinot
Sonsonate
San Miguel
EL SALVADOR
Usulután
Choluteca
Somotillo
Ciudad Darío
Sébaco
Mat
Mu
Gulf of Fonseca
Chinandega
NICA
Lago de Managua
Corinto
León
Tipit
Ju
MANAGUA
Mas
Gr
Jinotepe
Nandaime
Belén
Rivas
PACIFIC OCEAN
La C
Golfo de Papagayo
Filad
Pen
de N

Chipstmap grid letters: B C D E F G H (top and bottom), numbers 2 3 4 5 6 7 (left margin)

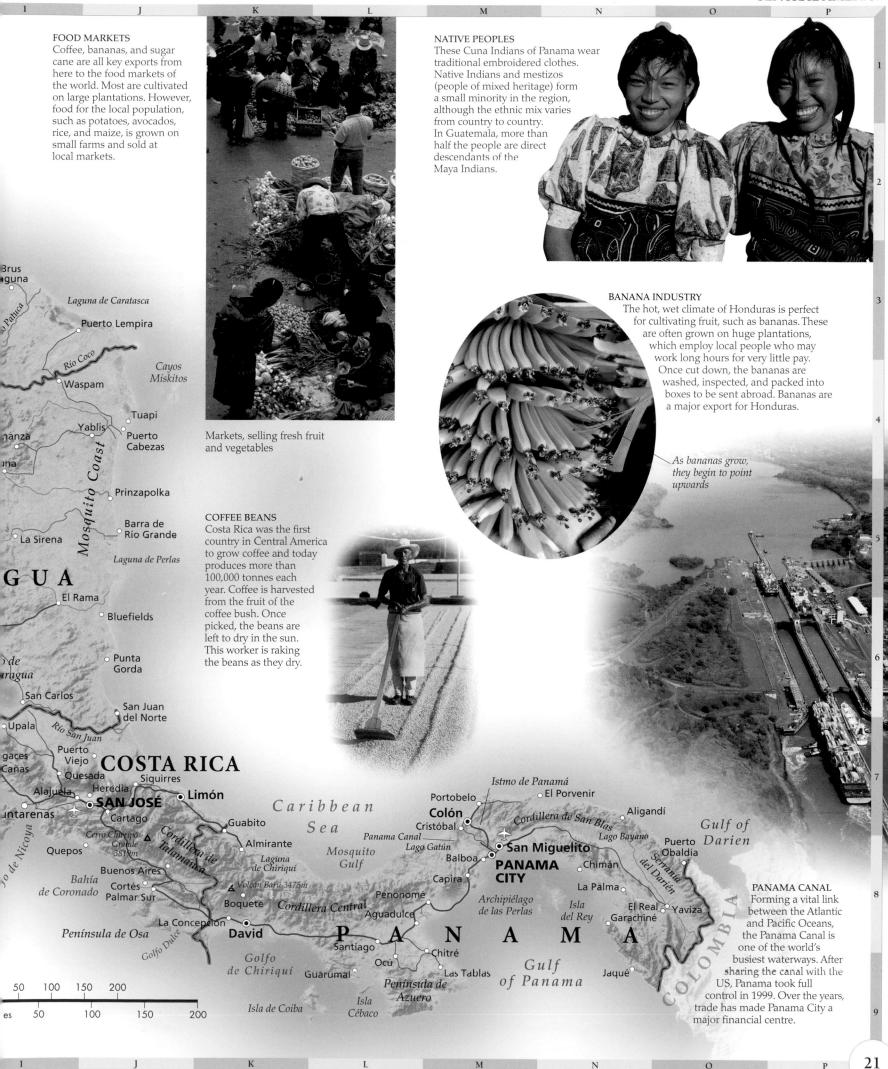

FOOD MARKETS
Coffee, bananas, and sugar cane are all key exports from here to the food markets of the world. Most are cultivated on large plantations. However, food for the local population, such as potatoes, avocados, rice, and maize, is grown on small farms and sold at local markets.

Markets, selling fresh fruit and vegetables

NATIVE PEOPLES
These Cuna Indians of Panama wear traditional embroidered clothes. Native Indians and mestizos (people of mixed heritage) form a small minority in the region, although the ethnic mix varies from country to country. In Guatemala, more than half the people are direct descendants of the Maya Indians.

BANANA INDUSTRY
The hot, wet climate of Honduras is perfect for cultivating fruit, such as bananas. These are often grown on huge plantations, which employ local people who may work long hours for very little pay. Once cut down, the bananas are washed, inspected, and packed into boxes to be sent abroad. Bananas are a major export for Honduras.

As bananas grow, they begin to point upwards

COFFEE BEANS
Costa Rica was the first country in Central America to grow coffee and today produces more than 100,000 tonnes each year. Coffee is harvested from the fruit of the coffee bush. Once picked, the beans are left to dry in the sun. This worker is raking the beans as they dry.

PANAMA CANAL
Forming a vital link between the Atlantic and Pacific Oceans, the Panama Canal is one of the world's busiest waterways. After sharing the canal with the US, Panama took full control in 1999. Over the years, trade has made Panama City a major financial centre.

Map labels:

Brus
Laguna
Laguna de Caratasca
Puerto Lempira
Río Coco
Cayos Miskitos
Waspam
Tuapi
Yablis
Puerto Cabezas
Prinzapolka
Barra de Río Grande
La Sirena
Laguna de Perlas
Mosquito Coast
GUA
El Rama
Bluefields
Punta Gorda
San Carlos
San Juan del Norte
Upala
Río San Juan
Puerto Viejo
gaces
Cañas
Quesada
Siquirres
Alajuela
Heredia
SAN JOSÉ
Limón
Cartago
Guabito
Cerro Chirripó Grande 3819m
Cordillera de Talamanca
Almirante
Quepos
Buenos Aires
Laguna de Chiriquí
Cortés
Palmar Sur
Volcán Barú 3475m
Bahía de Coronado
Boquete
Cordillera Central
Península de Osa
La Concepción
David
Golfo Dulce
Golfo de Chiriquí
Guarumal
Santiago
Ocú
Chitré
Las Tablas
Península de Azuero
Isla de Coiba
Isla Cébaco

COSTA RICA
Caribbean Sea
Mosquito Gulf
Istmo de Panamá
El Porvenir
Portobelo
Colón
Cristóbal
Cordillera de San Blas
Aligandí
Panama Canal
Lago Gatún
Lago Bayano
San Miguelito
Balboa
PANAMA CITY
Capira
Chimán
Penonomé
La Palma
Aguadulce
Archipiélago de las Perlas
Isla del Rey
Puerto Obaldía
Serranía del Darién
El Real
Garachiné
Yaviza
PANAMA
Gulf of Darien
Gulf of Panama
Jaqué
COLOMBIA

Scale bar:
50 100 150 200
es 50 100 150 200

The Caribbean

UNITED STATES
OF AMERICA

THIS REGION CONSISTS of thousands of islands stretching from Cuba in the west to Trinidad and Tobago in the southeast. European colonists wanted control of the islands in the 1500s, but the diseases they brought wiped out most of the local Carib and Arawak peoples. African slaves, imported to work on plantations, replaced local peoples and today most of the population are descended from those Africans. English, Spanish, and French are spoken in different countries, depending on which European power claimed the territory. Tourism and agriculture are major sources of employment.

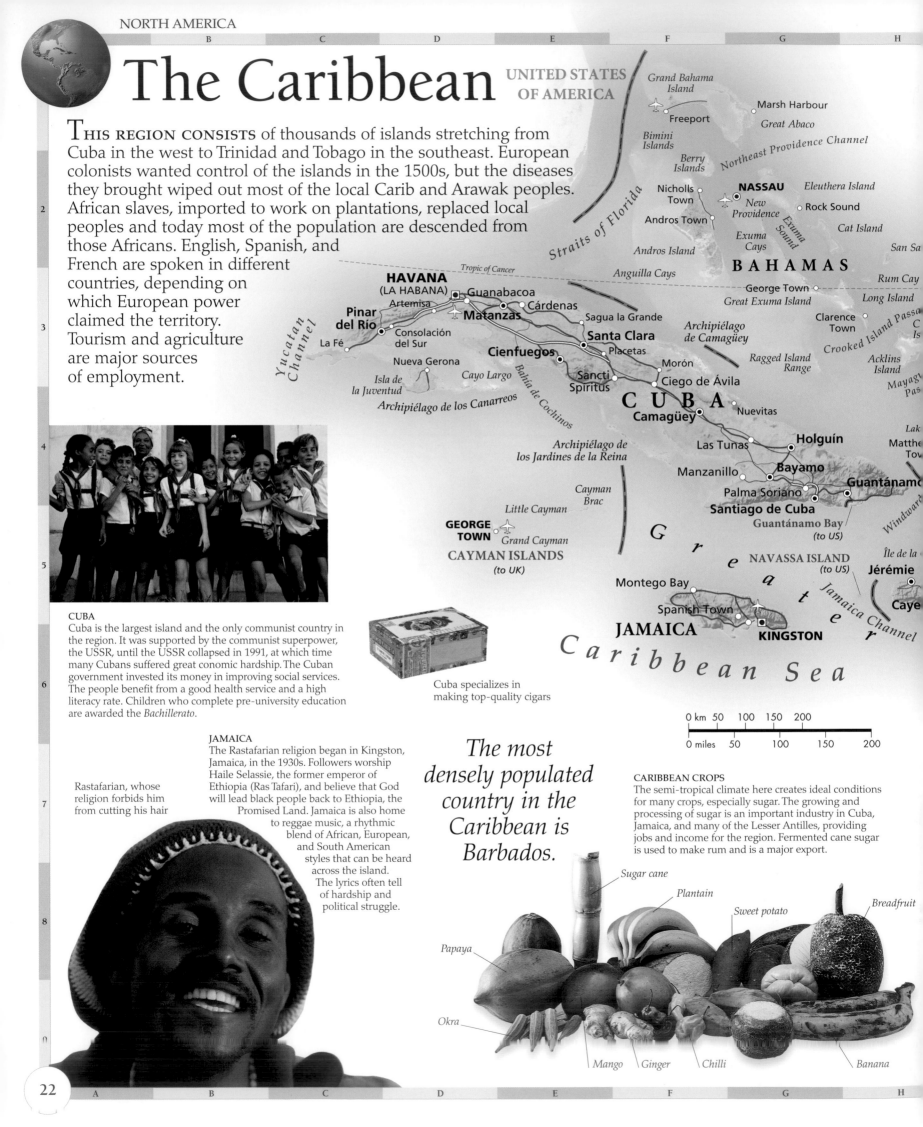

(Map labels)
Grand Bahama Island
Marsh Harbour
Freeport
Great Abaco
Bimini Islands
Northeast Providence Channel
Berry Islands
Nicholls Town
NASSAU
Eleuthera Island
New Providence
Rock Sound
Andros Town
Exuma Sound
Cat Island
San Sa
Andros Island
Exuma Cays
Straits of Florida
Tropic of Cancer
Anguilla Cays
BAHAMAS
Rum Cay
HAVANA (LA HABANA)
Guanabacoa
Artemisa
Cárdenas
George Town
Great Exuma Island
Long Island
Pinar del Río
Matanzas
Sagua la Grande
Archipiélago de Camagüey
Clarence Town
Crooked Island Passa
Consolación del Sur
Santa Clara
La Fé
Cienfuegos
Placetas
Ragged Island Range
Acklins Island
Nueva Gerona
Sancti Spíritus
Morón
Ciego de Ávila
Mayagu Pas
Isla de la Juventud
Cayo Largo
Bahía de Cochinos
CUBA
Archipiélago de los Canarreos
Camagüey
Nuevitas
Lak
Archipiélago de los Jardines de la Reina
Las Tunas
Holguín
Matthe Tov
Manzanillo
Bayamo
Cayman Brac
Palma Soriano
Guantánamo
Little Cayman
Santiago de Cuba
GEORGE TOWN
Grand Cayman
Guantánamo Bay (to US)
Windwar
CAYMAN ISLANDS (to UK)
Greater
Île de la
NAVASSA ISLAND (to US)
Jérémie
Montego Bay
Spanish Town
Caye
JAMAICA
KINGSTON
Jamaica Channel
Caribbean Sea

(Scale)
0 km 50 100 150 200
0 miles 50 100 150 200

CUBA
Cuba is the largest island and the only communist country in the region. It was supported by the communist superpower, the USSR, until the USSR collapsed in 1991, at which time many Cubans suffered great conomic hardship. The Cuban government invested its money in improving social services. The people benefit from a good health service and a high literacy rate. Children who complete pre-university education are awarded the *Bachillerato*.

Cuba specializes in making top-quality cigars

JAMAICA
The Rastafarian religion began in Kingston, Jamaica, in the 1930s. Followers worship Haile Selassie, the former emperor of Ethiopia (Ras Tafari), and believe that God will lead black people back to Ethiopia, the Promised Land. Jamaica is also home to reggae music, a rhythmic blend of African, European, and South American styles that can be heard across the island. The lyrics often tell of hardship and political struggle.

Rastafarian, whose religion forbids him from cutting his hair

The most densely populated country in the Caribbean is Barbados.

CARIBBEAN CROPS
The semi-tropical climate here creates ideal conditions for many crops, especially sugar. The growing and processing of sugar is an important industry in Cuba, Jamaica, and many of the Lesser Antilles, providing jobs and income for the region. Fermented cane sugar is used to make rum and is a major export.

Sugar cane
Plantain
Sweet potato
Breadfruit
Papaya
Okra
Mango
Ginger
Chilli
Banana

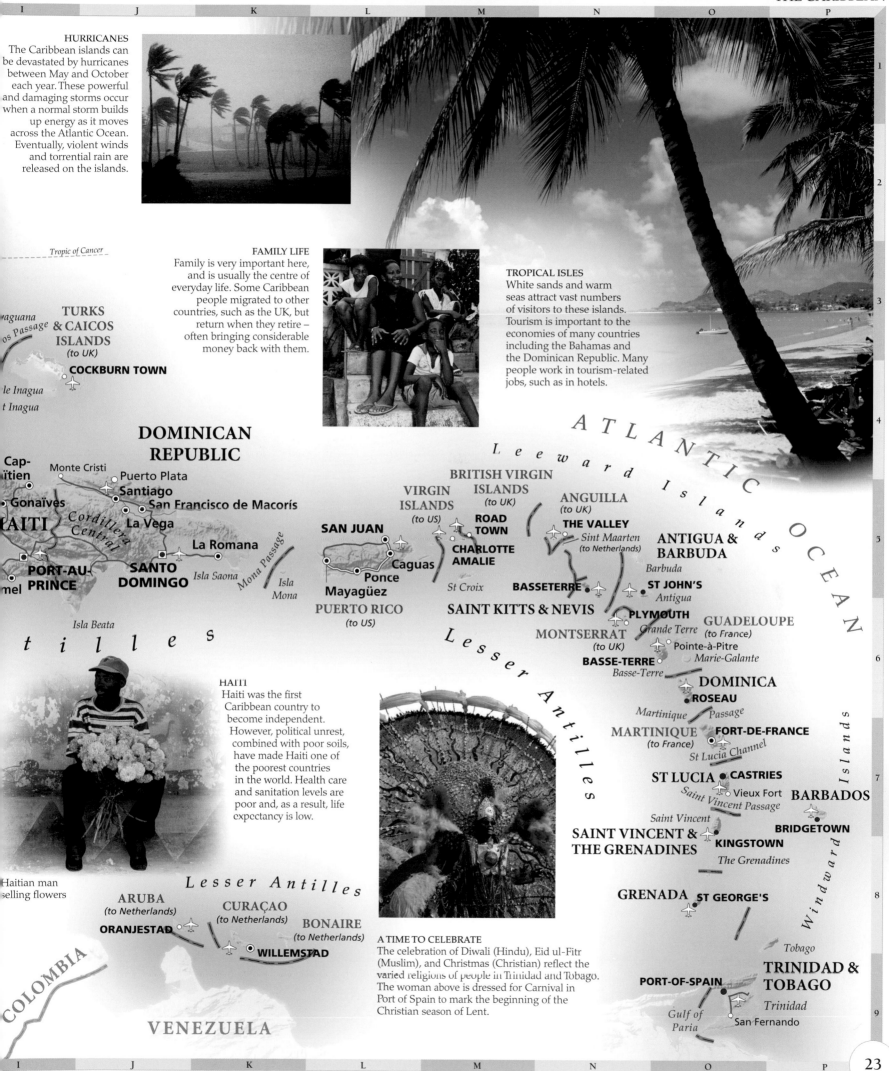

HURRICANES

The Caribbean islands can be devastated by hurricanes between May and October each year. These powerful and damaging storms occur when a normal storm builds up energy as it moves across the Atlantic Ocean. Eventually, violent winds and torrential rain are released on the islands.

Tropic of Cancer

FAMILY LIFE

Family is very important here, and is usually the centre of everyday life. Some Caribbean people migrated to other countries, such as the UK, but return when they retire – often bringing considerable money back with them.

TROPICAL ISLES

White sands and warm seas attract vast numbers of visitors to these islands. Tourism is important to the economies of many countries including the Bahamas and the Dominican Republic. Many people work in tourism-related jobs, such as in hotels.

HAITI

Haiti was the first Caribbean country to become independent. However, political unrest, combined with poor soils, have made Haiti one of the poorest countries in the world. Health care and sanitation levels are poor and, as a result, life expectancy is low.

Haitian man selling flowers

A TIME TO CELEBRATE

The celebration of Diwali (Hindu), Eid ul-Fitr (Muslim), and Christmas (Christian) reflect the varied religions of people in Trinidad and Tobago. The woman above is dressed for Carnival in Port of Spain to mark the beginning of the Christian season of Lent.

aguana
os Passage
le Inagua
t Inagua

TURKS & CAICOS ISLANDS
(to UK)

COCKBURN TOWN

DOMINICAN REPUBLIC

Cap-
ïtien
Monte Cristi
Puerto Plata
Santiago
San Francisco de Macorís
Gonaïves
Cordillera Central
La Vega
La Romana
HAITI
Mona Passage
Isla Saona
Isla Mona
PORT-AU-PRINCE
SANTO DOMINGO
mel
Isla Beata

tilles

Lesser Antilles

ARUBA
(to Netherlands)
CURAÇAO
(to Netherlands)
BONAIRE
(to Netherlands)
ORANJESTAD
WILLEMSTAD

COLOMBIA

VENEZUELA

VIRGIN ISLANDS
(to US)
SAN JUAN
Caguas
Ponce
Mayagüez
PUERTO RICO
(to US)

BRITISH VIRGIN ISLANDS
(to UK)
ROAD TOWN
CHARLOTTE AMALIE
St Croix

ANGUILLA
(to UK)
THE VALLEY
Sint Maarten (to Netherlands)

ANTIGUA & BARBUDA
Barbuda
BASSETERRE
ST JOHN'S
Antigua
SAINT KITTS & NEVIS
PLYMOUTH
MONTSERRAT
(to UK)
Grande Terre
GUADELOUPE
(to France)
BASSE-TERRE
Pointe-à-Pitre
Marie-Galante
Basse-Terre

Leeward Islands

ATLANTIC OCEAN

Lesser Antilles

DOMINICA
ROSEAU
Martinique   Passage
MARTINIQUE
(to France)
FORT-DE-FRANCE
St Lucia Channel

ST LUCIA
CASTRIES
Vieux Fort
Saint Vincent Passage
Saint Vincent
SAINT VINCENT & THE GRENADINES
KINGSTOWN
The Grenadines

BARBADOS
BRIDGETOWN

Windward Islands

GRENADA
ST GEORGE'S

Tobago

TRINIDAD & TOBAGO
PORT-OF-SPAIN
Trinidad
Gulf of Paria
San Fernando

SOUTH AMERICA

Although South America is much poorer than its northern neighbour, it is rich in natural resources. Its mineral wealth led to its invasion by the Portuguese and Spanish in the 1500s, and their languages and culture still shape the lives of the people here. The nations below are listed in order of area, headed by Brazil – the world's fifth largest country.

Brazil
- 8,514,877 sq km
  3,287,612 sq miles
- 194,000,000
- Brasília
- Portuguese, German, Italian, Spanish, Polish, Japanese, Amerindian languages

Venezuela
- 912,050 sq km
  352,144 sq miles
- 28,600,000
- Caracas
- Spanish, Amerindian languages

Latin American culture is world famous, thanks to its infectious music and dance. Here a couple in Buenos Aires, Argentina, demonstrate the art of the tango.

Bolivia
- 1,098,581 sq km
  424,164 sq miles
- 9,860,000
- La Paz
- Aymara, Quechua, Spanish

Chile
- 756,102 sq km
  291,933 sq miles
- 17,000,000
- Santiago
- Spanish, Amerindian languages

Argentina
- 2,780,400 sq km
  1,073,518 sq miles
- 40,300,000
- Buenos Aires
- Spanish, Italian, Amerindian languages

Paraguay
- 406,752 sq km
  157,048 sq miles
- 6,350,000
- Asunción
- Guaraní, Spanish, German

Ecuador
- 283,561 sq km
  109,484 sq miles
- 13,600,000
- Quito
- Spanish, Quechua, other Amerindian languages

Peru
- 1,285,216 sq km
  496,225 sq miles
- 29,200,000
- Lima
- Spanish, Quechua, Aymara

Guyana
- 214,969 sq km
  83,000 sq miles
- 762,500
- Georgetown
- English Creole, Hindi, Tamil, Amerindian languages, English

Uruguay
- 176,215 sq km
  68,037 sq miles
- 3,360,000
- Montevideo
- Spanish

Colombia
- 1,138,914 sq km
  439,737 sq miles
- 45,700,000
- Bogotá
- Spanish, Wayuu, Páez, and other Amerindian languages

Football is a national passion in Brazil. Most of these barefoot boys on Ipanema beach, Rio de Janeiro, will be dreaming of playing for Brazil in the World Cup.

Suriname
- 163,820 sq km
  63,251 sq miles
- 519,700
- Paramaribo
- Sranan (creole), Dutch, Javanese, Sarnami Hindi, Saramaccan (creole), Chinese, Carib

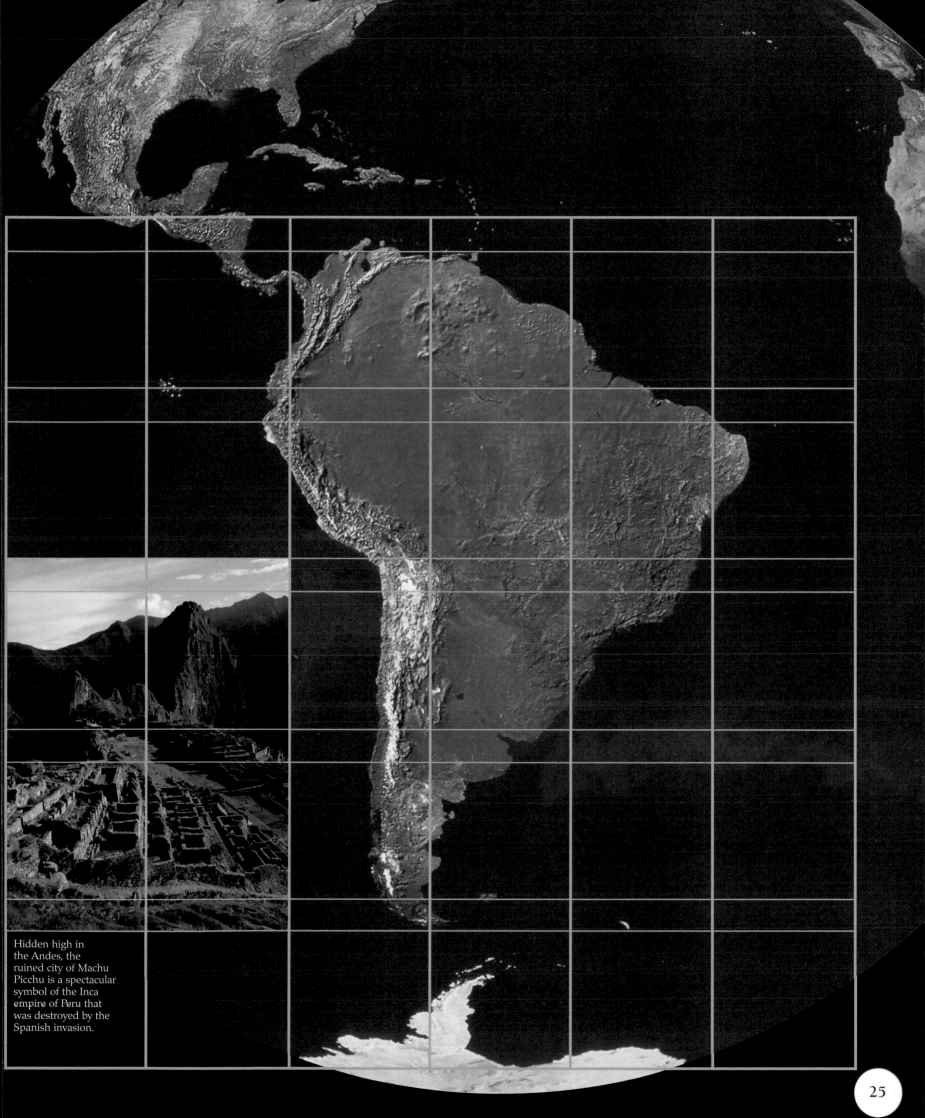

Hidden high in the Andes, the ruined city of Machu Picchu is a spectacular symbol of the Inca empire of Peru that was destroyed by the Spanish invasion.

Northwest South America

HIGH MOUNTAINS AND PLATEAUS, dense tropical rainforest, and coastal swamps are found in this region. In the 16th century, promises of untold riches attracted the Spanish to the countries here. They found the vast empire of the Incas, which stretched from what is now Peru into northern Colombia. To the north and east, other colonizers – Dutch, English, and French – arrived. Today, although the countries are independent, with the exception of French Guiana, Spanish remains the main language. The population is mainly a mix of native peoples and Europeans, except along the Caribbean coast where descendants of former African slaves live.

ANDES MOUNTAINS
The Andes, the world's longest mountain chain, extends 7,250 km (4,505 miles) down the western edge of South America. Barley, wheat, and potatoes grow well in highland areas, and are cultivated on the terraced hillsides.

FRENCH GUIANA
French Guiana is the only remaining colony in South America, and is governed by France. Tropical forests cover more than four-fifths of its land. In 1968, the European Space Agency established a launch site on the coast at Kourou, which is still used today.

CARACAS
Venezuela's population is growing rapidly and more than 88 per cent of the people now live in cities. The oil industry brings in considerable wealth, but many people are still poor. Although Caracas, Venezuela's capital city, is an important financial centre, it has many shantytowns.

Map labels

Caribbean Sea

Santa Marta
Barranquilla
Riohacha
Soledad
Cartagena
Valledupar
Sincelejo
Montería
Medellín
Dabeiba
Quibdó
Manizales
Pereira
Armenia
Tuluá
Buenaventura
Cali
Palmira
Popayán
Pasto
Nuquí
Tumaco
Esmeraldas
Santo Domingo de los Colorados
Ibarra
Tulcán
QUITO
Manta
Portoviejo
Ambato
Riobamba
Guayaquil
Milagro
Cuenca
Machala

Puerto López
Punto Fijo
Coro
Maracaibo
Cabimas
Barquisimeto
Ciudad Ojeda
Valera
Mérida
El Vigía
Bucaramanga
San Cristóbal
Cúcuta
Barrancabermeja
Aguachica
Yarumal
Bello
Caucasia
Tunja
Zipaquirá
BOGOTÁ
Sogamoso
Yopal
Villavicencio
Ibagué
Neiva
Garzón
Florencia
Pitalito
Mocoa
San José del Guaviare
Mitú

COLOMBIA
ECUADOR

Gulf of Darién
PANAMA

Valencia
CARACAS
Maracay
Acarigua
Guanare
Barinas
San Fernando
Valle de la Pascua
Puerto Carreño
Puerto Ayacucho
Puerto Inírida

VENEZUELA

La Asunción
Isla de Margarita
Porlamar
Cumaná
Carúpano
Puerto La Cruz
Barcelona
Maturín
Anaco
El Tigre
Ciudad Bolívar
Ciudad Guayana
Upata
El Callao
El Dorado
Tucupita

Isla Blanquilla
Isla de Aves
Tobago
Trinidad
TRINIDAD & TOBAGO

ATLANTIC OCEAN

Charity
GEORGETOWN
New Amsterdam
PARAMARIBO
St-Laurent-du-Maroni
CAYENNE
Ouanary
Kourou
Sinnamary
Grand-Santi
St-Georges
Camopi

GUYANA
SURINAME
FRENCH GUIANA (to France)

Matthews Ridge
Aurora
Linden
Peters Mine
Kamarang
Kurupukari
Lethem
Oreallá
Apoera
Totness

Angel Falls

Pakaraima Mountains

Guiana Highlands

Tumuc-Humac Mountains

BRAZIL

Río Orinoco
Río Meta
Río Caura
Río Caroní
Río Arauca
Río Apure
Río Guaviare
Río Vaupés
Río Putumayo
Río Napo
Río Caquetá
Río Apaporis
Essequibo River
Courantyne
Embalse de Guri

Cordillera Central
Cordillera Occidental

(Venezuela claims all of Guyana west of Essequibo River)

(claimed by Suriname)

Equator

PACIFIC OCEAN

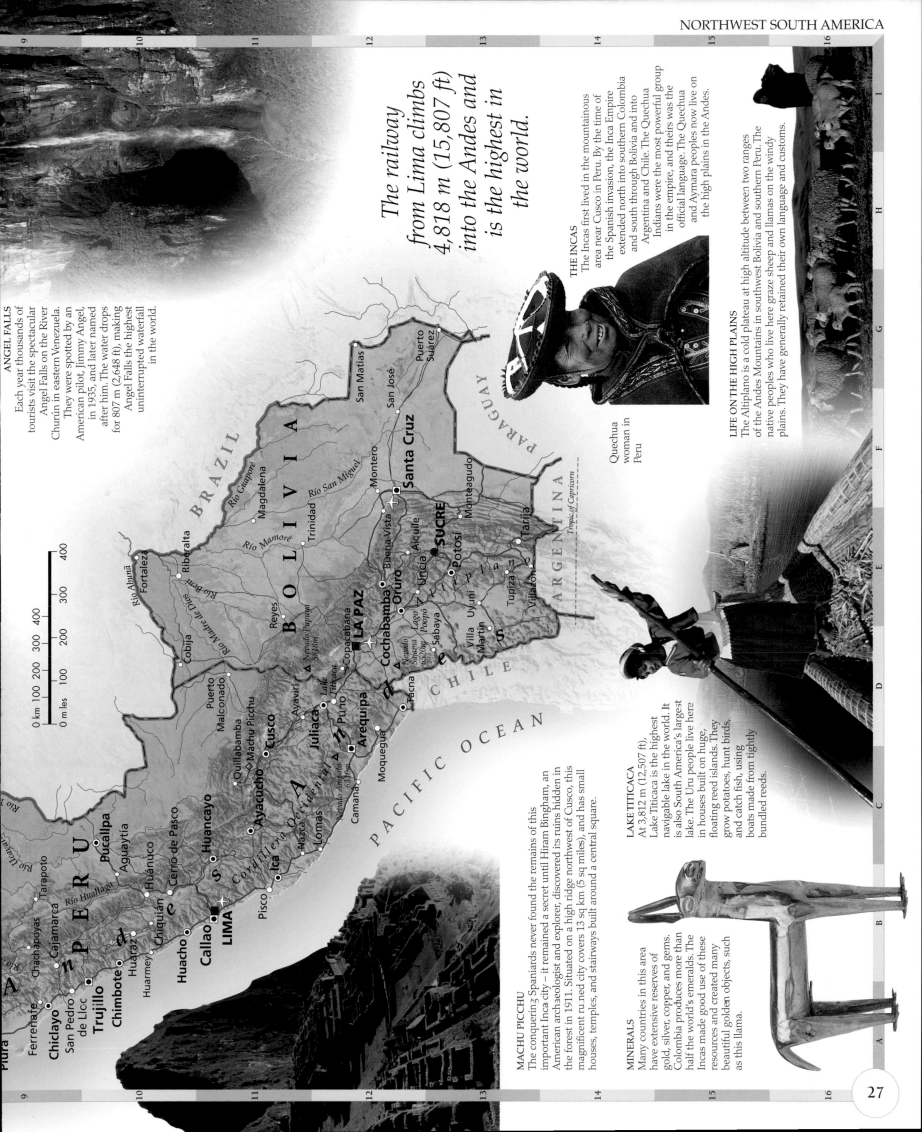

The railway from Lima climbs 4,818 m (15,807 ft) into the Andes and is the highest in the world.

ANGEL FALLS

Each year thousands of tourists visit the spectacular Angel Falls on the River Churún in eastern Venezuela. They were spotted by an American pilot, Jimmy Angel, in 1935, and later named after him. The water drops for 807 m (2,648 ft), making Angel Falls the highest uninterrupted waterfall in the world.

THE INCAS

The Incas first lived in the mountainous area near Cusco in Peru. By the time of the Spanish invasion, the Inca Empire extended north into southern Colombia and south through Bolivia and into Argentina and Chile. The Quechua Indians were the most powerful group in the empire, and theirs was the official language. The Quechua and Aymara peoples now live on the high plains in the Andes.

Quechua woman in Peru

LIFE ON THE HIGH PLAINS

The Altiplano is a cold plateau at high altitude between two ranges of the Andes Mountains in southwest Bolivia and southern Peru. The native peoples who live here graze sheep and llamas on the windy plains. They have generally retained their own language and customs.

MACHU PICCHU

The conquering Spaniards never found the remains of this important Inca city – it remained a secret until Hiram Bingham, an American archaeologist and explorer, discovered its ruins hidden in the forest in 1911. Situated on a high ridge northwest of Cusco, this magnificent ruined city covers 13 sq km (5 sq miles), and has small houses, temples, and stairways built around a central square.

MINERALS

Many countries in this area have extensive reserves of gold, silver, copper, and gems. Colombia produces more than half the world's emeralds. The Incas made good use of these resources and created many beautiful golden objects, such as this llama.

LAKE TITICACA

At 3,812 m (12,507 ft), Lake Titicaca is the highest navigable lake in the world. It is also South America's largest lake. The Uru people live here in houses built on huge, floating reed islands. They grow potatoes, hunt birds, and catch fish, using boats made from tightly bundled reeds.

Map labels

PACIFIC OCEAN

PERU
BRAZIL
BOLIVIA
PARAGUAY
ARGENTINA
CHILE

Piura
Ferreñafe
Chachapoyas
Tarapoto
Chiclayo
Cajamarca
San Pedro de Lloc
Trujillo
Chimbote
Huaraz
Chiquián
Huarmey
Huánuco
Bucallpa
Aguaytía
Cerro de Pasco
Huacho
Huancayo
Ayacucho
Callao
LIMA
Pisco
Ica
Cusco
Quillabamba
Machu Picchu
Juliaca
Ayaviri
Puno
Arequipa
Camaná
Lomas
Moquegua
Tacna

Río Ucayali
Río Huallaga
Río Marañón

Cordillera Occidental
Cordillera Oriental
Andes

Nevado Ampato 6310m
Nevado Sajama 6520m
Nevado Sarata 6310m
Nevado Payuya 5535m

Lake Titicaca
Copacabana
LA PAZ
Cochabamba
Oruro
Uncía
Potosí
Sucre
SUCRE
Villa Martín
Uyuni
Sabaya
Tupiza
Villazón
Tarija
Montaeagudo

Lago Poopó
Altiplano

Aicule

Buena Vista
Montero
Santa Cruz
San José
San Matías
Puerto Suárez

Trinidad
Río San Miguel
Reyes
Magdalena
Riberalta
Cobija
Puerto Maldonado
Fortaleza
Río Bení
Río Madre de Dios
Río Guaporé
Río Mamoré
Río Abuná

Tropic of Capricorn

0 km 100 200 300 400
0 miles 100 200 300 400

Brazil

THE VIBRANT CULTURE OF BRAZIL – with its fusion of music and dance – reflects the rich mix of its ethnic groups. The country also boasts immense natural resources with well-developed mining and manufacturing industries. Brazil grows all its own food and exports large quantities of coffee, sugar cane, soya beans, oranges, and cotton. However, the wealth is not evenly distributed, with some people living in luxury while most struggle with poverty. São Paulo is home to almost 10 million people, but poverty and lack of housing means that many live in shantytowns without running water or sanitation. Brazil was colonized in the 16th century by the Portuguese, who established their language and their Roman Catholic faith. It remains a deeply Catholic country with a strong emphasis on family life.

COFFEE
Brazil produces about one-quarter of the world's coffee, which is grown on large plantations in the states of Paraná and São Paulo. However, because world coffee prices go up and down so much, Brazilians are now growing other crops for export as well.

AMAZON RAINFOREST
Covering more than one-third of Brazil, the rainforest is home to a huge variety of animal and plant life. At one time, more than 5 million native Indians also lived here, but now only about 200,000 remain. Over the years, vast areas of forest have been cut down to provide timber for export, to make way for farmland, or to mine minerals such as gold, silver, and iron. The Kaxinawa Indians (left) still cultivate root vegetables as a food crop.

Brazilian morpho butterfly with brilliant blue wings, lives in rainforests from Brazil to Venezuela.

BRASÍLIA
Brasília replaced Rio de Janeiro as Brazil's capital in 1960 as part of a scheme to develop the interior of the country. Situated on land that was once rainforest, the city is laid out in the shape of an aeroplane. Government buildings are in the "cockpit", and residential areas are in the "wings".

FOOTBALL ENTHUSIASTS
Brazilians are passionate about football, which is played everywhere from beaches to shantytowns. There is fervent support for the national team, which has won the World Cup more times than any other country, most recently in 2002.

PEOPLE OF BRAZIL
Brazilians come from a variety of different ethnic groups, including descendants of the original native Indians, the Portuguese colonizers, African slaves brought over to work in the sugar plantations, and European migrants.

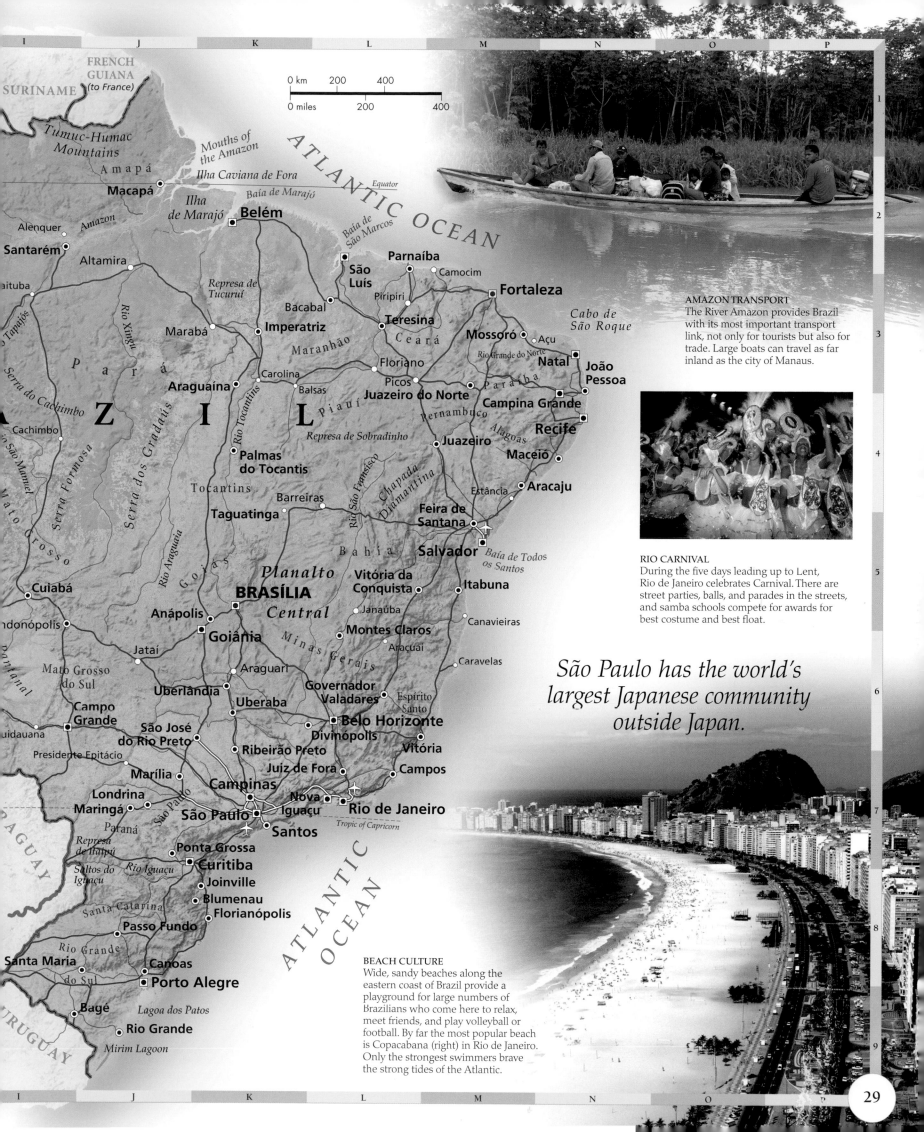

FRENCH GUIANA (to France)

SURINAME

Tumuc-Humac Mountains

Amapá

Mouths of the Amazon

Ilha Caviana de Fora

Equator

Baía de Marajó

Macapá

Alenquer

Amazon

Santarém

Altamira

aituba

Ilha de Marajó

Belém

ATLANTIC OCEAN

Baía de São Marcos

São Luís

Parnaíba

Camocim

Bacabal

Teresina

Piripiri

Fortaleza

Represa de Tucuruí

Imperatriz

Maranhão

Ceará

Mossoró

Açu

Cabo de São Roque

Marabá

Carolina

Floriano

Balsas

Natal

Rio Grande do Norte

Rio Xingu

Araguaína

Picos

Juazeiro do Norte

Piauí

Paraíba

João Pessoa

B R A Z I L

Serra do Cachimbo

Pará

Cachimbo

Rio Tapajós

Serra dos Gradaús

Rio Tocantins

Represa de Sobradinho

Campina Grande

Pernambuco

Recife

Rio São Francisco

Juazeiro

Alagoas

Maceió

Palmas do Tocantis

Chapada Diamantina

Tocantins

Estância

Aracaju

Serra Formosa

Taguatinga

Barreiras

Feira de Santana

Bahia

Salvador

Baía de Todos os Santos

Mato Grosso

Rio Araguaia

Goiás

Planalto

Vitória da Conquista

Itabuna

Cuiabá

ndonópolis

Anápolis

BRASÍLIA

Central

Janaúba

Canavieiras

Goiânia

Jataí

Minas

Araçuaí

Mato Grosso do Sul

Araguari

Gerais

Montes Claros

Caravelas

uidauana

Uberlândia

Uberaba

Governador Valadares

Espírito Santo

Campo Grande

São José do Rio Preto

Ribeirão Preto

Belo Horizonte

Divinópolis

Vitória

Presidente Epitácio

Marília

Juiz de Fora

Campos

Londrina

Campinas

Nova Iguaçu

Maringá

São Paulo

São Paulo

Iguaçu

Rio de Janeiro

Paraná

Santos

Tropic of Capricorn

Represa de Itaipú

Ponta Grossa

PARAGUAY

Curitiba

ATLANTIC OCEAN

Saltos do Iguaçu

Rio Iguaçu

Joinville

Santa Catarina

Blumenau

Florianópolis

Passo Fundo

Rio Grande

Santa Maria

Canoas

do Sul

Porto Alegre

URUGUAY

Bagé

Lagoa dos Patos

Rio Grande

Mirim Lagoon

0 km 200 400
0 miles 200 400

AMAZON TRANSPORT
The River Amazon provides Brazil with its most important transport link, not only for tourists but also for trade. Large boats can travel as far inland as the city of Manaus.

RIO CARNIVAL
During the five days leading up to Lent, Rio de Janeiro celebrates Carnival. There are street parties, balls, and parades in the streets, and samba schools compete for awards for best costume and best float.

São Paulo has the world's largest Japanese community outside Japan.

BEACH CULTURE
Wide, sandy beaches along the eastern coast of Brazil provide a playground for large numbers of Brazilians who come here to relax, meet friends, and play volleyball or football. By far the most popular beach is Copacabana (right) in Rio de Janeiro. Only the strongest swimmers brave the strong tides of the Atlantic.

Southern South America

TOWERING MOUNTAINS, vast grassy plains, and hot deserts create a very diverse geographical landscape. The four countries in this region – Chile, Paraguay, Uruguay, and Argentina – were once Spanish colonies but gained their independence in the early 1800s. Each country has an elected government but their economies remain fragile. Most of the population speak Spanish and are "mestizo" – of mixed Spanish and native Indian descent – except for Argentina, where up to 97 per cent are descended from Europeans.

Mix of Colonial Spanish, Italian, and Art Deco styles of architecture shows Montevideo's rich history

URUGUAY'S CAPITAL
The capital of Uruguay, Montevideo, is home to nearly half the country's population. It is also the main port and economic centre. This lively capital lies on the east bank of the Río de la Plata, and is a popular holiday resort because of its white sandy beaches.

ITAIPÚ DAM
The enormous Itaipú dam on the Paraná River in Paraguay is one of the world's largest hydroelectric projects. It can generate 90 per cent of the electricity Paraguay needs as well as large amounts for export.

ATACAMA DESERT
Sandwiched between the high Andes and the sea, the Atacama Desert in northern Chile is one of the hottest and driest areas in the world. Rain hardly ever falls here. This harsh landscape, however, is rich in copper deposits.

CHILEAN EDUCATION
Chile has a relatively high literacy rate (ability to read and write). This may be because schooling is both free and compulsory.

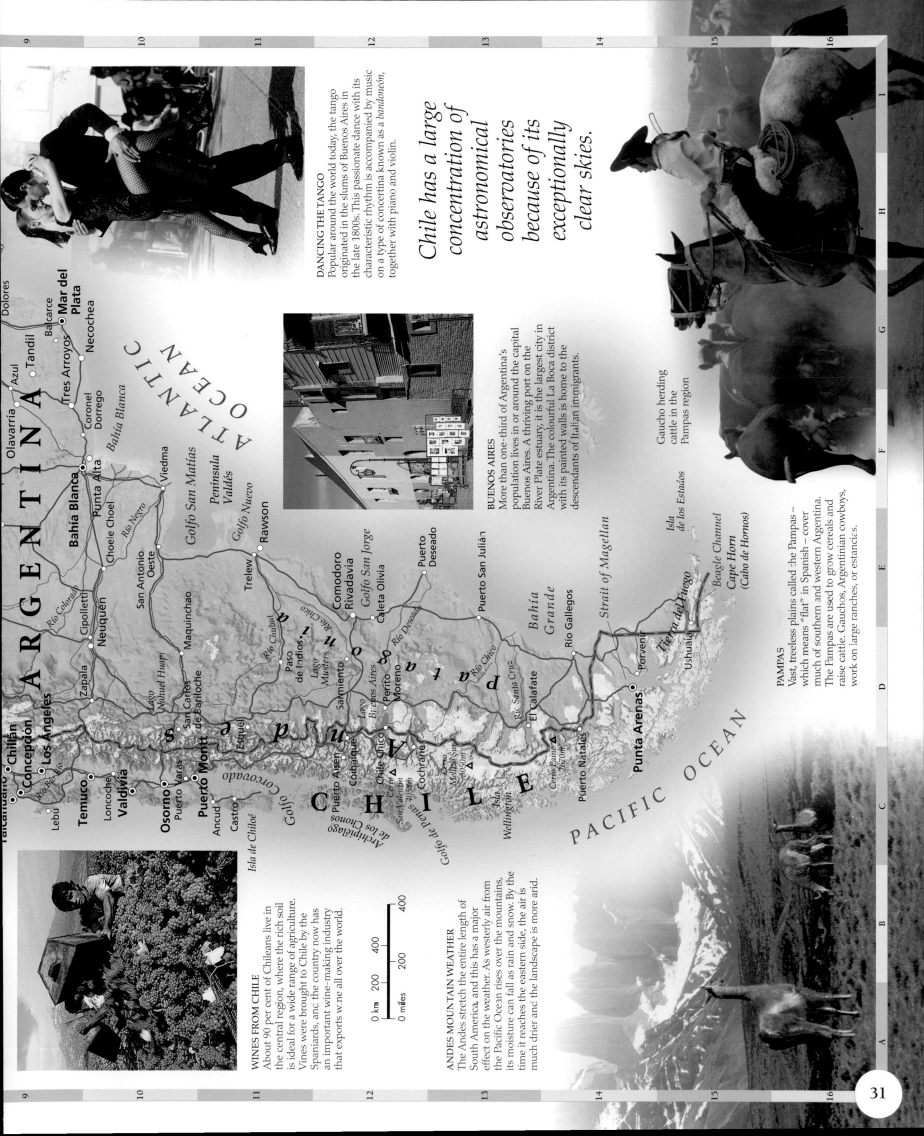

DANCING THE TANGO
Popular around the world today, the tango originated in the slums of Buenos Aires in the late 1800s. This passionate dance with its characteristic rhythm is accompanied by music on a type of concertina known as a *bandoneón*, together with piano and violin.

Chile has a large concentration of astronomical observatories because of its exceptionally clear skies.

BUENOS AIRES
More than one-third of Argentina's population lives in or around the capital Buenos Aires. A thriving port on the River Plate estuary, it is the largest city in Argentina. The colourful La Boca district with its painted walls is home to the descendants of Italian immigrants.

Gaucho herding cattle in the Pampas region

WINES FROM CHILE
About 90 per cent of Chileans live in the central region, where the rich soil is ideal for a wide range of agriculture. Vines were brought to Chile by the Spaniards, and the country now has an important wine-making industry that exports wine all over the world.

ANDES MOUNTAIN WEATHER
The Andes stretch the entire length of South America, and this has a major effect on the weather. As westerly air from the Pacific Ocean rises over the mountains, its moisture can fall as rain and snow. By the time it reaches the eastern side, the air is much drier and the landscape is more arid.

PAMPAS
Vast, treeless plains called the Pampas – which means "flat" in Spanish – cover much of southern and western Argentina. The Pampas are used to grow cereals and raise cattle. Gauchos, Argentinian cowboys, work on large ranches, or estancias.

Scale bar:
0 km 200 400
0 miles 200 400

Map labels:

ARGENTINA
CHILE
ATLANTIC OCEAN
PACIFIC OCEAN
Patagonia
Los Andes

Dolores
Balcarce
Azul
Tandil
Olavarría
Tres Arroyos
Necochea
Mar del Plata
Coronel Dorrego
Bahía Blanca
Punta Alta
Viedma
Bahía Blanca
Golfo San Matías
Península Valdés
Golfo Nuevo
Rawson
Río Negro
Choele Choel
San Antonio Oeste
Cipolletti
Río Colorado
Neuquén
Maquinchao
Golfo San Jorge
Comodoro Rivadavia
Caleta Olivia
Puerto Deseado
Río Chubut
Trelew
Río Chico
Río Deseado
Puerto San Julián
Zapala
Paso de Indios
Lago Musters
Sarmiento
Río Chico
Río Santa Cruz
Bahía Grande
Río Gallegos
Strait of Magellan
Isla de los Estados
Nahuel Huapi
San Carlos de Bariloche
Esquel
Lago Buenos Aires
Perito Moreno
Puerto Aisén
Coihaique
Chile Chico
Cochrane
Cerro San Valentín 4058m
Isla Wellington
Cerro Lautaro 3050m
Melimoyu
Puerto Natales
Punta Arenas
Porvenir
Tierra del Fuego
Ushuaia
Beagle Channel
Cape Horn (Cabo de Hornos)
El Calafate
Cerro Paine 2670m
Talcahuano
Chillán
Concepción
Los Ángeles
Lebu
Temuco
Loncoche
Valdivia
Río Bío Bío
Osorno
Puerto Varas
Puerto Montt
Ancud
Castro
Isla de Chiloé
Golfo Corcovado
Cerro Corcovado
Archipiélago de los Chonos
Golfo de Penas
Azul
Zapala

B   C   D   E   F   G   H

Atlantic Ocean

THE WORLD'S SECOND-LARGEST OCEAN, the Atlantic separates the Americas from Europe and Africa. The Atlantic is the world's youngest ocean, starting to form about 180 million years ago, as the continental plates began to separate. This movement continues today, as the oceanic plates that meet at the Mid-Atlantic Ridge continue to pull apart. The Atlantic is a major source of fish but, due to overfishing, stocks are now low. Many shipping routes cross the Atlantic, and pollution is an international problem as ships dump chemicals and waste. There are substantial reserves of oil and gas in the Gulf of Mexico, off the coast of west Africa, and in the north Atlantic.

GREENLAND
The largest island in the world, Greenland is a self-governing part of Denmark. Most Greenlanders live on the southwest coast. Mainly Inuit, with some Danish-Norwegian influences, they make their living by seal hunting, fishing, and fur trapping.

Fishing for halibut

TOURISM
The volcanic islands and black beaches of the eastern Atlantic, especially the Canaries (left), Madeira, and the Azores, are popular with tourists, who are attracted by the scenery and subtropical climate.

WARM CURRENTS
The Gulf Stream flows up the east coast of North America and across the Atlantic. It brings warm water and a mild climate to northern Europe, which would otherwise be cooler.

Mid-Atlantic Ridge

Tristan da Cunha island

At the centre of the ridge is a valley at least 16 km (10 miles) wide

UNDERWATER MOUNTAINS
The Mid-Atlantic Ridge is a great underwater mountain chain that runs the entire length of the Atlantic. It was formed by magma that oozed up from the sea bed, cooled to create solid rock, and gradually built up to form a ridge. Some peaks are so high that they break the surface to form volcanic islands, such as the country of Iceland.

ATLANTIC FISHING INDUSTRY
The Atlantic Ocean contains more than half the world's total stock of fish. Herring, anchovy, sardine, cod, flounder, and tuna are among the most important fish found here. However, overfishing, particularly of cod and tuna, has caused a significant decline in numbers.

WHALES
Many whales live in the Atlantic, migrating from summer feeding grounds in the cold polar regions to warmer waters in the Caribbean for the winter. They give birth and mate again before returning north.

Humpback whale breaching

FALKLANDS
Set in the windy south Atlantic off the coast of Argentina, the Falkland Islands belong to the UK but are also claimed by Argentina. Fishing and sheep farming are important. The land is rocky, mountainous, boggy, and almost treeless.

NORTH AMERICA

BERMU (to

Gulf of Mexico

Hatteras Plain

Greater Antilles

Puerto Trench

Caribbean Sea

Colombian Basin

Lesser Ar

Guatemala Basin

Panama Basin

Galápagos Islands (to Ecuador)

Peru-Chile Trench

Peru Basin

SOUT

PACIFIC OCEAN

Andes

Chile Basin

Peru-Chile Trench

Chile Rise

A   B   C   D   E   H

GREENLAND
(to Denmark)
Labrador
Sea
Denmark Strait
ICELAND
REYKJAVIK
FAEROE ISLANDS
(to Denmark)
Labrador
Basin
Reykjanes
Basin
Iceland
Basin
British
Isles
North
Sea
Baltic Sea
EUROPE
Charlie-Gibbs Fracture Zone
Rockall Bank
Bay of
Biscay
Alps
Newfoundland
Grand Banks of
Newfoundland
Newfoundland
Basin
Azores
(to Portugal)
East Azores Fracture Zone
Mediterranean Sea
Sohm
Plain
Madeira
(to Portugal)
Atlas Mountains
argasso
Sea
Great Meteor
Tablemount
Canary Islands
(to Spain)
Madeira
Plain
Sahara
Cape Verde
Plain
Kane Fracture Zone
Cape Verde
Basin
PRAIA
CAPE
VERDE
Sahel
ATLANTIC
AFRICA
Doldrums Fracture Zone
Sierra
Leone
Rise
Sierra
Leone
Basin
OCEAN
Mid
Guinea
Basin
Gulf of
Guinea
Amazon
Fan
Ceará Plain
Pernambuco
Plain
Ascension Fracture Zone
ASCENSION ISLAND
(to St Helena)
MERICA
Fernando de
Noronha
(to Brazil)
Brazil
Basin
Atlantic
ST HELENA
(to UK)
Zubov
Seamount
Angola
Basin
Vitória
Seamount
Ilha da
Trindade
(to Brazil)
Ridge
Santos
Plateau
Walvis Ridge
Orange Fan
Cape
Basin
Rio Grande
Rise
Cape of
Good Hope
Argentine
Basin
TRISTAN DA CUNHA
(to St Helena)
Gough Island
(to Tristan da Cunha)
f of San Matías
f of San Jorge
FALKLAND ISLANDS
(to UK)
Zapiola Ridge
Gough Fracture Zone
BOUVET
ISLAND
(to Norway)
Scotia
Sea
SOUTH SANDWICH
ISLANDS
(to UK)
SOUTH GEORGIA
(to UK)
SOUTHERN OCEAN
ape
orn
Drake Passage
East Scotia
Basin

Mineral-rich waters
in the Blue Lagoon,
Iceland, are said to
be beneficial to
people's health

ICELAND
Iceland is situated in the north Atlantic on
the Mid-Atlantic Ridge. As a result, it has at
least 20 active volcanoes and suffers frequent
earthquakes. There are numerous thermal
springs with boiling mud lakes and geysers.
Water from hot springs (above) is used to
provide hot water and heating for much of
Iceland's population, most of whom live
on the coast. The warm Gulf Stream
ensures that the country's ports
stay ice-free in winter.

*The Atlantic
covers one-fifth
of Earth's
surface.*

ICEBERGS
Icebergs in the Atlantic Ocean are
formed when icesheets and glaciers
reach the sea. Parts break off and start
to drift, driven by winds and currents.

AFRICA

Covering one-fifth of the world's land area, Africa has a rapidly growing populat███ Many of its 52 nations – listed below in order of size – are desperately poor. This is partly due to hostile climates, especially in and around the vast Sahara desert, but also because of a history of political turmoil, ethnic tennsion or conflict and, in some countries, war. Despite this, African culture is among the most vibrant on Earth.

Sudan
- 2,505,813 sq km
  967,500 sq miles
- 42,300,000
- Khartoum
- Arabic, Dinka, Nuer, Nubian, Beja, Zande, Bari, Fur, Shilluk, Lotuko

Chad
- 1,284,000 sq km
  495,755 sq miles
- 11,200,000
- N'Djamena
- French, Sara, Arabic, Maba

Ethiopia
- 1,104,300 sq km
  426,373 sq miles
- 82,800,000
- Addis Ababa
- Amharic, Tigrinya, Galla, Sidamo, Somali, English, Arabic (Oromu)

Namibia
- 824,292 sq km
  318,261 sq miles
- 2,170,000
- Windhoek
- Ovambo, Kavango, English, Bergdama, German, Afrikaans

Madagascar
- 587,041 sq km
  226,658 sq miles
- 19,600,000
- Antananarivo
- Malagasy, French

Zimbabwe
- 390,757 sq km
  150,872 sq miles
- 12,500,000
- Harare
- Shona, isiNdebele, English

Algeria
- 2,381,741 sq km
  919,595 sq miles
- 34,900,000
- Algiers
- Arabic, Tamazight (Berber: Kabyle, Shawia, Tamashek), French

Niger
- 1,267,000 sq km
  489,191 sq miles
- 15,300,000
- Niamey
- Hausa, Djerma, Fula, Tuareg, Teda, French

Mauritania
- 1,030,700 sq km
  397,955 sq miles
- 3,290,000
- Nouakchott
- Hassaniyah Arabic, Wolof, French

Mozambique
- 799,380 sq km
  308,642 sq miles
- 22,900,000
- Maputo
- Makua, Xitsonga, Sena, Lomwe, Portuguese

Botswana
- 581,730 sq km
  224,607 sq miles
- 1,950,000
- Gaborone
- Setswana, English, Shona, San, Khoikhoi, isiNdebele

Ivory Coast
- 322,463 sq km
  124,504 sq miles
- 21,100,000
- Yamoussoukro
- Akan, French, Kru, Voltaïque

Congo, Dem Rep of
- 2,344,858 sq km
  905,355 sq miles
- 66,000,000
- Kinshasa
- Kiswahili, Tshiluba, Kikongo, Lingala, French

Angola
- 1,246,700 sq km
  481,354 sq miles
- 18,500,000
- Luanda
- Portuguese, Umbundu, Kimbundu, Kikongo

Egypt
- 1,001,450 sq km
  386,662 sq miles
- 83,000,000
- Cairo
- Arabic, French, English, Berber

Zambia
- 752,618 sq km
  290,587 sq miles
- 12,900,000
- Lusaka
- Bemba, Tongan, Nyanja, Lozi, Lala-Bisa, Nsenga, English

Kenya
- 580,367 sq km
  224,081 sq miles
- 39,800,000
- Nairobi
- Kiswahili, English, Kikuyu, Luo, Kalenjin, Kamba

Burkina Faso
- 274,200 sq km
  105,869 sq miles
- 15,800,000
- Ouagadougou
- Mossi, Fulani, French, Tuareg, Diyula, Songhai

Congo, Republic of
- 2,344,858 sq km
  905,355 sq miles
- 3,680,000
- Brazzaville
- Kikongo, Teke, Lingala, French

Mali
- 1,240,192 sq km
  478,841 sq miles
- 13,000,000
- Bamako
- Bambara, Fula, Senufo, Soninke, French

Tanzania
- 947,300 sq km
  365,755 sq miles
- 43,700,000
- Dodoma
- Kiswahili, Sukuma,Kichagga, Nyamwezi, Hehe, Makonde, Yao, Sandawe, English

Somalia
- 637,657 sq km
  246,201 sq miles
- 9,130,000
- Mogadishu
- Somali, Arabic, English, Italian

Cameroon
- 475,440 sq km
  183,568 sq miles
- 19,500,000
- Yaoundé
- Bamileke, Fang, Fula, French, English

Gabon
- 267,667 sq km
  103,347 sq miles
- 1,470,000
- Libreville
- Fang, French, Punu, Sira, Nzebi, Mpongwe

Libya
- 1,759,540 sq km
  679,362 sq miles
- 6,420,000
- Tripoli
- Arabic, Tuareg

South Africa
- 1,219,090 sq km
  470,693 sq miles
- 50,100,000
- Tshwane
- English, isiZulu, isiXhosa, Afrikaans, Sepedi, Setswana, Sesotho, Xitsonga, siSwati, ███████████████

Nigeria
- 923,768 sq km
  356,669 sq miles
- 155,000,000
- Abuja
- Hausa, English, Yoruba, Igbo

Central African Republic
- 622,984 sq km
  240,535 sq miles
- 4,420,000
- Bangui
- Sango, Banda, Gbaya, French

Morocco
- 446,550 sq km
  172,414 sq miles
- 32,000,000
- Rabat
- Arabic, Tamazight (Berber), French, Spanish

Guinea
- 245,857 sq km
  94,926 sq miles
- 10,100,000
- Conakry
- Pulaar, Malinké, Sousou, French

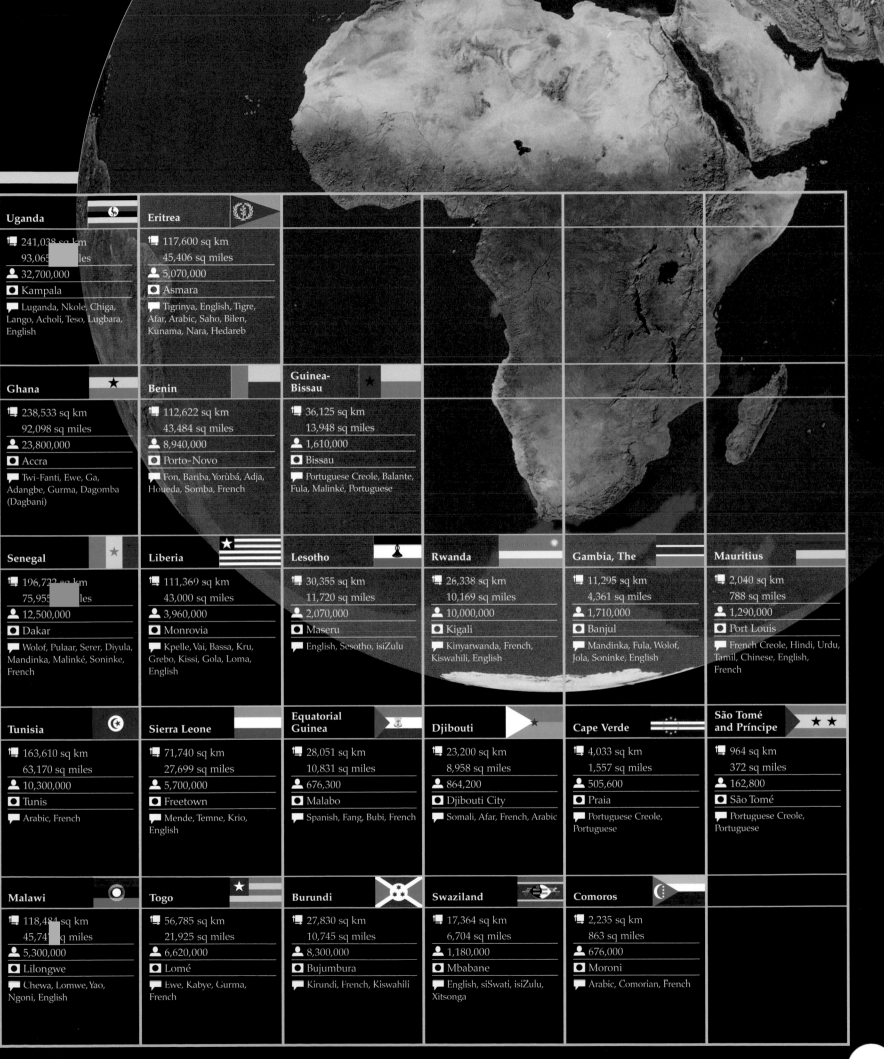

Uganda
- 241,038 sq km
  93,065 sq miles
- 32,700,000
- Kampala
- Luganda, Nkole, Chiga, Lango, Acholi, Teso, Lugbara, English

Eritrea
- 117,600 sq km
  45,406 sq miles
- 5,070,000
- Asmara
- Tigrinya, English, Tigre, Afar, Arabic, Saho, Bilen, Kunama, Nara, Hedareb

Ghana
- 238,533 sq km
  92,098 sq miles
- 23,800,000
- Accra
- Twi-Fanti, Ewe, Ga, Adangbe, Gurma, Dagomba (Dagbani)

Benin
- 112,622 sq km
  43,484 sq miles
- 8,940,000
- Porto-Novo
- Fon, Bariba, Yorùbá, Adja, Houeda, Somba, French

Guinea-Bissau
- 36,125 sq km
  13,948 sq miles
- 1,610,000
- Bissau
- Portuguese Creole, Balante, Fula, Malinké, Portuguese

Senegal
- 196,722 sq km
  75,955 sq miles
- 12,500,000
- Dakar
- Wolof, Pulaar, Serer, Diyula, Mandinka, Malinké, Soninke, French

Liberia
- 111,369 sq km
  43,000 sq miles
- 3,960,000
- Monrovia
- Kpelle, Vai, Bassa, Kru, Grebo, Kissi, Gola, Loma, English

Lesotho
- 30,355 sq km
  11,720 sq miles
- 2,070,000
- Maseru
- English, Sesotho, isiZulu

Rwanda
- 26,338 sq km
  10,169 sq miles
- 10,000,000
- Kigali
- Kinyarwanda, French, Kiswahili, English

Gambia, The
- 11,295 sq km
  4,361 sq miles
- 1,710,000
- Banjul
- Mandinka, Fula, Wolof, Jola, Soninke, English

Mauritius
- 2,040 sq km
  788 sq miles
- 1,290,000
- Port Louis
- French Creole, Hindi, Urdu, Tamil, Chinese, English, French

Tunisia
- 163,610 sq km
  63,170 sq miles
- 10,300,000
- Tunis
- Arabic, French

Sierra Leone
- 71,740 sq km
  27,699 sq miles
- 5,700,000
- Freetown
- Mende, Temne, Krio, English

Equatorial Guinea
- 28,051 sq km
  10,831 sq miles
- 676,300
- Malabo
- Spanish, Fang, Bubi, French

Djibouti
- 23,200 sq km
  8,958 sq miles
- 864,200
- Djibouti City
- Somali, Afar, French, Arabic

Cape Verde
- 4,033 sq km
  1,557 sq miles
- 505,600
- Praia
- Portuguese Creole, Portuguese

São Tomé and Príncipe
- 964 sq km
  372 sq miles
- 162,800
- São Tomé
- Portuguese Creole, Portuguese

Malawi
- 118,484 sq km
  45,745 sq miles
- 5,300,000
- Lilongwe
- Chewa, Lomwe, Yao, Ngoni, English

Togo
- 56,785 sq km
  21,925 sq miles
- 6,620,000
- Lomé
- Ewe, Kabye, Gurma, French

Burundi
- 27,830 sq km
  10,745 sq miles
- 8,300,000
- Bujumbura
- Kirundi, French, Kiswahili

Swaziland
- 17,364 sq km
  6,704 sq miles
- 1,180,000
- Mbabane
- English, siSwati, isiZulu, Xitsonga

Comoros
- 2,235 sq km
  863 sq miles
- 676,000
- Moroni
- Arabic, Comorian, French

Northwest Africa

FOUR COUNTRIES, plus the disputed area of Western Sahara, make up this part of Africa. Algeria, Libya, and Tunisia have rich supplies of oil and natural gas that boost their economies. Morocco relies on tourism, phosphates used for chemicals and fertilizer, and agriculture. In the fertile valleys of the Atlas Mountains, farmers grow grapes, citrus fruit, dates, and olives. The area also attracts tourists to its colourful markets, historical sites, and sandy beaches. The Sahara Desert dominates the region, particularly in Algeria and Libya.

SUN AND SEA
Many tourists visit Tunisia and Morocco each year to enjoy the warm climate and sandy beaches. Tourism provides jobs for the local people and brings much-needed income.

ARAB INFLUENCE
Arab invasions during the 7th and 11th centuries have influenced the culture, religion (Islam), architecture, and language of northwest Africa. Today, Arabic is the main language, and more than 95 per cent of the people here are Muslim.

MOROCCAN MARKET
In a souk, or market, craftworkers sell handmade products to tourists. Goods are displayed in booths along the bustling streets.

Muslims going to worship at the Hassan II mosque in Casablanca, Morocco

BERBERS
The Berber people were the original inhabitants of northwest Africa. Most now live in the Atlas Mountains or the desert. Although most Berbers converted to Islam when the Arabs arrived, they kept their own language and way of life. In 2001, Algeria recognized Berber (Tamazight) as an official language.

Berber woman working on the land in the Atlas Mountains

DATE PALMS

Dates are an important crop for Algeria and Tunisia. Date palms are often grown at oases, where water lies close to the surface of the desert. Here, the clusters of dates are shown ripening beneath polythene. Leaves from the trees can be used for thatch and the trunk is cut for timber.

ANCIENT RUINS

Phoenicians, Romans, and Greeks from ancient times have all left their mark on this part of Africa. Today, tourists come to admire the historical sites along the coast. These ruins of Carthage, near Tunis, date from 146 BCE, when Romans laid waste to this city. The Romans went on to control all of the north African coast.

The stones from dates can be roasted and ground to make a traditional date coffee.

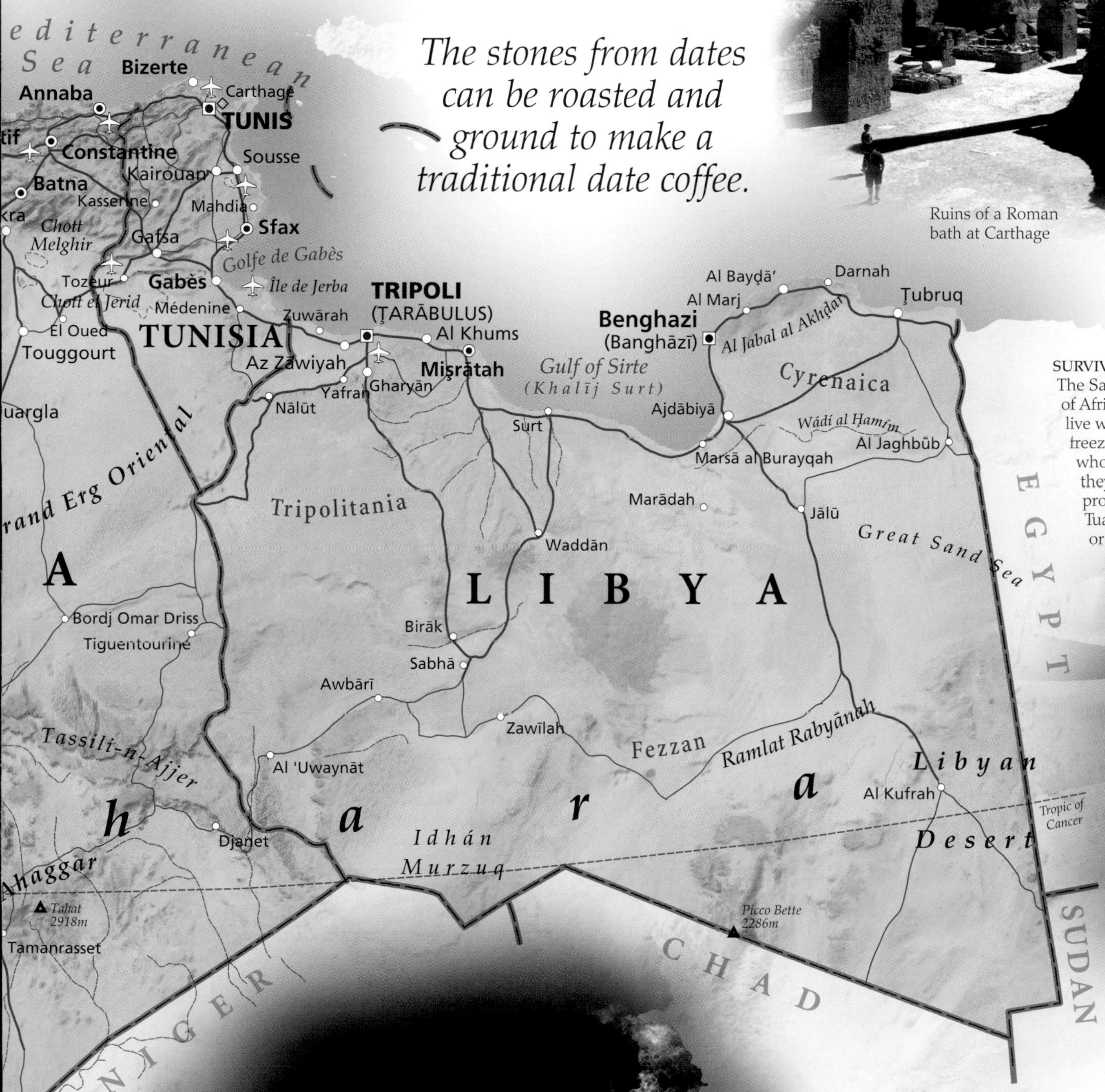

Ruins of a Roman bath at Carthage

Map labels

Mediterranean Sea
Bizerte
Annaba
Carthage
TUNIS
Constantine
Kairouan
Sousse
Batna
Kasserine
Mahdia
Gafsa
Sfax
Chott Melghir
Golfe de Gabès
Tozeur
Gabès
Île de Jerba
Chott el Jerid
Médenine
Zuwārah
TRIPOLI (ṬARĀBULUS)
El Oued
Touggourt
TUNISIA
Az Zāwiyah
Al Khums
Benghazi (Banghāzī)
 Al Bayḍā'
Al Marj
Darnah
Ṭubruq
Al Jabal al Akhḍar
Cyrenaica
uargla
Gharyān
Yafran
Miṣrātah
Gulf of Sirte (Khalīj Surt)
Ajdābiyā
Wādī al Ḥamīm
Nālūt
Surt
Al Jaghbūb
Marsā al Burayqah
Tripolitania
Marādah
Jālū
Great Sand Sea
Grand Erg Oriental
A
Waddān
LIBYA
E G Y P T
Bordj Omar Driss
Tiguentourine
Birāk
Sabhā
Awbārī
Fezzan
Ramlat Rabyānah
Libyan
Tassili-n-Ajjer
Zawīlah
Al 'Uwaynāt
Al Kufrah
Tropic of Cancer
h
a
r
a
Desert
Ahaggar
Djanet
Idhán
Murzuq
Talat 2918m
Tamanrasset
Picco Bette 2286m
N I G E R
C H A D
S U D A N

SURVIVAL IN THE SAHARA

The Sahara Desert covers almost one-third of Africa and is an inhospitable place to live with high daytime temperatures and freezing nights. The Tuareg are nomads for whom the desert is home. Traditionally, they keep camels for transport and to provide meat, milk, and hides. Many Tuareg now live in mountain areas or dwell in the cities.

Tuareg nomads in the Sahara carry salt to trade in markets

0 km 100 200
0 miles 100 200

Libyan oil field

LIBYAN OIL RESOURCES

The discovery of oil and gas in 1959 brought considerable wealth to Libya, and oil and gas currently make up 95 per cent of the country's exports. As a result, Libya's cities have grown as people have moved from rural areas to find work in the oil industry. Some of the money from oil is being spent on better healthcare and education for Libyans.

Northeast Africa

THIS REGION, KNOWN AS the Horn of Africa, contains the oldest civilizations in the continent, and some of its poorest countries. The borders that divide the countries today were mostly created by colonial rulers in the last hundred years. Pastoral nomads with their herds of animals often cross these borders in search of pasture. Most people still live in the countryside and farm the land, but many people now live in the cities. Tourism and agriculture are important sources of income for Egypt and Kenya, two of the richest and fastest-growing countries in the region. Elsewhere, tribal rivalries and disputes over land and resources have sometimes erupted into full-scale war and these, together with drought and poverty, have blighted the lives of millions of people in this region.

RIVER NILE

The Nile is the world's longest river. It flows north from Burundi to run along the Tanzania–Rwanda border, then through Uganda, Sudan, and Egypt to the coast. Most of Egypt's population lives around the valley and delta of the Nile, which provides the region's water. The river also provides irrigation for local crops, such as cotton.

SUEZ CANAL

The Suez Canal, opened in 1869, is one of the world's longest and most important artificial waterways. It links the Mediterranean Sea with the Gulf of Suez and the Red Sea, providing a crucial shortcut from Europe to India and east Asia. The tolls from the canal are a great source of income for Egypt.

LOSING FARMLAND

As the population grows in Ethiopia, forests are cut down for firewood, or to cultivate new areas for food crops. The soil, no longer held firm by the trees, is easily blown or washed away, and valuable farmland is lost.

Ploughing fields in Ethiopia

ABU SIMBEL

Tourists come to Egypt to see the pyramids at Giza and the temples along the Nile, such as these two built at Abu Simbel, south of Aswan. Tourism brings in money to preserve these historical sites.

Map labels

Mediterranean Sea

Nile Delta

Alexandria
Al ʿAlamayn
Sîdi Barrâni
Qattâra Depression –133m
Siwah

Dumyât
Port Said
Suez Canal
Al Ismâʿîlîyah
Suez
Az Zaqâzîq
Giza
CAIRO
Beni Suef
Al Minyâ
Mallawī
Asyût
Sawhâj
Qinâ
Luxor
Isnâ
Idfû
Aswân
Akhmîm
Hurghada
Gulf of Suez
▲ Gebel Mûsa 2285m
Tropic of Cancer
Lake Nasser
Aswan Dam

Qasr Farâfra
Bawîti
El Khârga

Saḥarâ al Gharbîya (Western Desert)

EGYPT

Sahara al Gharbîya

Great Sand Sea

Gilf Kebir Plateau

▲ Jabal al ʿUwaynât 1907m

El Atrun

Tropic of Cancer

LIBYA

CHAD

Darfur

Kebkabiya
El Geneina
Umm Burū
El Fasher
Sodiri
El Obeid

(administered by Egypt)

(administered by Sudan)

Wadi Halfa
Akasha
Delgo
Argo
Dongola
Ed Debba
Merowe

Wadi Oko

Red Sea

Port Sudan
Suakin
Tokar
Haiya
Abu Hamed
Shereik
Atbara
Ed Damer
Shendi

Nubian Desert

Abu Hamed

SUDAN

Omdurman
KHARTOUM
Wad Medani
Umm Ruwaba

Wâdi el Milk

Wâdi Howar

Nile

ERITREA
ASMARA
Massawa
Zula
Teseney
Mekʿelē
Maychew
Gedaref
Kassala
Khashm el Girba
Sennar
Gonder
Aseb

Dunakil Desert

Blue Nile

DJIBOUTI

Gulf of Aden

Caluula

Water makes up almost one-fifth of the surface area of Uganda.

RELIGIOUS BELIEFS
The Ethiopian Orthodox Union Church has existed since the 4th century CE. It is a branch of the Coptic Church and mixes Christian beliefs, such as Catholic saints, with some traditional African spiritual beliefs.

Coptic cross

TEA IN KENYA
Kenya is an important world producer of tea, which is grown on plantations in the highland areas (such as this one below). High rainfall here ensures a good crop. Coffee is also a valuable export.

Kenyan workers carefully select tea leaves for picking.

CAIRO
The largest city in Africa is Cairo, the capital of Egypt, with a population of more than 15 million. Here, Arab, African, and European influences exist alongside more traditional Egyptian customs.

Busy street bazaar in Cairo

SUDANESE DINKA
There are more than 500 different tribes in Sudan, who speak more than 100 languages and dialects. Like many tribal people here, the Dinka are nomadic – their cattle graze on the plains east of the Nile. Cattle are central to their lives – young Dinka men officially become adults with an initiation ceremony in which they are given an ox of their own.

Young Dinka man

MOUNTAIN GORILLAS
The Volcanoes National Park in Rwanda is one of the few places where you can still see a mountain gorilla (right) in the wild. These animals are threatened with extinction because of poachers and the destruction of their habitat. Tanzania and Kenya also have many important game reserves, which preserve the wildlife of the savannah.

0 km   100   200   400
0 miles   100   200   300   400

West Africa

0 km 100 200 300 400

0 miles 100 200 300 400

DRAMATICALLY **DIFFERENT CLIMATES** and landscapes influence life in west Africa. In the hot, dry north, it is difficult to grow crops. Only oases in the Sahara and seasonal rainfall in the Sahel make crop-growing possible. To the south, the climate is warm and wet, and crops such as cocoa and coffee are grown on large plantations. This region also has many valuable minerals. Despite these rich resources, most countries are poor. Since independence from colonial powers, there has been much political unrest, often sparked by poverty and tribal rivalries in the region. West Africa is also divided by religion, with Islam dominant in the north and Christianity in the south.

GAMBIA
In recent years, tourism has become increasingly important to the economy of Gambia. Visitors come to see wildlife along the River Gambia and to visit the Atlantic coast beaches. These safari tourists are admiring a giant termite mound.

PEOPLE OF GHANA
Family ties and a sense of community are important to the people of Ghana, and ceremonies throughout each year mark the events of childbirth, puberty, marriage, and death. About half of Ghanaians are Ashanti people whose ancestors developed one of the richest and most notable civilizations in Africa.

DIAMONDS AND GOLD
West Africa has many valuable minerals, including diamonds, uranium, copper, and gold. In Sierra Leone, where diamonds (left) provide crucial income, the mines were a focus of fighting in the civil war between rebel groups and the government.

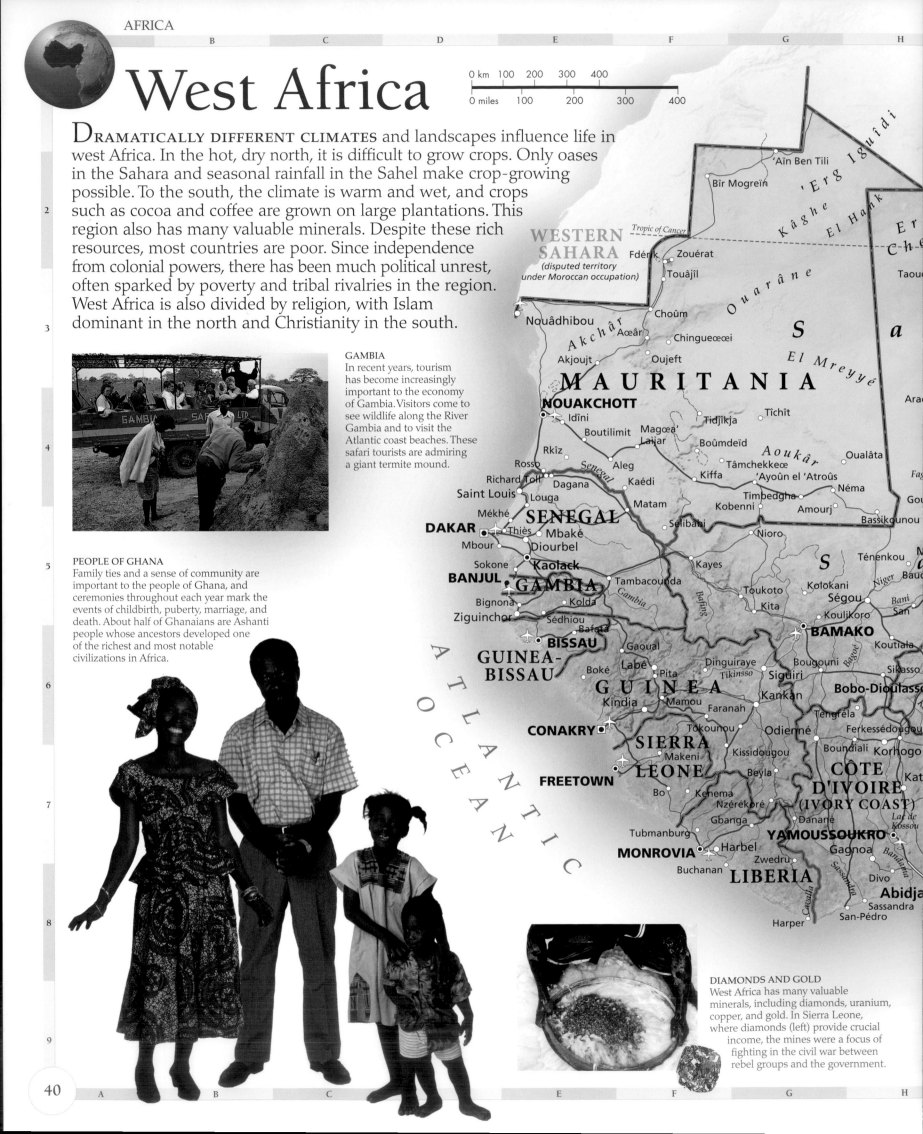

ATLANTIC OCEAN

WESTERN SAHARA
(disputed territory under Moroccan occupation)

MAURITANIA

NOUAKCHOTT

SENEGAL

DAKAR

BANJUL

GAMBIA

GUINEA-BISSAU

BISSAU

GUINEA

CONAKRY

SIERRA LEONE

FREETOWN

LIBERIA

MONROVIA

CÔTE D'IVOIRE (IVORY COAST)

YAMOUSSOUKRO

'Aïn Ben Tili
Bîr Mogreïn
Fdérik Zouérat
Touâjîl
Nouâdhibou
Choûm
Aœâr Chingueœœi
Akjoujt Oujeft
Idîni
Boutilimit Magœa' Laïjar
Rkîz
Rosso Aleg Boûmdeïd
Richard Toll Dagana Kaédi
Saint Louis Louga Kiffa
Mékhé Matam
Thiès Mbaké
Mbour Diourbel Sélibabi
Sokone Kaolack Nioro
Tambacounda Kayes
Bignona Kolda
Ziguinchor Sédhiou Toukoto
Bafatá Kita
Gaoual Koulikoro
Boké Labé Pita BAMAKO
Dinguiraye Bougouni
Kindia Tikinsso Siguiri
Mamou Kankan Bobo-Dioulasso
Faranah Tengréla
Tokounou Odienné Ferkessédougou
Makeni Kissidougou Boundiali Korhogo
Beyla
Bo Kenema Danané Lac de Kossou
Nzérékoré Gagnoa
Gbanga Divo
Tubmanburg Harbel Abidja
Buchanan Zwedru Sassandra
Harper San-Pédro

Tropic of Cancer

'Erg Iguîdi
Kâghe El Hank
Ouarâne
El Mreyyé
Aoukâr
Tidjîkja Tîchît
Kobenni Amourj
'Ayoûn el 'Atroûs Néma
Oualâta
Bassikounou
Ténenkou
Kolokani
Ségou
Koutiala
Sikasso
Korhogo

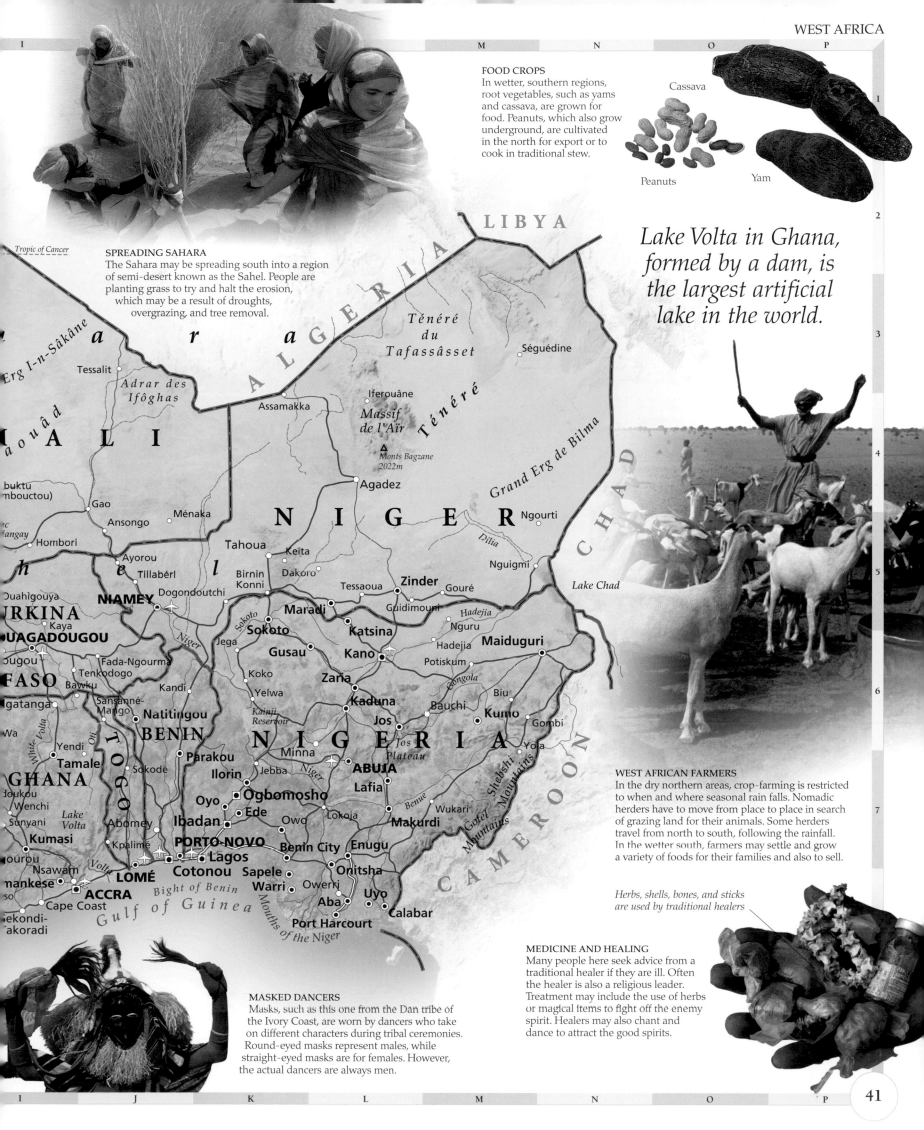

FOOD CROPS
In wetter, southern regions, root vegetables, such as yams and cassava, are grown for food. Peanuts, which also grow underground, are cultivated in the north for export or to cook in traditional stew.

Cassava

Peanuts

Yam

SPREADING SAHARA
The Sahara may be spreading south into a region of semi-desert known as the Sahel. People are planting grass to try and halt the erosion, which may be a result of droughts, overgrazing, and tree removal.

Lake Volta in Ghana, formed by a dam, is the largest artificial lake in the world.

WEST AFRICAN FARMERS
In the dry northern areas, crop-farming is restricted to when and where seasonal rain falls. Nomadic herders have to move from place to place in search of grazing land for their animals. Some herders travel from north to south, following the rainfall. In the wetter south, farmers may settle and grow a variety of foods for their families and also to sell.

Herbs, shells, bones, and sticks are used by traditional healers

MEDICINE AND HEALING
Many people here seek advice from a traditional healer if they are ill. Often the healer is also a religious leader. Treatment may include the use of herbs or magical items to fight off the enemy spirit. Healers may also chant and dance to attract the good spirits.

MASKED DANCERS
Masks, such as this one from the Dan tribe of the Ivory Coast, are worn by dancers who take on different characters during tribal ceremonies. Round-eyed masks represent males, while straight-eyed masks are for females. However, the actual dancers are always men.

41

Central Africa

ALL EIGHT COUNTRIES IN central Africa were European colonies with a painful history of slavery. Since the 1960s, independence has brought them mixed success. Rich mineral deposits and the discovery of offshore oil have provided income for Cameroon, Congo, and Gabon, while civil war and repressive governments have damaged other countries in the region. These include Chad and the Central African Republic, two of the world's poorest countries. Although the north is mainly arid, Africa's largest tropical rainforest dominates the south, with the powerful Congo River linking the interior with the coast. The tiny, volcanic country of São Tomé and Príncipe lies off the coast of Gabon.

RELIGIOUS BELIEFS
Although Christianity is the main religion here, many people also follow traditional beliefs. These suggest that natural objects, such as mountains and rivers, have a spirit. Masks, like this Bambuku head, are sometimes used to scare off evil spirits.

VILLAGE LIFE
Most people in rural areas live in villages or small towns. Some grow crops, such as cotton or cassava, for sale, but many exist just by growing food just for their family.

Mud-brick home

FISHING IN LAKE CHAD
Lake Chad is an important source of food, but it is shrinking at an alarming rate. A shallow lake, it is now only about 2–4 m (6.5–13 ft) deep on average. Its surface area has also reduced, due to droughts and the demand for water to irrigate the land.

0 km 100   200   300   400
0 miles   100   200   300   400

PEOPLE OF CHAD
With almost half the country lying in the arid Sahara Desert, more than 70 per cent of Chadians work on farmland near the River Chari in the south. Across Chad there are large numbers of ethnic groups, speaking more than 100 languages. Women here live an average of just 50 years and have 6.2 children.

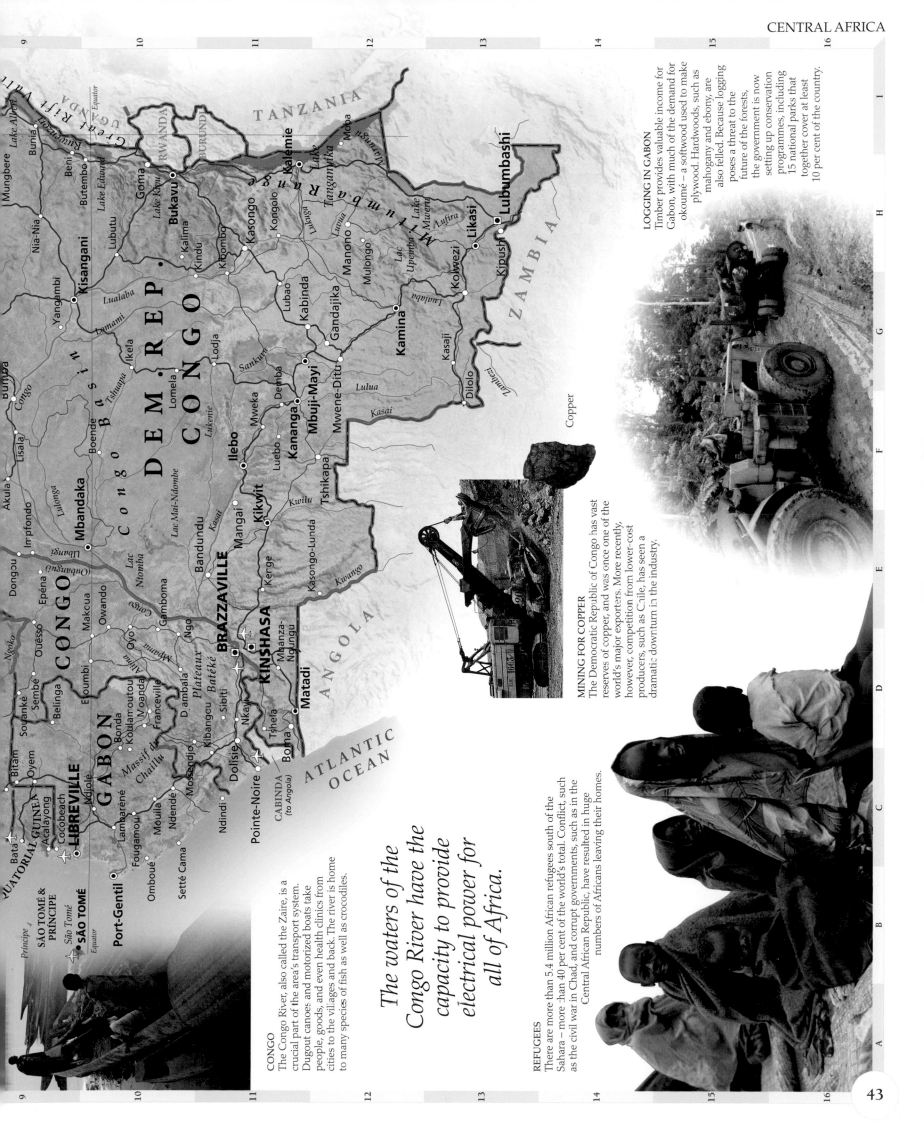

LOGGING IN GABON
Timber provides valuable income for Gabon, with much of the demand for okoumé – a softwood used to make plywood. Hardwoods, such as mahogany and ebony, are also felled. Because logging poses a threat to the future of the forests, the government is now setting up conservation programmes, including 15 national parks that together cover at least 10 per cent of the country.

MINING FOR COPPER
The Democratic Republic of Congo has vast reserves of copper, and was once one of the world's major exporters. More recently, however, competition from lower-cost producers, such as Chile, has seen a dramatic downturn in the industry.

Copper

CONGO
The Congo River, also called the Zaire, is a crucial part of the area's transport system. Dugout canoes and motorized boats take people, goods, and even health clinics from cities to the villages and back. The river is home to many species of fish as well as crocodiles.

The waters of the Congo River have the capacity to provide electrical power for all of Africa.

REFUGEES
There are more than 5.4 million African refugees south of the Sahara – more than 40 per cent of the world's total. Conflict, such as the civil war in Chad, and corrupt governments, such as in the Central African Republic, have resulted in huge numbers of Africans leaving their homes.

TANZANIA

UGANDA

RWANDA

BURUNDI

ZAMBIA

ANGOLA

ATLANTIC OCEAN

DEM. REP. CONGO

CONGO

GABON

EQUATORIAL GUINEA

SÃO TOMÉ & PRÍNCIPE

Great Rift Valley

Congo Basin

Equator

Lake Albert
Lake Edward
Lake Kivu
Lake Tanganyika
Lake Mweru
Lake Upemba

Mungbere
Bunia
Beni
Butembo
Nia-Nia
Goma
Bukavu
Lubutu
Kisangani
Yangambi
Lualaba
Lomami
Kindu
Kalima
Kasongo
Kongolo
Kibombo
Ikela
Lodja
Sankuru
Lubao
Kabinda
Manono
Kalemie
Moba
Mitumba
Likasi
Lubumbashi
Kipushi
Kolwezi
Kasaji
Dilolo
Zambezi
Lufira
Lac Upemba
Kamina
Gandajika
Mwene-Ditu
Mbuji-Mayi
Lulua
Kananga
Denba
Mweka
Lukenie
Luebo
Tshikapa
Kasai
Kasongo-Lunda
Kwango
Kwilu
Kerge
Kikwit
Mangai
Bandundu
Kasai
Lac Mai-Ndombe
Boende
Tshuapa
Mbandaka
Lisala
Akula
Bumba
Congo
Lulonga
Ubangi
Ilebo
Matadi
KINSHASA
Mbanza-Ngungu
BRAZZAVILLE
Ngo
Gamboma
Owando
Makcua
Oyo
Oubangui
Dongou
Impfondo
Epéna
Ouésso
Sembé
Souanké
Belinga
Eboumbi
Makokou
Mékambo
Franceville
Moanda
Koulamoutou
Bitam
Oyem
Mitzic
LIBREVILLE
Ndjolé
Lambaréné
Fougamou
Mouila
Ndendé
Ndindi
Setté Cama
Port-Gentil
Omboué
Cocobeach
Acalayong
Bata
Ngoko
Ivindo
Batéké Plateaux
Massif du Chaillu
Pointe-Noire
CABINDA (to Angola)
Boma
Tshela
Dolisie
Nkay
Kibangou
Sibiti
D'ambala
Mossendjo
Principe
São Tomé
SÃO TOMÉ
Equator
ZAMBIA

Southern Africa

FROM THE DRAMATIC Namib and Kalahari deserts in the west, to the tropical forests in the north, southern Africa is a region of contrasts. Oil, diamonds, gold, and other precious metals are all mined here. There are huge inland plains that are home to a variety of wildlife, and large areas devoted to agriculture. But flooding and droughts, together with civil unrest, have hampered development so that, despite an abundance of natural resources, many countries remain poor.

SAN BUSHMEN
One of the few groups of hunter-gatherers left in Africa, the San people roam the Kalahari Desert. Also known as Bush people, many San are now changing to a more settled life, often working on cattle ranches.

San hunter using a poison-tipped arrow

The Okavango River does not run out to sea like most rivers, but runs inland into the Kalahari Desert.

Tunnels transport water between dams

Dams are marked in black

LESOTHO
Water is a valuable resource in southern Africa, and Lesotho makes good use of its mountainous land and numerous rivers. The Highlands Water Scheme uses dams and tunnels to transport water to neighbouring South Africa.

JOHANNESBURG, SOUTH AFRICA
With a population of more than 7.5 million, Johannesburg is the fourth largest city in Africa after Cairo, Lagos, and Kinshasa. Many people have moved here from the surrounding countryside in search of work.

GOLD MINING
Gold, first discovered near Johannesburg in 1886, brought a great deal of wealth to the region. South Africa currently produces about 12 per cent of the world's gold.

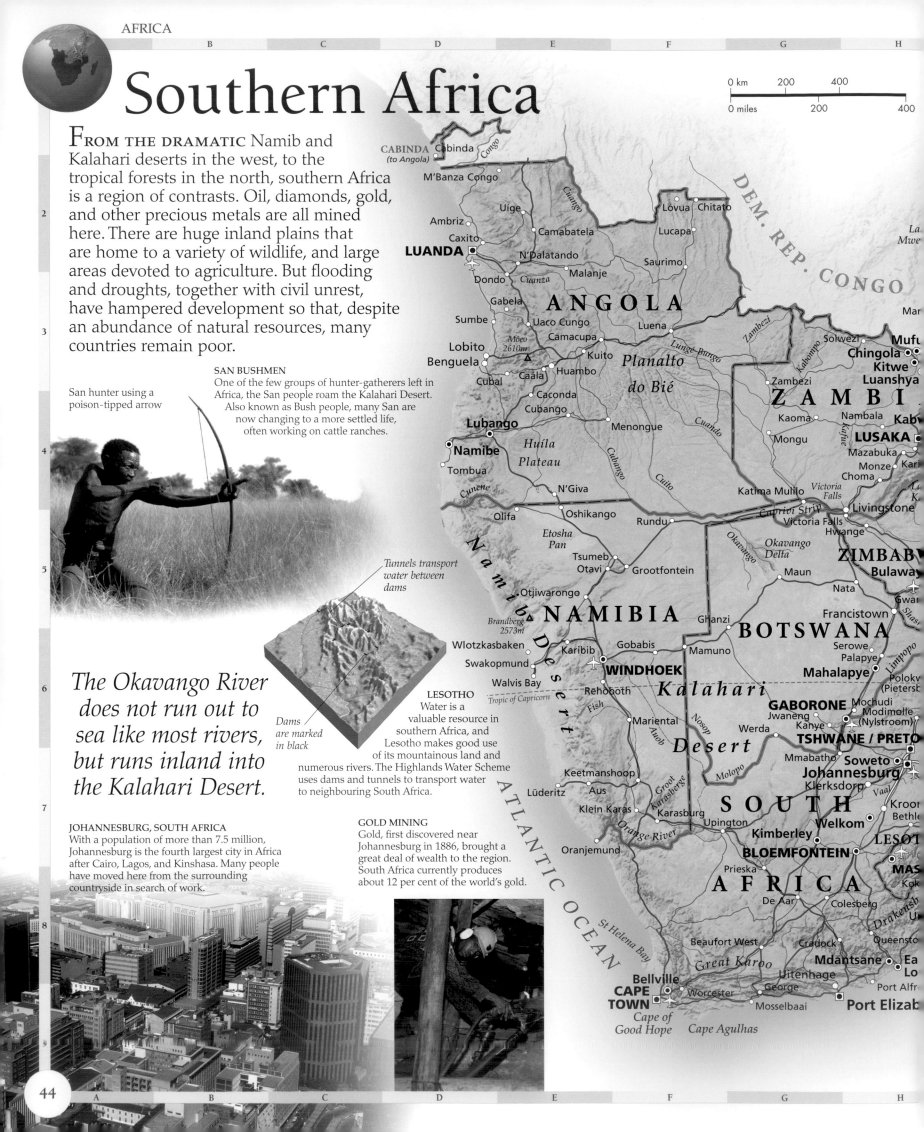

Map labels

0 km 200 400
0 miles 200 400

CABINDA (to Angola)
Cabinda
Congo
M'Banza Congo
Uige
Cuango
Ambriz
Camabatela
Lóvua Chitato
Caxito
Lucapa
LUANDA
N'Dalatando
Saurimo
Dondo
Cuanza
Malanje
Gabela
ANGOLA
Sumbe
Uaco Cungo
Luena
Lobito
Camacupa
Zambezi
Benguela
Môco 2610m
Kuito
Planalto do Bié
Caála Huambo
Cubal
Caconda
Cubango
Lubango
Menongue
Cuando
Namibe
Huíla Plateau
Cubango
Tombua
Cuito
Katima Mulilo
Cunene
N'Giva
Olifa
Oshikango
Rundu
Caprivi Strip
Victoria Falls
Etosha Pan
Tsumeb
Okavango
Okavango Delta
Otavi
Grootfontein
Maun
Nata
Otjiwarongo
NAMIBIA
Ghanzi
Francistown
Brandberg 2573m
BOTSWANA
Wlotzkasbaken
Karibib
Gobabis
Serowe
Palapye
Swakopmund
Mamuno
Mahalapye
Walvis Bay
WINDHOEK
Kalahari
Tropic of Capricorn
Rehoboth
Fish
GABORONE
Mochudi
Mariental
Nosop
Werda
Jwaneng Modimolle (Nylstroom)
Auob
Desert
Kanye
TSHWANE / PRETO
Keetmanshoop
Groot Karasberge
Mmabatho
Soweto
Lüderitz
Aus
Johannesburg
Klein Karas
Karasburg
Upington
Klerksdorp
Vaal
Orange River
Molopo
Kimberley
Welkom
SOUTH
Oranjemund
Prieska
BLOEMFONTEIN
AFRICA
De Aar
Colesberg
Drakensb
St Helena Bay
Beaufort West
Cradock
Queenstow
Great Karoo
Mdantsane
Uitenhage
Bellville
Worcester
George
Port Alfr
CAPE TOWN
Mosselbaai
Port Elizab
Cape of Good Hope
Cape Agulhas

ATLANTIC OCEAN

DEM. REP. CONGO

Solwezi
Mufu
Chingola
Kitwe
Luanshya
ZAMBI
Zambezi
Kaoma
Nambala
Kab
Mongu
LUSAKA
Mazabuka
Monze
Choma
Kari
Victoria Falls
Livingstone
Victoria Falls
Hwange
ZIMBAB
Bulaway

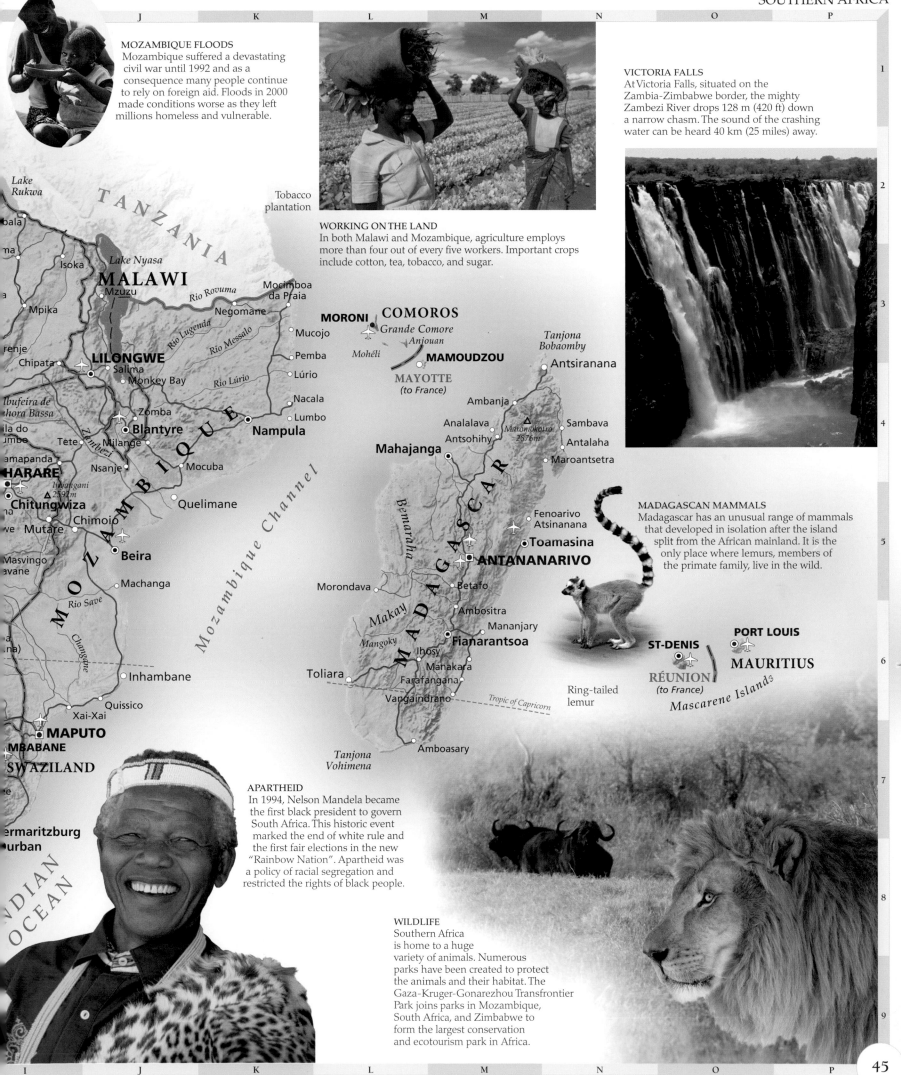

MOZAMBIQUE FLOODS
Mozambique suffered a devastating civil war until 1992 and as a consequence many people continue to rely on foreign aid. Floods in 2000 made conditions worse as they left millions homeless and vulnerable.

Tobacco plantation

WORKING ON THE LAND
In both Malawi and Mozambique, agriculture employs more than four out of every five workers. Important crops include cotton, tea, tobacco, and sugar.

VICTORIA FALLS
At Victoria Falls, situated on the Zambia-Zimbabwe border, the mighty Zambezi River drops 128 m (420 ft) down a narrow chasm. The sound of the crashing water can be heard 40 km (25 miles) away.

MADAGASCAN MAMMALS
Madagascar has an unusual range of mammals that developed in isolation after the island split from the African mainland. It is the only place where lemurs, members of the primate family, live in the wild.

Ring-tailed lemur

APARTHEID
In 1994, Nelson Mandela became the first black president to govern South Africa. This historic event marked the end of white rule and the first fair elections in the new "Rainbow Nation". Apartheid was a policy of racial segregation and restricted the rights of black people.

WILDLIFE
Southern Africa is home to a huge variety of animals. Numerous parks have been created to protect the animals and their habitat. The Gaza-Kruger-Gonarezhou Transfrontier Park joins parks in Mozambique, South Africa, and Zimbabwe to form the largest conservation and ecotourism park in Africa.

Lake Rukwa

TANZANIA

Lake Nyasa

Isoka

Mpika

MALAWI
Mzuzu

Negomane

Rio Rovuma

Mocimboa da Praia

Chipata

Rio Lugenda

Rio Messalo

LILONGWE

Salima

Monkey Bay

Mucojo

Pemba

MORONI   COMOROS
Grande Comore
Anjouan

Mohéli

MAMOUDZOU

MAYOTTE
(to France)

Tanjona Bobaomby

Antsiranana

Rio Lúrio

Lúrio

Nacala

Zomba

Lumbo

Ambanja

Analalava

Antsohihy

Sambava

renje

Ilbufeira de hora Bassa

Tete

Milange

Blantyre

Nampula

Mahajanga

Maromokotro 2876m

Antalaha

Maroantsetra

Nsanje

Mocuba

HARARE

Inyangani 2592m

Quelimane

Chitungwiza

Bemaraha

Fenoarivo Atsinanana

Mutare

Chimoio

Toamasina

Beira

ANTANANARIVO

Morondava

Betafo

Machanga

Rio Save

Masvingo

Ambositra

Makay

Ambositra

Mananjary

Mangoky

Fianarantsoa

Ihosy

PORT LOUIS

ST-DENIS

MAURITIUS

RÉUNION
(to France)

Mascarene Islands

Toliara

Manakara

Farafangana

Inhambane

Vangaindrano

Tropic of Capricorn

Quissico

Xai-Xai

MAPUTO

MBABANE

SWAZILAND

ermaritzburg
urban

INDIAN OCEAN

Tanjona Vohimena

Amboasary

MOZAMBIQUE

Mozambique Channel

MADAGASCAR

Zambezi

Changane

EUROPE

Separated from Asia by the ridge of the Ural Mountains, Europe is a continent of very different nations, listed below in order of their land area. Each nation has its own language and culture, but they share a 2,000-year history of civilization that has inspired some of the world's greatest political ideas, works of art, and innovations in technology.

Russian Federation
- 17,098,242 sq km
- 6,601,668 sq miles
- 141,000,000
- Moscow
- Russian, Tatar, Ukrainian, Chuvash, various other national languages

Germany
- 357,022 sq km
- 137,847 sq miles
- 82,200,000
- Berlin
- German, Turkish

United Kingdom
- 243,610 sq km
- 94,058 sq miles
- 61,600,000
- London
- English, Welsh, Scottish Gaelic, Irish Gaelic

Iceland
- 103,000 sq km
- 39,769 sq miles
- 322,700
- Reykjavík
- Icelandic

Serbia
- 77,474 sq km
- 29,913 sq miles
- 7,750,000
- Belgrade
- Serbian, Hungarian (Magyar)

Bosnia and Herzegovina
- 51,197 sq km
- 19,767 sq miles
- 3,770,000
- Sarajevo
- Bosnian, Serbian, Croatian

France
- 643,427 sq km
- 248,429 sq miles
- 62,300,000
- Paris
- French, Provençal, German, Breton, Catalan, Basque

Finland
- 338,145 sq km
- 130,559 sq miles
- 5,330,000
- Helsinki
- Finnish, Swedish, Sami

Romania
- 238,391 sq km
- 92,043 sq miles
- 21,300,000
- Bucharest
- Romanian, Hungarian (Magyar), Romany, German

Hungary
- 93,028 sq km
- 35,918 sq miles
- 9,990,000
- Budapest
- Hungarian (Magyar)

Ireland
- 70,273 sq km
- 27,133 sq miles
- 4,520,000
- Dublin
- English, Irish Gaelic

Slovakia
- 49,035 sq km
- 18,933 sq miles
- 5,410,000
- Bratislava
- Slovak, Hungarian (Magyar), Czech

Ukraine
- 603,550 sq km
- 233,032 sq miles
- 45,700,000
- Kiev
- Ukrainian, Russian, Tatar

Norway
- 323,802 sq km
- 125,021 sq miles
- 4,810,000
- Oslo
- Norwegian (Bokmål, "book language", and Nynorsk "new Norsk"), Sami

Belarus
- 207,600 sq km
- 180,155 sq miles
- 9,630,000
- Minsk
- Belarussian, Russian

Portugal
- 92,090 sq km
- 35,556 sq miles
- 10,700,000
- Lisbon
- Portuguese

Lithuania
- 65,300 sq km
- 25,212 sq miles
- 3,290,000
- Vilnius
- Lithuanian, Russian

Estonia
- 45,228 sq km
- 17,463 sq miles
- 1,340,000
- Tallinn
- Estonian, Russian

Spain
- 505,370 sq km
- 195,124 sq miles
- 44,900,000
- Madrid
- Spanish, Catalan, Galician, Basque

Poland
- 312,685 sq km
- 120,728 sq miles
- 38,100,000
- Warsaw
- Polish

Greece
- 131,957 sq km
- 50,949 sq miles
- 11,200,000
- Athens
- Greek, Turkish, Macedonian, Albanian

Austria
- 83,871 sq km
- 32,383 sq miles
- 8,360,000
- Vienna
- German, Croatian, Slovenian, Hungarian (Magyar)

Latvia
- 64,589 sq km
- 24,938 sq miles
- 2,250,000
- Riga
- Latvian, Russian

Denmark
- 43,094 sq km
- 16,639 sq miles
- 5,470,000
- Copenhagen
- Danish

Sweden
- 450,295 sq km
- 173,860 sq miles
- 9,250,000
- Stockholm
- Swedish, Finnish, Sami

Italy
- 301,340 sq km
- 116,348 sq miles
- 59,900,000
- Rome
- Italian, German, French, Rhaeto-Romanic, Sardinian

Bulgaria
- 110,879 sq km
- 42,811 sq miles
- 7,540,000
- Sofia
- Bulgarian, Turkish, Romany

Czech Republic
- 78,867 sq km
- 30,451 sq miles
- 10,400,000
- Prague
- Czech, Slovak, Hungarian (Magyar)

Croatia
- 56,594 sq km
- 21,851 sq miles
- 4,420,000
- Zagreb
- Croatian

Netherlands
- 41,543 sq km
- 16,040 sq miles
- 16,600,000
- Amsterdam
- Dutch, Frisian

Switzerland
- 41,277 sq km
- 15,937 sq miles
- 7,570,000
- Bern
- German, Swiss-German, French, Italian, Romansh

Slovenia
- 20,273 sq km
- 7,827 sq miles
- 2,020,000
- Ljubljana
- Slovenian

Moldova
- 33,851 sq km
- 13,070 sq miles
- 3,600,000
- Chisinau
- Moldovan, Ukrainian, Russian

Montenegro
- 13,812 sq km
- 5,333 sq miles
- 624,200
- Podgorica
- Montenegrin, Serbian, Albanian, Bosnian, Croatian

Belgium
- 30,528 sq km
- 11,787 sq miles
- 10,600,000
- Brussels
- Dutch, French, German

The cathedral dome of Santa Maria del Fiore dominates the skyline of Florence, Italy – one of the world's most beautiful cities.

Albania
- 28,748 sq km
- 11,100 sq miles
- 3,160,000
- Tirana
- Albanian, Greek

Kosovo
- 10,887 sq km
- 4,203 sq miles
- 2,100,000
- Pristina
- Albanian, Serbian, Bosnian, Gorani, Romany, Turkish

Luxembourg
- 2,586 sq km
- 998 sq miles
- 486,200
- Luxembourg
- Luxembourgish, German, French

Malta
- 316 sq km
- 122 sq miles
- 408,700
- Valletta
- Maltese, English

San Marino
- 61 sq km
- 24 sq miles
- 31,400
- San Marino
- Italian

Vatican City
- 0.44 sq km
- 0.17 sq miles
- 800
- Vatican City
- Italian, Latin

Macedonia
- 25,713 sq km
- 9,928 sq miles
- 2,040,000
- Skopje
- Macedonian, Albanian, Turkish, Romany, Serbian

Cyprus
- 9,251 sq km
- 3,572 sq miles
- 871,000
- Nicosia
- Greek, Turkish

Andorra
- 468 sq km
- 181 sq miles
- 82,200
- Andorra la Vella
- Spanish, Catalan, French, Portuguese

Liechtenstein
- 160 sq km
- 62 sq miles
- 35,000
- Vaduz
- German, Alemannisch dialect, Italian

Monaco
- 2 sq km
- 0.77 sq miles
- 32,000
- Monaco
- French, Italian, Monégasque, English

Scandinavia and Finland

THE THREE SCANDINAVIAN countries of Norway, Sweden, and Denmark, along with neighbouring Finland, are among the most northerly countries in Europe. Here the winters are long and cold. In the far north above the Arctic Circle, the Sun remains below the horizon for up to two months a year. Perhaps because of the harsh climate and the geographical isolation, Scandinavia has attracted little immigration, so the population is not very ethnically diverse. Finland is the most densely forested country in Europe, and wood accounts for 30 per cent of its exports. All four countries are highly industrialized and are among the wealthiest in the world.

SKIING
During the winter months, much of Scandinavia is covered with snow, so skiing is one of the easiest forms of transport. It is also a very popular sport.

Sami man in traditional costume

LAPLAND
Northern Sweden and Finland are known as Lapland. Here, the local Sami people survive the cold and inhospitable climate by herding reindeer, which they breed for their meat, milk, and skins.

URBAN POPULATIONS
Scandinavia has a high urban population. Many people live in towns and cities, with less than one-fifth living in the countryside. Since the region is covered in lakes, fjords, and surrounded by sea, many people also live near the water.

Copenhagen in Denmark is the second-largest city in Scandinavia after Stockholm, Sweden.

Map labels

RUSSIAN FEDERATION

FINLAND

SWEDEN

NORWAY

Barents Sea

ARCTIC OCEAN

Norwegian Sea

Gulf of Bothnia

Lapland

Kvitoja

Arctic Circle

North Cape (Nordkapp)

Magerøya

Varangerfjorden
Varangerhalvøya
Kirkenes
Tana
Vadsø
Vardø
Porsangen

Finnmarksvidda

Ringvassøya
Kvaløya
Senja
Andøya
Søroya

Tromsø
Talvik
Alta
Lakselv
Karasjok
Karigasniemi
Kaamanen
Inarijärvi
Ivalo
Saariselkä
Kittilä
Sattanen
Sodankylä
Kuusamo
Suomussalmi

Vesterålen
Lofoten
Harstad
Narvik
Hinnøya
Ofotfjorden
Bodø
Fauske
Mo i Rana
Mosjøen
Vega

Kaaresuvanto
Muonio
Muonionjoki
Kolari
Tornionjoki
Kittilä
Ounasjoki
Kemijärvi
Rovaniemi
Kemijoki
Pudasjärvi
Kajaani

Kiruna
Torneträsk
Gällivare
Malmberget
Skalka
Jokkmokk
Kebnekaise 2117 m
Kalixälven
Luleälven
Haparanda
Tornio
Kemi
Kalix
Luleå
Piteå
Hailuoto
Raahe
Oulu
Oulujoki
Oulujärvi
Kempele

Skellefteå
Skellefteälven
Arvidsjaur
Lycksele
Umeälven
Umeå
Vasa (Vaasa)
Kokkola (Karleby)
Jakobstad (Pietarsaari)
Lapua
Seinäjoki
Närpes (Närpiö)

Storuman
Storuman
Vilhelmina
Dorotea
Hoting
Strömsund
Örnsköldsvik
Härnösand
Sundsvall
Timrå

Borgefjellet
Namsos
Steinkjer
Verdalsøra
Levanger
Stjørdal
Trondheim
Trondheimsfjorden
Frohavet
Hitra
Frøya
Smøla
Kristiansund
Molde
Åndalsnes
Ålesund

Dovrefjell
Røros
Heimdal
Støren
Storsjön
Östersund
Ånge
Ratan

Ångermanälven
Kvarnbergs vattnet

Kjusele

0 km 100 200
0 miles 100 200

INDUSTRIAL STRENGTH

Manufacturing is an important source of employment and wealth throughout Scandinavia. Many of the goods produced, such as cars in Sweden, electronic goods in Finland (above), and mobile phones in Finland, are exported all over the world. In Denmark, many people also work in agriculture, fish processing, and brewing.

NORWEGIAN FJORDS

The west coast of Norway has thousands of deep inlets, known as fjords, gouged out of the mountains by glaciers during the last ice age and then flooded by the sea. The fjords run inland between high mountains and make a favourite destination for cruise ships bringing tourists to admire the stunning scenery.

THE SAUNA

The sauna, or steam bath, was invented in Finland about 1,000 years ago as a way of cleaning and relaxing the body. After a hot sauna, many Finns cool off by plunging into an icy pool (below) or a snowdrift.

BUILDING WITH WOOD

Much of Norway and Sweden, and two-thirds of Finland, is covered by dense forests of birch, pine, spruce, and other trees. Finland has more than 16 times more forested land per person than the European average. Many people in the region work in the forestry industry, producing wood for the construction and furniture industries. This great natural resource is also used to build homes and churches, like this medieval stave church (left) in Norway.

SAVING THE ENVIRONMENT

The people of Scandinavia are very environmentally conscious and recycle as many household items as they can. Strict national laws protect the environment from industrial waste and pollution, although there is growing concern about the levels of pollution in the Baltic Sea.

Bergen
Kouvola
Kotka
Riihimäki
Porvoo
Hyvinkää
HELSINKI
Vantaa
Espoo
Gulf of Finland
Turku (Åbo)
Salo
Hanko (Hangö)
Åland
Ålands Hav
Norrtälje
Uppsala
Tierp
Sandviken
Gävle
Sala
Täby
STOCKHOLM
Mälaren
Sollentuna
Södertälje
Nyköping
Gotland
Visby
Norrköping
Linköping
Öland
Oskarshamn
Borgholm
Kalmar
Karlskrona
Baltic Sea
Hanöbukten
Bornholm
Rönne

Rättvik
Leksand
Falun
Borlänge
Mora
Malung
Lucvika
Avesta
Nora
Klarälven
Västerås
Örebro
Karlstad
Säffle
Hjälmaren
Askersund
Flipstad
Grums
Mariestad
Vänern
Lidköping
Vättern
Jönköping
Växjö
Borås
Varberg
Ljungby
Lahorm
Kungsbacka
Mölndal
Halmstad
Ljungby
Kristianstad
Helsingborg
Lund
Malmö
Møn
Falster
Sjælland
Nykøbing

Geilo
Eidfjord
Hardangerfjorden
Gol
Gjøvik
Hamar
Hønefoss
Kongsberg
Sandvika
Drammen
Moss
Ski
OSLO
Lillestrøm
Mjøsa
Hardangervidda
Haukeligrend
Leirvik
Haugesund
Sandnes
Stavanger
Moi
Evje
Liknes
Kristiansand
Setesdal
Porsgrunn
Skien
Arendal
Horten
Fredrikstad
Sarpsborg
Halden
Strömstad
Mellerud
Uddevalla
Trollhättan
Gothenburg (Göteborg)
Kungälv
Laesø
Randers
Århus
DENMARK
Hjørring
Aalborg
Hobro
Viborg
Holstebro
Ringkøbing Fjord
Jutland (Jylland)
Varde
Esbjerg
Kolding
Odense
Fyn
Slagelse
COPENHAGEN (KØBENHAVN)
Storebælt
Lolland
Rømø
GERMANY

North Sea
Skagerrak
Kattegat

The British Isles

FOR SUCH A SMALL GROUP OF ISLANDS, the British Isles has a very rich history. This is evident from its legacy of ancient ruins, medieval castles, dramatic cathedrals, and grand country houses. Once a leading industrial and colonial power, British monarchs ruled an empire that circled the globe. As a result, English is still widely spoken around the world. Today, many traditional industries, such as shipbuilding, mining, and engineering, have declined, and the emphasis is now on banking and insurance, as well as pharmaceuticals. The British Isles consists of two countries: the United Kingdom of Great Britain and Northern Ireland (the UK), and the Republic of Ireland.

Wales has more than 200 castles.

IRELAND
Tourists visit Ireland, attracted by its unspoiled countryside and lively cities, such as Dublin (left). Once part of Britain, Ireland gained independence in 1922. In 2005–2007, it had one of the fastest-growing economies in Europe, but its economy shrank along with Europe's in 2008–2010.

HORSE BREEDING
Lush pastures and a mild climate have encouraged the breeding of thoroughbred racehorses in Ireland. Stud farms here raise some of the best racehorses in the world.

Irish horse and rider on a training run

SCOTLAND
Scotland and England united as a single country in 1707. Today, however, Scotland is a self-governing part of the UK, with its own parliament and distinct legal and educational systems. Edinburgh, above, is a popular city with a magnificent castle. Each summer, the city hosts an international arts festival.

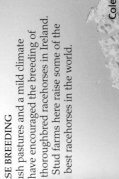

NORTH SEA ENERGY
Beneath the shallow seas around Britain, there are supplies of oil and natural gas. Oil rigs raise oil and gas to the surface, where it is pumped by pipeline to be refined on the mainland. Production has declined and supplies are now running low, but more distant reserves still wait to be exploited. However, few businesses are willing to take on further costly exploration.

MONEY MATTERS
The City of London is the UK's financial centre. Before the banking crash of 2008, more than 500 banks had offices there. Lloyd's Insurance Building (right) is one of the city's most distinctive skyscrapers. Built of steel and glass, it has lifts on the outside.

Map labels

Shetland Islands — Unst, Yell, Fetlar, Mainland, Lerwick

Fair Isle

Orkney Islands — Sanday, Kirkwall, Mainland, Hoy

John o'Groats, Wick, Thurso

ATLANTIC OCEAN

North Sea

North West Highlands — Ben Hope 927 m, Ullapool, Stromeferry, Mallaig, Fort William, Oban

The Minch, The Little Minch

Isle of Lewis, Stornoway, Harris, North Uist, South Uist, Barra, St Kilda, Outer Hebrides

Isle of Skye, Rhum, Eigg, Coll, Tiree, Isle of Mull, Firth of Lorn, Jura, Islay, Kintyre, Isle of Arran

Inner Hebrides

Elgin, Inverness, Loch Ness, Aviemore, Spey, Dee, Grampian Mountains

Moray Firth, Fraserburgh, Peterhead, **Aberdeen**, Montrose, Arbroath, Forfar, **Dundee**, St Andrews

SCOTLAND, Perth, Tay, Firth of Forth, Dunfermline, **Edinburgh**, Stirling, Forth, Clyde, Hamilton, **Glasgow**, Paisley, Greenock, East Kilbride, Kilmarnock, Prestwick, Ayr, Loch Lomond, Ben Nevis 1343 m

Berwick-upon-Tweed, Galashiels, Hawick, Cheviot Hills, Southern Uplands, Dumfries, Stranraer

Newcastle upon Tyne, South Shields, **Sunderland**, Tyne, Durham, Hartlepool, Darlington, Tees, **Middlesbrough**, Northallerton, Whitby, Scarborough, Bridlington, Beverley

Carlisle, Penrith, Lake District, Workington, Whitehaven, Kendal, Ribble, Pennines

Barrow-in-Furness, Lancaster, **York**, Harrogate, Ouse

NORTHERN IRELAND, Coleraine, Londonderry, Stranorlar, Strabane, Omagh, Newtownabbey, **Belfast**, Bangor, Newtownards, Downpatrick, Downpatrick, Lough Neagh, Armagh, Portadown, Newry

Donegal, Donegal Bay, Sligo, Colloney, Boyle, Lower Lough Erne, Upper Lough Erne, Enniskillen

UNITED KINGDOM

DOUGLAS

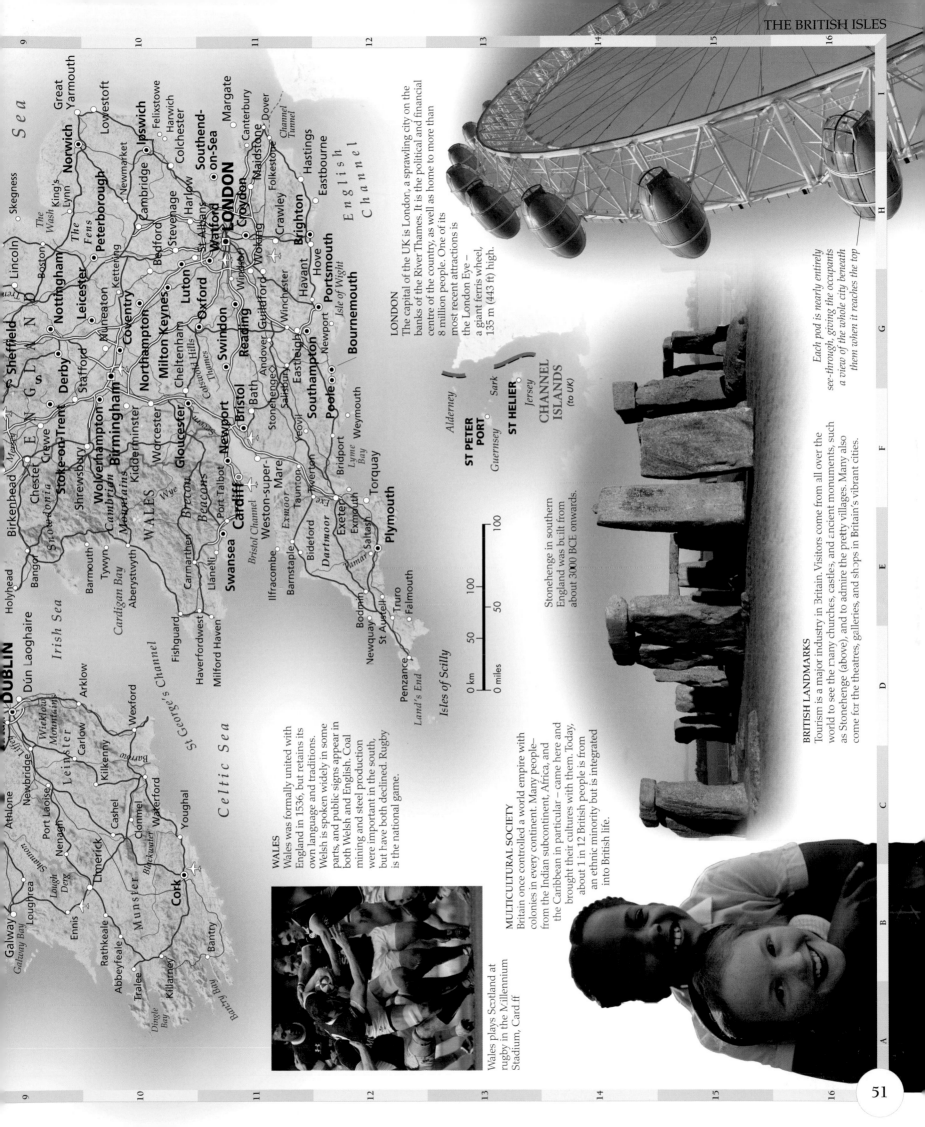

LONDON
The capital of the UK is London, a sprawling city on the banks of the River Thames. It is the political and financial centre of the country, as well as home to more than 8 million people. One of its most recent attractions is the London Eye – a giant ferris wheel, 135 m (443 ft) high.

Each pod is nearly entirely see-through, giving the occupants a view of the whole city beneath them when it reaches the top

BRITISH LANDMARKS
Tourism is a major industry in Britain. Visitors come from all over the world to see the many churches, castles, and ancient monuments, such as Stonehenge (above), and to admire the pretty villages. Many also come for the theatres, galleries, and shops in Britain's vibrant cities.

Stonehenge in southern England was built from about 3000 BCE onwards.

WALES
Wales was formally united with England in 1536, but retains its own language and traditions. Welsh is spoken widely in some parts, and public signs appear in both Welsh and English. Coal mining and steel production were important in the south, but have both declined. Rugby is the national game.

MULTICULTURAL SOCIETY
Britain once controlled a world empire with colonies in every continent. Many people– from the Indian subcontinent, Africa, and the Caribbean in particular – came here and brought their cultures with them. Today, about 1 in 12 British people is from an ethnic minority but is integrated into British life.

Wales plays Scotland at rugby in the Millennium Stadium, Cardiff

Scale
0 km   50   100
0 miles   50   100

Map labels

Sea (North Sea)

Great Yarmouth
Lowestoft
Felixstowe
Harwich
Ipswich
Norwich
Skegness
King's Lynn
Colchester
Newmarket
Cambridge
Peterborough
The Wash
The Fens
Boston
Lincoln
Bedford
Stevenage
St Albans
Watford
LONDON
Croydon
Maidstone
Margate
Canterbury
Dover
Channel Tunnel
Folkestone
Hastings
Eastbourne
Brighton
Hove
Crawley
Woking
Guildford
Southend-on-Sea
Harlow
Luton
Milton Keynes
Northampton
Kettering
Nottingham
Leicester
Derby
Muneaton
Coventry
Sheffield
ENGLAND
Birkenhead
Chester
Crewe
Stoke-on-Trent
Stafford
Shrewsbury
Wolverhampton
Birmingham
Kidderminster
Worcester
Gloucester
Cheltenham
Oxford
Swindon
Reading
Windsor
Winchester
Andover
Salisbury
Stonehenge
Cotswold Hills
Bath
Bristol
Newport
Cardiff
Swansea
Llanelli
Carmarthen
Brecon Beacons
Cambrian Mountains
Snowdonia
Bangor
Barmouth
Tywyn
Aberystwyth
Cardigan Bay
WALES
Wye
Bristol Channel
Weston-super-Mare
Taunton
Exmoor
Tiverton
Exe
Bridport
Lyme Bay
Weymouth
Poole
Bournemouth
Isle of Wight
Newport
Portsmouth
Havant
Southampton
Eastleigh
Yeovil
Dartmoor
Exmouth
Exeter
Torquay
Plymouth
Saltash
Tamar
Bideford
Barnstaple
Ilfracombe
Truro
Falmouth
Penzance
Land's End
Newquay
St Austell
Bodmin
Isles of Scilly

Milford Haven
Haverfordwest
Fishguard
St George's Channel
Holyhead
Irish Sea
Celtic Sea

Port Talbot

Ireland side:
DUBLIN
Dún Laoghaire
Wicklow Mountains
Arklow
Wexford
Carlow
Kilkenny
Kildare
Newbridge
Athlone
Port Laoise
Nenagh
Leinster
Barrow
Clonmel
Waterford
Youghal
Cork
Cashel
Limerick
Ennis
Shannon
Munster
Rathkeale
Abbeyfeale
Tralee
Killarney
Bantry
Bantry Bay
Dingle Bay
Galway
Galway Bay
Loughrea
Lough Derg
Blackwater
Liffey

English Channel

Alderney
Guernsey
ST PETER PORT
Sark
Jersey
ST HELIER
CHANNEL ISLANDS
(to UK)

The Low Countries

THE NETHERLANDS, BELGIUM, AND LUXEMBOURG are known as the Low Countries because the land is so flat and low-lying. In the case of the Netherlands, much of the land is below sea level – *Netherlands* is Dutch for "nether lands". The three countries are among the richest in Europe and, while farming still plays an important part, they all have strong, modern economies based on manufacturing and trade. Luxembourg in particular is known as a tax haven and is a major centre for international finance. Their location at the mouth of the River Rhine and other major European rivers places the three countries at the heart of western European trade and politics – all three were founder members of the European Economic Community (now the European Union, or EU), established in 1957.

ROTTERDAM, NETHERLANDS
Every year, more than 30,000 sea-going ships and 110,000 barges call at the port of Rotterdam. Lying at the mouth of the River Rhine, this port is the largest in the world and is where vast container ships from all over the world load or unload their cargoes. The smaller barges help to transport goods farther inland. With the port's ultra-modern Vessel Traffic Service (VTS) it's possible to track ships on a radar screen up to 60 km (37 miles) off the coast and 40 km (25 miles) inland.

Tulips were introduced to the Netherlands from Turkey in 1562. Black tulips were the most valuable.

Dutch tulips

CROPS
Fertile soil and good irrigation have helped the Netherlands become a major exporter of agricultural products, with vegetables and tomatoes forming important crops. It is also famous for its bulbs and cut flowers, notably tulips.

RECLAIMING THE LAND
Over the centuries, the Dutch have reclaimed land from the sea. They did this by building huge dykes, or dams, to keep out the sea, and then draining the surface water into canals. Windmills originally pumped out the water, but electric pumps are now used.

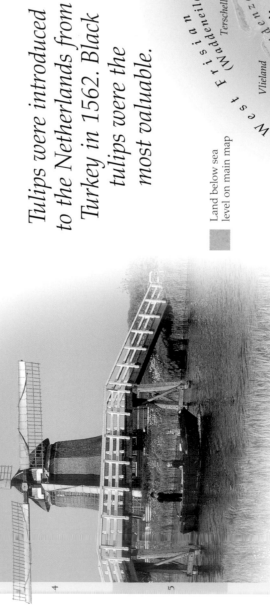

DUTCH PEOPLE
The Dutch once ruled a vast empire in Indonesia, the Caribbean, and South America. As a result, many nationalities now live here. Ethnic minorities make up about 20 per cent of the people and in some cities, the majority of primary school children have a non-Dutch background.

Land below sea level on main map

GERMANY

NETHERLANDS

West Frisian Islands (Waddeneilanden)

Waddenzee

IJsselmeer

Flevoland

Texel

Vlieland

Terschelling

Ameland

Schiermonnikoog

Delfzijl
Appingedam
Groningen
Haren
Zuidbroek
Vlagtwedde
Borger
Emmen
Coevorden
Hardenberg
Den Ham
Tubbergen
Almelo
Rijssen
Goor
Hengelo
Enschede
Deventer

Eemshaven
Loppersum
Winsum
Zuidhorn
Zuidlaren
Assen
Hoogeveen
Beilen

Eemshaven

Dokkum
Winsum
Leeuwarden
Drachten
Heerenveen
Wolvega
Steenwijk
Meppel
Staphorst
Zwolle
Nunspeet
Apeldoorn
Vaassen
Vaassen

Harlingen
Menaldum
Sneek
Joure

Nieuwolde
Den Ham

Harlingen
Menaldum
Leeuwarden

Den Helder
Schagen
Opmeer
Hoorn
Emmeloord
Lelystad
Almere
Zeewolde
Baarn

Alkmaar
Castricum
Purmerend
Zaanstad
Amstelveen
Hilversum

Velsen-Noord
Haarlem
AMSTERDAM

Noordwijk aan Zee
Leiden
Sassenheim

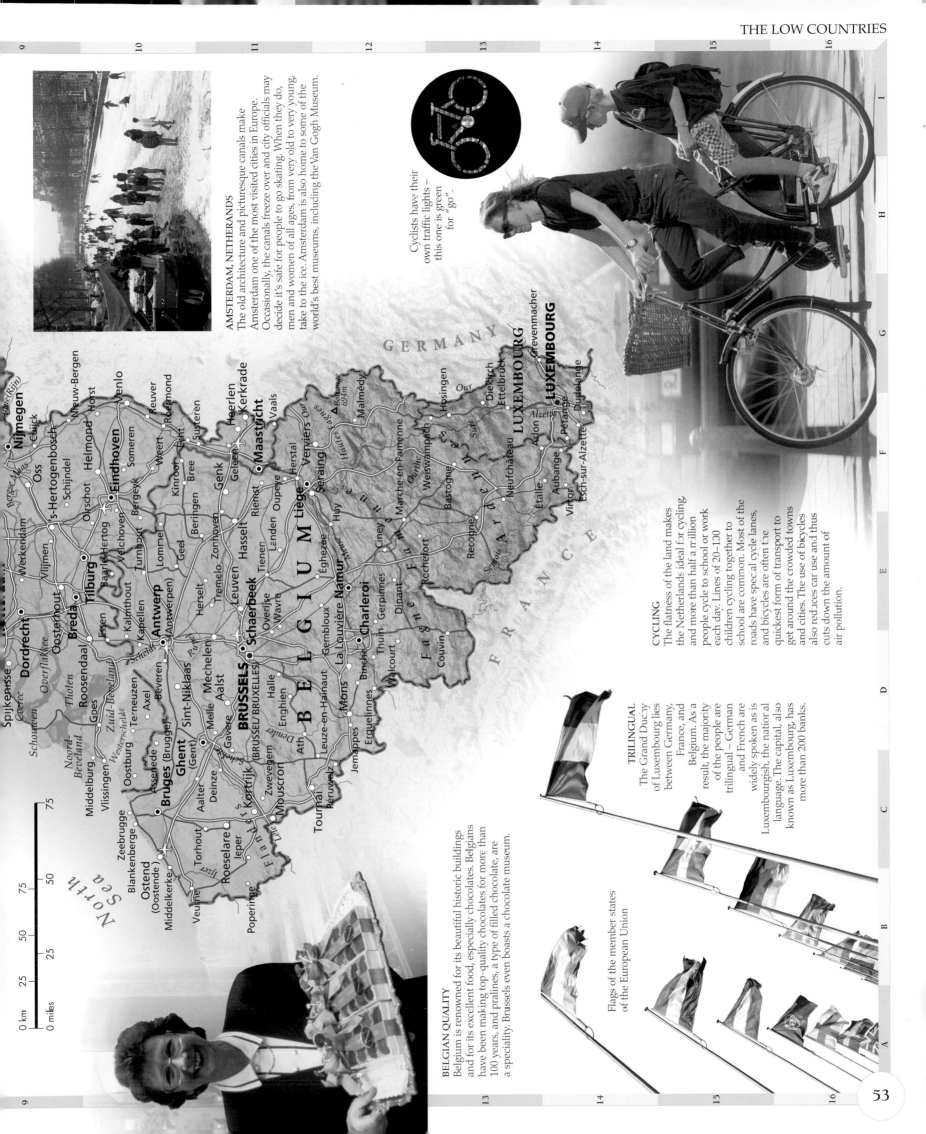

AMSTERDAM, NETHERLANDS
The old architecture and picturesque canals make Amsterdam one of the most visited cities in Europe. Occasionally, the canals freeze over and city officials may decide it's safe for people to go skating. When they do, men and women of all ages, from very old to very young, take to the ice. Amsterdam is also home to some of the world's best museums, including the Van Gogh Museum.

Cyclists have their own traffic lights – this one is green for "go".

CYCLING
The flatness of the land makes the Netherlands ideal for cycling, and more than half a million people cycle to school or work each day. Lines of 20–100 children cycling together to school are common. Most of the roads have special cycle lanes, and bicycles are often the quickest form of transport to get around the crowded towns and cities. The use of bicycles also reduces car use and thus cuts down the amount of air pollution.

TRILINGUAL
The Grand Duchy of Luxembourg lies between Germany, France, and Belgium. As a result, the majority of the people are trilingual – German and French are widely spoken as is Luxembourgish, the national language. The capital, also known as Luxembourg, has more than 200 banks.

Flags of the member states of the European Union

BELGIAN QUALITY
Belgium is renowned for its beautiful historic buildings and for its excellent food, especially chocolates. Belgians have been making top-quality chocolates for more than 100 years, and pralines, a type of filled chocolate, are a speciality. Brussels even boasts a chocolate museum.

France

IN DIRECT CONTRAST TO ITS mainly rural landscape, France is a modern nation with most people now living in towns and cities. It has flourishing industries and is the fifth richest economy in the world after the USA, Japan, Germany, and the UK. A country of varied scenery, from gently rolling farmland in the north to a stretch of dry, warm Mediterranean coast in the south, France also shares two mountain ranges – the Pyrenees and the Alps. Each of the 22 regions within France, which includes the island of Corsica, has its own distinct identity and culture. The tiny countries of Andorra and Monaco lie next to France.

Boules, the national game of France, is still played in village squares around the country.

NUCLEAR POWER

Three-quarters of France's electricity is produced by nuclear power plants (above), making the country largely self-sufficient in energy and one of the main producers of nuclear power in Europe. Hydroelectric plants are also an important source of power.

HIGH-SPEED TRAVEL

France has Europe's fastest train, the TGV – *train à grande vitesse* – which travels at up to 300 kph (186 mph) during normal services. In 2007, a modified TGV even set a speed record for conventional trains of 574.8 kph (357.2 mph). The TGV network connects Paris with all the country's major cities, which makes it easier to commute or visit relatives. It also extends to Germany, Italy, Belgium, Switzerland, and through the Channel Tunnel to Britain.

STREETS OF PARIS

Tourists flock to Paris to visit its world-famous museums and art galleries, shop in its elegant stores, and soak up its vibrant atmosphere. Montmartre, which overlooks the city, is famous for its artists. Close by, in the Place du Tertre (above), visitors can have their portrait painted.

GERMANY

BELGIUM

LUX.

SWITZERLAND

English Channel

Strait of Dover

Channel Tunnel

ATLANTIC OCEAN

CHANNEL ISLANDS (to UK)

Brest
Morlaix
Landerneau
Plérin
Quimper
Concarneau
Quimperlé
Pontivy
Lorient
Hennebont
Auray
Vannes
Loudéac
St-Brieuc
St-Malo
Dinan
Redon
Châteaubriant
Vitré
Laval
Rennes
Fougères
Avranches
Granville
Coutances
St-Lô
Cherbourg
Bayeux
Caen
Lisieux
le Havre
Fécamp
Dieppe
Abbeville
le Portel
Boulogne-sur-Mer
Berck-Plage
Calais
Dunkerque
Tourcoing
Roubaix
Lille
Douai
St-Omer
Valenciennes
Cambrai
Hirson
Charleville-Mézières
Sedan
Reims
Laon
St-Quentin
Noyon
Compiègne
Château-Thierry
Beauvais
Amiens
Arras
Albert
Rouen
Barentin
Louviers
Évreux
PARIS
Pontoise
Argenteuil
Nanterre
Créteil
Versailles
Antony
Melun
Fontainebleau
Sens
Montargis
Nemours
Auxerre
Chartres
Châteaudun
Orléans
Olivet
Blois
Vendôme
Tours
Châteauroux
Bourges
Vierzon
Cosne-Cours-sur-Loire
Nevers
Alençon
le Mans
la Flèche
Trélazé
Angers
Saumur
Thouars
Châtellerault
Cholet
les Herbiers
Challans
la Roche-sur-Yon
Rezé
Nantes
St-Nazaire
la Baule-Escoublac
Belle Île
Île d'Yeu
Île d'Ouessant
Golfe de St-Malo
Baie de la Seine

Metz
Thionville
Hagondange
Hayange
Bar-le-Duc
Toul
Nancy
Saverne
Haguenau
Schiltigheim
Strasbourg
Sélestat
Colmar
Mulhouse
St-Louis
Audincourt
Montbéliard
Belfort
Vesoul
Langres
Chaumont
Dijon
Beaune
Troyes
Châlons-en-Champagne
Épinal
St-Dié
Cernay
Besançon

*Ardennes
Artois
Picardie
(Normandie)
Maine
Anjou
Berry
Touraine
Orléanais
Île-de-France
Champagne
Lorraine
Alsace
Bourgogne (Burgundy)
Côte-d'Or
Franche-Comté
Vosges
Morvan
Poitou
Brittany (Bretagne)
Iroise*

*Seine
Somme
Oise
Marne
Meuse
Moselle
Yonne
Loire
Cher
Creuse
Sarthe
Indre*

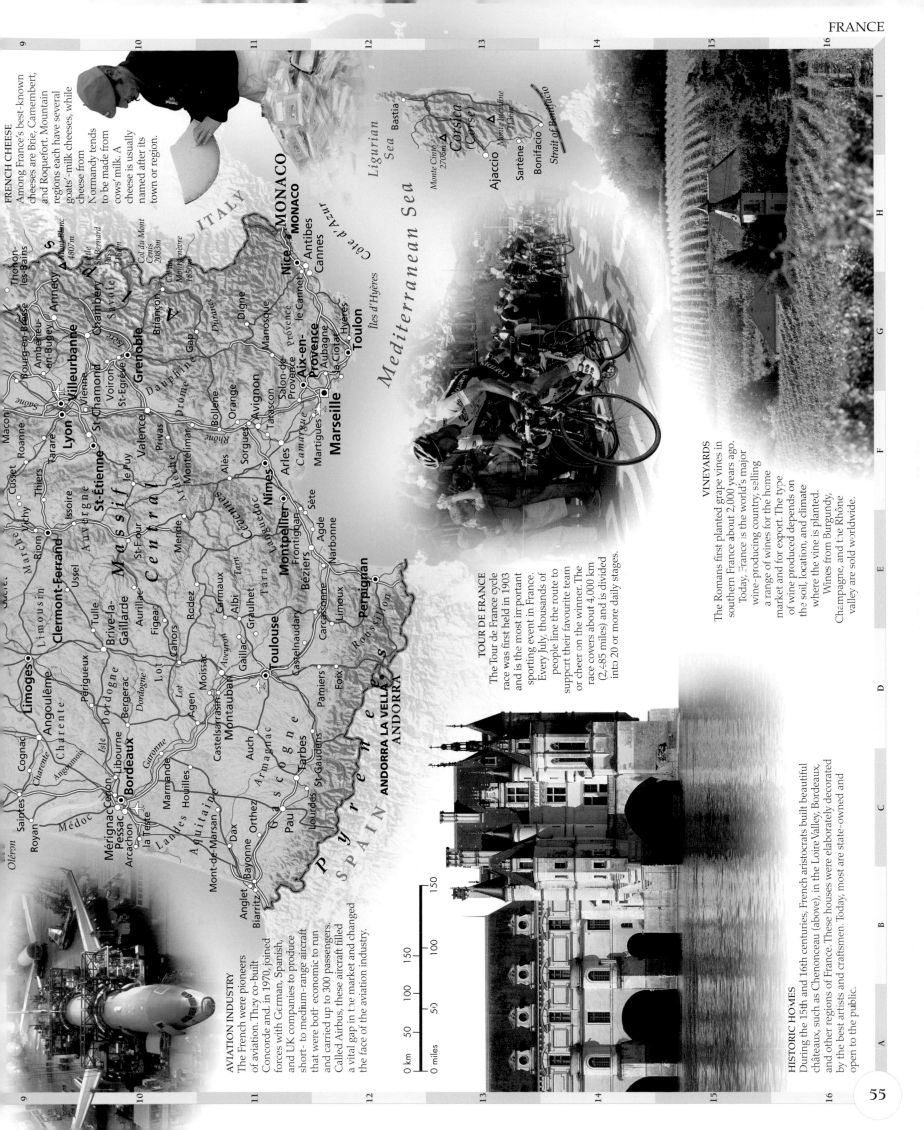

FRENCH CHEESE

Among France's best-known cheeses are Brie, Camembert, and Roquefort. Mountain regions each have several goats'-milk cheeses, while cheese from Normandy tends to be made from cows' milk. A cheese is usually named after its town or region.

AVIATION INDUSTRY

The French were pioneers of aviation. They co-built Concorde and, in 1970, joined forces with German, Spanish, and UK companies to produce short- to medium-range aircraft that were both economic to run and carried up to 300 passengers. Called Airbus, these aircraft filled a vital gap in the market and changed the face of the aviation industry.

TOUR DE FRANCE

The Tour de France cycle race was first held in 1903 and is the most important sporting event in France. Every July, thousands of people line the route to cheer on the winner. The race covers about 4,000 km (2,485 miles) and is divided into 20 or more daily stages.

VINEYARDS

The Romans first planted grape vines in southern France about 2,000 years ago. Today, France is the world's major wine-producing country, selling a range of wines for the home market and for export. The type of wine produced depends on the soil, location, and climate where the vine is planted. Wines from Burgundy, Champagne, and the Rhône valley are sold worldwide.

HISTORIC HOMES

During the 15th and 16th centuries, French aristocrats built beautiful châteaux, such as Chenonceau (above), in the Loire Valley, Bordeaux, and other regions of France. These houses were elaborately decorated by the best artists and craftsmen. Today, most are state-owned and open to the public.

Map labels

ITALY

Mediterranean Sea

Ligurian Sea

Corsica (Corse)
Bastia
Monte Cinto 2706m
Monte Incudine 2136m
Ajaccio
Sartène
Bonifacio
Strait of Bonifacio

Côte d'Azur

MONACO
MONACO
Nice
Antibes
Cannes
le Cannet
Îles d'Hyères
Hyères
Toulon
la Ciotat
Aubagne
Marseille
Martigues
Aix-en-Provence
Salon-de-Provence
Arles
Tarascon
Avignon
Orange
Bollène
Sorgues
Montélimar
Privas
Valence
Digne
Manosque
Gap
Briançon
Grenoble
Voiron
St-Égrève
Vienne
Chambéry
St-Chamond
Villeurbanne
Lyon
Bourg-en-Bresse
Amberieu-en-Bugey
Annecy
Thonon-les-Bains
Mont Blanc 4807m
Col du Mont Cenis 2083m
Little St Bernard Pass 2188m
Mont Genèvre 1850m

Savoie
Isère
Drôme
Dauphiné
Durance
Ardèche
Provence
Camargue
Rhône
Saône
Mâcon
Roanne
Tarare
Thiers
Vichy
Cusset
Riom
Clermont-Ferrand
Issoire
Ussel
Tulle
Brive-la-Gaillarde
Aurillac
Figeac
Rodez
Millau
Mende
Le Puy
St-Four
Graulhet
Carmaux
Albi
Gaillac
Montauban
Castelsarrasin
Moissac
Cahors
Agen
Bergerac
Périgueux
Limoges
Angoulême
Cognac
Saintes
Royan
Oléron
Pessac
Mérignac
Bordeaux
Libourne
Arcachon
la Teste
Médoc
Marmande
Dax
Mont-de-Marsan
Orthez
Pau
St-Gaudens
Tarbes
Lourdes
Auch
Houilles
Anglet
Bayonne
Biarritz
SPAIN
ANDORRA
ANDORRA LA VELLA
PYRÉNÉES
Foix
Pamiers
Carcassonne
Castelnaudary
Toulouse
Limoux
Perpignan
Narbonne
Béziers
Agde
Sète
Montpellier
Frontignan
Nîmes
Alès
Cévennes
Roussillon
Languedoc
Tarn
Aveyron
Lot
Dordogne
Isle
Charente
Angoumois
Aquitaine
Gascogne
Armagnac
Landes
Garonne
Lot
Limousin
Marche
Massif Central
Auvergne
St-Étienne

AVIATION INDUSTRY
TOUR DE FRANCE

0 km 50 100 150
0 miles 50 100 150

Germany and the Alpine States

LYING AT THE VERY HEART OF EUROPE, Germany is one of the world's wealthiest nations. It is also Europe's leading industrial power. To its south lie the Alpine states of Switzerland, Austria, Liechtenstein, and Slovenia. The region is famed for its beautiful Alpine scenery, mountains, and lakes. German is the main language in all but Slovenia. However, each of the five countries has its own distinct history, culture, and national identity. Indeed, since 1815, Switzerland has been recognized as a neutral nation, and has stayed out of all the wars that have affected Europe.

THE JOY OF UNIFICATION
After World War II, Germany was split, with a US-backed capitalist state in the west and a Russian-backed state in the east. Built in 1961, the Berlin Wall was 155 km (96 miles) long and was designed to stop East Germans from leaving for a better life in the West. The wall divided Berlin and separated families, friends, and a nation for 28 years. When Germany was unified (reunited) in 1990, the wall was demolished.

Celebrations at the Brandenburg Gate mark the 10th anniversary of the fall of the Berlin Wall.

GENEVA
Geneva lies on the shores of Lake Geneva, Europe's largest Alpine lake. This orderly city is a global centre for banking and finance. It is also a base for many international organizations, such as the Red Cross.

The Swiss speak German, French, Italian, and Romansh.

GERMAN INDUSTRY
With its coal and iron mines, the Ruhr Valley was once the powerhouse of the German economy. Today's industry ranges from engineering to high-tech goods. Quality assembly and design make Germany the third-largest car producer in the world.

FOOD AND DRINK
The annual Munich *Oktoberfest* is Germany's biggest beer festival. Entertainment includes parades and music.

Baltic Sea

DENMARK

POLAND

NETHERLANDS

BELGIUM

GERMANY

SWISS WATCHES
The Swiss invented the first wristwatch, the first quartz watch, and the first waterresistant watch. With their worldwide reputation for quality and style, timepieces make up the country's third largest export.

SLOVENIA
After centuries of rule by overlords, Slovenia became independent in 1991. Although the population is only 2 million, the national culture is strong. The famous Lipizzaner show horses are named after the Slovenian farm where they were first bred.

VIENNA, AUSTRIA
Vienna is a city of baroque buildings, palaces, and famous concert halls. Grand balls with traditional waltzes are still customary. These are a reminder of when the city was the centre of the Austro-Hungarian Empire, which controlled large parts of east and central Europe.

The opera ball in Vienna

The high and graceful stride of the Lipizzaner horses makes them excel in competitions.

ALPS
The Alps run from southeast France and spread eastwards through Switzerland and northern Italy into Austria and Slovenia. A popular tourist destination, the Alps are famous for dramatic scenery and winter sports.

57

B   C   D   E   F   G   H

Spain and Portugal

THE COUNTRIES OF SPAIN AND PORTUGAL share an area of land called the Iberian Peninsula. In the north, this land is cut off from the rest of Europe by the Pyrenees Mountains, while to the south, it is separated from Africa by the Strait of Gibraltar. The region was once ruled by Islamic people from north Africa, known as the Moors. Evidence of their occupation can still be seen in buildings in the cities of Andalucía. The Moors were eventually defeated in 1492, and for a while, Portugal came under Spanish control, as did much of Europe. During the 20th century, both countries were ruled by brutal dictatorships, which were overthrown in the 1970s. They are now modern democracies.

Spanish families tend to eat dinner late, at around 9 PM. So after school, children eat a snack called a merienda.

HARVESTING CORK
Cork is made from the outer bark of the evergreen cork oak tree. The bark is carefully stripped off, flattened, laid out in sheets, and then left to dry. The cork is used for many products, such as stoppers for wine bottles, matting, and tiles. Portugal is the world's leading exporter of cork.

LISBON
Portugal's capital city is Lisbon, which is situated at the mouth of the River Tagus on a series of steep hills and valleys. In 1755, two-thirds of the city was completely destroyed by an earthquake and tidal wave but was rebuilt with beautiful squares and public buildings. Many explorers have set sail from Lisbon in their quest to find new lands.

Trams are a feature of Lisbon streets and a popular form of transport for both the locals and tourists.

FISHING
Spain and Portugal have well-developed fishing industries with large-scale fleets and many smaller local fleets. However, overfishing along Portugal's coast and out in the north Atlantic has put many people's livelihoods at risk. A massive oil spill off the coast of Galicia in 2002 also hit fish stocks, but the Portuguese government and thousands of volunteers restored beaches to their former beauty.

A Coruña (La Coruña)
Ferrol
Luarca   Avilés   Gijón (Xixón)   Costa V
Betanzos   Pravia   Tineo   Villaviciosa   Ll
Laracha   Vilalba   Oviedo   Mieres del Cam
Santa Comba   Asturias   Cantab
Cabo Fisterra   Outes   Galicia   Lugo   Pola de Lena   Cabañaquinta
Muros   Santiago   Cordillera Cantábrica
Ribeira   Lalín   Chantada   Monforte   Ponferrada   León
Pontevedra   O Carballiño   Astorga
Marín   Ourense (Orense)   Castilla-León
Vigo   Ponteareas   Xinzo de Limia   Benavente   Palencia
Viana do Castelo   Ponte da Barca   Bragança   Embalse de Ricobayo
Braga   Chaves   Zamora   Valladolid
Póvoa de Varzim   Guimarães   Toro   Duero
Vila do Conde   Vila Real   Medina del Campo
Matosinhos   Embalse de Almendra
Porto (Oporto)   Douro   Lamego   Salamanca   Se
Vila Nova de Gaia   São João da Madeira
Ovar   Albergaria-a-Velha   Viseu   Ávila
Aveiro   Ciudad-Rodrigo   S
Ílhavo   Alto da Torre 1993m   Guarda   Béjar   Sistema Cent
Coimbra   Serra da Estrela   Covilhã   Sierra de Gredos
Figueira da Foz   Plasencia   Talavera de la Reina
PORTUGAL   Coria
Leiria   Castelo Branco   Tagus   Embalse de Valdecañas
Tomar   Cáceres
Entroncamento   Abrantes   Embalse de Alcántara   Trujillo
Peniche   Caldas da Rainha   Herrera del Duq
Torres Vedras   Santarém   Portalegre   Extremadura
Coruche   Mérida   Villanueva de la Serer
Sintra   LISBON (LISBOA)   Estremoz   Elvas   Don Benito
Cascais   Évora   Badajoz   Castuera   Puerto
Almada   Barreiro   Serra d'Ossa   Almendralejo   Villafranca de los Barros
Setúbal   Alcácer do Sal   Zafra   Pozoblan
Baía de Setúbal   Azuaga
Jeréz de los Caballeros
Sines   Beja   Sierra Morena   Córdoba
Ourique   Cortegana   Monto
Valverde del Camino   Nerva   Palma del Rí
Algarve   La Algaba   Carmona   Ecija   Andalu
Portimão   Ayamonte   Lepe   Seville (Sevilla)   Osuna   Lucena
Cabo de São Vicente   Faro   Isla Cristina   Huelva   Dos Hermanas   Archid
Lagos   Tavira   Las Cabezas de San Juan   Antequera
Olhão   Gulf of Cadiz (Golfo de Cádiz)   Lebrija   Olvera   Álora
Ubrique   Ronda   M
Coín
Cádiz   Jeréz de la Frontera   Fuengirola   Marbella
San Fernando   Estepona   Costa de
Costa de la Luz   Barbate de Franco
Algeciras   GIBRALTA (to UK)
Strait of Gibraltar   Ceuta (to Spai
MOROCCO

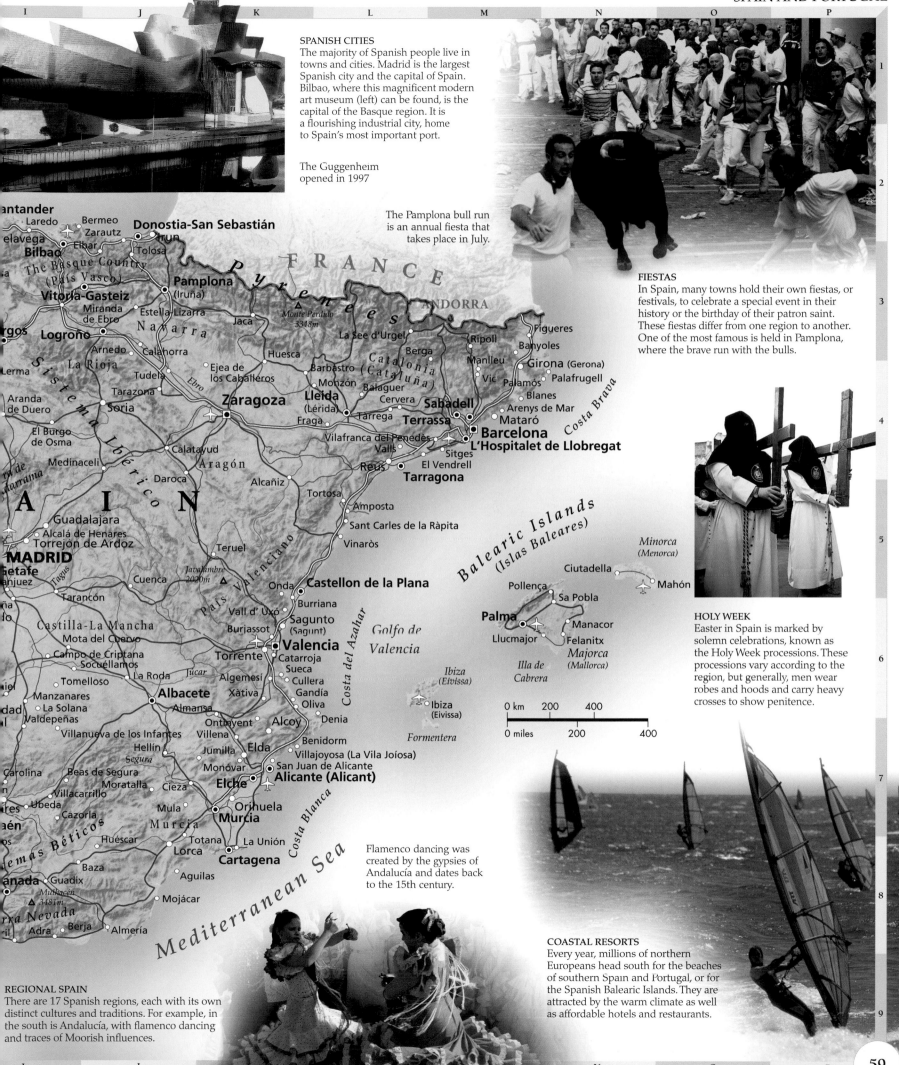

SPANISH CITIES
The majority of Spanish people live in towns and cities. Madrid is the largest Spanish city and the capital of Spain. Bilbao, where this magnificent modern art museum (left) can be found, is the capital of the Basque region. It is a flourishing industrial city, home to Spain's most important port.

The Guggenheim opened in 1997

The Pamplona bull run is an annual fiesta that takes place in July.

FIESTAS
In Spain, many towns hold their own fiestas, or festivals, to celebrate a special event in their history or the birthday of their patron saint. These fiestas differ from one region to another. One of the most famous is held in Pamplona, where the brave run with the bulls.

HOLY WEEK
Easter in Spain is marked by solemn celebrations, known as the Holy Week processions. These processions vary according to the region, but generally, men wear robes and hoods and carry heavy crosses to show penitence.

COASTAL RESORTS
Every year, millions of northern Europeans head south for the beaches of southern Spain and Portugal, or for the Spanish Balearic Islands. They are attracted by the warm climate as well as affordable hotels and restaurants.

Flamenco dancing was created by the gypsies of Andalucía and dates back to the 15th century.

REGIONAL SPAIN
There are 17 Spanish regions, each with its own distinct cultures and traditions. For example, in the south is Andalucía, with flamenco dancing and traces of Moorish influences.

Map labels

Santander • Laredo • Bermeo • Zarautz • Donostia-San Sebastián
elavega • Bilbao • Eibar • Tolosa • Irun
The Basque Country (País Vasco)
Pamplona (Iruña) • Vitoria-Gasteiz • Miranda de Ebro
Estella-Lizarra • Navarra
rgos • Logroño • Arnedo • Calahorra • Tudela • Jaca • Huesca
La Rioja • Tarazona • Soria
Lerma • Sistema Ibérico • Ejea de los Caballeros • Barbastro • Monzón • Balaguer
El Burgo de Osma • Zaragoza • Lleida (Lérida) • Cervera • Sabadell • Arenys de Mar
Aranda de Duero • Fraga • Tárrega • Terrassa • Mataró
Medinaceli • Calatayud • Aragón • Vilafranca del Penedès • Barcelona
ra de arrama • Daroca • Valls • L'Hospitalet de Llobregat
A I N • Guadalajara • Alcañiz • Sitges • El Vendrell
Alcalá de Henares • Teruel • Tortosa • Reus • Tarragona
Torrejón de Ardoz • Javalambre 2020m • Amposta
MADRID • etafe • Cuenca • Sant Carles de la Ràpita
anjuez • Tarancón • Vinaròs
ña • Castilla-La Mancha • Onda • Castellon de la Plana
lo • Mota del Cuervo • Burriana • Golfo de Valencia
Campo de Criptana • Vall d'Uxó • Sagunto (Sagunt)
Socuéllamos • Buriassot
Tomelloso • La Roda • Torrente • Valencia • Catarroja • Costa del Azahar
Manzanares • Algemesí • Sueca
dad • La Solana • Albacete • Almansa • Xàtiva • Cullera
Valdepeñas • Gandía • Oliva
Villanueva de los Infantes • Onthyent • Villena • Alcoy • Denia
Hellín • Villajoyosa (La Vila Joíosa)
Jumilla • Elda • Benidorm
arolina • Beas de Segura • Monóvar • San Juan de Alicante
Moratalla • Cieza • Elche • Alicante (Alicant)
Villacarrillo • Mula • Orihuela
aén • Ubeda • Cazorla • Murcia • Costa Blanca
res • Huéscar • Totana • La Unión
Sistemas Béticos • Lorca • Cartagena
ranada • Baza • Aguilas
Guadix • Mojácar
Mulhacén 3481m
rra Nevada • Adra • Berja • Almería

FRANCE • Pyrenees • ANDORRA
Monte Perdido 3348m
Figueres • Ripoll • Banyoles • Girona (Gerona) • Palafrugell
Berga • Manlleu • Palamós • Blanes • Costa Brava
Catalonia (Cataluña) • Vic

Balearic Islands (Islas Baleares)
Minorca (Menorca) • Ciutadella • Mahón
Pollença • Sa Pobla
Palma • Manacor • Felanitx
Llucmajor • Majorca (Mallorca)
Illa de Cabrera
Ibiza (Eivissa)
Ibiza (Eivissa)
Formentera

Mediterranean Sea

0 km 200 400
0 miles 200 400

Italy

Vatican City has a permanent population of only about 800 people, although more than 3,000 come to work in the city-state each day.

Carnival masks

Andrea Bocelli

THE BOOT-SHAPED COUNTRY of Italy stretches from the mountainous north down to the Mediterranean Sea. For much of its history, Italy consisted of city-states – such as Florence and Venice – and was united only in 1870. Regional differences in Italy are huge, as each region has its own cuisine, customs, and dialect, and is geographically quite distinct. As a result, many Italians identify themselves first by region and then by country. The largest division, however, is between the rich north and the poorer south – a rugged region with several active volcanoes and the occasional severe earthquake. The mainland of Italy includes two tiny independent states – San Marino and Vatican City.

COLOSSEUM
One of Rome's greatest sights is the Colosseum, which opened in CE 80. Deadly gladiatorial combats and animal fights were staged here before crowds of up to 55,000 people.

HOME OF OPERA
The idea of setting drama to music originated in Italy during the 16th century. Since then, Italian composers, such as Rossini, Verdi, and Puccini, have made opera the most popular musical form in Italy. Many cities have their own opera houses.

CITY OF CANALS
The beautiful city of Venice is made up of 118 islands, 177 canals, and 400 bridges. The only way to get around is to walk or take a boat: a *vaporetto*, *motoscafo*, or *motonave*. The most distinctive boat, however, is the gondola. Each year, in the days before Ash Wednesday, Venice hosts a carnival when the city celebrates with fireworks and everyone wears spectacular masks.

FOOTBALL FANS
Italians are mad about football and fanatically follow the performance of teams such as Juventus, AC Milan, Inter, and Roma. Italian teams frequently win major European competitions, and the national team has won the World Cup four times – in 1934, 1938, 1982, and 2006.

The oval-shaped Colosseum stood at 189 m (620 ft) high.

SLOVENIA
CROATIA
AUSTRIA
SWITZERLAND
FRANCE
MONACO

Brenner Pass 1374m

Trieste
Tarvisio
Montalcone
Cortina d'Ampezzo
Gemona del Friuli
Udine
Pordenone
Portogruaro
Treviso
Venice (Venezia)
Gulf of Venice
Mestre
Chioggia
Bressanone
Merano
Bolzano
Dolomites
Trento
Vicenza
Padova
Rovigo
Foci del Po
Adige
Monselice
Ostiglia
Po
Edolo
Arco
Lake Garda
Bassano del Grappa
Verona
Mantova
Comacchio
Imola
Ferrara
Ravenna
Forlì
Cesena
Rimini
SAN MARINO
SAN MARINO
Pesaro
Fano
Ancona
Falconara Marittima
Civitanova Marche
Fermo
Ascoli Piceno
Teramo
Giulianova
Marche
Appennino
Umbro-Marchigiano
Lake Como
Como
Lombardy (Lombardia)
Bergamo
Sesto San Giovanni
Brescia
Cremona
Parma
Reggio nell'Emilia
Modena
Bologna
Faenza
Carpi
Piacenza
Pavia
Monza
Milan (Milano)
Rho
Lake Maggiore
Varese
Novara
Vercelli
Pisa
Prato
Pistoia
Florence (Firenze)
Arezzo
Arno
Chianti
Siena
Perugia
Foligno
Todi
Terni
Lago Trasimeno
Tuscany (Toscana)
Grosseto
Lago di Bolsena
Viterbo
Orbetello
Archipelago Toscano
Portoferraio
Isola d'Elba
Piombino
Cecina
Livorno
Viareggio
Lucca
Massa
Carrara
La Spezia
Savona
Genoa (Genova)
Gulf of Genoa
Finale Ligure
Imperia
San Remo
Ventimiglia
Liguria
Gulf of Genoa
Asti
Alessandria
Casteggio
Appennino Ligure
Mondovì
Cuneo
Savigliano
Moncalieri
Rivoli
Susa
Turin (Torino)
Piemonte
Aosta
Gran Paradiso 4061m
Little St-Bernard Pass 2188m
Great Saint Bernard Pass 2469m
Mont Blanc 4807m
Rhône
Alps
Apennines
Po Valley
Piombino

Adriatic Sea

Strait of Otranto

Brindisi
Lecce
Maglie
Taranto
Manduria
Gallipoli
Golfo di Taranto
Bari
Molfetta
Barletta
Manfredonia
Andria
Bitonto
Altamura
Matera
Puglia
Ciro Marino
Crotone
Catanzaro
Siderno
La Sila
Rossano
Castrovillari
Cosenza
Amantea
Lamezia
Palmi
Reggio di Calabria
Strait of Messina
Ionian Sea

San Severo
Foggia
Cerignola
Campobasso
Isernia
Benevento
Avellino
Caserta
Torre del Greco
Salerno
Battipaglia
Agropoli
Sapri
Lauria
Consilina
Sala
Appennino Lucano
Potenza
Campania
Volturno
Gaeta
Golfo di Gaeta
(ROMA)
Anzio
Latina
Terracina
Isole Ponziane
Naples
(Napoli)
Isola di Capri
Gulf of Salerno
Vesuvius 1277 m

Tyrrhenian Sea

Isola Stromboli
Isole Eolie
Isola Lipari
Isola Vulcano

Messina
Catania
Monti Etna 3340 m
Simeto
Cefalù
Palermo
Alcamo
Marsala
Trapani
Castelvetrano
Caltanissetta
Agrigento
Gela
Vittoria
Ragusa
Modica
Pozzallo
Siracusa
Sicily (Sicilia)
Strait of Sicily

MALTA
VALLETTA
Gozo
Malta Channel
Isole Pelagie
Isola di Pantelleria

Mediterranean Sea

(Sardegna)
Porto Torres
Alghero
Sassari
Tempio Pausania
Olbia
Ozieri
Siniscola
Nuoro
Macomer
Oristano
Iglesias
Carbonia
Villacidro
Cagliari
Quartu Sant' Elena
Punta La Marmora 1834 m

Olive harvesters gather olives in nets

OLIVE HARVEST
Italy is a big producer of olive oil, producing around 3.6 million tonnes, which is second only to Spain in Europe. The oil is produced by first pressing the fruits of the olive tree between steel or stone rollers, then squeezing oil from the pulp using a press. Olive trees flourish in the fertile soils and the mild, frost-free climate of southern Italy.

VATICAN CITY
This tiny state in Rome is the centre of the Roman Catholic Church and home to the Pope. As well as St Peter's Basilica and the surrounding buildings and gardens, the Vatican boasts Michelangelo's Sistine Chapel. The state has its own flag, postage stamps, and coins.

Swiss guards, in their red, yellow, and blue striped costumes, stand at the gates into Vatican City.

RENAISSANCE ITALY
Florence (below) sits either side of the River Arno. During the 15th century, a new movement in art and architecture, known as the Renaissance, or rebirth, began in Italy. Painters and sculptors, such as Leonardo da Vinci, Michelangelo, and Raphael, created beautiful works of art using improved techniques of perspective and realism. Many of these can still be seen in the galleries and churches of Florence.

HOME LIFE
Family life is important in Italy, and most people live at home until they marry. This is partly due to lack of cheap housing. Lunch (*pranzo*) is often the main meal of the day.

0 km 50 100
0 miles 50 100

Central Europe

FOUR COUNTRIES LIE at the heart of central Europe – Poland, the Czech Republic, Slovakia, and Hungary. The region is typically composed of wide plains broken by gentle hills and the Carpathian mountain range in the south. In the late 1980s, these countries broke away from years of communist rule. The new democratic governments were faced with the problems of trying to modernize their countries. These changes are ongoing, but in some of the countries, such as the Czech Republic, there are signs of improvement and a rise in living standards.

TRADITIONAL TRADES
The countries of central Europe, except Slovakia, are heavily industrialized. Vast coal mines, steel works (above), and engineering works dominate the urban landscape. Although some of these sites are old and poorly equipped, these countries are trying to update machinery and introduce measures to improve standards of environmental pollution.

FAMILY FARMS
Poland has one of the largest agricultural sectors in Europe, with more than one-quarter of the workforce employed on the land. Most farms are still small, family-run businesses, growing grains, sugar beet, and potatoes. Large numbers of pigs and other animals are also kept.

RELIGION
The Roman Catholic Church is very strong throughout central Europe. Attending mass on Sunday and observing religious holidays, such as Christmas and Easter, are important features of family life.

GOLDEN PRAGUE
Prague, the capital of the Czech Republic, is one of Europe's most beautiful cities. It contains many old buildings with golden roofs and grand squares. Unlike other central European cities, Prague escaped serious damage during both world wars and thus retains much of its charm.

Part of Prague's colourful history is preserved in buildings around the Old Town Square.

BELARUS

KALININGRAD
(to Russian Federation)

Suwałki
Gołdap
Augustów
Kuźnica
Sokółka
Giżycko
Ełk
Grajewo
Białystok
Łapy
Pisz
Zambrów
Bielsk Podlaski
Siemiatycze
Biała Podlaska
Bartoszyce
Kętrzyn
Szczytno
Łomża
Ostrów
Radzyń Podlaski
Dobre Miasto
Nidzica
Mazowiecka
Międzyrzec Podlaski
Biskupiec
Olsztyn
Mława
Ostrołęka
Wyszków
Łuków
Krasnystaw
Chełm
Lidzbark
Warmiński
Pułtusk
Garwolin
Puławy
Lublin
Włodawa
Elbląg
Ostróda
Iława
Ciechanów
Płońsk
WARSAW
(WARSZAWA)
Góra
Kalwaria
Ryki
Świdnik
Zamość
Braniewo
Malbork
Kwidzyn
Brodnica
Rypin
Sierpc
Nowy Dwór Mazowiecki
Pruszków
Grójec
Skarżysko-
Kamienna
Ostrowiec
Świętokrzyski
Sandomierz
Tomaszów Lubelski
Gulf of Danzig
Vistula Lagoon
Gdynia
Rumia
Tczew
Grudziądz
Lipno
Włocławek
Płock
Kutno
Łódź
Tomaszów
Mazowiecki
Starachowice
Kielce
Stalowa Wola
Gdańsk
Lębork
Chojnice
Świecie
Chełmża
Toruń
Inowrocław
Zgierz
Piotrków
Trybunalski
Radomsko
Częstochowa
Tarnobrzeg
Zawiercie
Wejherowo
Kościerzyna
Bytów
Czersk
Żnin
Mogilno
Konin
Pabianice
Bełchatów
Wieluń
Kłobuck
Jędrzejów
Władysławowo
Słupsk
Szczecinek
Wałcz
Gniezno
Września
Pleszew
Sieradz
Radomsko
Lubliniec
Opole
Bytom
Ząbkowice Śląskie
Ustka
Sławno
Piła
Oborniki
Poznań
Kalisz
Ostrów
Wielkopolski
Leszno
Rawicz
Kępno
Kluczbork
Brzeg
Wrocław
Koszalin
Białogard
Choszczno
Trzcianka
Środa
Wielkopolski
Głogów
Lubin
Legnica
Świdnica
Wałbrzych
Kołobrzeg
Świdwin
Nowogard
Stargard Szczeciński
Międzyrzecz
Sulechów
Nowa Sól
Żagań
Bolesławiec
Jelenia Góra
Świnoujście
Goleniów
Pyrzyce
Sulęcin
Krosno
Odrzańskie
Żary
Zgorzelec
Liberec
Szczecin
Słubice
Świebodzin
Lutsko
Szprotawa
Gorzów Wielkopolski
Zielona Góra
Pomeranian
Bay
Baltic Sea

Mazury
Mazowiecki
Radom
Wyżyna Lubelska
Wyżyna Małopolska
Śląsk
Sudety
Śnieżka
1602m

Oder (Odra)
Narew
Bug
Wisła
Warta
Noteć
Jezioro
Śniardwy

GERMANY

Ústí nad Labem
Teplice
Děčín
Chomutov
Most
Lovosice

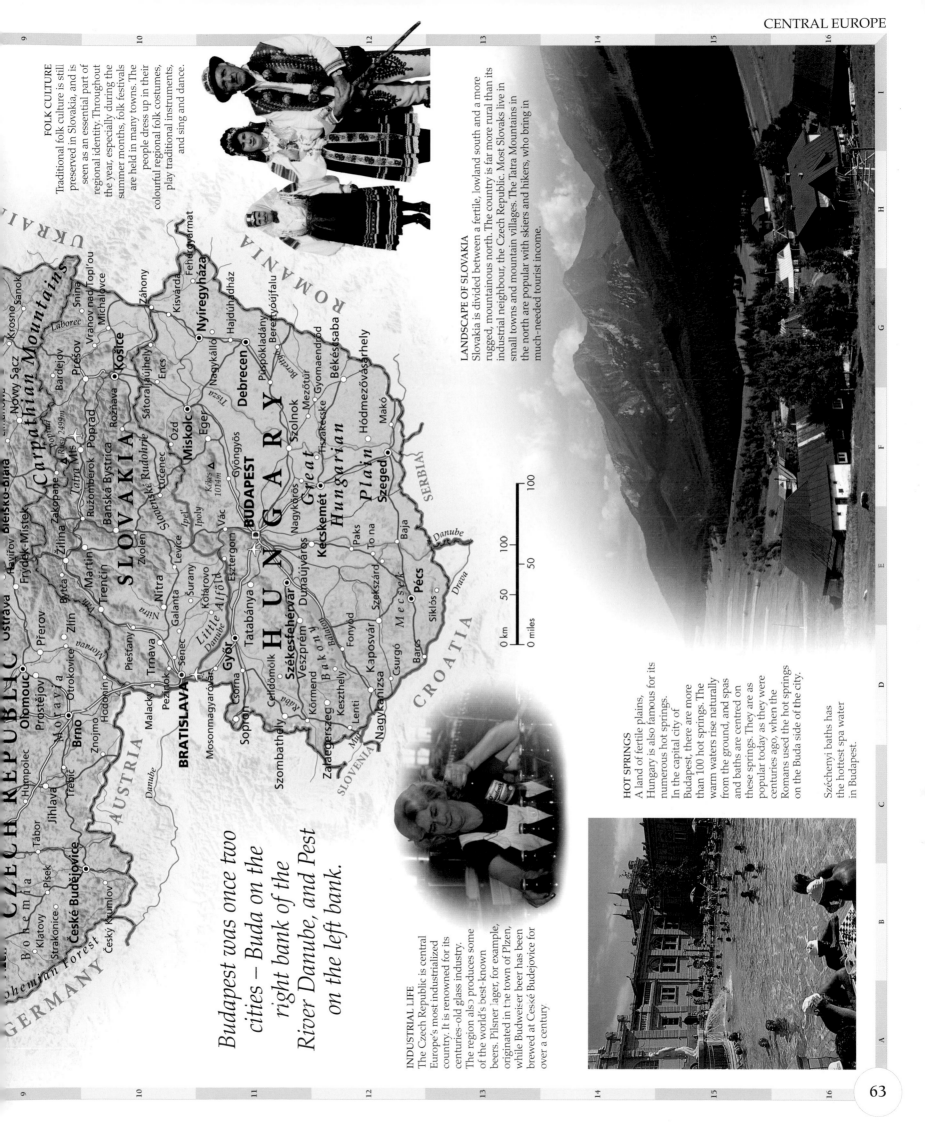

FOLK CULTURE
Traditional folk culture is still preserved in Slovakia, and is seen as an essential part of regional identity. Throughout the year, especially during the summer months, folk festivals are held in many towns. The people dress up in their colourful regional folk costumes, play traditional instruments, and sing and dance.

LANDSCAPE OF SLOVAKIA
Slovakia is divided between a fertile, lowland south and a more rugged, mountainous north. The country is far more rural than its industrial neighbour, the Czech Republic. Most Slovaks live in small towns and mountain villages. The Tatra Mountains in the north are popular with skiers and hikers, who bring in much-needed tourist income.

Budapest was once two cities – Buda on the right bank of the River Danube, and Pest on the left bank.

INDUSTRIAL LIFE
The Czech Republic is central Europe's most industrialized country. It is renowned for its centuries-old glass industry. The region also produces some of the world's best-known beers. Pilsner lager, for example, originated in the town of Plzeň, while Budweiser beer has been brewed at České Budějovice for over a century.

HOT SPRINGS
A land of fertile plains, Hungary is also famous for its numerous hot springs. In the capital city of Budapest, there are more than 100 hot springs. The warm waters rise naturally from the ground, and spas and baths are centred on these springs. They are as popular today as they were centuries ago, when the Romans used the hot springs on the Buda side of the city.

Széchenyi baths has the hottest spa water in Budapest.

Southeast Europe

UNTIL 1991, CROATIA, Bosnia and Herzegovina, Serbia, Montenegro, and Macedonia were all part of Yugoslavia. Ethnic tensions between the Serbs and other peoples in Yugoslavia caused a series of bloody wars that broke up the country. Peace was eventually restored in 1999, but all five countries have suffered intense economic problems as a result. So, too, has Albania since its communist government collapsed. The six nations do, however, have huge potential, with considerable agricultural and mineral resources. In the north, the River Danube is an important trading route for both Croatia and Serbia, while Croatia has a flourishing tourist industry along its beautiful Adriatic coast.

THE ADRIATIC

The long Adriatic coastline of Croatia is one of the most beautiful in Europe. The wooded hillsides, pretty beaches, such as Markarska (right), islands, and historic towns once attracted tourists from all over Europe. Now that the country is no longer involved in the war, tourists are returning, contributing vital income to the national economy.

GROWING FOOD

The most fertile area in this region lies along the River Danube in northern Serbia and eastern Croatia. Here, vegetables, fruit, maize, and cereals are grown, as well as grapes for wine-making. Most farms are small-scale family businesses growing a wide range of crops.

Family-run allotments

DIFFERENT SCRIPTS

Croatian and Serbian languages are very similar but the people of Croatia, a predominantly Roman Catholic country, write in Roman script, as do Bosnians. Serbians are mainly Eastern Orthodox and write using both Roman and Russian Cyrillic scripts.

Magazine with Cyrillic script

Magazine with Roman script

SPORTING ACHIEVEMENT

Croatia is a great sporting nation. Skier Janica Kostelic is not only Croatia's first triple Olympic champion, she is the most successful female Alpine skier of all time, winning three gold medals at the 2002 Winter Olympics and another gold and silver medal in 2006.

Janica Kostelic

The Dalmatian dog is named after the coastal region of Dalmatia in Croatia, its first known home.

Map labels

ROMANIA

HUNGARY

SLOVENIA

CROATIA

BOSNIA & HERZEGOVINA

SERBIA

REPUBLIKA SRPSKA

Vojvodina

Subotica, Kanjiža, Senta, Ada, Kikinda, Bačka Topola, Sombor, Srbobran, Vrbas, Bačka Palanka, Temerin, Zrenjanin, Mužlja, Bečej, Tisza, Novi Sad, Indija, Stara Pazova, Batajnica, Zemun, BELGRADE (BEOGRAD), Pančevo, Vršac, Bela Crkva, Smederevo, Požarevac, Velika Morava, Smederevska Palanka, Mladenovac, Arandelovac, Valjevo, Loznica, Šabac, Sremska Mitrovica, Ruma, Putog, Borovo, Vukovar, Županja, Sremska, Bijeljina, Zvornik, Srebrenica, Tuzla, Brčko, Modriča, Derventa, Doboj, Gradačac, Bosanski Samac, Maglaj, Zenica, Zavidovići, Visoko, SARAJEVO, Livno, Jajce, Travnik, Banja Luka, Ključ, Sana, Prijedor, Bosanski Novi, Bosanska Gradiška, Bosanska Dubica, Kozara, Vrbas, Nova Gradiška, Slavonska Požega, Slavonski Brod, Đakovo, Osijek, Beli Manastir, Drava, Slatina, Virovitica, Papuk, Bjelovar, Koprivnica, Čakovec, Varaždin, Krapina, ZAGREB, Sesvete, Sisak, Kutina, Petrinja, Karlovac, Glina, Una, Bihać, Cazin, Unac, Dinara, Troglav 1913m, Knin, Sinj, Gospić, Velebit, Zadar, Šibenik, Pag, Rijeka, Crikvenica, Senj, Ogulin, Krk, Cres, Lošinj, Kvarner, Pula, Opatija, Istra, Rovinj, Poreč, Dugi Otok, Adriatic, Sava, Drava, Drina, Bosna, Kolpa

Danube (Duna)

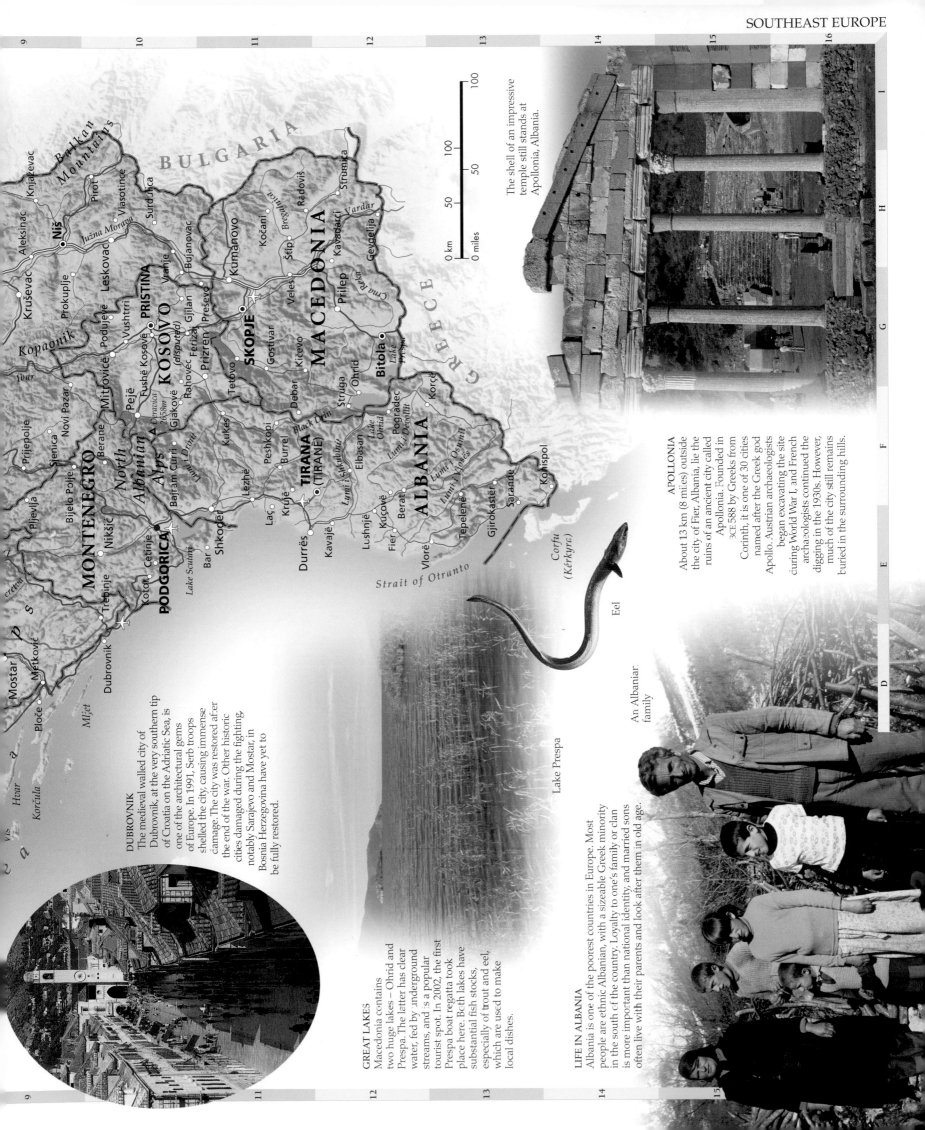

BULGARIA

Balkan Mountains

Knjaževac
Pirot
Vlasotince
Niš
Aleksinac
Kruševac
Južna Morava
Leskovac
Prokuplje
Surdulica
Kopaonik
Novi Pazar
Vranje
Bujanovac
PRISTINA
Podujevë
Vushtrri
Presevo
Kumanovo
Ibar
Mitrovicë
Fushë Kosovë
Gjilan
KOSOVO
(disputed)
Ferizaj
SKOPJE
Kočani
Štip
Radoviš
Strumica
Prijepolje
Berane
Pejë
Rahovec
Prizren
Tetovo
Gostivar
Veles
Kavadarci
Gevgelija
Vardar
Sjenica
North
Peshkopi
Kičevo
Debar
Ohrid
Prilep
Crna Reka
Bijelo Polje
Albanian
Bajram Curri
Gjakovë
Deravica
2658m
Alps
Kukës
Struga
Bitola
Lake
Ohrid
Lake
Prespa
MACEDONIA
Pljevlja
MONTENEGRO
Nikšić
Lumi i Drini
Lezhë
Burrel
Black Drin
Lumi i Shkumbini
Pogradec
Korçë
Trebinje
Cetinje
PODGORICA
Laç
Krujë
Elbasan
Lumi i
Devollit
Lake Scutari
Kotor
Shkodër
Bar
TIRANA
(TIRANË)
G R E E C E
Mostar
Metković
Dubrovnik
Durrës
Kavajë
Lushnjë
Fier
Berat
Lumi i Osumit
Lumi i Vjosës
Tepelenë
Ploče
Mljet
Kučovë
Vlorë
ALBANIA
Gjirokastër
Sarandë
Korçula
Hvar
Vis
Strait of Otranto
Corfu
(Kérkyra)
Kolispol

km 100
100
50
50
0 km
0 miles

The shell of an impressive temple still stands at Apollonia, Albania.

APOLLONIA
About 13 km (8 miles) outside the city of Fier, Albania, lie the ruins of an ancient city called Apollonia. Founded in 3CE 588 by Greeks from Corinth, it is one of 30 cities named after the Greek god Apollo. Austrian archaeologists began excavating the site during World War I, and French archaeologists continued the digging in the 1930s. However, much of the city still remains buried in the surrounding hills.

Eel

An Albaniar family

DUBROVNIK
The medieval walled city of Dubrovnik, at the very southern tip of Croatia on the Adriatic Sea, is one of the architectural gems of Europe. In 1991, Serb troops shelled the city, causing immense damage. The city was restored after the end of the war. Other historic cities damaged during the fighting, notably Sarajevo and Mostar, in Bosnia Herzegovina have yet to be fully restored.

GREAT LAKES
Macedonia contains two huge lakes – Ohrid and Prespa. The latter has clear water, fed by underground streams, and is a popular tourist spot. In 2002, the first Prespa boat regatta took place here. Both lakes have substantial fish stocks, especially of trout and eel, which are used to make local dishes.

Lake Prespa

LIFE IN ALBANIA
Albania is one of the poorest countries in Europe. Most people are ethnic Albanian, with a sizeable Greek minority in the south of the country. Loyalty to one's family or clan is more important than national identity, and married sons often live with their parents and look after them in old age.

Bulgaria and Greece

FOR MORE THAN FOUR CENTURIES Bulgaria and Greece were ruled by the Ottoman Turks. Bulgaria gained independence in 1908, while southern Greece became independent in 1832 and was joined by northern Greece in 1913. After World War II, Bulgaria became a communist state. Both states are now democracies and members of the European Union (EU). Bulgaria remains relatively poor while in 2010, it emerged that Greece had a huge national deficit due to spending more than it had been collecting in taxes. The EU lent Greece 112 billion euros to restore its economy. Although they border each other, Bulgaria and Greece are quite different; the Greek mainland is mountainous with only one-third of the land suitable for cultivation. By contrast, Bulgaria is more fertile with a strong agricultural tradition. Tourism is an important source of income to both countries, with visitors flocking to the Black Sea resorts in Bulgaria, to the Greek mainland to see the ancient ruins, and to the Greek islands in search of sandy beaches.

First held in Athens in 1896, the modern Olympic Games were staged there again in 2004.

BULGARIAN AGRICULTURE

Wheat, maize, and other cereals grow in the fertile Danube river valley in the north of the country. Tobacco (right) grows in the Maritsa river valley in the southeast, while grapes for the wine industry flourish on the slopes of the Balkan Mountains. The festival of Kukerov Dan, with traditional processions, celebrates the start of the agricultural year.

CITY LIFE

Bulgarians make up about 85 per cent of the total population of the country. The rest are Turkish, Macedonian, or Roma. Most people live in apartment blocks in the main towns and cities. They are more likely to use public transport as not all households have a car.

Trams provide an efficient way for people to get around the city of Sofia.

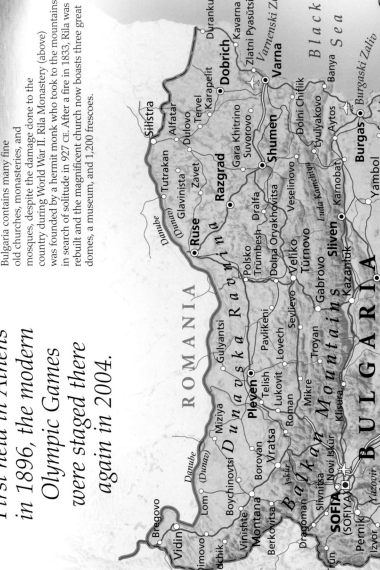

ARCHITECTURE

Bulgaria contains many fine old churches, monasteries, and mosques, despite the damage done to the country during World War II. Rila Monastery (above) was founded by a hermit monk who took to the mountains in search of solitude in 927 CE. After a fire in 1833, Rila was rebuilt and the magnificent church now boasts three great domes, a museum, and 1,200 frescoes.

LANGUAGE

The 24 characters in the Greek alphabet date from the 8th century BCE, when the first texts were written in classical Greek. Since then the language has evolved and is now spoken by 11 million people around the world.

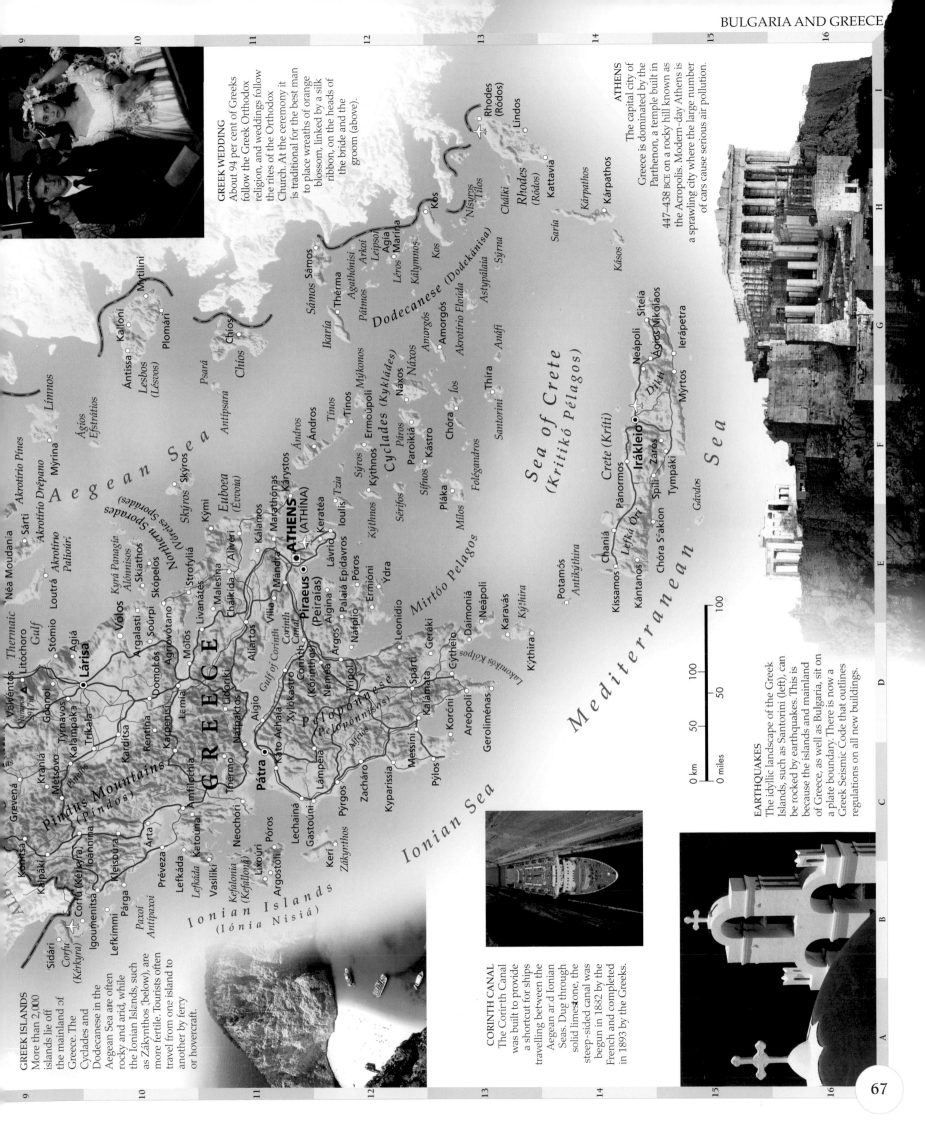

GREEK ISLANDS

More than 2,000 islands lie off the mainland of Greece. The Cyclades and Dodecanese in the Aegean Sea are often rocky and arid, while the Ionian Islands, such as Zákynthos (below), are more fertile. Tourists often travel from one island to another by ferry or hovercraft.

GREEK WEDDING

About 94 per cent of Greeks follow the Greek Orthodox religion, and weddings follow the rites of the Orthodox Church. At the ceremony it is traditional for the best man to place wreaths of orange blossom, linked by a silk ribbon, on the heads of the bride and the groom (above).

ATHENS

The capital city of Greece is dominated by the Parthenon, a temple built in 447–438 BCE on a rocky hill known as the Acropolis. Modern-day Athens is a sprawling city where the large number of cars cause serious air pollution.

CORINTH CANAL

The Corinth Canal was built to provide a shortcut for ships travelling between the Aegean and Ionian Seas. Dug through solid limestone, the steep-sided canal was begun in 1882 by the French and completed in 1893 by the Greeks.

EARTHQUAKES

The idyllic landscape of the Greek Islands, such as Santorini (left), can be rocked by earthquakes. This is because the islands and mainland of Greece, as well as Bulgaria, sit on a plate boundary. There is now a Greek Seismic Code that outlines regulations on all new buildings.

Aegean Sea

Ionian Sea

Ionian Islands
(Iónia Nisiá)

Mediterranean Sea

Mirtóo Pélagos

Sea of Crete
(Kritikó Pélagos)

GREECE

Peloponnese
(Pelopónnisos)

Dodecanese (Dodekánisa)

Cyclades (Kykládes)

Crete (Kríti)

Lakonikós Kólpos

Pindus Mountains
(Píndos)

Northern Sporades
(Vóreies Sporádes)

Thermaic Gulf

Gulf of Corinth

67

Ukraine, Moldova, & Romania

THROUGHOUT MUCH OF THE LAST CENTURY, Ukraine and Moldova formed part of the Soviet Union, while Romania was ruled for 20 years by the dictator Nicolae Ceausescu. In 1989, Ceausescu was overthrown, while Ukraine and Moldova became independent in 1991. Today, the three countries are struggling to come to terms with their communist inheritance and transform themselves into modern democracies. All three lack modern technology and face serious economic and environmental problems arising from outdated industry. They also face increasing ethnic tensions with their minority populations – Hungarians in Romania, as well as Russians left behind in Ukraine and Moldova after the collapse of the Soviet Union.

CITY LIFE
Romania has many cities and towns with a mix of old and new buildings. Sibiu (left) was founded in the 12th century and, at one time, had 19 guilds – each representing a different craft – within its city walls. Much remains from this colourful history, especially in the painted buildings of the old town.

FOLK CUSTOMS
Despite years of communist rule, folk customs thrived in the rural areas of Romania and Ukraine. In Ukraine, singers perform *dumas*, historical epics that tell of slavery under the Turks. One of the traditional instruments is a bandura (left), a stringed instrument that sounds like a harpsichord.

DRACULA'S CASTLE
Situated in Transylvania, Bran Castle is a favourite tourist destination. This is where author Bram Stoker's fictional blood-drinking Count Dracula lived. The story is probably based on a 15th-century Romanian prince, Vlad Dracula, who reigned for less than 10 years but caused more than 50,000 deaths.

The word Transylvania means "land beyond the forests".

EASTER BREAD
In Romania, Easter is celebrated with a meal of roast lamb served with a bread called *cozonac*. This is made by pounding nuts, raisins, and even cocoa, into the dough.

INDUSTRY IN THE UKRAINE
Ukraine is the world's eighth largest producer of steel and has a large coal industry as well as reserves of oil and gas. Today, however, much of its industry is out of date and inefficient. Most of the heavy industry is situated in the central Dnieper river valley.

Liquid iron ore

HOLIDAYS BY THE SEA
The Black Sea resorts of the Crimea, in southern Ukraine, were once a favourite holiday destination for Russians heading south for the summer sun. Today, resorts such as Yalta (below), are growing again in popularity, sometimes as a budget alternative to Mediterranean destinations. The quality of facilities is improving as tourist numbers increase.

Children of the Maramures region of Transylvania.

PEOPLE OF ROMANIA
Romanians speak Romanian – a language closely related to French, Italian, and Spanish. The country also has sizeable Hungarian and Roma minorities, which have both been discriminated against in recent years. Most Hungarian speakers live in the region of Romania known as Transylvania.

RICH SOILS OF MOLDOVA
Moldova consists of partially wooded plains intercut with rivers and streams. About 75 per cent of the land is rich in chernozem (black) soil, which is very fertile. Wine and sunflower production is important here. Fruit and vegetables, such as pumpkins (left), also grow well

Baltic States and Belarus

THE THREE BALTIC STATES, Estonia, Latvia, and Lithuania, all share a small stretch of coast on the Baltic Sea. Belarus lies between Poland, Ukraine, and the Russian Federation. Following independence from the Soviet Union in 1991, all these countries faced problems such as price rises, food shortages, and pollution. However, the Baltic States have since tried to reform their societies and economies along Western lines. Belarus has kept close links with Russia and has been the slowest to reform. This mainly rural country remains isolated from the rest of Europe and, with few natural resources, remains one of its poorest nations.

Political rally in Tallinn

SINGING REVOLUTION
Estonia is known for its classical music tradition – most notably its choirs. This love of music was most powerful when people raised their voices during the Singing Revolution in 1988 (right), part of their move towards independence.

TALLINN OLD TOWN
With its colourful buildings, turreted walls, and gabled roofs, Tallinn is one of the best-preserved capital cities in Europe. All the winding, cobbled streets lead to the Town Hall Square (left).

AMBER
Two-thirds of the world's amber, the fossilized resin of pine trees, is washed up from the sea bed along the Baltic coast. Amber is used to make jewellery, among other things.

Belarus used to be known as Belorussia, a name that means "White Russia".

RUSSIAN FEDERATION

Map labels

Gulf of Finland

Baltic Sea

Gulf of Riga

ESTONIA

LATVIA

LITHUANIA

POLAND

Narva Bay

Narva Reservoir

Lake Peipus

Lake Pskov

TALLINN
Paldiski, Maardu, Loksa, Raasiku, Aegviidu, Kunda, Rakvere, Rakke, Tapa, Kohtla-Järve, Narva, Sillamäe, Kallaste, Palamuse, **Tartu**, Võnnu, Räpina

Keila-Tir, Risti, Rapla, Paide, Viljandi, Põltsamaa, Otepää, Põlva, Võru

Hiiumaa, Kärdla, Vormsi, Haapsalu, Lihula, Rapla, Pärnu-Jaagupi, Audru, Sindi, **Pärnu**, Uulu, Kilingi-Nõmme, Mõisaküla, Valga, Tõrva, Valka, Rõngu

Vainameri, Emmaste, Orissaare, Kuressaare, Virtsu, Kihnu, Ruhnu

Saaremaa, Sääre, Kolka, Roja, Mērsrags, Engure, Ainaži, Salacgrīva, Staicele, Ruijena, Aloja, Burtnieku Ezers, Valmiera, Cēsis, Smiltene

Kolkasrags, Ventspils, Mazirbe, Ugāle, Talsi, Tukums, Jūrmala, **RĪGA**, Sigulda, Jelgava, Iecava, Bauska, Aizkraukle, Pļaviņas, Madona, Lubāns, Varakļāni, Rēzekne, Ludza

Usmas Ezers, Kuldīga, Kandava, Saldus, Dobele, Brocēni, Auce, Jaunpiebalga, Gulbene, Balvi, Rugāji, Kārsava, Viļaka

Kurzeme, Pāvilosta, Liepāja, Grobiņa, Durbe, Skuodas, Mažeikiai, Telšiai, Papilė, Joniškis, Radviliškis, Pakruojis, Biržai, Pasvalys, Rokiškis, Nereta, Viesīte, Viesite, Jēkabpils, Līvāni, Spogi, **Daugavpils**, Dagda, Krāslava

Šeduva, Pāvilosta, Priekulė, Gargždai, Plungė, Kretinga, **Klaipėda**, Šilutė, Šilalė, Kelmė, **Šiauliai**, Skaudvilė, Raseiniai, Naujamiestis, Subačius, **Panevėžys**, Anykščiai, Utena, Zarasai, Visaginas, Obeliai

Nida, Courland Lagoon, Rucava, Neman, Tauragė, Jurbarkas, Neman, Dotnuva, Jonava, Ukmergė, Giedraičiai, Vidzy

Zelenogradsk, **Kaliningrad** (to Russian Federation), Gvardeysk, Cherryakhovsk, **Kaunas**, Vilkija, Kaišiadorys, Neris, **VILNIUS**, Trakai, Širvintos, Druskininkai

Pionerskiy, Primorsk, Mamonovo, Bagrationovsk, Zheleznodorozhnyy, Gusev, Vilkaviškis, Marijampolė, Kalvarija, Prienai, Alytus, Rūdiškės, Merkinė, Varėna, Druskininkai

KALININGRAD (to Russian Federation)

Navapolatsk, Polatsk, Yukhavichy, Bihosava, Vyerkhnyadzvinsk, Drysa, Western Dvina, Vyetryna, Hlybokaye, Yezyaryshcha

Žemaičių Aukštumas

MINSK
The capital of Belarus, Minsk, was destroyed during World War II and then rebuilt in a starkly modern style. Minsk is the country's economic centre: Cars, lorries and tractors, chemicals, timber products, and a range of high-tech goods are all produced here. Farm produce (above) is also sold in the markets.

RUSSIAN FEDERATION

POLAND

UKRAINE

B E L A R U S

GYMNASTICS
The former Soviet Union worked its young athletes and gymnasts extremely hard in order to win Olympic medals and thus national glory. Many of the most famous gymnasts came from Belarus, notably Olga Korbut and, more recently, Svetlana Boginskya (right), who has won three gold, one silver, and one bronze Olympic medals.

FORESTS AND LAKES
All four countries are low-lying with many moors, bogs, unspoiled lakes, and fir and pine forests. Forestry is an important industry, providing wood pulp for paper making, and timber for furniture and houses.

Ferns thrive in this Latvian forest

TEXTILES
Development of the textile industry (above) in these countries is strong, with foreign investment helping growth. Clothes, bedlinen, curtains, and towels are just some of the items made for export.

FARMING
The fertile soils and flat landscapes make this region good for farming. The Baltic States, particulary Latvia (left), have large dairy farms. Belarus is a major producer of flax, which is used to make linen and other products. Potatoes – used to make vodka – sugar beet, and other root crops are also grown here.

LITHUANIAN COSTUME
In some Lithuanian villages people still wear traditional folk costume, especially for festive occasions. Women's clothing is generally colourful (left) and might include a white linen shirt, a skirt, and an apron. The decoration and style of the costume shows which region of Lithuania the wearer comes from.

European Russia

SEPARATED FROM ASIAN RUSSIA by the Ural Mountains, European Russia is so large that it spans four time zones. The climate and landscape range from cold desert and frozen tundra in the north to the warm coast of the Black Sea in the southwest. Forests and grassy steppes cover huge areas. More than 100 million people – two-thirds of the total Russian population – live in European Russia, most of them in cities such as the capital, Moscow. Since the collapse of communism in 1991, many Russians have experienced a fall in their standard of living. Shortages of food and manufactured goods occurred, and crime and unemployment rates rose. As a result, Russia was the only European country in which life expectancy fell. As the country recovered, it was hit by deep recession in 2009.

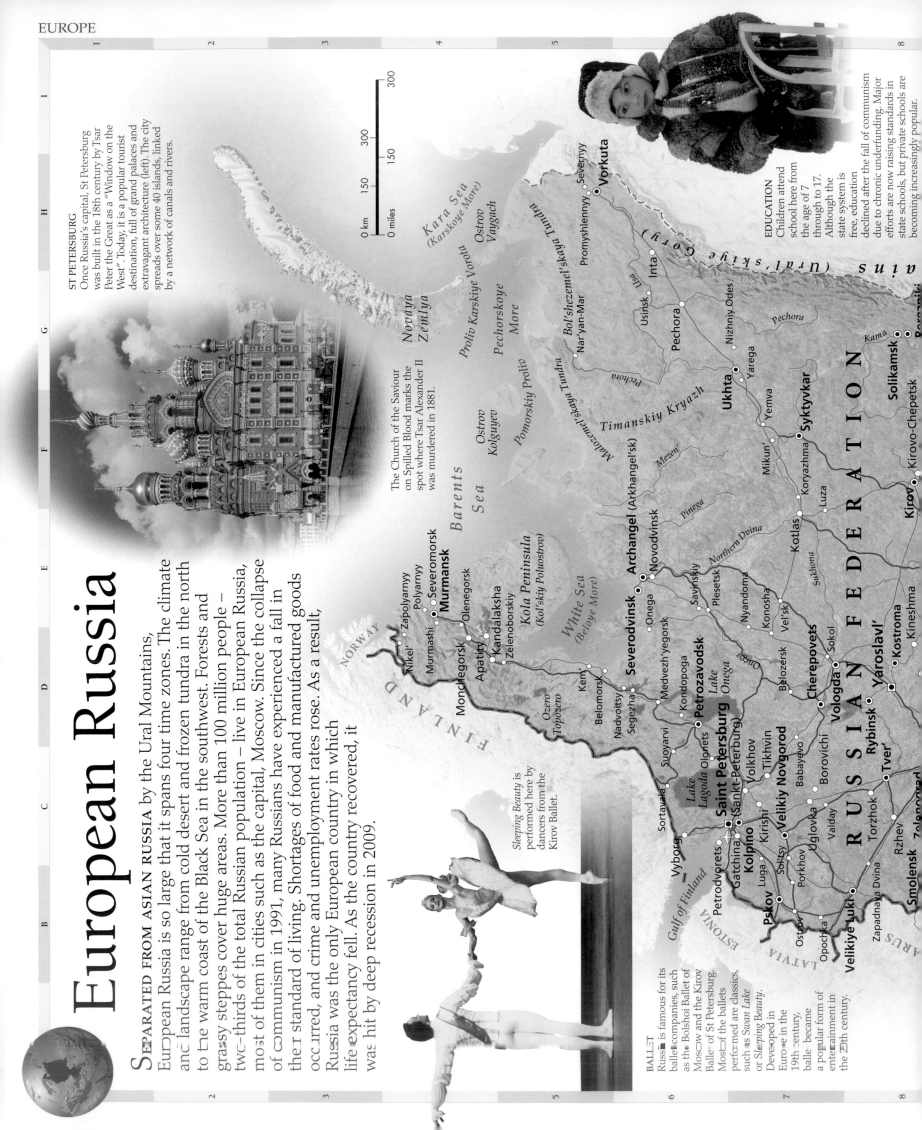

ST PETERSBURG
Once Russia's capital, St Petersburg was built in the 18th century by Tsar Peter the Great as a "Window on the West". Today, it is a popular tourist destination, full of grand palaces and extravagant architecture (left). The city spreads over some 40 islands, linked by a network of canals and rivers.

The Church of the Saviour on Spilled Blood marks the spot where Tsar Alexander II was murdered in 1881.

Sleeping Beauty is performed here by dancers from the Kirov Ballet.

BALLET
Russia is famous for its ballet companies, such as the Bolshoi Ballet of Moscow and the Kirov Ballet of St Petersburg. Most of the ballets performed are classics, such as Swan Lake or Sleeping Beauty. Developed in Europe in the 19th century, ballet became a popular form of entertainment in the 20th century.

EDUCATION
Children attend school here from the age of 7 through to 17. Although the state system is free, education declined after the fall of communism due to chronic underfunding. Major efforts are now raising standards in state schools, but private schools are becoming increasingly popular.

Scale
0 km   150   300
0 miles   150   300

Map labels

Kara Sea (Karskoye More)
Novaya Zemlya
Ostrov Vaygach
Proliv Karskiye Vorota
Pechorskoye More
Pomorskiy Proliv
Ostrov Kolguyev
Barents Sea
White Sea (Beloye More)
Kola Peninsula (Kol'skiy Poluostrov)

NORWAY
FINLAND
ESTONIA
LATVIA

Gulf of Finland

Severnyy
Promyshlennyy
Vorkuta
Bol'shezemel'skaya Tundra
Nar'yan-Mar
Inta
Usa
Usinsk
Pechora
Nizhniy Odes
Pechora
Kama
Yarega
Ukhta
Yemva
Mikun'
Syktyvkar
Koryazhma
Kirovo-Chepetsk
Kirov
Solikamsk
Malozemel'skaya Tundra
Timanskiy Kryazh
Mezen'
Pinega
Northern Dvina
Kotlas
Luza
Sukhona
Archangel (Arkhangel'sk)
Novodvinsk
Severodvinsk
Onega
Savinskiy
Plesetsk
Nyandoma
Konosha
Vel'sk
Kineshma
Kostroma
Yaroslavl'
Vologda
Cherepovets
Sokol
Belozersk
Onega
Medvezh'yegorsk
Kondopoga
Petrozavodsk
Lake Onega
Severomorsk
Murmansk
Polyarnyy
Zapolyarnyy
Nikel'
Murmashi
Monchegorsk
Olenegorsk
Apatity
Kandalaksha
Zelenoborskiy
Kem'
Belomorsk
Nadvoitsy
Segezha
Ozero Topozero
Suoyarvi
Sortavala
Lake Ladoga
Olonets
Lodeynoye
Vyborg
Petrodvorets
Gatchina
Kolpino
Saint Petersburg (Sankt-Peterburg)
Velikiy Novgorod
Volkhov
Tikhvin
Kirishi
Babayevo
Borovichi
Uglovka
Valday
Torzhok
Tver'
Rybinsk
Zapadnaya Dvina
Rzhev
Smolensk
Velikiye Luki
Pskov
Luga
Soltsy
Porkhov
Ostrov
Opochka
Velikiye Luki

RUSSIAN FEDERATION
Ural Mountains (Ural'skiye Gory)

Industrial smog casts a haze over Moscow.

RURAL LIFE
Rural life has become extremely tough since the economic collapse of large-scale farms in the 1990s, with many people living in poverty. Smaller cooperatives and farms (above) have sprung up, and the agricultural industry is going through a painful period of reform. Due to the harsh climate, only 10 per cent of the land is suitable for agriculture.

Icons, common in the Russian Orthodox Church, are religious images painted on wooden panels.

THE TATARS
Russia's largest ethnic minority, the Tatars (below), are an Islamic people descended from the Mongols. Their largest population lives in the Tatarstan Republic, midway between Moscow and the Urals.

The title tsar, or czar, once used for Russian rulers, means "emperor" and comes from the ancient Roman title "Caesar".

THE RUSSIAN CHURCH
The main religion in Russia is the Russian Orthodox Church. Under communism, all religion was banned. The new freedom means that many Russians now attend church services on a regular basis. New churches are being built, old ones restored, and seminaries reopened to train new priests.

MOSCOW METRO
Not many underground railways can claim to be tourist attractions, but Moscow's metro can. Built in the 1930s, many of its stations are decorated with beautiful chandeliers, mosaics, paintings, and sculptures. One of the busiest, most efficient metros in the world, it is used by more than 7 million people daily.

POLLUTION
The communists invested heavily in industry, but their outdated methods of production have affected the environment. Rivers such as the Volga are badly polluted, and many cities are covered in a permanent and poisonous smog. Chest infections and other diseases related to air pollution are common.

ASIA

The vast continent of Asia is dominated by two giant nations – China and India, each with more than a billion people and a rich and colourful history. Both are being transformed by rapid economic growth, and so are many other Asian countries, listed below in order of size. Yet in some regions of central Asia life has barely changed in a thousand years.

China
- 9,596,961 sq km
- 3,705,387 sq miles
- 1,350,000,000
- Beijing
- Mandarin, Wu, Cantonese, Hsiang, Min, Hakka, Kan

Iran
- 1,648,195 sq km
- 636,368 sq miles
- 74,200,000
- Tehran
- Farsi, Azeri, Luri, Gilaki, Mazandarani, Kurdish, Turkmen, Arabic, Balochi

Afghanistan
- 652,230 sq km
- 251,826 sq miles
- 28,100,000
- Kabul
- Pashto, Tajik, Dari, Farsi, Uzbek, Turkmen

Iraq
- 438,317 sq km
- 169,234 sq miles
- 30,700,000
- Baghdad
- Arabic, Kurdish, Turkic languages, Armenian, Assyrian

Philippines
- 300,000 sq km
- 115,830 sq miles
- 92,000,000
- Manila
- Filipino, English, Tagalog, Cebuano, Ilocano, Hiligaynon, many other local languages

Nepal
- 147,181 sq km
- 56,827 sq miles
- 29,300,000
- Kathmandu
- Nepali, Maithili, Bhojpuri

India
- 3,287,263 sq km
- 1,269,212 sq miles
- 1,200,000,000
- New Delhi
- Hindi, English, Urdu, Bengali, Marathi, Telugu, Tamil, Bihari, Gujarati, Kannada.

Mongolia
- 1,564,116 sq km
- 603,905 sq miles
- 2,670,000
- Ulan Bator
- Khalkha Mongolian, Kazakh, Chinese, Russian

Yemen
- 527,968 sq km
- 203,848 sq miles
- 23,600,000
- Sanaak
- Arabic

Japan
- 377,915 sq km
- 145,913 sq miles
- 127,000,000
- Tokyo
- Japanese, Korean, Chinese

Laos
- 236,800 sq km
- 91,428 sq miles
- 6,320,000
- Vientiane
- Lao, Mon-Khmer, Yao, Vietnamese, Chinese, French

Bangladesh
- 143,998 sq km
- 55,598 sq miles
- 162,000,000
- Dhaka
- Bengali, Urdu, Chakma, Marma (Magh), Garo, Khasi, Santhali, Tripura, Mru

Kazakhstan
- 2,724,900 sq km
- 1,052,084 sq miles
- 15,600,000
- Astana
- Kazakh, Russian, Ukrainian, German, Uzbek, Tatar, Uyghur

Pakistan
- 796,095 sq km
- 307,372 sq miles
- 181,000,000
- Islamabad
- Punjabi, Sindhi, Pashtu, Urdu, Balochi, Brahui

Thailand
- 513,120 sq km
- 198,116 sq miles
- 67,800,000
- Bangkok
- Thai, Chinese, Malay, Khmer, Mon, Karen, Miao

Vietnam
- 331,210 sq km
- 127,880 sq miles
- 88,100,000
- Hanoi
- Vietnamese, Chinese, Thai, Khmer, Muong, Nung, Miao, Yao, Jarai

Kyrgyzstan
- 199,951 sq km
- 77,201 sq miles
- 5,480,000
- Bishkek
- Kyrgyz, Russian, Uzbek, Tatar, Ukrainian

Tajikistan
- 143,100 sq km
- 55,251 sq miles
- 6,950,000
- Dushanbe
- Tajik, Uzbek, Russian

Saudi Arabia
- 2,149,690 sq km
- 829,995 sq miles
- 25,700,000
- Riyadh
- Arabic

Turkey
- 783,562 sq km
- 302,533 sq miles
- 74,800,000
- Ankara
- Turkish, Kurdish, Arabic, Circassian, Armenian, Greek, Georgian, Ladino (Judaeo-Spanish)

Turkmenistan
- 488,100 sq km
- 188,455 sq miles
- 5,110,000
- Ashgabat
- Turkmen, Uzbek, Russian, Kazakh, Tatar

Malaysia
- 329,847 sq km
- 127,354 sq miles
- 27,500,000
- Kuala Lumpur
- Bahasa Malaysia, Malay, Chinese, Tamil, English

Syria
- 185,180 sq km
- 71,498 sq miles
- 21,900,000
- Damascus
- Arabic, French, Kurdish, Armenian, Circassian, Turkic languages, Assyrian, Aramaic

North Korea
- 120,538 sq km
- 46,540 sq miles
- 23,900,000
- Pyongyang
- Korean

Indonesia
- 1,904,569 sq km
- 735,354 sq miles
- 230,000,000
- Jakarta
- Javanese, Sundanese, Madurese, Bahasa Indonesia, Dutch

Myanmar (Burma)
- 676,578 sq km
- 261,227 sq miles
- 50,000,000
- Nay Pyi Taw
- Burmese, Shan, Karen, Rakhine (Arakanese), Chin, Yangbye, Kachin, Mon

Uzbekistan
- 447,400 sq km
- 172,741 sq miles
- 27,500,000
- Tashkent
- Uzbek, Russian, Tajik, Kazakh

Oman
- 309,500 sq km
- 119,498 sq miles
- 2,850,000
- Muscat
- Arabic, Balochi, Farsi, Hindi, Punjabi

Cambodia
- 181,035 sq km
- 69,898 sq miles
- 14,800,000
- Phnom Penh
- Khmer, French, Chinese, Vietnamese, Cham

South Korea
- 99,720 sq km
- 38,502 sq miles
- 48,300,000
- Seoul
- Korean

Jordan

- 89,342 sq km
  34,495 sq miles
- 6,320,000
- Amman
- Arabic

Sri Lanka

- 65,610 sq km
  25,332 sq miles
- 20,200,000
- Colombo
- Sinhala, Tamil,
  Sinhala-Tamil, English

Azerbaijan

- 86,600 sq km
  33,436 sq miles
- 8,830,000
- Baku
- Azerbaijani, Russian

Bhutan

- 38,394 sq km
  14,824 sq miles
- 697,300
- Thimphu
- Dzongkha, Nepali,
  Assamese

Israel

- 20,770 sq km
  8,019 sq miles
- 7,170,000
- Jerusalem
- Hebrew, Arabic, Yiddish,
  German, Russian, Polish,
  Romanian, Persian

Qatar

- 11,586 sq km
  4,473 sq miles
- 1,410,000
- Doha
- Arabic

United Arab Emirates

- 83,600 sq km
  32,278 sq miles
- 4,600,000
- Abu Dhabi
- Arabic, Farsi, Indian and
  Pakistani languages, English

Taiwan

- 35,980 sq km
  13,892 sq miles
- 23,000,000
- Taipei
- Amoy Chinese, Mandarin
  Chinese, Hakka Chinese

Kuwait

- 17,818 sq km
  6,880 sq miles
- 2,990,000
- Kuwait City
- Arabic, English

Lebanon

- 10,400 sq km
  4,015 sq miles
- 4,220,000
- Beirut
- Arabic, French, Armenian,
  Assyrian

Bahrain

- 741 sq km
  286 sq miles
- 791,500
- Manama
- Arabic

Seychelles

- 455 sq km
  176 sq miles
- 84,600
- Victoria
- French Creole, English,
  French

Georgia

- 69,700 sq km
  26,911 sq miles
- 4,260,000
- T'bilisi
- Georgian, Russian, Azeri,
  Armenian, Mingrelian, Ossetian,
  Abkhazian

Armenia

- 29,743 sq km
  11,484 sq miles
- 3,080,000
- Yerevan
- Armenian, Azeri, Russian

East Timor

- 14,874 sq km
  5,743 sq miles
- 1,130,000
- Dili
- Tetum (Portuguese/
  Austronesian), Bahasa
  Indonesia, Portuguese

Brunei

- 5,765 sq km
  2,226 sq miles
- 399,700
- Bandar Seri Begawan
- Malay, English, Chinese

Singapore

- 697 sq km
  269 sq miles
- 4,740,000
- Singapore
- Mandarin, Malay, Tamil,
  English

Maldives

- 298 sq km
  115 sq miles
- 309,400
- Malé
- Dhivehi (Maldivian),
  Sinhala, Tamil, Arabic

Turkey and the Caucasus

TURKEY LIES IN BOTH ASIA and Europe – separated by the Bosphorus – and was once part of the powerful Ottoman Empire. Although the Turks are 99 per cent Muslim, modern Turkey is a country with no official religion. Western Turkey is relatively industrialized, with a tourist industry along the Mediterranean coast that brings in considerable income. Many farmers and herders in the centre and east, however, struggle to make a living in the arid environment. To the northeast lie the Caucasus countries of Georgia, Azerbaijan, and Armenia. Once part of the USSR, they are now independent.

ISTANBUL
The different faces of Turkey can be seen in its former capital, Istanbul, which lies on both sides of the Bosphorus waterway. Churches, mosques, and ancient buildings in both European and Islamic styles sit side by side with modern shops and offices. Bridges link the two parts of the city. In 1923, Ankara became the new capital.

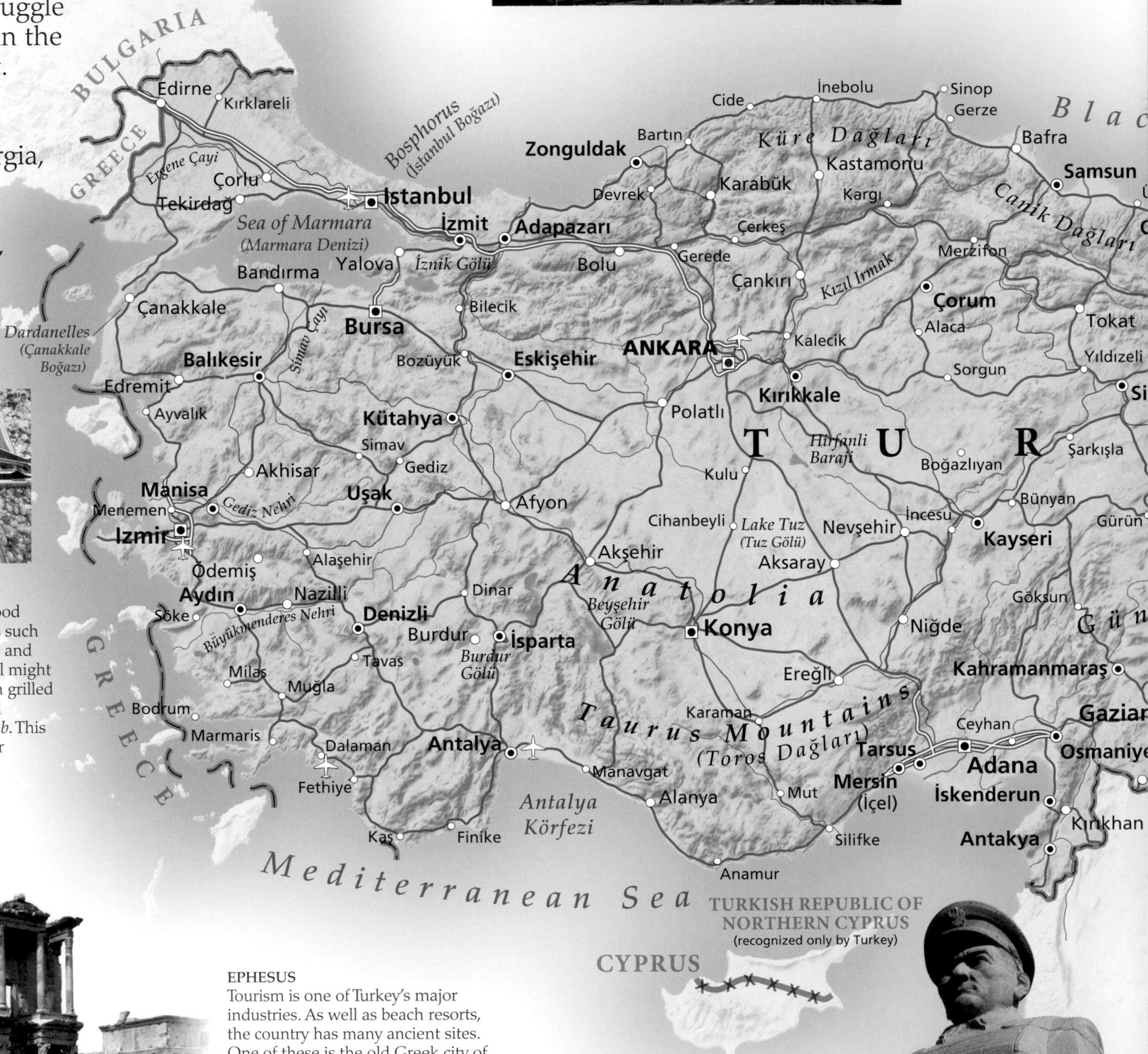

TURKISH FOOD
Turkey is self-sufficient in food and grows specialized crops such as aubergines, peppers, figs, and dates. A typical Turkish meal might consist of spiced lamb, often grilled on a skewer with onion and tomato to make a *shish kebab*. This would be served with rice or cracked wheat.

EPHESUS
Tourism is one of Turkey's major industries. As well as beach resorts, the country has many ancient sites. One of these is the old Greek city of Ephesus, which lies 56 km (35 miles) south of modern-day Izmir on the Aegean coast. The city was famous for its Temple of Artemis, which was considered one of the seven wonders of the world.

Visitors to Ephesus admiring the remains of the Library of Celsus

FATHER OF THE TURKS
Mustafa Kemal Atatürk (1881–1938), founder of the modern Turkish state, became its first president in 1923. He introduced many reforms, including more equality for women and better education for all. He also declared that Islam was no longer to be the official religion.

Map labels:

BULGARIA, GREECE, Edirne, Kırklareli, Çorlu, Tekirdağ, Ergene Çayı, Istanbul, İzmit, Adapazarı, Sea of Marmara (Marmara Denizi), Bandırma, Yalova, İznik Gölü, Bolu, Gerede, Çanakkale, Bilecik, Bursa, Simav Çayı, Bozüyük, Eskişehir, ANKARA, Dardanelles (Çanakkale Boğazı), Balıkesir, Edremit, Ayvalık, Kütahya, Simav, Gediz, Polatlı, Kırıkkale, Akhisar, Manisa, Uşak, Afyon, Kulu, Menemen, Gediz Nehri, İzmir, Ödemiş, Alaşehir, Akşehir, Anatolia, Beyşehir Gölü, Konya, Büyükmenderes Nehri, Nazilli, Dinar, Söke, Aydın, Denizli, Burdur, Isparta, Burdur Gölü, Ereğli, Milas, Tavas, Karaman, Muğla, Bodrum, Marmaris, Dalaman, Antalya, Taurus Mountains (Toros Dağları), Tarsus, Mersin (İçel), Adana, İskenderun, Fethiye, Manavgat, Alanya, Mut, Kaş, Finike, Antalya Körfezi, Silifke, Antakya, Anamur, Mediterranean Sea

Bosphorus (İstanbul Boğazı), Zonguldak, Bartın, Cide, İnebolu, Sinop, Gerze, Black [Sea], Küre Dağları, Bafra, Devrek, Karabük, Kastamonu, Kargı, Samsun, Çerkeş, Çankırı, Kızıl Irmak, Merzifon, Canik Dağları, Çorum, Alaca, Tokat, Kalecik, Yıldızeli, TURKEY, Hirfanli Barajı, Sorgun, Boğazlıyan, Şarkışla, Cihanbeyli, Lake Tuz (Tuz Gölü), Nevşehir, İncesu, Bünyan, Kayseri, Gürün, Aksaray, Niğde, Göksun, Kahramanmaraş, Gaziantep, Ceyhan, Osmaniye, Kırıkhan

TURKISH REPUBLIC OF NORTHERN CYPRUS (recognized only by Turkey)

CYPRUS

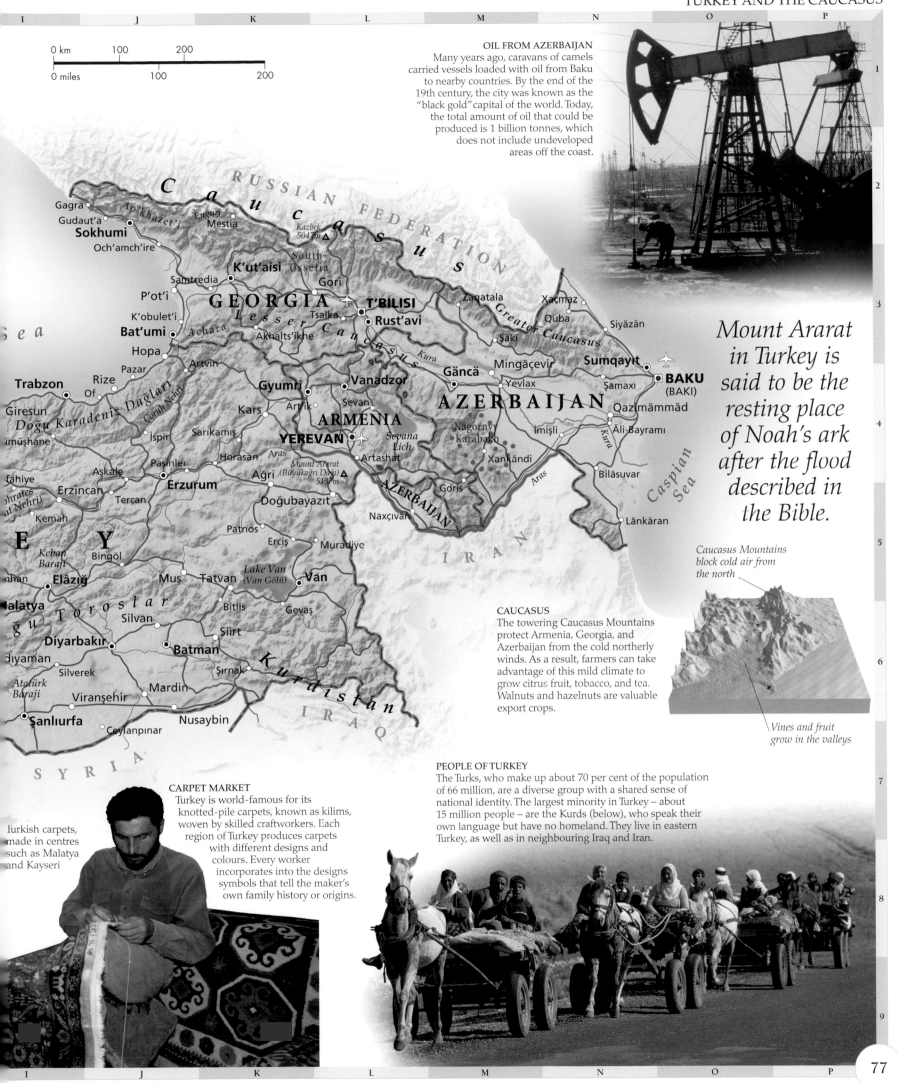

0 km   100   200
0 miles   100   200

OIL FROM AZERBAIJAN
Many years ago, caravans of camels carried vessels loaded with oil from Baku to nearby countries. By the end of the 19th century, the city was known as the "black gold" capital of the world. Today, the total amount of oil that could be produced is 1 billion tonnes, which does not include undeveloped areas off the coast.

Mount Ararat in Turkey is said to be the resting place of Noah's ark after the flood described in the Bible.

Caucasus Mountains block cold air from the north

CAUCASUS
The towering Caucasus Mountains protect Armenia, Georgia, and Azerbaijan from the cold northerly winds. As a result, farmers can take advantage of this mild climate to grow citrus fruit, tobacco, and tea. Walnuts and hazelnuts are valuable export crops.

Vines and fruit grow in the valleys

PEOPLE OF TURKEY
The Turks, who make up about 70 per cent of the population of 66 million, are a diverse group with a shared sense of national identity. The largest minority in Turkey – about 15 million people – are the Kurds (below), who speak their own language but have no homeland. They live in eastern Turkey, as well as in neighbouring Iraq and Iran.

CARPET MARKET
Turkey is world-famous for its knotted-pile carpets, known as kilims, woven by skilled craftworkers. Each region of Turkey produces carpets with different designs and colours. Every worker incorporates into the designs symbols that tell the maker's own family history or origins.

Turkish carpets, made in centres such as Malatya and Kayseri

77

Russia and Kazakhstan

THE RUSSIAN FEDERATION is the biggest country in the world, almost twice as big as either the USA or China. It extends halfway around the world, crosses two continents, and spans 11 time zones. The vast region of Siberia alone is larger than Canada. Kazakhstan lies to its south and is a large but sparsely populated country. From 1917 to 1991, both countries were part of the Union of Soviet Socialist Republics (USSR), the world's first communist state. When the USSR collapsed, Russia, Kazakhstan, and the 13 other member republics gained independence. Since then, Russia and Kazakhstan have begun to transform themselves from communist states into democratic nations. Both countries have a lot of fertile land, huge mineral deposits, and many other natural resources. However, Russia still has a very low life expectancy rate compared to other industrialized countries.

Lake Baikal is up to 1,940 m (6,365 ft) deep and contains more than 20 per cent of the world's freshwater supply.

Kazakh man hunting with a trained golden eagle

KAZAKH CULTURE
The majority of people in Kazakhstan are Kazakh Muslims. They were once a nomadic people who travelled around on horseback, herding their sheep. Although most Kazakhs live in rural areas of the country, retaining a strong loyalty to their clans and families, the new, modern capital city of Astana is growing quickly, due to wealth generated by oil and gas.

Coal miners in Siberia

NATURAL WEALTH
Siberia contains almost one-third of the world's natural gas reserves and has vast deposits of oil, as well as abundant minerals such as coal and precious metals including gold. However, many of these resources are inaccessible or in remote places, and the extreme winters make it difficult to extract them.

0 km 400 800
0 miles 400 800

Franz Josef Land

North Cape (Nordkapp)

ARCTI

Barents Sea

FINLAND

Murmansk
Kandalaksha
Kola Peninsula
Novaya Zemlya
Kara Sea (Karskoye More)
Ostrov Belyy
Ostrov Kolguyev
Dik

LAT.
EST.
Saint Petersburg (Sankt-Peterburg)
Lake Lagoda
Petrozavodsk
White Sea
Severodvinsk
Arkhangel'sk
Nar'yan-Mar
Yamal Peninsula

BELARUS
Pskov
Velikiy Novgorod
Lake Onega
Cherepovets
Smolensk
Severnaya Dvina
Vel'sk
Kotlas
Syktyvkar
Ukhta
Vorkuta
Salekhard
Obskaya Guba
Tal

MOSCOW (MOSKVA)
Tver'
Vologda
Yaroslavl'
Kineshma
Vladimir
Nizhniy Novgorod
Kirov
Glazov
Solikamsk
Nadym
Nori
Igar

UKRAINE
Bryansk
Tula
Belgorod
Ryazan'
Voronezh
Tambov
Penza
Kazan'
Izhevsk
Perm'
Serov
Khanty-Mansiysk
Nyagan'
West
Ural Mountains

Black Sea
Rostov-na-Donu
Ul'yanovsk
Saratov
Tol'yatti
Samara
Naberezhnyye Chelny
Yekaterinburg
Surgut
Nizhnevartovsk
Siberian
Plain
RUSSIA

Krasnodar
Volgograd
Stavropol'
Elbrus 5642m
Nal'chik
Vladikavkaz
Groznyy
Makhachkala
GEORGIA
Caucasus
Sochi
Sterlitamak
Ufa
Tyumen'
Tobol'sk
Ishim
Ishim
Irtysh
Chelyabinsk
Magnitogorsk
Ural'sk
Orenburg
Astrakhan'
Atyrau
Aktobe (Aktyubinsk)
Orsk
Alga
Rudnyy
Kostanay
Petropavlovsk
Omsk
Tomsk
Ob'
Krasnoy
Kemero

AZERBAIJAN
Caspian Sea
Fort-Shevchenko
Emba
Chelkar
Aktau
Zhanaozen
Ustyurt Plateau
Aral Sea
KAZAKHSTAN
Atbasar
Kokshetau
Shchuchinsk
ASTANA
Kulunda Steppe
Novosibirsk
Barnaul
Novokuznetsk
Ab

TURKMENISTAN
Syr Darya
Aral'sk
Novokazalinsk
Temirtau
Saran'
Karaganda
Pavlodar
Semipalatinsk
Leninogorsk
Zyryanovsk
Gora Belu 4506m
Altai Mounta

Kyzyl Kum
Dzhusaly
Kyzylorda
Zhezkazgan
Kazakh Uplands
Shar
Ust'-Kamenogorsk
Balkhash
Ayaguz
Ozero Zaysan
UZBEKISTAN
Turkestan
Kentau
Karatau
Arys'
Shu
Lake Balkhash
Taldykorgan
Tekeli

Shymkent
Taraz
Kirghiz Range
Almaty (Alma-Ata)
KYRGYZSTAN
CHINA

TAIGA FOREST
Russia's forests cover more than two-fifths of the country's territory. The taiga forest type extends across the Urals to cover much of Siberia. This type of forest is formed by small, widely spaced trees, with large areas of poorly drained marsh grasses.

Nenets man guiding a sledge and reindeer

NATIVE PEOPLES
During the winter months, temperatures in Siberia regularly drop to below –43°C (–45°F). The native people who live here, such as the Nenets people of the Yamal Peninsula region, have adapted well to their environment and survive by herding reindeer, hunting, and fishing.

RUSSIAN LANGUAGE
Russian is the official language of the Russian Federation, but many of the 152 other nationalities inside the federation speak their own language as well. The Russian language uses the Cyrillic alphabet, which was devised by Greek missionaries.

РУССКОЕ БИСТРО

OLD CUSTOMS
The communists tried to impose a Russian national culture on the native peoples of Siberia, but many of their customs survived in remote areas. Today, traditional costume, music, and dance are all flourishing throughout Siberia.

Russian dancer in traditional dress

Trans-Siberian Railway train

Siberian tiger

TRANS-SIBERIAN RAILWAY
The longest railway in the world runs 9,310 km (5,785 miles) from Moscow's Yaroslavl Station in the west, across Siberia to the Pacific port of Vladivostok in the east. The railway was started in 1891 and took 14 years to finish. Trains take eight days to complete the journey and cross eight time zones.

SIBERIAN WILDLIFE
Siberia is home to a huge range of wildlife, including the rare Siberian tiger (the biggest tiger in the world), wolves, reindeer, and black and brown bears. The Baikal seal – found only in Lake Baikal – is the world's only freshwater seal.

Map labels

OCEAN

Bering Strait

Chukchi Sea

East Siberian Sea

New Siberian Islands

Ostrov Oktyabr'skoy Revolyutsii

Ostrov Novaya Sibir'

trov omolets

naya lya

trov hevik

Ostrov Kotel'nyy

Ostrov Bol'shoy Lyakhovskiy

Ekvyvatapskiy Khrebet

Anadyrskiy Zaliv

Pevek

Anadyr'

Anadyr'

Ambarchik

Cherskiy

Alazeya

Indigirka

Kolyma

Koryakskoye Nagor'ye

Kolymskoye Nagor'ye

Bering Sea

Laptev Sea

Taymyr Peninsula

Ozero Taymyr

-Sibirskaya Nizmennost'

Kheta

Ust'-Oleněk

Tiksi

Kazach'ye

Yana

Adycha

Susuman

Atka

Ossora

Ostrov Karaginskiy

Zaliv Shelikhova

Ust'-Kamchatsk

Vidkan

Klyucheyskaya Sopka 4688m △

plato orana

Kotuy

Anabar

Oleněk

Oleněk

Verkhoyanskiy Khrebet

Khrebet Cherskogo

Magadan

Okhotsk

Atlasovo

Mil'kovo

Kamchatka Peninsula

Petropavlovsk-Kamchatskiy

Central Siberian Uplands

aya Tunguska

Lena

Aldan

Yakutsk

Nyurba

Vilyuy

Amga

Aldan

S I B E R I A

Pervyy Kuril'skiy Proliv

Ostrov Paramushir

Mirnyy

Suntar

Oleěkminsk

Sea of Okhotsk (Okhotskoye More)

(S I B I R ')

Angara

Olyokma

Lena

Neryungri

Shantarskiye Ostrova

Ostrov Sakhalin

F E D E R A T I O N

Ust'-Ilimsk

Bodaybo

Ostrov Urup

Ostrov Iturup

Kurile Islands (Kuril'skiye Ostrova)

nsk

Ust'-Kut

Tynda

Skovorodino

Komsomol'sk-na-Amure

Kuril'sk

Bratsk

Lake Baikal (Ozero Baykal)

Vityim

Yablonovyy Khrebet

Amur

Svobodnyy

Khabarovsk

Yuzhno-Sakhalinsk

Tulun

Shilka

Khrebet Sikhote-Alin'

La Perouse Strait

(administered by Russian Federation, claimed by Japan)

Usol'ye-Sibirskoye

Angarsk

Blagoveshchensk

Birobidzhan

Khor

Sea of Japan (East Sea)

n Sayans

Irkutsk

Ulan-Ude

Chita

Olovyannaya

Bikin

Ussuri

Kyakhta

Krasnokamensk

Zabaykal'sk

C H I N A

Ussuriysk

JAPAN

M O N G O L I A

Vladivostok

Nakhodka

The Near East

ISRAEL, JORDAN, SYRIA, AND LEBANON are the countries collectively known as the Near East. This is a land that is dominated by desert but also has fertile coastal plains. Lack of water is a constant problem here, although Israel has introduced computerized irrigation systems to extend the land suitable for agriculture. The creation of the Jewish state of Israel in 1948, in what was previously Arab-dominated Palestine, has led to almost continuous conflict in the region. Arabs and Israelis have fought four major wars, which have cost many lives. The Mediterranean island of Cyprus has also suffered a violent recent history.

The map on Cyprus's flag is copper-coloured because Cyprus means "island of copper".

SYRIAN MARKET
Damascus is one of the oldest inhabited cities in the world. At its centre is a massive souk (bazaar) where the streets are full of stalls and small shops selling everything from carpets, textiles, and jewellery to household goods and fresh produce.

DAILY LIFE
Even in a war-torn country such as Israel, people continue to live as normal a life as possible. Children listen to pop music and watch their favourite sports stars, either live or on Television. In a peaceful break, these Palestinian boys play football in a Jerusalem street.

LEBANON REBUILT
Beirut, the capital of Lebanon, was once the commercial and banking centre of the Arab world, but it was devastated by the civil war that ravaged the country from 1975 to the early 1990s. Today, the country is largely at peace and Beirut is regaining much of its former glory. Lebanon remains dominated, however, by its two powerful neighbours – Syria and Israel.

CYPRUS
Cyprus became independent from Britain in 1960. However, conflict between Greeks and Turks caused Turkey to invade the island in 1974. Since then, Cyprus has been split between a Turkish Cypriot north and a Greek Cypriot south. Most Cypriots make a living from farming grapes, citrus fruit, and olives. Women often sell hand-made lace items to tourists.

Map labels

IRAQ
TURKEY
S Y R I A

Tigris
Al Mālikīyah
Al Qāmishlī
Al Jazīrah
Al Ḩasakah
Ash Shadādah
Aş Şuwār
Al Manāşif
Subaykhān
Abū Ḩardān
Abū Kamāl
Ra's al 'Ayn
Al Mayādīn
Al 'Ashārah
Jabal 'Abd al 'Azīz
Dayr az Zawr
At Tibnī
Jabal Bishrī
As Sukhnah
Ar Raqqah
As Sabkhah
Tudmur (Palmyra)
At Tall al Abyaḑ
Nahr Balīkh
Madīnat ath Thawrah
Lake Assad (Buḩayrat al Asad)
Ar Rāmī
Al Bāridah
Jarābulus
Euphrates
Manbij
Sabkhat al Jabbūl
Salamiyah
Ar Rāmī
Aleppo (Halab)
A'zāz
Al Bāb
Abū aḑ Ḑuhūr
Ma'arrat an Nu'mān
Ḩamāh
Ḩimş (Homs)
Al Quşayr
Afrīn
Ḩārim
Idlib
Arīḩā
Salamiyah
Jibāl as Sāḩilīyah
Jablah
Baniyās
Maşyāf
Tall Kalakh
Ţarţūs
Qoubaÿāt
El Mina
Tripoli
Lādhiqiyah (Latakia)
Jebel Liban

Mediterranean Sea

Agialoúsa (Yenierenköy)
TURKISH REPUBLIC OF NORTHERN CYPRUS
(recognized only by Turkey)
Ammóchostos (Gazimağusa) (Famagusta)
Sovereign Base Area (to UK)
Keryneia (Girne)
Kythréa (Değirmelik)
Lápithos (Lapta)
NICOSIA
Dekeleia
Lárnaka
CYPRUS
Lemmasol
Nórfou (Güzelyurt)
Pólis
Tróodos
Pafos
Sovereign Base Area

100
100
50
50
0 km
0 miles

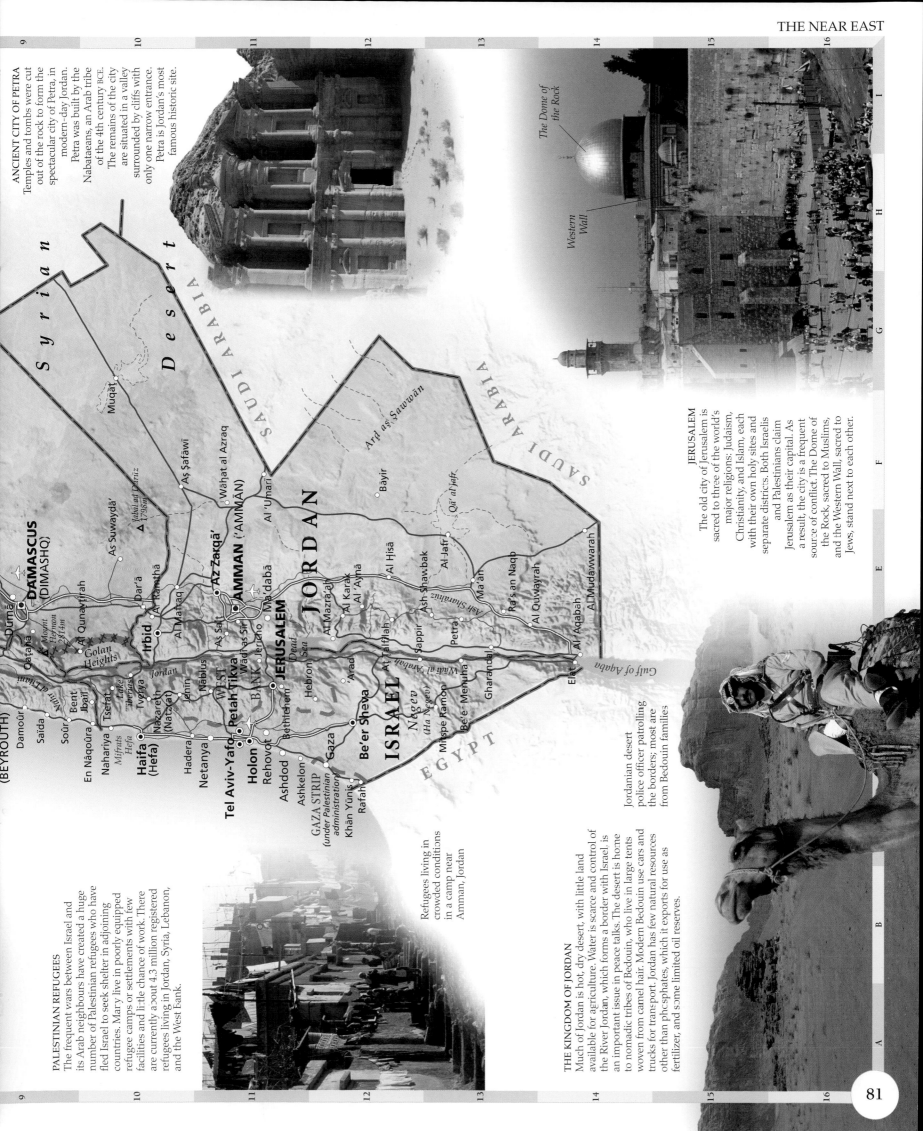

ANCIENT CITY OF PETRA
Temples and tombs were cut out of the rock to form the spectacular city of Petra, in modern-day Jordan. Petra was built by the Nabataeans, an Arab tribe of the 4th century BCE. The remains of the city are situated in a valley surrounded by cliffs with only one narrow entrance. Petra is Jordan's most famous historic site.

The Dome of the Rock

Western Wall

JERUSALEM
The old city of Jerusalem is sacred to three of the world's major religions: Judaism, Christianity, and Islam, each with their own holy sites and separate districts. Both Israelis and Palestinians claim Jerusalem as their capital. As a result, the city is a frequent source of conflict. The Dome of the Rock, sacred to Muslims, and the Western Wall, sacred to Jews, stand next to each other.

PALESTINIAN REFUGEES
The frequent wars between Israel and its Arab neighbours have created a huge number of Palestinian refugees who have fled Israel to seek shelter in adjoining countries. Many live in poorly equipped refugee camps or settlements with few facilities and little chance of work. There are currently about 4.3 million registered refugees living in Jordan, Syria, Lebanon, and the West Bank.

Refugees living in crowded conditions in a camp near Amman, Jordan

THE KINGDOM OF JORDAN
Much of Jordan is hot, dry desert, with little land available for agriculture. Water is scarce and control of the River Jordan, which forms a border with Israel, is an important issue in peace talks. The desert is home to nomadic tribes of Bedouin, who live in large tents woven from camel hair. Modern Bedouin use cars and trucks for transport. Jordan has few natural resources other than phosphates, which it exports for use as fertilizer, and some limited oil reserves.

Jordanian desert police officer patrolling the borders; most are from Bedouin families

Map labels

Syrian Desert

SAUDI ARABIA

SAUDI ARABIA

JORDAN

ISRAEL

EGYPT

Negev (Ha Negev)

WEST BANK

GAZA STRIP (under Palestinian administration)

Golan Heights

Ard aṣ Ṣawwān

Ash Sharāh

Wādī al 'Arabah

Dead Sea

Jordan

Gulf of Aqaba

DAMASCUS (DIMASHQ)
(BEYROUTH)
Duma
Qaṭanā
Saïda
Soûr
Bent Jbaïl
En Nâqoûra
Nahariya
Haifa (Hefa)
Hadera
Netanya
Tel Aviv-Yafo
Holon
Rehovot
Ashdod
Ashkelon
Gaza
Khān Yūnis
Rafaḥ
Be'er Sheva
Be'é Menuha
Mispe Ramon
Gharandal
Elat
Al 'Aqabah
Al Mudawwarah
Ra's an Naqb
Al Quwayrah
Ma'ān
Petra
Sappir
At Ṭafīlah
Al Ḥisā
Ash Shawbak
Al-Jafr
Qā' al Jafr
Bāyir
Al Mazra'ah
Al Karak
Al 'Aynā
Ma'dabā
AMMAN ('AMMĀN)
Az Zarqā'
As Salt
Al 'Umarī
Wāḥat al Azraq
Aṣ Ṣafāwī
Muqāt
As Suwaydā'
Jabal ad Durūz 1798m
Dar'ā
Ar Ramthā
Irbid
Al Mafraq
Wādī as Sir
Jericho
JERUSALEM
Bethlehem
Hebron
Arad
Nāblus
Jenin
Nazareth (Naẕerat)
Tveṛya
Petaḥ Tiqva
Lake Tiberias
Mifrats Ḥefa
Tserat
Al Qunayṭrah
Mount Hermon 2814m
Nahr el Līṭani
Oaṭaha

The Middle East

THE MIDDLE EAST IS HOME to the world's oldest civilizations, which grew up in the Tigris and Euphrates river valleys of present-day Iraq more than 6,000 years ago. The world's first towns and cities were built here. Since then, many powerful empires have dominated the region, all leaving a wealth of buildings and monuments behind them. Today, the Middle East is at the centre of the Islamic world. The population of every country is Arab and speaks Arabic, except Iran, where half the population are Farsi-speaking Persians.

DESERT WARS
Most international boundaries in the Middle East are just lines drawn in the sand by the former European colonial powers, and have often caused conflict. Iraq and Iran fought a bitter eight-year war along their common border from 1980. Since then, further conflicts between Iraq and international forces have caused much suffering.

ROLE OF WOMEN
Family life is important throughout the Muslim world. The role of women varies from country to country – traditionally, women stay at home and look after the family, but some now work. In public, many cover their head, or whole body with a burqa.

THE IRANIANS
About half the total population of Iran are Persians, who live in the centre and north of the country. Large numbers of Azeris live in the northwest, while Kurds live in the west and Baluchis in the southeast. The official language of Iran is Farsi, but many other languages are also spoken.

The Persian language is written in Arabic script

OIL PRODUCTION
The Middle East is the world's major oil producer – Saudi Arabia alone produces more than 10 per cent of the world's supply. Oil has brought great wealth to the region, in particular to Saudi Arabia and the Gulf States.

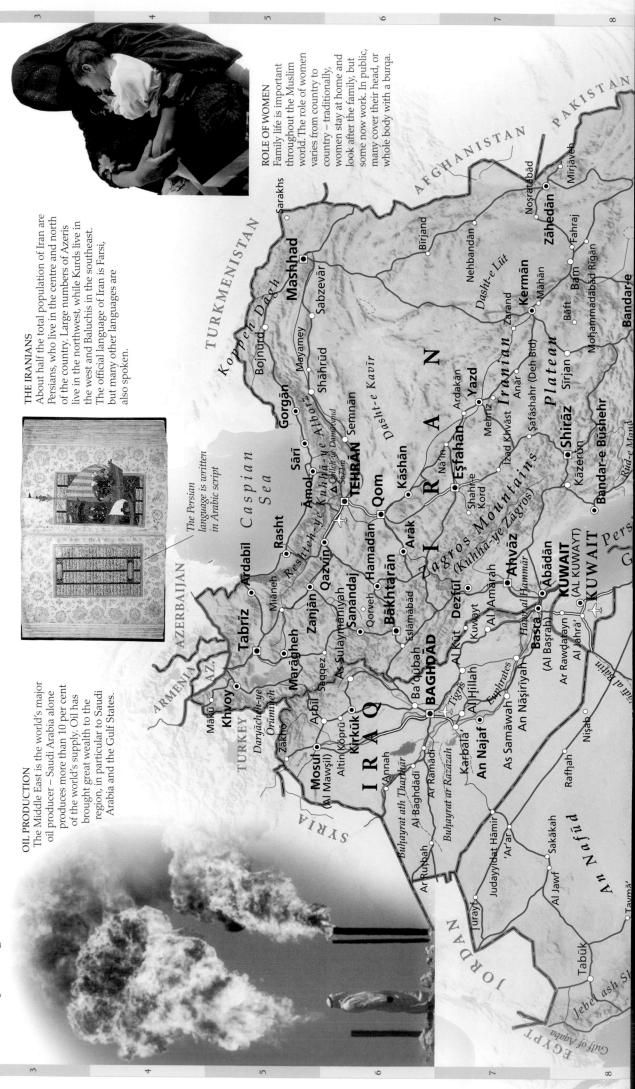

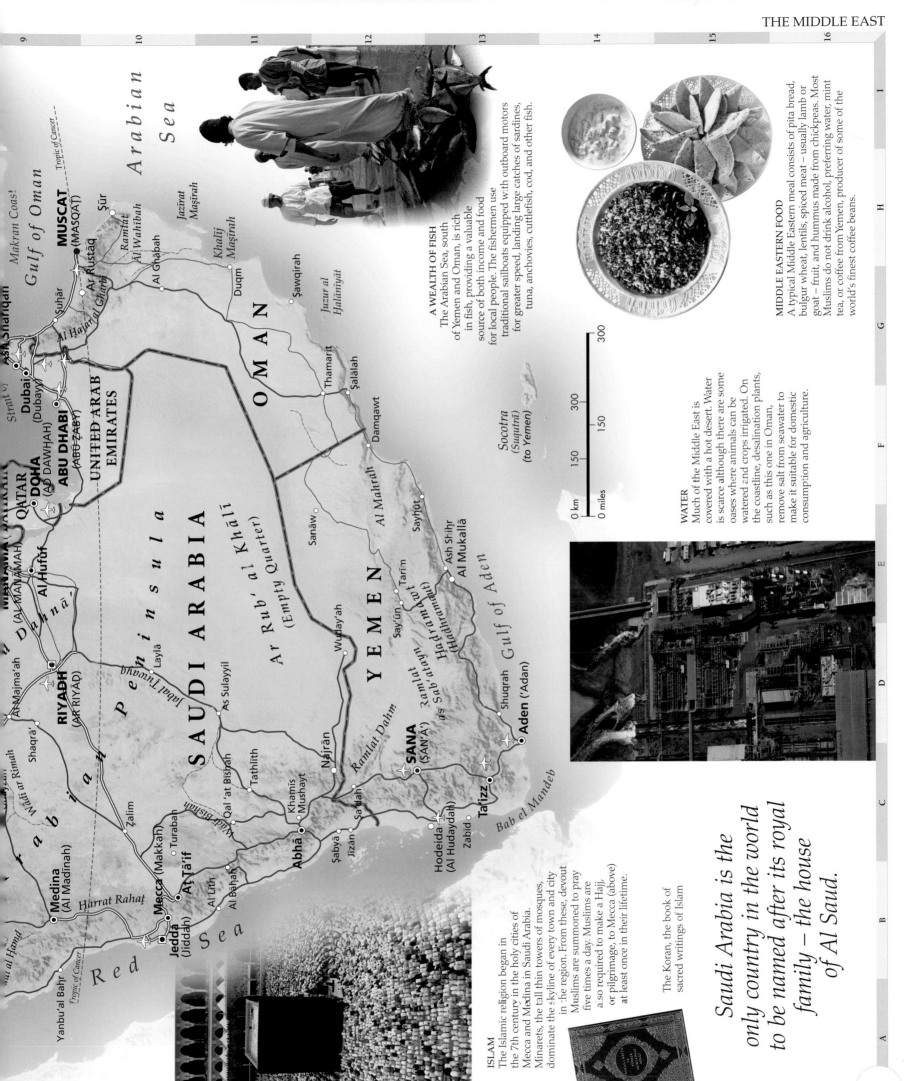

A WEALTH OF FISH
The Arabian Sea, south of Yemen and Oman, is rich in fish, providing a valuable source of both income and food for local people. The fishermen use traditional sailboats equipped with outboard motors for greater speed, landing large catches of sardines, tuna, anchovies, cuttlefish, cod, and other fish.

MIDDLE EASTERN FOOD
A typical Middle Eastern meal consists of pita bread, bulgur wheat, lentils, spiced meat – usually lamb or goat – fruit, and hummus made from chickpeas. Most Muslims do not drink alcohol, preferring water, mint tea, or coffee from Yemen, producer of some of the world's finest coffee beans.

WATER
Much of the Middle East is covered with a hot desert. Water is scarce although there are some oases where animals can be watered and crops irrigated. On the coastline, desalination plants, such as this one in Oman, remove salt from seawater to make it suitable for domestic consumption and agriculture.

300
300
150
150
0 km
0 miles

ISLAM
The Islamic religion began in the 7th century in the holy cities of Mecca and Medina in Saudi Arabia. Minarets, the tall thin towers of mosques, dominate the skyline of every town and city in the region. From these, devout Muslims are summoned to pray five times a day. Muslims are also required to make a Hajj, or pilgrimage, to Mecca (above) at least once in their lifetime.

The Koran, the book of sacred writings of Islam

Saudi Arabia is the only country in the world to be named after its royal family – the house of Al Saud.

Arabian Sea

Gulf of Oman

Makran Coast

Tropic of Cancer

MUSCAT
(MASQAŢ)

Şūr
Ar Rustāq
Suḩār
Al Ghābah
Al Waḩībah
Ramlat
Jazīrat Maşīrah
Khalij Maşīrah
Juzur al Ḩalāniyāt

OMAN

Aş Sharīqah
Dubai (Dubayy)
Abu Dhabi (ABU ZABY)
Al Hajar al Gharbī

UNITED ARAB EMIRATES

Strait of Hormuz

QATAR
DOHA (AD DAWḨAH)

BAHRAIN
(AL MANĀMAH)
Al Hufūf

(AL DAHNĀ')

SAUDI ARABIA

Arabian Peninsula

Ar Rub' al Khālī (Empty Quarter)

Duqm
Şawqirah
Thamarit
Şalālah
Damqawt
Al Mahrah
Sayḩūt
Ash Shiḩr
Al Mukallā

Socotra (Suquṭrā) (to Yemen)

Gulf of Aden

Sanāw
Tarīm
Say'ūn
Ḩaḍramawt (Ḩaḍramaut)
Wuday'ah
Ramlat as Sab'atayn

YEMEN

Ramlat Daḩm
Najrān
SANA (ŞAN'Ā')
Al Maḩrah
Sayḩūt
Shuqrah
Aden ('Adan)
Bab el Mandeb

Riyadh (AR RIYĀḌ)
Jabal Ṭuwayq
Layla
As Sulayyil
Shaqrā'
Zalim
Turaban
Al Lith
Al Bāḩaḩ
Abhā
Khamīs Mushayt
Qal 'at Bīshah
Tathlīth
Sabyā
Jizān
Hodeida (Al Hudaydah)
Zabīd
Ṣa'dah
Ta'izz
Wādī Bīshah

Medina (Al Madīnah)
Mecca (Makkah)
Aṭ Ṭā'if
Jedda (Jiddah)
Harrat Rahaṭ
Yanbu' al Bahr

Red Sea

Tropic of Cancer

Al Majma'ah
Shaqrā'

Ad Dahnā'

Wādī ar Rimah

Central Asia

THE FIVE CENTRAL ASIAN NATIONS rise up from hot deserts in the west and south to cold, high mountain ranges in the east. The area has oil, gas, and mineral reserves, as well as other natural resources, but water is often scarce and agriculture is limited. The four northern nations were once part of the Soviet Union and are now independent nations. Afghanistan is a landlocked country and three-quarters of its land is inaccessible terrain. It was invaded by the Soviet Union in 1979, prompting a civil war that has lasted for more than 20 years. In 2002, American and other Western forces overthrew a fundamentalist Islamic regime in Afghanistan because of its support for international terrorism. The country, however, has been wrecked by these years of continuous warfare, making it one of the poorest and most deprived nations on Earth.

One of the world's largest gold mines is at Muruntau in the Kyzyl Kum desert in Uzbekistan.

FESTIVALS IN AFGHANISTAN
Despite the horrors of recent years, the Afghans still celebrate important Islamic festivals, notably Eid ul-Fitr, which marks the end of the holy month of Ramadan. People visit friends and family and eat a festive meal together. The art of storytelling still flourishes in Afghanistan, as does the *attan*, the national dance.

An Afghan refugee carries bread with which to break the Ramadan fast.

Children in Kabul, Afghanistan, made homeless by war

LIFE EXPECTANCY
As a result of war, drought, and poverty, people in Afghanistan can expect to live an average of only 45 years, one of the lowest life expectancy rates in the world. Infant mortality is extremely high. Health services have almost completely collapsed and few trained doctors and nurses are available to help the sick. Sadly, there are not enough orphanages to cope with the increasing number of children made homeless by war.

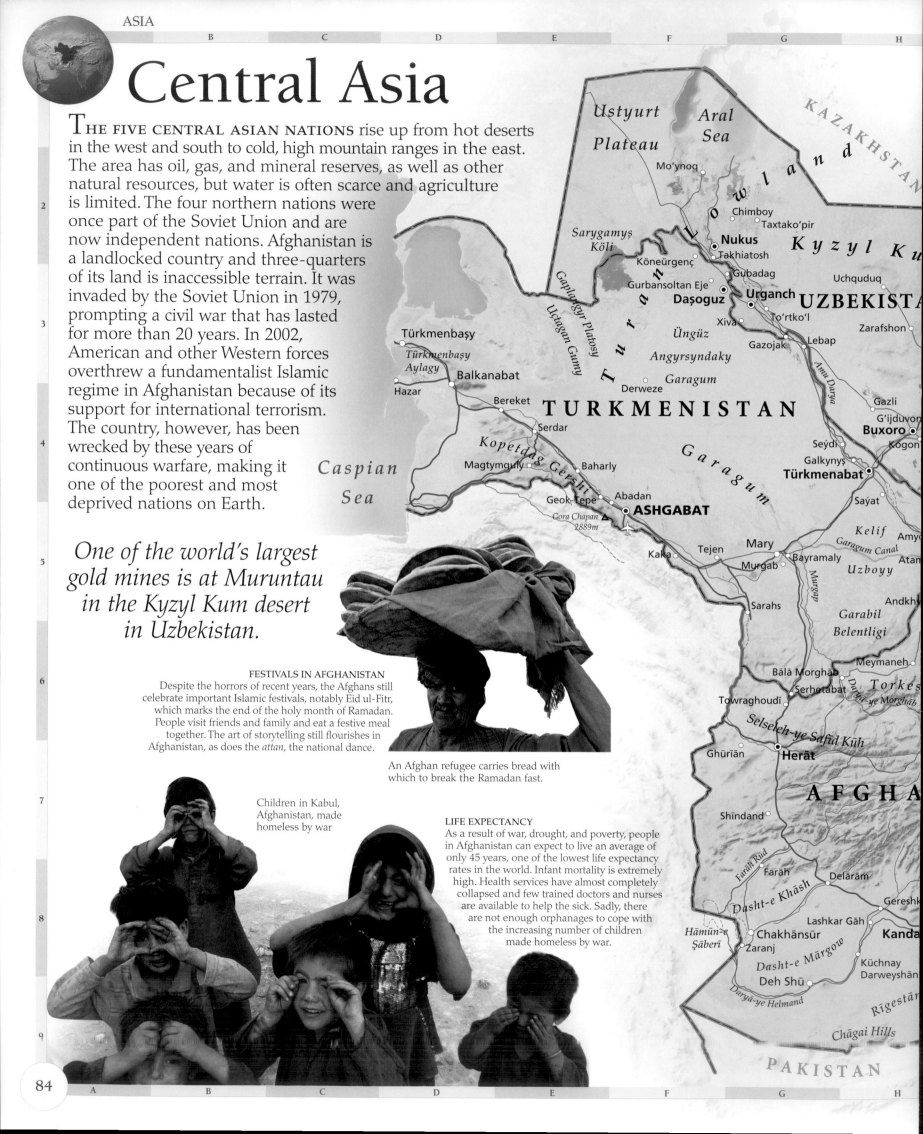

Map labels

KAZAKHSTAN
Ustyurt Plateau
Aral Sea
Lowland
Mo'ynoq
Sarygamyş Köli
Chimboy
Taxtako'pir
Nukus
Takhiatosh
Kyzyl Kum
Köneürgenç
Gubadag
Uchquduq
Gurbansoltan Eje
Daşoguz
Urganch
UZBEKISTAN
Xiva
To'rtko'l
Zarafshon
Üngüz
Gazojak
Lebap
Angyrsyndaky
Anıu Darya
Gazli
Garagum
Derweze
G'ijduvon
Türkmenbaşy
Türkmenbaşy Aylagy
Uçtagan Gumy
Gaplaňgyr Platosy
Turan
Buxoro
Balkanabat
Kogon
Hazar
Bereket
TURKMENISTAN
Seýdi
Serdar
Garagum
Galkynyş
Türkmenabat
Kopetdag Gershi
Baharly
Sayat
Caspian Sea
Magtymguly
Abadan
Geok-Tepe
ASHGABAT
Gora Chapan 2889m
Kelif
Amy
Garagum Canal
Kaka
Tejen
Mary
Bayramaly
Atan
Murgab
Murgap
Uzboyy
Sarahs
Andkh
Garabil Belentligi
Bālā Morghāb
Meymaneh
Serhetabat
Torkes
Towraghoudi
Daryā-ye Morghāb
Selseleh-ye Safid Kūh
Ghūrīān
Herāt
AFGHA
Shīndand
Farāh Rūd
Farāh
Delārām
Dasht-e Khāsh
Gereshk
Lashkar Gāh
Hāmūn-e Şāberī
Chakhānsūr
Kanda
Zaranj
Küchnay Darweyshān
Dasht-e Mārgow
Deh Shū
Daryā-ye Helmand
Rīgestān
Chāgai Hills
PAKISTAN

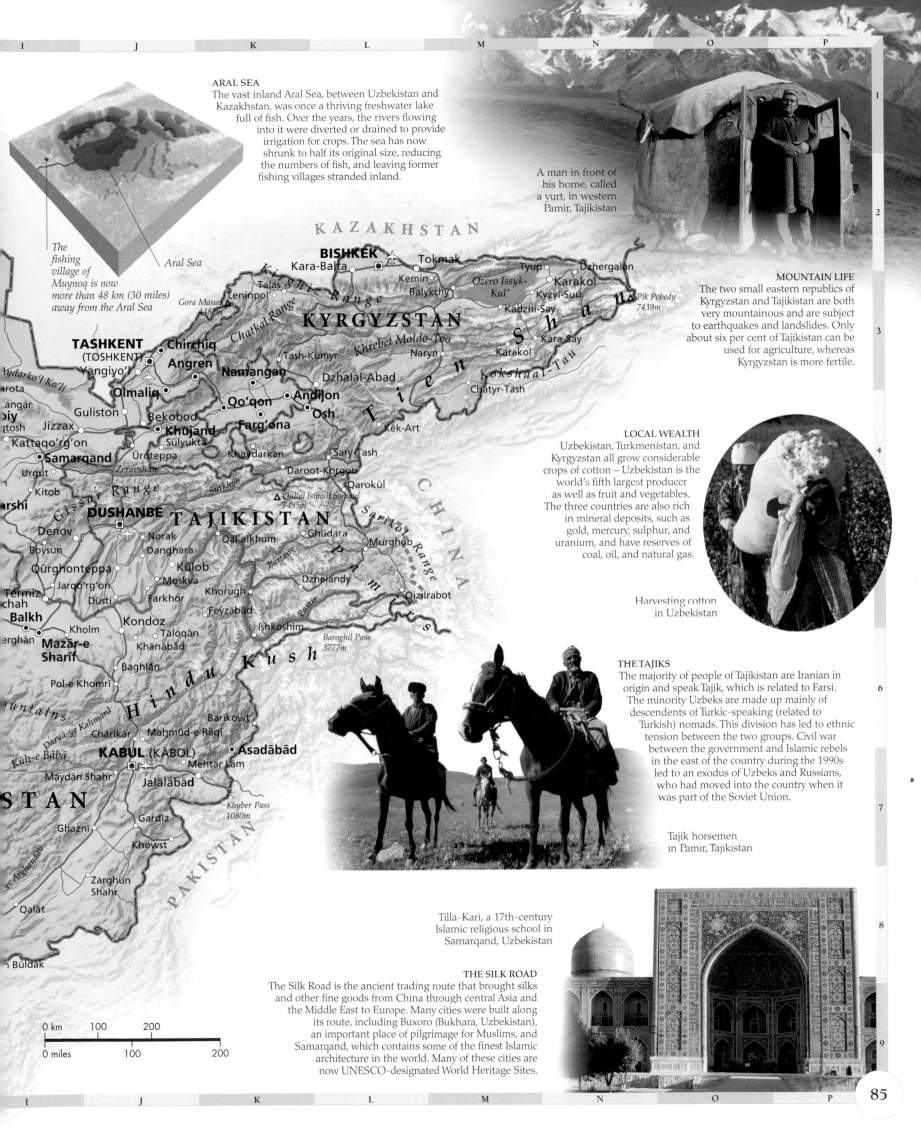

ARAL SEA
The vast inland Aral Sea, between Uzbekistan and Kazakhstan, was once a thriving freshwater lake full of fish. Over the years, the rivers flowing into it were diverted or drained to provide irrigation for crops. The sea has now shrunk to half its original size, reducing the numbers of fish, and leaving former fishing villages stranded inland.

The fishing village of Muynoq is now more than 48 km (30 miles) away from the Aral Sea

A man in front of his home, called a yurt, in western Pamir, Tajikistan

MOUNTAIN LIFE
The two small eastern republics of Kyrgyzstan and Tajikistan are both very mountainous and are subject to earthquakes and landslides. Only about six per cent of Tajikistan can be used for agriculture, whereas Kyrgyzstan is more fertile.

LOCAL WEALTH
Uzbekistan, Turkmenistan, and Kyrgyzstan all grow considerable crops of cotton – Uzbekistan is the world's fifth largest producer as well as fruit and vegetables. The three countries are also rich in mineral deposits, such as gold, mercury, sulphur, and uranium, and have reserves of coal, oil, and natural gas.

Harvesting cotton in Uzbekistan

THE TAJIKS
The majority of people of Tajikistan are Iranian in origin and speak Tajik, which is related to Farsi. The minority Uzbeks are made up mainly of descendents of Turkic-speaking (related to Turkish) nomads. This division has led to ethnic tension between the two groups. Civil war between the government and Islamic rebels in the east of the country during the 1990s led to an exodus of Uzbeks and Russians, who had moved into the country when it was part of the Soviet Union.

Tajik horsemen in Pamir, Tajikistan

Tilla-Kari, a 17th-century Islamic religious school in Samarqand, Uzbekistan

THE SILK ROAD
The Silk Road is the ancient trading route that brought silks and other fine goods from China through central Asia and the Middle East to Europe. Many cities were built along its route, including Buxoro (Bukhara, Uzbekistan), an important place of pilgrimage for Muslims, and Samarqand, which contains some of the finest Islamic architecture in the world. Many of these cities are now UNESCO-designated World Heritage Sites.

0 km	100	200
0 miles	100	200

Indian Subcontinent

SEPARATED FROM the rest of Asia by the Himalayas, the Indian subcontinent is home to almost one-quarter of the world's population – a staggering 1.15 billion people. They have a long and complex history, form many different ethnic groups, speak a wide variety of languages, and worship many different gods. While some people in these countries are wealthy, many others live in poverty. Tensions between and within countries in this region have sometimes erupted in warfare. The Indian subcontinent is often affected by natural disasters, notably cyclones in the Bay of Bengal, and earthquakes and floods in Pakistan. However, India, the most heavily populated nation and once prone to famine, is now more than self-sufficient in food. All but Nepal and Bhutan were once ruled by the British, whose legacy can be seen in the common language of English, in the architecture, the vast railway system, and in sport – most notably cricket.

MONSOON
From May/June to September, warm, moist southerly winds sweep up from the Indian Ocean and the Bay of Bengal across the subcontinent. Once these winds meet dry land, moisture falls as monsoon rainfall. Although this irrigates the land and replenishes the water supply, it can also cause severe flooding.

FAMILY LIFE IN PAKISTAN
Pakistanis have strong ties to their extended families, and often many generations live and work together in family-run businesses. Smaller family units, however, are becoming more common in urban areas. Although some women hold prominent positions in public and commercial life, such as Benazir Bhutto who was prime minister twice before she was assassinated in December 2007, most women do not work outside the home.

SRI LANKA
In 1983, civil war erupted in Sri Lanka between the Buddhist majority Sinhalese, who dominate the government, and the Hindu minority Tamils, who wanted to establish their own independent state in the north of the island. The civil war, which ended in 2009 when the government defeated the Tamil Tigers, has cost many lives and disrupted the island's economy. Yet Sri Lanka still has one of the highest literacy rates in the world and high levels of health care.

School child, Sri Lanka

*one of
rol"
greed
een
and
tan
72)*

SAI CHIN
*stered by China,
ned by India)*

DEMCHOK/
DÊMQOG
*(administered
by China, claimed
by India)*

THE HIMALAYAS
The highest chain of mountains in the world, the Himalayas have eight peaks that are more than 8,000 m (26,247 ft) high. Everest, the world's highest mountain at 8,850 m (29,035 ft), is on the border of Nepal and Tibet. Mountaineers come from far and wide to scale these massive peaks.

Bhutanese people

ARUNACHAI
PRADESH
(claimed by China)

BHUTAN
Hidden away in the Himalayas, the people of Bhutan are devoutly Buddhist and have little contact with the outside world. A minority of the population are Nepalese Hindus who came to the country in the first half of the last century. Most Bhutanese live in the fertile river valleys of the centre and south of the country. Traditional dress – the *kira* for women and the *gho* for men – is widely worn.

The name Bhutan means "Land of the Thunder Dragon" in Dzongkha, the country's official language.

RELIGION
Two of the world's great religions – Hinduism and Buddhism – began in India more than 2,500 years ago. Most Pakistanis and Bangladeshis are Muslim, most Indians and Nepalese are Hindu, and most Sri Lankans and Bhutanese are Buddhist.

Hindus bathe in the River Ganges, which is considered sacred

BOLLYWOOD
More films are produced in Mumbai (Bombay), India – more than 800 a year – than in the whole of the USA, turning "Bollywood", as it is known, into a major cultural centre. Bollywood films generally have historical, religious, or social themes, and are famous for their song and dance routines and glamorous stars. These films are an important export to central Asia, the Middle East, and Africa.

TEA IN SRI LANKA
Sri Lanka is the world's largest exporter of tea. The plantations are located mainly in the centre of the island and employ women to pick the delicate, green shoots of the bushes.

North Andaman

Middle Andaman

Port Blair
Andaman Islands
(to India)

South Andaman

Little Andaman

Nicobar Islands
(to India)

Car Nicobar

Katchall Island

Little Nicobar
Great Nicobar

Indira Point

Andaman Sea

INDIAN OCEAN

Map labels
NEPAL
CHINA
Sālyān
Annapurna 8091m
Mount Everest 8850m
Kula Kangri 755-m
Pokharā
Bhaktapur
THIMPHU
BHUTAN
Dibrugarh
KATHMANDU
Lalitpur
Darjiling
Bongaigaon
Jorhāt
Faizābād
Birātnagar
Shiliguri
Brahmaputra
Lucknow
Uttar Pradesh
Gorakhpur
Chhapra
Dinajpur
Rangpur
Meghālaya
Guwāhāti
Kohima
Imphāl
Allahābād
Patna
Jamalpur
Sylhet
Silchar
Kānpur
Ganges
Bihār
Varānasi
Gaya
Rajshahi
BANGLADESH
Sāgar
Madhya Pradesh
Jharkhand
Pabna
DHAKA
Tropic of Cancer
Murwāra
Dhanbād
Āsānsol
Jessore
Comilla
Jabalpur
Chota Nāgpur
Rānchi
West Bengal
Khulna
Chittagong
Bilāspur
Jamshedpur
Kolkata (Calcutta)
Barisal
Korba
Raulakela
Kharagpur
Chhattisgarth
Mouths of the Ganges
Gondia
Sambalpur
Bāleshwar
Bay of Bengal
Raipur
Orissa
Mahānadi
Chandrapur
Cuttack
Bhubaneshwar
Puri
Jagdalpur
Brahmapur
Karimnagar
Andhra Pradesh
Vizianagaram
Eastern Ghats
Godavari
Visākhapatnam
Warangal
Rājahmundry
Vijayawāda
Chīrala
Ongole
Kāvali
Nellore
dapah
Chennai (Madras)
Kānchīpuram
Pondicherry
iruchchirāppalli
Palk Strait
Jaffna
Mannar
SRI LANKA
Trincomalee
Puttalam
Batticaloa
Kandy
COLOMBO
Sri Jayewardanapura Kotte
Galle
MYANMAR (BURMA)
Himalayas
Bareilly
Uttarakhand
erut
hu
nir
IA
al
gpur
mābād
Varangal
yderābād
ool
atri
rai
Murai
orin
of
nar
ombo
lutara

Western China and Mongolia

CHINA IS A LAND of great geographical diversity and amazing landscapes. More than 90 per cent of the population are Han Chinese – descendents of people who settled here more than 5,000 years ago. This region includes western China, Mongolia, and Tibet. Mongolia gained its independence from China in 1911 and is now an independent democracy. Tibet is currently governed by China. Compared with eastern China, this region is sparsely populated and characterized by vast deserts, remote mountains, and extreme temperatures.

DESERT LANDS
The cold, rocky Gobi Desert (right) stretches for more than 1,000,000 sq km (400,000 sq miles) through Mongolia and northeast China. Many dinosaur bones and eggs have been found here, making it one of the richest dinosaur fossil regions in the world.

THE MONGOLIANS
Most of the people living in Mongolia are Khalkh Mongols. About half of these people now live in urban areas, but some still lead traditional lives as nomadic herders. They live in large felt tents, called *yurts*. Smoke from the central iron stove escapes through a chimney in the roof.

In traditional Mongolian khoomi singing, men are able to sing several notes at once.

CHINESE WRITING
The Chinese alphabet is not made up of letters. Instead, separate symbols stand for individual words or parts of words. There are more than 40,000 characters in the Chinese language. The same symbols are used everywhere in China, and no matter what Chinese language or dialect people speak, they can all read the same script.

兒童百科全書

Chinese symbols, whose strokes have to be written in a certain order

MONASTERIES IN MONGOLIA
Under communism, Mongolians were forbidden to practise their traditional Buddhist faith, which was viewed as superstitious and unscientific. Since the democratic government was set up in 1990, about 100 monasteries have reopened. Most people, however, no longer follow any religion.

Map labels

Hövsgöl Nuur
Uvs Nuur
Ulaangom
Ölgiy
Altay
Hyargas Nuur
Halban
Har Us Nuur
Har Nuur
Hovd
Hangayn N
Tset
M O
Altay
Bayanh
KAZAKHSTAN
Altai Mountains
Aj Bogd Uul 3802m
Karamay
Gurbantünggüt Shamo
Kuytun
Borohoro Shan
Shihezi
Fukang
Jimsar
Atas Bogd 2695m
Yining
Ürümqi
Qitai
Turpan
Hami
KYRGYZSTAN
Tien Shan
Tomür Feng 7443m
Turpan Pendi
Korla
Bosten Hu
Xingxingxia
Kashi
Tarim He
Tarim Basin
Kuruktag
GANSU
Yengisar
XINJIANG
Laojunmiao
Shache
Qilian Sh
Yecheng
Takla Makan Desert
Ruoqiang
Danghe Nanshan
(claimed by India)
Pishan
Moyu
Qira
Altun Shan
C H I N
Hotan
Qaidam Pendi
TAJIKISTAN
Karakoram Range
K2 8611m
Kunlun Shan
Golmud
Dul
AKSAI CHIN
Burhan Budai Shan
QINGHAI
PAKISTAN
AKSAI CHIN (administered by China, claimed by India)
Plateau of Tibet (Qingzang Gaoyuan)
Tongtian He
Bayan Har Sh
Indus
Rutog
Yushu
DEMCHOK/DÊMQOG (administered by China, claimed by India)
Tanggula Shan
Mekong
INDIA
Gar Xincun
Gozhê
Siling Co
Amdo
Qamdo
Zanda
Tangra Yumco
Gyaring Co
Nagqu
Salu
Brahmaputra
Ngangzê Co
Nam Co
Damxung
Nyainqêntanglha Shan
Lhazê
Xigazê
Maizhokunggar
NEPAL
Himalayas
Lhasa
Gyangzê
Gonggar
ARUNÁCHAL PRADESH (claimed by China)
Mount Everest 8850m
BHUTAN
INDIA
MYAN BURMA

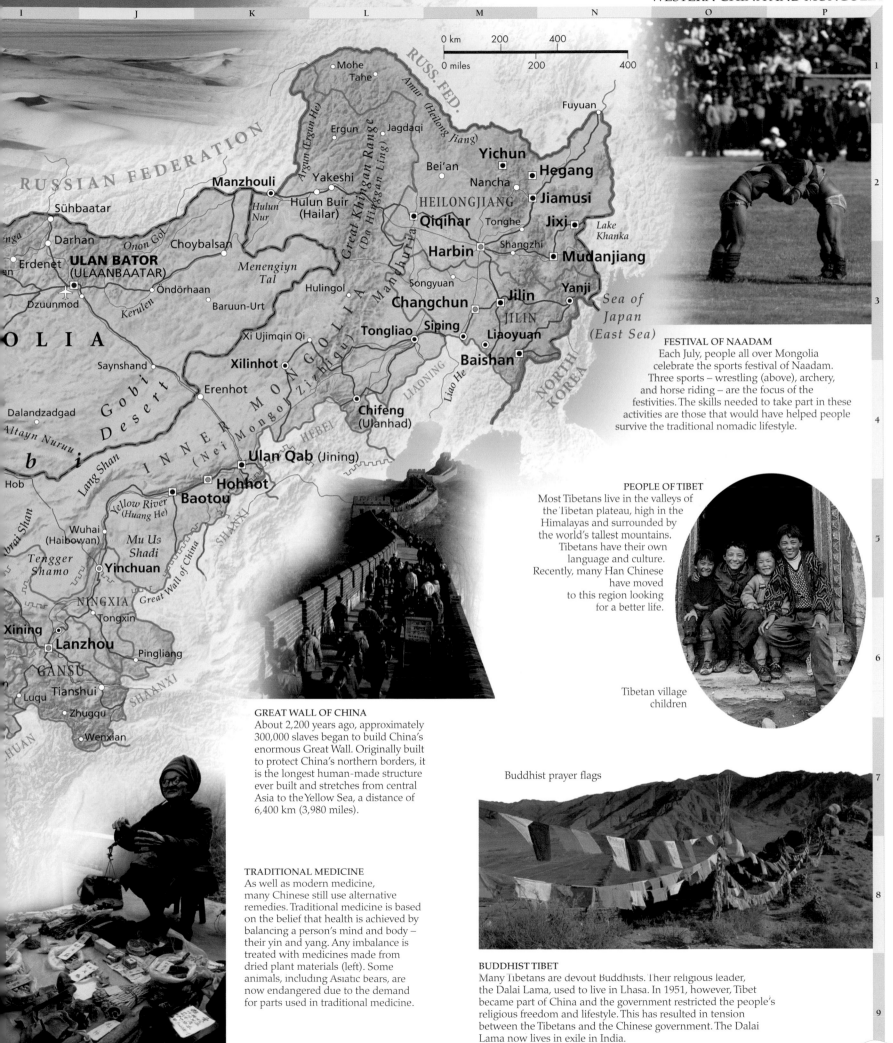

FESTIVAL OF NAADAM
Each July, people all over Mongolia celebrate the sports festival of Naadam. Three sports – wrestling (above), archery, and horse riding – are the focus of the festivities. The skills needed to take part in these activities are those that would have helped people survive the traditional nomadic lifestyle.

PEOPLE OF TIBET
Most Tibetans live in the valleys of the Tibetan plateau, high in the Himalayas and surrounded by the world's tallest mountains. Tibetans have their own language and culture. Recently, many Han Chinese have moved to this region looking for a better life.

Tibetan village children

GREAT WALL OF CHINA
About 2,200 years ago, approximately 300,000 slaves began to build China's enormous Great Wall. Originally built to protect China's northern borders, it is the longest human-made structure ever built and stretches from central Asia to the Yellow Sea, a distance of 6,400 km (3,980 miles).

Buddhist prayer flags

TRADITIONAL MEDICINE
As well as modern medicine, many Chinese still use alternative remedies. Traditional medicine is based on the belief that health is achieved by balancing a person's mind and body – their yin and yang. Any imbalance is treated with medicines made from dried plant materials (left). Some animals, including Asiatic bears, are now endangered due to the demand for parts used in traditional medicine.

BUDDHIST TIBET
Many Tibetans are devout Buddhists. Their religious leader, the Dalai Lama, used to live in Lhasa. In 1951, however, Tibet became part of China and the government restricted the people's religious freedom and lifestyle. This has resulted in tension between the Tibetans and the Chinese government. The Dalai Lama now lives in exile in India.

Eastern China and Korea

CHINA HAS A LARGE population of more than 1.3 billion, with two-thirds living in eastern China. For thousands of years, powerful emperors ruled China. During this period, Chinese civilization was very advanced, but much of the population lived in poverty. In 1949, after a communist revolution, the People's Republic of China was established. Food, education, and health care became available to more people, but there was also a loss of freedom. Today, Chinese people have more freedom, but the government still has tight control over their lives. The Korean peninsula is divided politically into north and south, and political tensions continue to exist between the two governments. Since 1949, Taiwan has been in dispute with China over who governs the mountainous island of Taiwan.

NEW YEAR CELEBRATIONS

Chinese New Year, also known as the Spring Festival, is the country's most important festival. It is usually held in January or February. Good-luck messages decorate buildings and there are feasts, fireworks, fairs, and processions. People wear red clothes for good luck and give gifts of coins to symbolize wealth.

Chinese New Year parade

HONG KONG

For 100 years, Hong Kong was a British colony. Then, in 1997, it was returned to China. These small islands are some of the most densely populated parts of the world. Most people live and work in high-rise buildings. It has a prosperous economy at the heart of global finance and the people there have one of the world's highest life expectancies.

Skyline of Hong Kong with a Chinese junk in the foreground

ONE-CHILD FAMILIES

Many Chinese children do not have brothers or sisters. This is due to policies brought in by the Chinese goverment in 1979. To try and control the rising population, the government offers special benefits to couples with only one child. Although this has slowed down the rate of growth, China's population still grows by millions each year.

PADDY FIELDS

Rice forms the basis of most Chinese meals. It grows in paddy fields in the southeast of the country. During the growing season, fields are flooded so farmers can grow more rice more quickly. In the drier regions, wheat is grown and used to make noodles, buns, and dumplings. Rice or wheat is combined with local vegetables, meats, and spices to create regional dishes.

NINGXIA
Tongchua
Xiany
QINGHAI
Bayan Har Shan
GANSU
Baoji
Xi'a
Hongyuan
Hanzhong SHAA
Yalong Jiang
Guangyuan
SICHUAN
Mianyang Wanyu
TIBET
Nanchong
Luhuo
Wanzh
Litang
Chengdu
Sichuan
Ya'an
Pendi
C H
Jinsha Jiang (Chang Jiang)
Leshan
Neijiang
Li
Chongqir
Zigong
CHONGQING SH
Hengduan Shan
Xichang
Tongzi
Zhongdian
Zunyi
Hua
Yangtze (Chang Jiang)
Zhoatong
GUIZHOU
Salween
Panzhihua
Guiyang
Dali
Anshun
Kai
Guanling
Duyun
Baoshan
Kunming
Dushan
MYANMAR (BURMA)
YUNNAN
Xingxi
Yuxi
Wuliang Shan
Bose
Liuzh
Kaiyuan
Wenshan
GUANGX
Gejiu
Mekong
Tropic of Cancer
Nanning
Jinghong
VIETNAM
Qinzhou
LAOS
Beiha

0 km 150 300

0 Miles 150 300

Gulf of Tongking

Danz

Dongfang

HAI

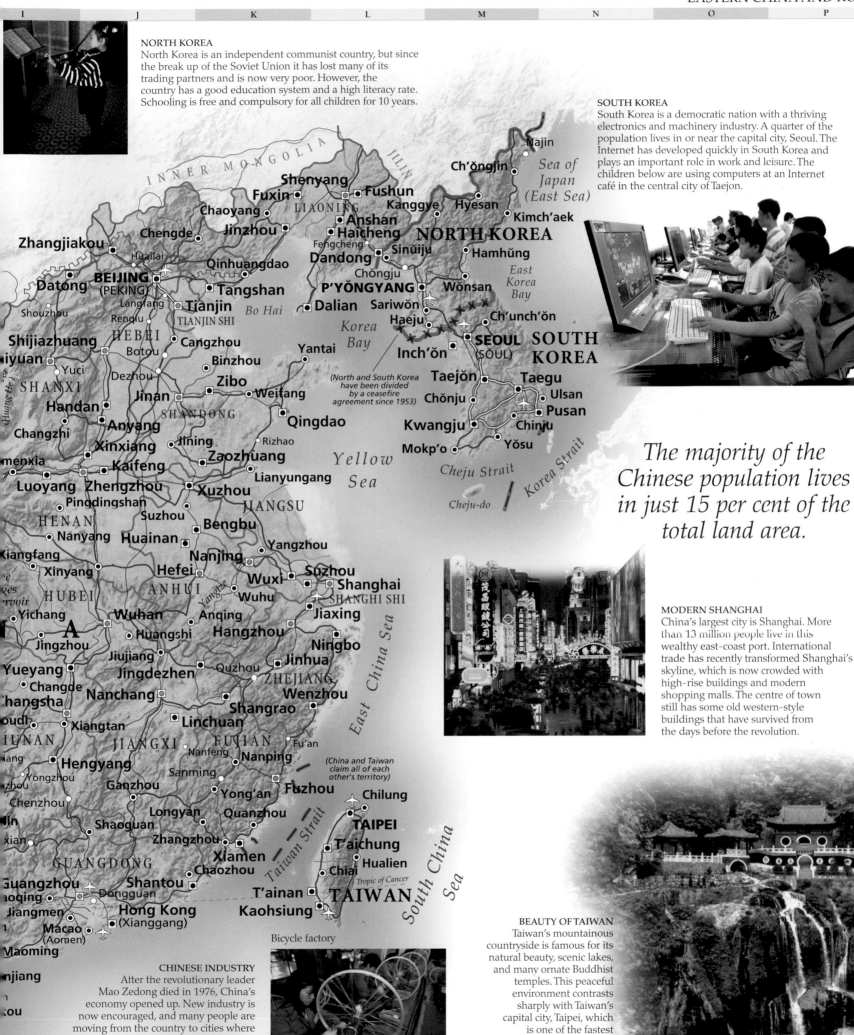

NORTH KOREA

North Korea is an independent communist country, but since the break up of the Soviet Union it has lost many of its trading partners and is now very poor. However, the country has a good education system and a high literacy rate. Schooling is free and compulsory for all children for 10 years.

SOUTH KOREA

South Korea is a democratic nation with a thriving electronics and machinery industry. A quarter of the population lives in or near the capital city, Seoul. The Internet has developed quickly in South Korea and plays an important role in work and leisure. The children below are using computers at an Internet café in the central city of Taejon.

The majority of the Chinese population lives in just 15 per cent of the total land area.

Map labels

INNER MONGOLIA

JILIN

Najin

Ch'ŏngjin

Sea of Japan (East Sea)

Shenyang
Fuxin
Fushun
Chaoyang
Kanggye
Hyesan
LIAONING
Anshan
Kimch'aek
Chengde
Jinzhou
Haicheng
Zhangjiakou
Fengcheng
Sinŭiju
Hamhŭng
Datong
Huailai
Qinhuangdao
Dandong
East Korea Bay
Langfang
Chŏngju
Shouzhou
BEIJING (PEKING)
Tangshan
P'YŎNGYANG
Wŏnsan
Renqiu
Tianjin
Bo Hai
Dalian
Sariwŏn
Shijiazhuang
TIANJIN SHI
Haeju
iyuan
Cangzhou
Korea Bay
Ch'unch'ŏn
Yuci
HEBEI
Botou
Yantai
Inch'ŏn
SEOUL (SOUL)
SOUTH KOREA
SHANXI
Dezhou
Binzhou
Jinan
Zibo
Weifang
(North and South Korea have been divided by a ceasefire agreement since 1953)
Taejŏn
Taegu
Handan
SHANDONG
Chŏnju
Ulsan
Changzhi
Anyang
Qingdao
Kwangju
Pusan
Xinxiang
Jining
Chinju
menxia
Kaifeng
Zaozhuang
Rizhao
Yellow Sea
Mokp'o
Yŏsu
Luoyang
Zhengzhou
Xuzhou
Lianyungang
Cheju Strait
Korea Strait
Pingdingshan
HENAN
Suzhou
JIANGSU
Cheju-do
Nanyang
Huainan
Bengbu
Xiangfang
Hefei
Nanjing
Yangzhou
Xinyang
Wuxi
Suzhou
HUBEI
ANHUI
Yangtze
Wuhu
Shanghai
Yichang
Wuhan
Anqing
Jiaxing
SHANGHI SHI
Huangshi
Hangzhou
Jingzhou
Jiujiang
Ningbo
Yueyang
Jingdezhen
Quzhou
Jinhua
Changde
Nanchang
ZHEJIANG
hangsha
Shangrao
Wenzhou
Xiangtan
Linchuan
UNAN
JIANGXI
FUJIAN
Fu'an
East China Sea
Hengyang
Nanfeng
Nanping
Yongzhou
Ganzhou
Sanming
Yong'an
(China and Taiwan claim all of each other's territory)
Chenzhou
Longyan
Quanzhou
Fuzhou
Chilung
Shaoguan
Zhangzhou
TAIPEI
GUANGDONG
Xiamen
T'aichung
Chaozhou
Hualien
Guangzhou
Shantou
Chiai
Dongguan
T'ainan
TAIWAN
South China Sea
aoqing
Hong Kong (Xianggang)
Kaohsiung
Jiangmen
Taiwan Strait
Macao (Aomen)
aoming
Tropic of Cancer

MODERN SHANGHAI

China's largest city is Shanghai. More than 13 million people live in this wealthy east-coast port. International trade has recently transformed Shanghai's skyline, which is now crowded with high-rise buildings and modern shopping malls. The centre of town still has some old western-style buildings that have survived from the days before the revolution.

BEAUTY OF TAIWAN

Taiwan's mountainous countryside is famous for its natural beauty, scenic lakes, and many ornate Buddhist temples. This peaceful environment contrasts sharply with Taiwan's capital city, Taipei, which is one of the fastest growing cities in Asia.

Bicycle factory

CHINESE INDUSTRY

After the revolutionary leader Mao Zedong died in 1976, China's economy opened up. New industry is now encouraged, and many people are moving from the country to cities where there are relatively well-paid jobs.

Japan

JAPAN IS SITUATED in the north Pacific Ocean off the coast of the Asian continent. It is made up of four main islands and more than 3,000 smaller ones. The Japanese people have a distinctive culture based on traditions built up over thousands of years. They have their own language and script. School children all learn to read and write both in the traditional script and using letters. Social rules in Japan are strict, and respect and politeness are considered very important. Most people bow when greeting one another, for example. Japan is a very modern country, however, with one of the world's most technologically advanced societies. Its economy is based on the development and production of cutting-edge electronics and vehicles, and most families have the latest consumer goods.

RELIGIONS OF JAPAN
Many Japanese people follow a mix of the Shinto and Buddhist religions, attending wedding blessings in Shinto shrines and funerals in Buddhist temples. Buddhism originated in India and arrived in Japan in the 6th century, whereas the Shinto faith is native to Japan. Respect for nature is especially important in the Shinto religion. Many natural locations, such as Mount Fuji, are considered sacred.

EARTHQUAKES
The islands of Japan are situated in an area where four of Earth's tectonic plates meet. This causes frequent earthquakes. Japanese school children are taught how to keep safe during an earthquake by sheltering in a doorway or under a table.

OVERCROWDING
Most of the country's 127 million people live in cities in the flatter, coastal areas. Tokyo and Osaka are very crowded, and homes here are usually very small and are designed to make the most of the limited space.

FASHION IN JAPAN
On ordinary days, Japanese people usually wear western-style clothes. Most children have a school uniform. On festival days, such as Children's Day, many people prefer to wear the traditional kimono. Women's kimonos are often made of colourful silk, decorated with beautiful designs.

Traditional and modern dresses

Japanese Temple

Mount Fuji is a dormant volcano.

Map labels

La Perouse Strait
Sea of Okhotsk
Kurile Islands
Ostrov Shikotan (Kurile Islands administered by Russian Federation, claimed by Japan)
Ostrov Kunashir

Rebun-tō
Rishiri-tō
Wakkanai
Nakagawa
Nayoro
Monbetsu
Shibetsu
Shirataki
Abashiri
Shari
Shintoku
Bekkai
Kitami
Kushiro
Obihiro
Hiroo
Asahikawa
Takikawa
Hokkaidō
Asahi-dake △ 2290m
△ Horoshiri-dake 2052m
Ebetsu
Chitose
Tomakomai
Noboribetsu
Muroran
Hakodate
Ishikari-wan
Otaru
Sapporo
Iwanai
Uchiura-wan
Setana
Okushiri-tō
Esashi
Fukushima
Tsugaru-kaikyō
Mutsu
Mutsu-wan
Aomori
Goshogawara
Hirosaki
Noshiro
Akita
Honjō
Sakata
Towada
Hachinohe
Kuji
Fudi
Miyako
Kuroishi
Odate
Iwate
Morioka
Hanamaki
Kesennuma
Gojōme
Yokote
Shizugawa
Yuzawa
Shinjō
Ishinomaki
Akkeshi
Nemuro

0 km   100   200
0 miles 100 200

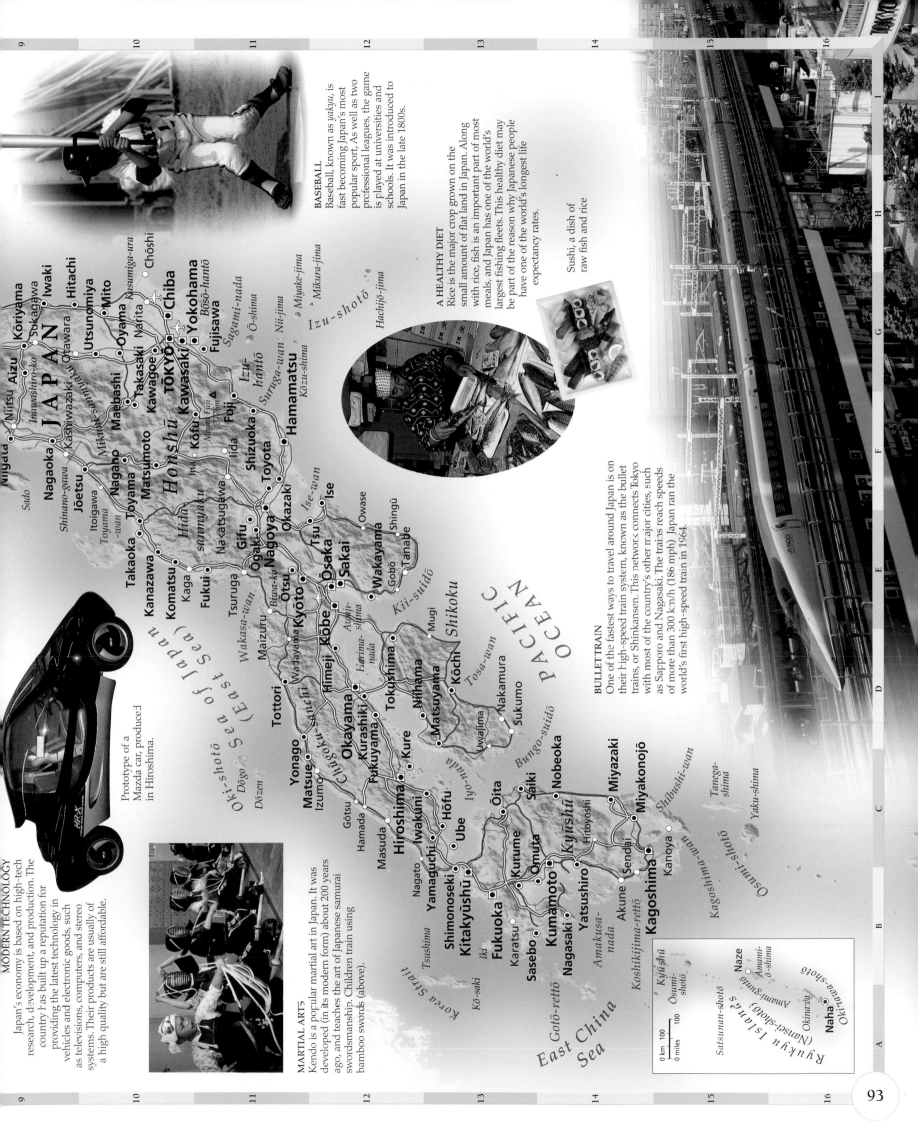

MODERN TECHNOLOGY

Japan's economy is based on high-tech research, development, and production. The country has built up a reputation for providing the latest technology in vehicles and electronic goods, such as televisions, computers, and stereo systems. Their products are usually of a high quality but are still affordable.

Prototype of a Mazda car, produced in Hiroshima.

MARTIAL ARTS

Kendo is a popular martial art in Japan. It was developed (in its modern form) about 200 years ago, and teaches the art of Japanese samurai swordsmanship. Children train using bamboo swords (above).

BASEBALL

Baseball, known as *yakyu*, is fast becoming Japan's most popular sport. As well as two professional leagues, the game is played at universities and schools. It was introduced to Japan in the late 1800s.

A HEALTHY DIET

Rice is the major crop grown on the small amount of flat land in Japan. Along with rice, fish is an important part of most meals, and Japan has one of the world's largest fishing fleets. This healthy diet may be part of the reason why Japanese people have one of the world's longest life expectancy rates.

Sushi, a dish of raw fish and rice

BULLET TRAIN

One of the fastest ways to travel around Japan is on their high-speed train system, known as the bullet trains, or Shinkansen. This network connects Tokyo with most of the country's other major cities, such as Sapporo and Nagasaki. The trains reach speeds of more than 300 km/h (186 mph) Japan ran the world's first high-speed train in 1964.

Mainland SE Asia

THE PENINSULA of Southeast Asia lies directly to the south of India and China, between the Pacific and Indian oceans. It is made up of Myanmar (Burma), Thailand, Vietnam, Cambodia, and Laos. Over thousands of years, the influence of people from nearby India, China, and Arabian countries has helped to give this region a diverse mix of cultures and religions. Much of the land here is mountainous, with half the region covered in forest. Most people live in coastal or lowland regions, where they can grow crops such as rice, raise cattle, and catch fish. In recent years, the electronics industry has also become an important part of southeast Asian economies, especially in Thailand.

GROWING RICE
Rice is the most important crop in southeast Asia. It grows well in wet lowland areas, such as the Mekong River delta in Vietnam, where the plants can be grown in paddy fields. Most rice is planted and harvested by women.

ORPHANS IN CAMBODIA
Cambodia has a very high percentage of widows and orphans, mainly because many men were killed in civil wars in recent decades.

Cambodian orphanage

RURAL LIVING
Most people in southeast Asia live in rural areas rather than cities, and farming is the most common occupation. The steep, mountainous regions are often unsuitable for growing crops or raising cattle, however, and many farming communities are based in the fertile river valleys and deltas. There are more than 200 villages on and around this lake (right) in Myanmar.

KAREN TRIBE
There are 600,000 tribespeople living in the northeastern hills of Thailand. The Karen are the largest hill tribe. They originated from Myanmar, but moved into Thailand to escape political unrest.

Padaung women, who are part of the Karen tribe, wear distinctive gold neck rings

CHINA

Hengduan Shan

Hkakabo Razi
5885m

Kumon Range

INDIA

Nmai Hka

Mali Hka

Myitkyina

Mogaung

Bhamo

Katha

Banmauk

Maingkwan

Chindwin

Irrawaddy

MYANMAR (BURMA)

Shwebo

Monywa

Sagaing Mandalay
Amarapura
Kyaukse
Myingyan
Meiktila

Pakokku

Chauk

Yenangyaung

Magway

Minbu

Thayetmyo

Pyay

Myanaung

Thandwe

Chin Hills

Arakan Yoma

Falam

Tamu

Ramree Island

Chedubá Island

Bay of Bengal

Sittwe

Kyaukpyu

BANGLADESH

Tropic of Cancer

Lashio

Pyin-Oo-Lwin

NAY PYI TAW

Taunggyi

Loikaw

Pawn

Taungdwingyi

Aunglan

Paungde

Phyu

Taungoo

Nyaunglebin

Pyuntaza

Hinthada

Bago

Sittaung

Salween

Shan Plateau

Keng Tung

Muang Sing

Muang Namo

Louangnamtha

Viangphoukha

Houayxay

Chiang Rai

Fang

Chiang Mai

Phayao

Lampang

Phrae

Nan

Lampang

Mae Nam Ping

Mae Nam Ping

Nam Yom

Nam Nan

Sirikit Reservoir

Korat

Black River

Lai Châu

Điện Biên

Nam On

Phôngsali

Xam Nua

Sop Hao

Muong Xieng Ngeun

Louangphabang

Xaignabouli

LAOS

Pak Lay

Ban Hin Heup

VIENTIANE (VIANGCHAN)

Loei

Nong Khai

Ang Nam Ngum

Paksan

Tha Khek

Hoang Liên Son

Lao Cai

Ha Giang

Cao Bằng

Lang Son

Thai Nguyên

Việt Trì

HA NOI

Hoa Binh

Ha Đông

Ha Binh

Nam Định

Tương Dương

Thanh Hoa

Đồng Hới

Vinh

Bắc Giang

Hồng Gai

Cẩm Pha

Hai Phong

Thai Binh

Gulf of Tongking

VIETNAM

Chaîne Annamitique

Tropic of Cancer

CHINA

Scale

| 0 km | 100 | 200 |
| 0 miles | 100 | 200 |

I

ANGKOR

The impressive temple complex of Angkor in Cambodia attracts visitors interested in its history and architecture. This combination of temples and palaces was built in 1113 CE by the Khmer king Suryavarman II. The buildings, such as Angkor Wat, below, are made of stone and brick and are decorated with relief sculptures showing mythical scenes of Hindu gods and great royal processions. The complex was uncovered in 1861 by French naturalist Henri Mouhot, following stories of a "lost city" in the jungle.

Angkor Wat

MONASTIC LIFE

The main religion in mainland southeast Asia is Buddhism. Nearly all Thai villages have their own temple, or wat, which is the centre of village life. Most young men spend some time in a monastery, where they have few possessions and spend much of their time in meditation.

FLOATING MARKET

The capital of Thailand, Bangkok, is a busy, crowded city with more than nine million inhabitants. The city was built on an island in the river, and has many canals. Boats, known as sampans, (above) act as floating markets from which traders sell fresh fruit and vegetables.

A large, previously unknown mammal, the Vu Quang ox, was only recently discovered in the forests of northern Vietnam.

THAI BEACHES

Tourism is now a major industry for Thailand. Popular destinations include the country's lively capital, Bangkok, and the beautiful island beach resorts (below). Phuket, Thailand's largest island, is often referred to as the "Pearl of the South".

Quang Ngai
Tam Ky
Quy Nhon
Tuy Hoa
Nha Trang
Cam Ranh
Phan Rang-Thap Cham
Phan Thiet
Da Lat
Di Linh
Vung Tau
Hô Chí Minh
Biên Hoa
My Tho
Tra Vinh
Long Xuyên
Cân Thơ
Soc Trăng
Bac Liêu
Ca Mau
Côn Dao
Mouths of the Mekong

V I E T N A M

Pley Cu
Kon Tum
Salavan
Muang Khôngxédôn
Pakxe
Champasak
Samakhixai
Virôchey
Tônle Srêpôk
Tônle Kong
Tônle San
Stœng Trêng
Phumi Kâmpóng Trábêk
Krâchéh
Kâmpóng Cham
Svay Riêng
Prey Vêng
Suông
Krâtié
Kâmpóng Chhnăng
Kâmpóng Saôm
Kâmpôt
Châu Dôc
Rach Gia
Vinh Rach Gia

PHNOM PENH (PNUM PÉNH)

C A M B O D I A

Mekong
Stœng Sên
Tônle Sap
Phumi Sâmraông
Krâlânh
Siem Reap
Angkor Wat
Bătdâmbâng
Poŭthisăt
Chuor Phnum Krâvanh
Ódôngk
Môung Roessei
Reăng Kesei

Chuor Phnum Dângrêk
Ó Lêt
T H A I L A N D

Ubon Ratchathani
Buriram
Surin
Nakhon Ratchasima
Sara Buri
Lop Buri
Nakhon Sawan
Nakhon Pathom
Ayutthaya
Ratchaburi
Phetchaburi
Srinagarind Reservoir
Chanthaburi
Rayong
Pattaya
Chon Buri
Samut Prakan
Ao Krung Thep
Ban Hua Hin

BANGKOK (KRUNG THEP)

Ko Chang

Gulf of Thailand

Chumphon
Lang Suan
Surat Thani
Sichon
Nakhon Si Thammarat
Pak Phanang
Phatthalung
Thale Luang
Songkhla
Pattani
Narathiwat
Yala
Hat Yai
Thung Song
Trang
Ko Lanta
Ko Samui
Ko Phangan
Ranong
Ko Pha Thong
Phang-Nga
Ko Phuket
Phuket
Andaman Sea
Ko Ta Ru Tao
Puau Langkawi

M A L A Y S I A

Bilauktaung Range
Isthmus of Kra
Tenasserim
Ye
Dawei
Mali Kyun
Kadan Kyun
Myeik
Daung Kyun
Letsôk-aw Kyun
Lanbi Kyun
Zadetkyi Kyun

Mergui Archipelago

South China Sea

Mouths of the Irrawaddy
Great Coco Island
Little Coco Island

B   C   D   E   F   G   H

Maritime SE Asia

To the south of the Asian mainland lies maritime southeast Asia. It includes Malaysia, Indonesia, East Timor, Singapore, and the Philippines. Part of Malaysia is connected to the mainland, but the rest of the region is made up of more than 20,000 islands that stretch across the Pacific and Indian Oceans. Lying near the Equator, the climate is mostly hot, wet, and humid. Most of the larger islands are mountainous and covered in dense forest, and many people live in villages near rivers or on the coast. Like the rest of southeast Asia, the population is made up of people from many different cultural backgrounds speaking hundreds of different languages. The most common religion is Islam, except in the Philippines, where most people are Roman Catholic.

GREAT APES
The orangutans are great apes that live only in Borneo and the northern corner of Sumatra. They spend most of their time in the trees, even building tree-top nests in which to sleep. Sadly, the orangutan is endangered because of deforestation.

PEOPLE OF MALAYSIA
Ethnic Malaysians make up 53 per cent of the population and are known as bumiputera, meaning "sons of the soil". Most Malaysians are Muslim. Ethnic Chinese form 26 per cent of the population.

Ubadiah Mosque, Malaysia

THE SULTAN OF BRUNEI
Brunei is ruled by a sultan who lives in the world's largest palace. The sultan is one of the wealthiest men in the world.

Sultan of Brunei

SINGAPORE
As the financial and industrial centre of southeast Asia, Singapore is one of the wealthiest countries in this region. It has a thriving high-tech industry and a high standard of living. There are strictly enforced laws forbidding littering and other small crimes. The death penalty is imposed for drug smuggling. The government also controls the press and restricts the Internet.

Skyscrapers in Singapore's financial district

KITE FLYING
After the harvest, the people of Malaysia celebrate with the Wau-flying (kite-flying) festival, where skilled people demonstrate the traditional Malaysian sport.

Map labels:

Andaman Sea
THAILAND
South China Sea
Banda Aceh
George Town
Butterworth
Kota Bharu
Sigli
Pulau Pinang
Kuala Terengganu
Langsa
Taiping
Dungun
Meulaboh
Ipoh
Cukai
Medan
Kuala Lipis
Kuantan
Pulau Simeulue
Tebingtinggi
Klang
KUALA LUMPUR
Kepulauan Natuna
Pematangsiantar
PUTRAJAYA
MALAYSIA
Kota Kinabal
BANDAR SERI BEGAWAN
BRUNEI
Miri
Gunung K
Ba
Kepulauan Banyak
Danau Toba
Seremban
Muar
Melaka
Keluang
Selat Serasan
Sibu
Batang Rajang
Bintulu
Sibolga
Batu Pahat
Kuching
Sungai
Pulau Nias
Johor Bahru
SINGAPORE
Sri Aman
Sarawak
Panyabungan
Pekanbaru
Singkawang
Sidas
Pegunungan Muller
Sungai M
Equator
Pontianak
Sungai Kapuas
Solok
Rengat
Kepulauan Lingga
Borneo
Padang
Kualatungkal
Balikpapan
Pulau Siberut
Batang Hari
Jambi
Bangka
Kalimantan
INDIAN OCEAN
Sungaipenuh
Pangkalpinang
Sampit
Sungai Barito
Am
Kepulauan Mentawai
Sumatra (Sumatera)
Palembang
Kandangan
I N D
Lahat
Banjarmasin
Bengkulu
Pulau Belitung
Kotabumi
Java Sea
Bandar Lampung
Cirebon
JAKARTA
Tegal
Pekalongan
Serang
Semarang
Pulau Madura
Selat Sunda
Bogor
Kudus
Sukabumi
Surabaya
Bandung
Java (Jawa)
Probolinggo
Tasikmalaya
Jember
Cilacap
Malang
Matara
Magelang
Kediri
Den
Yogyakarta
Madiun
Surakarta
Selat Karimata
Pulau

A   B   C   D   E   F   G   H

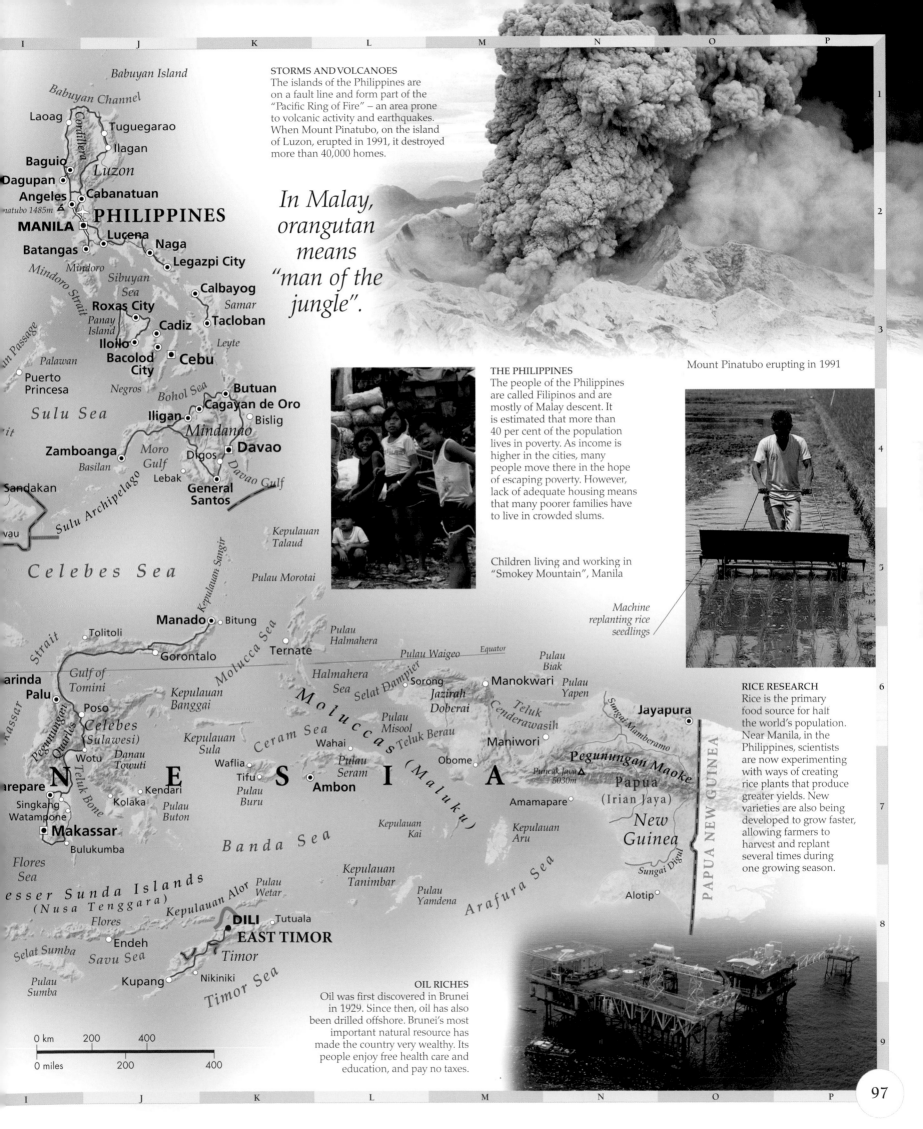

STORMS AND VOLCANOES

The islands of the Philippines are on a fault line and form part of the "Pacific Ring of Fire" – an area prone to volcanic activity and earthquakes. When Mount Pinatubo, on the island of Luzon, erupted in 1991, it destroyed more than 40,000 homes.

In Malay, orangutan means "man of the jungle".

Mount Pinatubo erupting in 1991

THE PHILIPPINES

The people of the Philippines are called Filipinos and are mostly of Malay descent. It is estimated that more than 40 per cent of the population lives in poverty. As income is higher in the cities, many people move there in the hope of escaping poverty. However, lack of adequate housing means that many poorer families have to live in crowded slums.

Children living and working in "Smokey Mountain", Manila

Machine replanting rice seedlings

RICE RESEARCH

Rice is the primary food source for half the world's population. Near Manila, in the Philippines, scientists are now experimenting with ways of creating rice plants that produce greater yields. New varieties are also being developed to grow faster, allowing farmers to harvest and replant several times during one growing season.

OIL RICHES

Oil was first discovered in Brunei in 1929. Since then, oil has also been drilled offshore. Brunei's most important natural resource has made the country very wealthy. Its people enjoy free health care and education, and pay no taxes.

Map labels

Babuyan Island
Babuyan Channel
Laoag
Tuguegarao
Ilagan
Baguio
Cordillera
Luzon
Dagupan
Angeles
Cabanatuan
Pinatubo 1485m
PHILIPPINES
MANILA
Lucena
Naga
Batangas
Legazpi City
Mindoro
Mindoro Strait
Sibuyan Sea
Calbayog
Roxas City
Samar
Panay Island
Cadiz
Tacloban
Iloilo
Cebu
Leyte
Bacolod City
Butuan
Palawan
Negros
Bohol Sea
Cagayan de Oro
Puerto Princesa
Iligan
Bislig
Sulu Sea
Mindanao
Davao
Zamboanga
Moro Gulf
Digos
Basilan
Davao Gulf
Sandakan
Lebak
General Santos
Sulu Archipelago
Kepulauan Talaud
Celebes Sea
Pulau Morotai
Manado
Bitung
Tolitoli
Kepulauan Sangir
Molucca Sea
Pulau Halmahera
Gorontalo
Ternate
Pulau Waigeo
Equator
Pulau Biak
Gulf of Tomini
Halmahera Sea
Selat Dampier
Sorong
Manokwari
Pulau Yapen
Palu
Molucca Sea
Jazirah Doberai
Teluk Cenderawasih
Jayapura
Kepulauan Banggai
Moluccas (Maluku)
Sungai Mamberamo
Celebes (Sulawesi)
Ceram Sea
Pulau Misool
Teluk Berau
Maniwori
Pegunungan Maoke
Poso
Kepulauan Sula
Wahai
Obome
Puncak Jaya 5030m
Papua (Irian Jaya)
Wotu
Danau Towuti
Waflia
Pulau Seram
New Guinea
Kendari
Tifu
Ambon
Amamapare
Kolaka
Pulau Buru
Singkang
Pulau Buton
Kepulauan Kai
Kepulauan Aru
Watampone
Banda Sea
Makassar
PAPUA NEW GUINEA
Bulukumba
Sungai Digul
Flores Sea
Kepulauan Tanimbar
Lesser Sunda Islands (Nusa Tenggara)
Pulau Wetar
Pulau Yamdena
Arafura Sea
Alotip
Kepulauan Alor
Flores
DILI
Tutuala
EAST TIMOR
Endeh
Selat Sumba
Savu Sea
Timor
Kupang
Nikiniki
Timor Sea
Pulau Sumba
INDONESIA

0 km 200 400
0 miles 200 400

Indian Ocean

THE THIRD LARGEST ocean in the world, the Indian Ocean is bounded by Africa, Asia, Australasia, and Antarctica. The ocean contains some 5,000 islands. Madagascar and Sri Lanka are large, but most of the islands are small and ringed by coral reefs. The people of the Maldives have very mixed origins, incorporating Indian, Sinhalese, Arab, and African heritage, while two-thirds of those living on Mauritius are Indian immigrants and their descendents. Altogether, about one-fifth of the world's population live on this ocean's warm shores. Those along the northern coasts are often threatened by monsoon rain and tropical storms, which can cause severe flooding.

THE MALDIVES
The Maldives is a low-lying archipelago of 1,300 small, coral islands, of which 202 are inhabited. The main industries are fishing – still carried out by traditional pole and line methods to conserve stocks – and tourism. Holiday resorts are on separate islands to those inhabited by the locals, so as not to disturb the Maldive peoples' traditional Muslim lifestyles.

CORAL ISLANDS
Coral is a living organism formed in warm water by tiny sea creatures known as polyps. These creatures build limestone skeletons around themselves, which accumulate over thousands of years. As sea levels change, this coral can be exposed as low-lying islands or submerged as reefs.

THE SEYCHELLES
The Seychelles consists of 115 islands – some are coral islands while others are mountainous and made of granite. Most Seychellois people are Creoles – people of mixed African, Asian, and European ancestry. There are also small Chinese and Indian communities.

Market on the largest Seychelles island, Mahé

ENVIRONMENT
Beautiful shells are for sale on this beach in South Africa. If the trader only collects empty shells, no harm is done, but in many parts of the world, dealers hunt live shellfish, sea turtles, and rare species of starfish and sea urchins. Nations such as the Maldives take great care to protect their environment.

LIMITED TOURISM
The tropical climate, sandy beaches, beautiful coral reefs, and abundant marine life make both the Seychelles and the Maldives ideal tourist destinations. These same features also make them extremely attractive to scuba divers. However, the fragile environment of both island nations means that they have deliberately tried to make them exclusive, attracting only limited numbers of wealthy visitors, instead of pursuing mass tourism.

Mediterranean Sea

Arabian Peninsula

Red Sea

Ethiopian Highlands

AFRICA

Somali

COMO

MAYO (to Fra

Mozambique Channel

Davie Ridge

Na Bas

Mozambique Pla

Africana Seamount

Agulhas Basin

Agulhas Plateau

Prince Edward Islan (to South Africa)

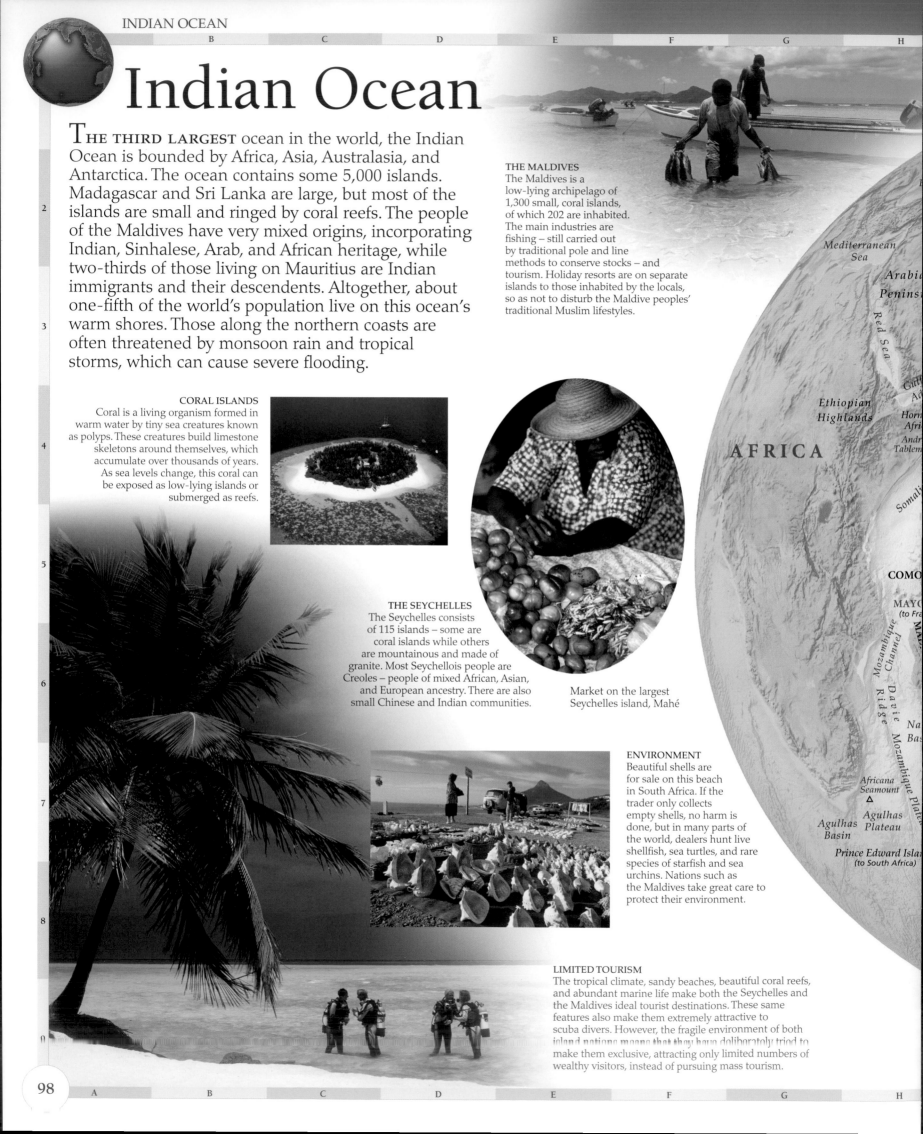

SALT FROM THE SEA
Salt is essential for life and has been traded here for centuries. People around the Indian Ocean make salt by flooding large, flat areas with sea water. As the water evaporates in the sun, salt crystals are left behind. These are then collected, drained, and cleaned.

Collecting salt in the Maldives

MANGROVES
A lot of the coast in the tropical part of the Indian Ocean is fringed with mangrove forests. These amazing trees live in brackish water and have long roots that trap sediment and protect the coast from erosion. Without these trees, settlements and land along the coast are in danger of being damaged by high tides and strong storms.

The moutia dance of the Seychelles was brought to the islands by African slaves in the 1700s.

INTERNATIONAL SEAWAYS
The Indian Ocean contains some of the busiest and most important shipping routes in the world. Smaller ships sail to and from the Mediterranean Sea and the ports of Europe and America through the Red Sea and Suez Canal, while larger freighters and oil tankers from the Persian Gulf sail around the Cape of Good Hope at the southern tip of Africa.

Norwegian freighter

Map labels:

Aral Sea · Caspian Sea · Tien Shan · Gobi · ASIA · Himalayas · Iranian Plateau · Yellow Sea · Gulf of Oman · Murray Ridge · Indus Fan · Ganges Fan · PACIFIC OCEAN · Arabian Sea · Bay of Bengal · Owen Fracture Zone · Arabian Basin · Laccadive Islands (to India) · Andaman Islands (to India) · Carlsberg Ridge · SRI LANKA · Gulf of Thailand · South China Sea · Nicobar Islands (to India) · MALDIVES · MALE · Chagos-Laccadive Plateau · Chagos Trench · Ceylon Plain · Andaman Sea · Sumatra · Borneo · East Indies · Celebes · VICTORIA · SEYCHELLES · Mid-Indian Basin · Cocos Basin · Java Sea · Java · Mid-Indian Ridge · BRITISH INDIAN OCEAN TERRITORY (to UK) · Kepulauan Mentawai · Ninetyeast Ridge · Investigator Ridge · COCOS ISLANDS (to Australia) · CHRISTMAS ISLAND (to Australia) · Java Trench · North Australian Basin · INDIAN · MAURITIUS · Argo Fracture Zone · Wharton Basin · Exmouth Plateau · REUNION (to France) · Egeria Fracture Zone · OCEAN · Cuvier Plateau · AUSTRALASIA & OCEANIA · Madagascar · East Indiaman Ridge · Perth Basin · Broken Ridge · Naturaliste Plateau · Diamantina Fracture Zone · Southwest Indian Ridge · Amsterdam Island · Crozet Basin · St Paul Island · Southeast Indian Ridge · FRENCH SOUTHERN & ANTARCTIC TERRITORIES (to France) · Crozet Islands · Kerguelen Plateau · Kerguelen · HEARD & McDONALD ISLANDS (to Australia) · South Indian Basin · Lena Tablemount · Banzare Seamounts · Enderby Plain · SOUTHERN OCEAN · ANTARCTICA

99

AUSTRALASIA & OCEANIA

Unknown to the outside world before the 17th century, Australia is a still a sparsely inhabited land where most people live in cities. At its heart is a great arid desert, in stark contrast to the islands of Oceania where all life revolves around the glittering ocean. The 3,000 named islands are grouped into nations, listed below in order of land area.

Australia
- 7,741,220 sq km
  2,988,902 sq miles
- 21,300,000
- Canberra
- English, Italian, Cantonese, Greek, Arabic, Vietnamese, Aboriginal languages

The thickly wooded Rock Islands of Palau near the Philippines are ancient reefs raised above sea level, fringed by coral sand beaches and blue lagoons.

Micronesia
- 702 sq km
  271 sq miles
- 110,700
- Palikir
- Trukese, Pohnpeian, Kosraean, Yapese, English

New Zealand
- 267,710 sq km
  103,363 sq miles
- 4,270,000
- Wellington
- English, Maori

Palau
- 459 sq km
  177 sq miles
- 20,400
- Melekeok
- Palauan, English, Japanese, Angaur, Tobi, Sonsorolese

Papa New Guinea
- 462,840 sq km
  178,704 sq miles
- 6,730,000
- Port Moresby
- Pidgin English, Papuan, English, Motu, 800 (est) native languages

Solomon Islands
- 28,896 sq km
  11,157 sq miles
- 523,200
- Honiara
- English, Pidgin English, Melanesian Pidgin, c. 120 other languages

Fiji
- 18,274 sq km
  7,056 sq miles
- 849,200
- Suva
- Fijian, English, Hindi, Urdu, Tamil, Telugu

Vanuatu
- 12,189 sq km
  4,706 sq miles
- 239,800
- Port-Vila
- Bislama (Melanesian Pidgin), English, French, other indigenous languages

Kiribati
- 811 sq km
  313 sq miles
- 99,482
- Bairiki (Tarawa atoll)
- English, Kiribati

Samoa
- 2,831 sq km
  1,093 sq miles
- 178,800
- Apia
- Samoan, English

Tonga
- 747 sq km
  288 sq miles
- 104,000
- Nuku'Alofa
- English, Tongan

Marshall Islands
- 181 sq km
  70 sq miles
- 65,859
- Majuro
- Marshallese, English, Japanese, German

Sydney's iconic Opera House and Harbour Bridge symbolize this Australian city's role as a centre of global culture.

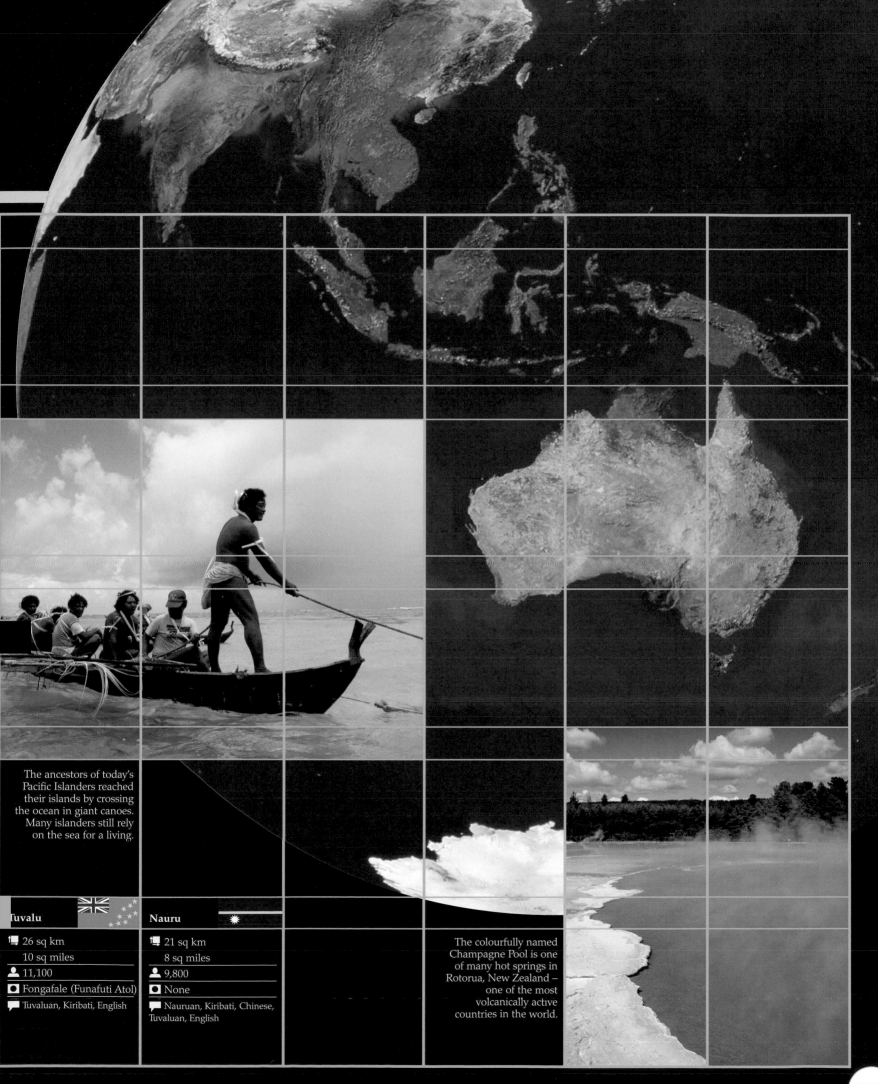

The ancestors of today's Pacific Islanders reached their islands by crossing the ocean in giant canoes. Many islanders still rely on the sea for a living.

The colourfully named Champagne Pool is one of many hot springs in Rotorua, New Zealand – one of the most volcanically active countries in the world.

SW Pacific

THE ISLANDS of the southwest Pacific are home to people of many different cultures and languages. The islands are divided into three general groups based on their location and the similarities between their peoples. The Polynesian islands to the east include Tonga, Samoa, the Cook Islands, and Tahiti. Melanesia includes Fiji, the Solomon Islands, and Vanuatu. The smallest group, Micronesia, includes the Marshall, Kiribati, and Caroline Islands. The first Europeans came to the southwest Pacific in the 1600s, several thousand years after Melanesians, Micronesians, and Polynesians first arrived.

ISLAND HOLIDAYS
White sandy beaches and warm water makes this region ideal for tourists.

NORTHERN MARIANA ISLANDS *(to US)*

Tinian *Saipan*
Rota

✈ **HAGATÑA**
GUAM
(to US)

Enewetak Atoll *Bikini Atoll* *Rongelap Atoll*

MARSHALL ISLAN

Ujelang Atoll
Kwajalein Atoll
Namu Atoll

Yap

MICRONESIA

Babeldaob

MELEKEOK

Chuuk Islands **PALIKIR** ✈
Pohnpei

PALAU

Caroline Islands

Ailinglaplap Atoll

Jaluit A

Kosrae *Ebo Ato*

LAND OF MANY LANGUAGES
Historically, the mountainous landscape of Papua New Guinea made contact between the villages difficult. As a result of many years of isolation, some villages developed their own individual languages. Nationwide, about 800 different languages evolved.

Equator

NAURU

Admiralty Islands *St.Matthias Group*

Bismarck Archipelago
Bismarck Sea *New Ireland*

INDONESIA

PAPUA NEW GUINEA

Central Range *Madang*
Mount Wilhelm 4509m *New Britain* *Bougainville Island*

New Guinea *Lae* *Choiseul*

Owen Stanley Range *Solomon Sea* *Santa Isabel*

SOLOMON

New Georgia Islands *Malaita*

Gulf of Papua

PORT MORESBY ◉ ✈ *D'Entrecasteaux Islands* **HONIARA** ● ✈ **ISLANDS**

Guadalcanal

Louisiade Archipelago *San Cristobal* *Santa Cr Islands*

Rennell

Men in Papua New Guinea wearing traditional make-up

Coral Sea

A MIX OF RELIGIONS
Christianity is the dominant religion on most southwest Pacific islands. However Islam and Hinduism are also practised. Many people also retain beliefs from traditional religions that existed before the islands were colonized by people from Europe and Asia.

CORAL SEA ISLANDS
(to Australia)

Ban Isla

VANUATU

Espiritu Santo
Malekula

PORT-VILA ✈

Beads, shells, and feathers form part of the decoration

NEW CALEDONIA
(to France)

Erromango
Tann An

Ouvéa

New Caledonia *Lifou*

Iles Loyauté

✈ **NOUMÉA**

Tropic of Capricorn

Vanuatu tribespeople dancing at a religious ceremony

FOOD CROPS

Most Pacific Islanders live in small villages near the sea. Inland areas are often mountainous, making farming difficult. Instead, people grow foods such as sweet potatoes, bananas, and coconuts in lowland areas. As well as providing milk, the coconut meat is used to produce copra, a substance for making soap and cosmetics.

Copra worker in Fiji scooping coconut kernels

THE KINGDOM OF TONGA

Tonga is the only Pacific nation never fully brought under foreign rule. Instead, it is run in the traditional way by its own king. All land is owned by the royal family and is allotted to households for their use. Now, some young, westernized Tongans have started calling for more democracy.

The Royal Palace in Tonga

Cook Islands family

FAMILY LIFE

Many Pacific people live in extended family groups. Recently, however, some islanders have migrated to countries such as New Zealand and the United States in order to look for work.

KINGMAN REEF (to US)

PALMYRA ATOLL (to US)

Teraina

Tabuaeran

BAKER & HOWLAND ISLANDS (to US)

JARVIS ISLAND (to US)

Kiritimati (Christmas Island)

International Dateline

PACIFIC OCEAN

BAIRIKI

Tungaru

Beru

Nikunau

Tamana

Arorae

Kanton

Enderbury Island

KIRIBATI

McKean Island

Birnie Island

Orona

Manra

Nikumaroro

KIRIBATI

Phoenix Islands

Mulden Island

Line Islands

Starbuck Island

Nanumea Atoll

Niutao

Nanumaga

Nui Atoll

Nukufetau

Nuku Hiva

Vostok Island

Millennium Island

FONGAFALE

Funafuti Atoll

TUVALU

Nukulaelae

Atafu Atoll

Nukunonu Atoll

Fakaofo Atoll

TOKELAU (to New Zealand)

Penrhyn

Rakahanga

Manihiki

Flint Island

Polynesia

Nuku Hiva

Marquesas Islands

Hiva Oa

Fatu Hiva

Niulakita

WALLIS & FUTUNA (to France)

MATĀ'UTU

Île Uvea

AMERICAN SAMOA (to US)

Northern Cook Islands

Rotuma

Île Futuna

SAMOA

Savai'i

'Upolu

ĀPIA

PAGO PAGO

Ta'ū

Tutuila

COOK ISLANDS (to New Zealand)

Tikehau

Takaroa

Fakarava

Makemo

FIJI

Cikobia

Vanua Levu

Niuatoputapu

Raiatea

PAPEETE

Tuamotu Islands

Amanu

Tatakoto

Nadi

Viti Levu

SUVA

TONGA

Lau Group

NIUE (to New Zealand)

ALOFI

Palmerston

Manuae

Tahiti

Archipel de la Société

Ahunui

Kadavu

Vava'u Group

Tofua

Ha'apai Group

Takutea

Southern Cook Islands

Mangaia

FRENCH POLYNESIA (to France)

Rururu

Tubuai

Vanavana

Marutea

Tureia

NUKU' ALOFA

Tongatapu

'Eua

International Dateline

AVARUA

Rarotonga

Îles Australes

Raevavae

Tropic of Capricorn

Fangataufa

Tongatapu Group

OUTRIGGER CANOES

Transport between many islands has traditionally been by outrigger canoes. Floats attached to the side provide extra stability, particularly useful for the fishermen who stand in the boats to cast their nets.

Islanders netfishing in an outrigger off the coast of Ifalik, Micronesia

Marotiri

0 km	300	600
0 miles	300	600

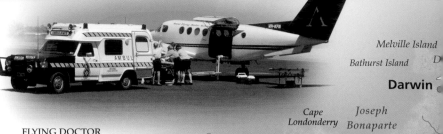

Australia

A HUGE, GENERALLY FLAT COUNTRY, Australia has relatively few inhabitants. This is mainly because most of the land is hot, semi-arid desert – known as the outback – unsuitable for towns or farms. In places where there is some vegetation, or the land has been irrigated, sheep and cattle are grazed. Wheat is grown in the fertile south. The first people to live here were the Aboriginals, who arrived from Asia at least 50,000 years ago. Today, most Australians are descendants of European immigrants, with a more recent addition of Asians.

FLYING DOCTOR
For anyone living in the remote Australian outback, the nearest doctor can be many hours away. When emergency help is needed, the Royal Flying Doctor Services can get to the scene to treat a patient or fly them to hospital.

AUSTRALIAN ABORIGINALS
The original inhabitants of Australia had an intimate understanding of their environment. This connection to the land, and its plants and animals, affects every aspect of their culture. When Europeans started arriving in the late 18th century, only the Aboriginals in remote areas escaped contact with the diseases they brought. Today, Aboriginals rarely live off the land, but work in factories or farms.

MINING
Australia has one of the world's most important mining industries, with resources including gold (left), coal, natural gas, iron ore, copper, and opals. However, damage to the environment, and Aboriginal claims over land used for mining, still need to be faced.

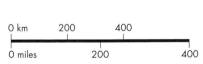

0 km   200   400
0 miles   200   400

AUSTRALIAN FOOTBALL
A popular sport here is Australian Rules Football. One of the rules is that players can kick or punch the ball but they must not throw it. Many Australians either play the game themselves or support their favourite team. As the name implies, the game originated in Australia, but it now has leagues in other countries, such as Great Britain and the USA.

OUTDOOR SPORTS
A warm climate, with easy access to beaches and wilderness areas, has made outdoor activities an important part of modern Australian life. Water sports, such as swimming, sailing, and surfing, are especially popular. Because of the danger of exposure to strong sunlight, people are told to cover up and always use sunscreen.

Melville Island
Bathurst Island
Darwin
Cape Londonderry
Joseph Bonaparte Gulf
Pine
Bonaparte Archipelago
Bigge Island
Wyndham
Victoria R.
Heywood Islands
Kununurra
Top Sp
Roadh
King Sound
Kimberley Plateau
Broome
Fitzroy Crossing
Halls Creek
Tana
Fitzroy River
Desc
INDIAN OCEAN
Eighty Mile Beach
Great Sandy Desert
Barrow Island
Dampier
Port Hedland
Percival Lakes
T
Exmouth Gulf
Onslow
Marble Bar
Fortescue River
Exmouth
Hamersley Range
WESTERN
Lake Mackay
Ma
Ashburton River
Newman
Tropic of Capricorn
Barlee Range
Lake Disappointment
A U S T
Gibson Desert
Lake Amadeus
Bernier Island
Gascoyne River
Uluru (Ayers Rock) 867m
Dorre Island
Carnarvon
Shark Bay
Denham
Murchison River
Robinson Range
Lake Carnegie
Dirk Hartog Island
Lake Wells
Musgrave Ra
Meekatharra
AUSTRALIA
Kalbarri
Mount Magnet
Great Victoria Desert
Lake Carey
Geraldton
Lake Barlee
Lake Moore
Lake Rebecca
Kalgoorlie
Zanthus
Reid
Moora
Southern Cross
Coolgardie
Nullarbor Plain
Gingin
Merredin
Lake Cowan
Eucla
Perth
Northam
Norseman
Fremantle
Brookton
Balladonia
Mandurah
Narrogin
Bunbury
Wagin
Collie
Katanning
Esperance
Great Australian Big
Busselton
Manjimup
Augusta
Albany

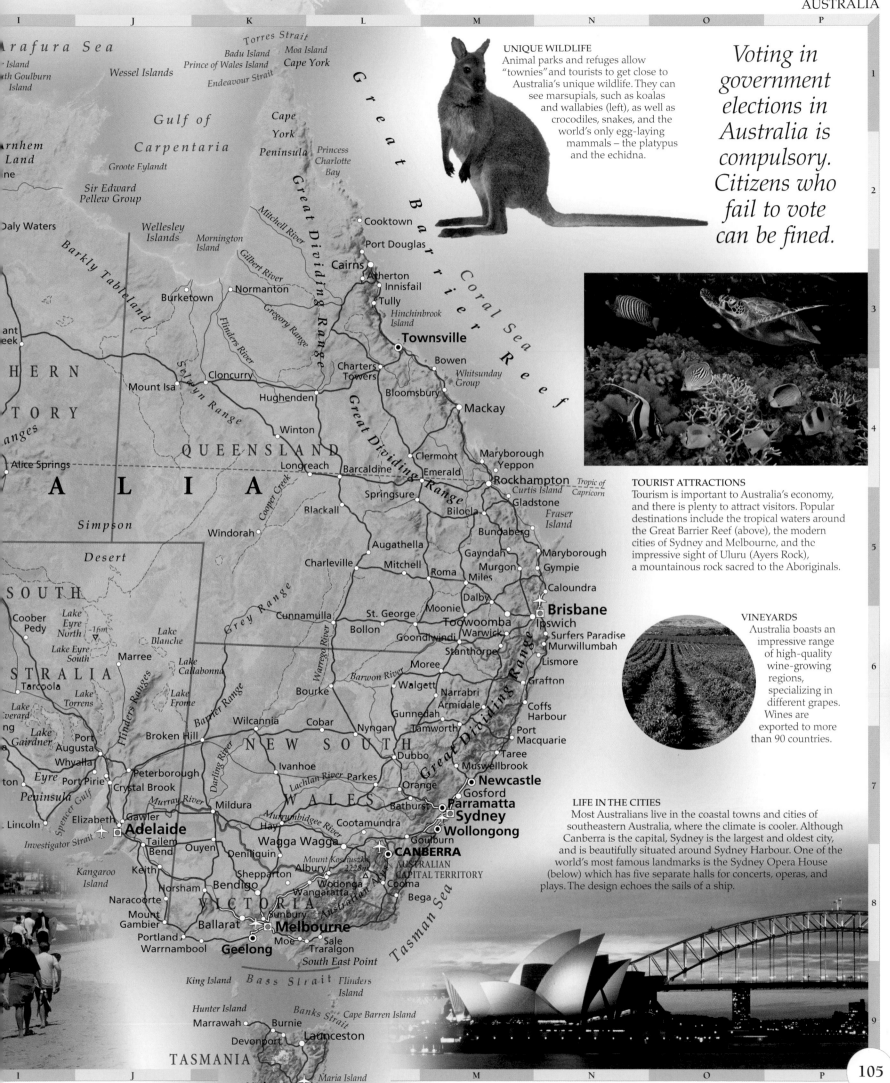

| | I | J | K | L | M | N | O | P |

Arafura Sea

Torres Strait
Badu Island   Moa Island
Prince of Wales Island   Cape York
Endeavour Strait

Wessel Islands

Island
th Goulburn
Island

Gulf of

Carpentaria

Sir Edward
Pellew Group

Groote Eylandt

Daly Waters

rnhem
Land
ne

ant
eek

Barkly Tableland

Wellesley
Islands

Mornington
Island

Cape
York
Peninsula

Princess
Charlotte
Bay

Cooktown

Port Douglas

Cairns

Atherton
Innisfail

Tully

Hinchinbrook
Island

Townsville

Bowen

Whitsunday
Group

Mackay

Burketown

Normanton

Gilbert River

Gregory Range

Mitchell River

Great Dividing Range

Great Barrier Coral Sea Reef

Cloncurry

Flinders River

Charters
Towers

Mount Isa

Hughenden

Selwyn Range

QUEENSLAND

Winton

Bloomsbury

Clermont

Maryborough
Yeppon

A L I A

Alice Springs

Longreach

Barcaldine

Emerald

Rockhampton

Tropic of
Capricorn

Curtis Island

Gladstone

Great Dividing Range

nges

Springsure

Biloela

Simpson

Blackall

Cooper Creek

Windorah

Augathella

Bundaberg

Fraser
Island

Desert

Charleville

Mitchell

Gayndah

Maryborough

SOUTH

Murgon
Miles

Gympie

Roma

Caloundra

Lake
Eyre
North

−16m

Coober
Pedy

Lake
Blanche

Grey Range

Cunnamulla

St. George

Moonie

Dalby

Toowoomba

Brisbane

Ipswich

Lake Eyre
South

Lake
Callabonna

Bollon

Goondiwindi

Warwick

Surfers Paradise

Murwillumbah

STRALIA

Marree

Lake
Frome

Warrego River

Moree

Stanthorpe

Lismore

Tarcoola

Flinders Ranges

Barwon River

Walgett

Narrabri

Grafton

Lake
everard
ng

Lake
Torrens

Barrier Range

Bourke

Armidale

Coffs
Harbour

Lake
Gairdner

Wilcannia

Cobar

Gunnedah

Port
Macquarie

Port
Augusta

Broken Hill

NEW SOUTH

Tamworth

Whyalla

Peterborough

Ivanhoe

Nyngan

Taree

Eyre

Port Pirie

Crystal Brook

Darling River

Parkes

Dubbo

Great Dividing Range

Muswellbrook

ton

Peninsula

Lachlan River

Orange

Newcastle

Lincoln

Elizabeth

Gawler

Murray River

Mildura

Hay

Bathurst

WALES

Gosford
Parramatta

Sydney

Spencer Gulf

Adelaide

Tailem
Bend

Ouyen

Deniliquin

Murrumbidgee River

Cootamundra

Goulburn

Wollongong

Investigator Strait

Keith

Shepparton

Albury

Mount Kosciuszko
2228m

CANBERRA

AUSTRALIAN
CAPITAL TERRITORY

Kangaroo
Island

Horsham

Bendigo

Wodonga
Wangaratta

Cooma

Naracoorte

Ballarat

VICTORIA

Sunbury

Australian Alps

Bega

Mount
Gambier

Portland

Moe

Melbourne

Sale
Traralgon

Tasman Sea

Warrnambool

Geelong

South East Point

King Island

Bass Strait

Flinders
Island

Hunter Island

Banks Strait

Cape Barren Island

Marrawah

Burnie

Launceston

Devonport

TASMANIA

Hobart

Maria Island

UNIQUE WILDLIFE
Animal parks and refuges allow
"townies" and tourists to get close to
Australia's unique wildlife. They can
see marsupials, such as koalas
and wallabies (left), as well as
crocodiles, snakes, and the
world's only egg-laying
mammals – the platypus
and the echidna.

Voting in
government
elections in
Australia is
compulsory.
Citizens who
fail to vote
can be fined.

TOURIST ATTRACTIONS
Tourism is important to Australia's economy,
and there is plenty to attract visitors. Popular
destinations include the tropical waters around
the Great Barrier Reef (above), the modern
cities of Sydney and Melbourne, and the
impressive sight of Uluru (Ayers Rock),
a mountainous rock sacred to the Aboriginals.

VINEYARDS
Australia boasts an
impressive range
of high-quality
wine-growing
regions,
specializing in
different grapes.
Wines are
exported to more
than 90 countries.

LIFE IN THE CITIES
Most Australians live in the coastal towns and cities of
southeastern Australia, where the climate is cooler. Although
Canberra is the capital, Sydney is the largest and oldest city,
and is beautifully situated around Sydney Harbour. One of the
world's most famous landmarks is the Sydney Opera House
(below) which has five separate halls for concerts, operas, and
plays. The design echoes the sails of a ship.

New Zealand

MADE UP OF TWO MAIN ISLANDS and several smaller ones, New Zealand is one of the most isolated countries in the world. Located in the southern Pacific, the country has a mild climate, with warm summers and cool, wet winters. Both main islands have mountains, short, swift-flowing rivers, forests, and fertile farmland. Until the Europeans arrived, most of the landscape was covered in dense forest, known as native bush. Today, although forests remain, much has been cleared for farming. Most New Zealanders live on North Island, which is warmer and less mountainous. Although New Zealanders are of mainly British descent, the Maoris – a people of Polynesian origin – were the first to arrive about 1,000 years ago. Today, non-Maori Polynesians and Asians are adding to the ethnic mix. The country has a liberal, clean, green image and a high standard of living.

AUCKLAND
With its safe harbour and nearby scenic islands, Auckland is known as the "city of sails". It boasts more pleasure boats per person than anywhere else in the world. The water that separates the bigger islands is home to dolphins, families of blue penguins, and the occasional whale.

MAORI CULTURE
Maoris make up almost 16 per cent of the population, with most living on North Island. Before the coming of the *Pakeha* (white man), Maori history was passed on orally to succeeding generations. This included many legends and *waiata* (songs). Their carvings in wood (left) and stone (right) were another way they recorded and remembered events. In recent years, interest in Maori culture has increased, and school children are now taught the Maori language.

Greenstone (jade) carving, an example of Maori art

In 1893, New Zealand was the first country to give women the vote.

PACIFIC OCEAN

Tasman Sea

North Island

0 km   50   100
0 miles   50   100

FILM INDUSTRY
New Zealand has a well-established film industry. Today, thanks to the acclaimed Tolkien trilogy, *Lord of the Rings* (above), the country has become increasingly popular with international studios for location work. The country offers an unusually wide range of scenery as well as technical experts.

AN AGRICULTURAL NATION
Agriculture is of prime importance, and accounts for more than half of national export earnings. Orchards produce a vast range of fruit from apples (above) to kiwi fruit (below). Cereals and other crops, such as sunflowers, add colour and variety to the landscape. Traditional sheep and cattle farming has expanded to include deer, goats, and even ostriches.

UNIQUE WILDLIFE
New Zealand has many unique and endangered animal species, especially birds. There were no mammal predators before humans introduced them, so many animal species have few means of defence, and some birds such as the kiwi cannot fly. Conservation schemes are now in place to protect endangered species.

Flightless Kiwi bird

VOLCANIC ACTIVITY
A fault line runs through New Zealand, where two major tectonic plates meet. It has caused devastating earthquakes, but has also helped to create breathtaking scenery. This includes South Island's Southern Alps, and many smaller volcanic mountains, hot springs, and geysers on North Island.

Lady Knox geyser, North Island

GREEN ENERGY
Most of the country's electricity comes from hydroelectric power. It is generated by river water gushing through turbines inside dams at power stations. New Zealand also has geothermal energy, using heat from inside Earth.

ADVENTURE SPORTS PARADISE
New Zealand offers a huge range of adventure sports and outdoor activities, from white-water rafting (below) to bungee jumping. The latter originated in Queenstown on South Island. The town is billed as the country's top adventure tourism destination because its surrounding lakes, mountains, and rivers, and its mostly dry climate, are ideal for outdoor pursuits.

Pacific Ocean

THE LARGEST OCEAN ON EARTH, the Pacific covers one-third of Earth's surface. The island nations of Japan, Indonesia, Australia, New Zealand, and many others are completely surrounded by this enormous ocean, which stretches from the Arctic in the north to the Antarctic in the south. The Pacific is also the world's deepest ocean – its greatest known depth is in the Mariana Trench, off Guam, which plunges steeply for 11,033 m (36,198 ft). Within the Pacific, there are many smaller seas that lie near land. These include the Tasman Sea, the South China Sea, and the Bering Sea. There are more than 30,000 islands in the Pacific. Most are too small or barren to be inhabited, but others are home to people of many different cultures and religions. The native island peoples fall into three main groups – Polynesians, Melanesians, and Micronesians. Although the word *pacific* means "peaceful", strong currents, tropical storms, and tsunamis can all make this ocean far from peaceful.

HAWAII
This chain of eight volcanic islands and 124 islets forms the 50th state of the United States of America, and was admitted to the union in 1959. The dramatic landscape and palm-fringed beaches make Hawaii a popular destination for tourists. Today, native Hawaiians are a minority in their own land.

Hawaiian conch shells, once blown to sound a warning

Marine iguana on black volcanic rocks, Galápagos Islands

GALÁPAGOS ISLANDS
When British naturalist Charles Darwin (1809–1882) went to the Galápagos Islands, he found many unusual animals. He also noticed differences between animals of the same species living elsewhere. This led him to believe that, over time, animals adapt, or evolve, to suit their habitats.

TSUNAMI
Earthquakes beneath the sea may cause giant waves called tsunamis. These can travel great distances across the ocean, building into a huge wall of water as they approach the coast. They can leave immense damage in their wake.

SURFING
The Hawaiian sport of surfing ranks as the oldest sport in the USA. It was first practised by the nobility as a form of religious ceremony until the 1820s when missionaries, who thought it immoral, tried to ban it. Today, surfing is one of the most popular watersports and can be seen all over the world, from Australia to the UK.

Black smoker chimney

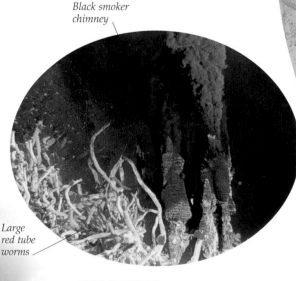

Large red tube worms

DEEP-SEA VENTS
Underwater exploration has revealed some amazing places deep in the Pacific. Large vents, formed by solidified minerals, act as chimneys for super-hot steam and gas that stream up from the sea bed. These vents are known as black smokers. Scientists have found a host of new creatures living in this hostile environment

ASIA

Sea of Japan (East Sea)

Japan

Yellow Sea

East China Sea

Ryukyu Trench

Shikoku Basin

Emperor Seamounts

Taiwan

Philippine Sea

NORTHERN MARIANA ISLANDS (to US)

South China Basin

Philippine Basin

GUAM (to US)

▽ Challenger Deep 11,034m

Philippines

PALAU

Caroline Islands

MICR

South China Sea

Celebes Sea

M

Borneo

Celebes

East Indies

New Guinea

Java Sea

Banda Sea

Java

Timor

Timor Sea

Arafura Sea

Torres Strait

Gr

INDIAN OCEAN

AUSTRALASIA & OCEANIA

Great Australian Bight

South Australian Basin

Bas Tas

The Pacific is larger than Earth's entire land surface.

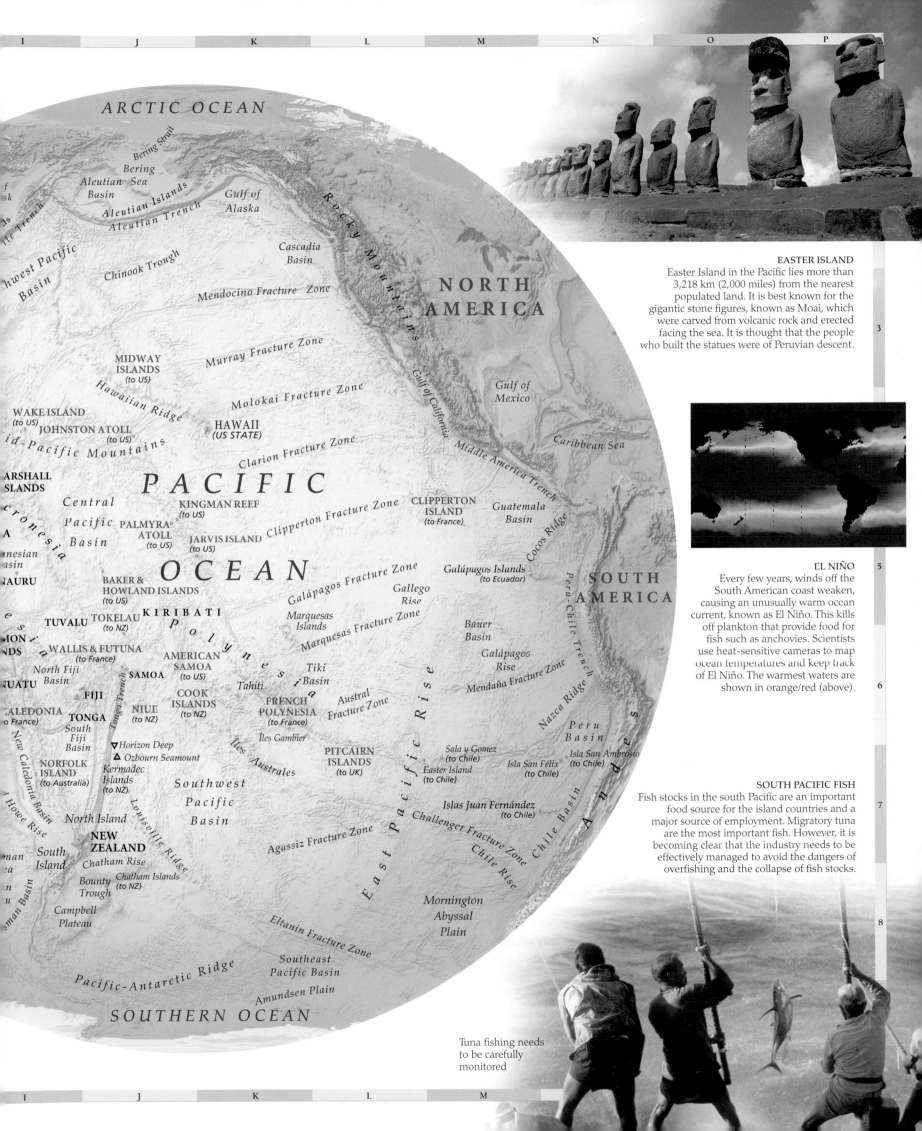

Map labels:

ARCTIC OCEAN

Bering Strait
Bering Sea
Aleutian Basin
Aleutian Islands
Aleutian Trench
Gulf of Alaska
Rocky Mountains

NORTH AMERICA

Northwest Pacific Basin
Chinook Trough
Cascadia Basin
Mendocino Fracture Zone
Murray Fracture Zone
MIDWAY ISLANDS (to US)
Hawaiian Ridge
Molokai Fracture Zone
WAKE ISLAND (to US)
JOHNSTON ATOLL (to US)
HAWAII (US STATE)
Mid-Pacific Mountains
Clarion Fracture Zone
Gulf of California
Gulf of Mexico
Caribbean Sea
Middle America Trench

MARSHALL ISLANDS
Central Pacific Basin
KINGMAN REEF (to US)
PALMYRA ATOLL (to US)
JARVIS ISLAND (to US)
Clipperton Fracture Zone
CLIPPERTON ISLAND (to France)
Guatemala Basin
Cocos Ridge

PACIFIC OCEAN

Micronesia
Melanesian Basin
NAURU
BAKER & HOWLAND ISLANDS (to US)
Galápagos Fracture Zone
Gallego Rise
Galápagos Islands (to Ecuador)
SOUTH AMERICA

TUVALU
TOKELAU (to NZ)
KIRIBATI
Polynesia
Marquesas Islands
Marquesas Fracture Zone
Bauer Basin
Galápagos Rise
Peru-Chile Trench

WALLIS & FUTUNA (to France)
AMERICAN SAMOA (to US)
Tiki Basin
Mendaña Fracture Zone

North Fiji Basin
SAMOA
Tonga Trench
Tahiti
COOK ISLANDS (to NZ)
FRENCH POLYNESIA (to France)
Austral Fracture Zone

FIJI
NIUE (to NZ)
VANUATU

CALEDONIA (to France)
TONGA
South Fiji Basin
Horizon Deep
Ozbourn Seamount
Iles Gambier
PITCAIRN ISLANDS (to UK)
Sala y Gomez (to Chile)
Easter Island (to Chile)
Isla San Félix (to Chile)
Isla San Ambrosio (to Chile)
Nazca Ridge
Peru Basin

NORFOLK ISLAND (to Australia)
Kermadec Islands (to NZ)
Iles Australes
East Pacific Rise
Islas Juan Fernández (to Chile)
Challenger Fracture Zone
Chile Basin
Andes

Lord Howe Rise
New Caledonia Basin
Louisville Ridge
Southwest Pacific Basin
Agassiz Fracture Zone
Chile Rise

NEW ZEALAND
North Island
South Island
Chatham Rise
Chatham Islands (to NZ)
Bounty Trough
Campbell Plateau
Eltanin Fracture Zone
Mornington Abyssal Plain

Tasman Basin
Southeast Pacific Basin
Amundsen Plain
Pacific-Antarctic Ridge

SOUTHERN OCEAN

EASTER ISLAND
Easter Island in the Pacific lies more than 3,218 km (2,000 miles) from the nearest populated land. It is best known for the gigantic stone figures, known as Moai, which were carved from volcanic rock and erected facing the sea. It is thought that the people who built the statues were of Peruvian descent.

EL NIÑO
Every few years, winds off the South American coast weaken, causing an unusually warm ocean current, known as El Niño. This kills off plankton that provide food for fish such as anchovies. Scientists use heat-sensitive cameras to map ocean temperatures and keep track of El Niño. The warmest waters are shown in orange/red (above).

SOUTH PACIFIC FISH
Fish stocks in the south Pacific are an important food source for the island countries and a major source of employment. Migratory tuna are the most important fish. However, it is becoming clear that the industry needs to be effectively managed to avoid the dangers of overfishing and the collapse of fish stocks.

Tuna fishing needs to be carefully monitored

Antarctica

THE FROZEN CONTINENT OF ANTARCTICA is covered by a vast icecap, many thousands of years old, and surrounded by the freezing seas of the Southern Ocean. It is the only continent with no permanent inhabitants – the only people who come here are scientists or tourists. Although the land is rich in oil and minerals, mining is prohibited under the laws of the Antarctic Treaty. This Treaty, agreed by 45 countries, made Antarctica a "continent for science" to be used for peaceful purposes only.

DAY TRIPPERS
Tourists visit Antarctica in summer. There are no resorts, so visitors generally stay on small cruise ships. When they come ashore, people have to wear insulated clothing and goggles to protect their eyes from glare off the ice.

OZONE HOLE
High in the atmosphere, ozone (a gas) forms a natural shield that protects us from the Sun's ultraviolet rays. Scientists at both poles have found holes in the ozone layer, caused by chemicals known as CFCs, once used in aerosols, fridges, and plastic packaging.

RESEARCH
The only people who stay in Antarctica are scientists. They come to study the climate, weather, and geology. By taking ice samples, for example, they can learn about changes in the world's climate over the years.

Scientist checking an ice core

KRILL
Tiny, shrimp-like creatures, krill are the primary food source for a great number of Antarctic animals. These include whales, seals, penguins, squid, and fish.

Antarctica is actually a desert.

FLOATING ICE
Icebergs are giant chunks of floating ice that break away, or calve, from ice sheets or glaciers. Most of their mass lies hidden below sea level.

Emperor penguins huddling for warmth

PENGUINS
Penguins walk awkwardly on land, but can swim swiftly to catch fish. Waterproof feathers and a thick layer of fat help keep them warm.

Map labels

SOUTHERN OCEAN

Orcadas (Argentina)
South Orkney Islands
Signy (UK)
South Shetland Islands
Esperanza (Argentina)
Capitán Arturo Prat (Chile)
Palmer (US)
Rothera (UK)
San Martin (Argentina)
Drake Passage
Antarctic Peninsula
Graham Land
Palmer Land
Weddell Sea
Ronne Ice Shelf
Berkner Island
Sanae (South Africa)
Georg von Neumayer (Germany)
Novolazarevskaya (Russian Federation)
Dronning Maud Land
Lützow Holmbukta
Syowa (Japan)
Molodezhnaya (Russian Federation)
Enderby Land
Mawson (Australia)
Halley (UK)
Coats Land
Belgrano II (Argentina)
Cape Darnley
Mackenzie Bay
Prydz Bay
Princess Elizabeth Land
Davis (Australia)
ANTARCTICA
Bellingshausen Sea
PETER I ISLAND (to Norway)
Vinson Massif 4897m
Ellsworth Land
West Antarctica
Transantarctic Mountains
Amundsen-Scott (US)
South Pole
East Antarctica
Mirny (Russ. Fed.)
Vostok (Russian Federation)
Shackleton Ice Shelf
Marie Byrd Land
Mount Kirkpatrick 4528m
Mount Markham 4351m
Mount Sidley 4181m
Amundsen Sea
Mount Siple 3100m
Roosevelt Island
Ross Ice Shelf
Scott Base (NZ)
McMurdo Base (US)
Mount Erebus 3794m
Ross Sea
Victoria Land
Wilkes Land
Casey (Australia)
Cape Poinsett
Terre Adélie
SOUTHERN OCEAN
Cape Adare
Leningradskaya (Russian Federation)
George V Land
Dumont d'Urville (France)
South Geomagnetic Pole
Antarctic Circle
Balleny Islands

0 km — 500
0 miles — 500

Arctic Ocean

THE SMALLEST OF THE WORLD'S oceans, the Arctic is almost entirely surrounded by the northern edges of North America, Europe, and Asia. For most of the year, its waters are covered by a thick sheet of ice, although warmer currents from the Pacific and Atlantic melt the ice along the continental coasts for a short time in summer. Despite the harsh conditions, the region is home to a range of wildlife, such as reindeer, musk ox, foxes, and wolves. Some people, including the Inuit of Canada and the Sami of northern Scandinavia, have also adapted to this tough environment.

LONG DAYS
Seasons at the poles are extreme. Polar summers are short but there can be sunshine for 24 hours a "day" as the Sun never dips below the horizon (above). This is because Earth rotates at an angle to the Sun.

ALASKAN OIL
Reserves of oil and gas in the Beaufort Sea, off the coast of Alaska, have attracted interest However, the introduction of ships and oil platforms brings problems. In a bid to protect the area, several environmental organizations are actively working to prevent drilling for more oil in this area.

Walruses breed off the Arctic coasts.

0 km 250 500
0 miles 250 500

ARCTIC SURVIVORS
Polar bears live along the Arctic coasts of Canada, Greenland, and Russia. They hunt seals and fish at points where the sea ice melts. With so much Arctic ice having melted away in recent years, the polar bear's habitat is slowly disappearing. An insulating layer of fat, called blubber, helps the bears survive the cold. Their white fur also provides essential camouflage on the ice.

NORTHERN LIGHTS
In midwinter, the north polar skies are sometimes lit up by dramatic curtains of red and green light. Known as the northern lights, these special effects are caused by disturbances in the upper atmosphere. The same happens near Antarctica, where the effect is called the southern lights.

Bering Strait
Arctic Circle
Chukchi Sea
Ostrov Vrangelya
East Siberian Sea
Beaufort Sea
Amundsen Gulf
Banks Island
Victoria Island
Melville Island
CANADA
Queen Elizabeth Islands
North Geomagnetic Pole
ARCTIC
North Pole
OCEAN
Ellesmere Island
Lancaster Sound
Nares Strait
Lincoln Sea
Knud Rasmussen Land
Kap Morris Jesup
Baffin Bay
Wandel Sea
Kong Frederik VIII Land
SVALBARD (to Norway)
Spitsbergen
LONGYEARBYEN
NUUK
GREENLAND (to Denmark)
Arctic Circle
Kong Christian IX Land
Greenland Sea
Bjørnøya (to Norway)
Barents Sea
JAN MAYEN (to Norway)
Norwegian Sea
Denmark Strait
ICELAND
REYKJAVÍK
Novosibirskiye Ostrova
RUSSIAN FEDERATION
Laptev Sea
Severnaya Zemlya
Franz Josef Land
Kara Sea

Gazetteer

HOW TO USE THE GAZETTEER

This gazetteer is a selection of the names in *Children's World Atlas*, and can be used to help you find places on the maps. For example, to find the city of Lisbon in Portugal, look up its name in the gazetteer. The entry reads:

Lisbon *Capital* Portugal 58 E6

The first number, 58, tells you that Lisbon appears on the map on page 58. The second number, E6, shows that it is in square E6. Turn to page 58. Trace down from the letter E along the top of the grid (or up from the letter E on the bottom of the grid), and then across from the number 6 on the side of the grid. You will find Lisbon in the area where the letter and number meet.

A

Aachen *Town* Germany 56 B7
Aalborg *Town* Denmark 49 B11
Aalen *Town* Germany 57 E9
Aalst *Town* Belgium 53 D11
Aalter *Town* Belgium 53 C10
Äänekoski *Town* Finland 48 G8
Aba *Town* Nigeria 41 L8
Aba *Town* Democratic Republic of Congo 42 I8
Ābādān *Town* Iran 82 E7
Abakan *Town* Russian Federation 78 H7
Abbeville *Town* France 54 E5
Abéché *Town* Chad 42 F6
Abengourou *Town* Côte d'Ivoire 41 I8
Aberdeen *Town* South Dakota, USA 12 G4
Aberdeen *Town* Maryland, USA 9 H8
Aberdeen *Town* Scotland, UK 50 F5
Aberystwyth *Town* Wales, UK 51 E10
Abhā *Town* Saudi Arabia 83 C11
Abidjan *Town* Côte d'Ivoire 40 H8
Abilene *Town* Texas, USA 17 K5
Åbo *see* Turku
Abomey *Town* Benin 41 J7
Abrantes *Town* Portugal 58 F6
Abu Dhabi *Capital* United Arab Emirates 83 F9
Abu Hamed *Town* Sudan 38 E6
Abuja *Capital* Nigeria 41 L7
Abū Kamāl *Town* Syria 80 I7
Abū Ẓaby *see* Abu Dhabi
Acapulco *Town* Mexico 19 J9
Acarigua *Town* Venezuela 26 D5
Accra *Capital* Ghana 41 I8
Aconcagua, Cerro *Mountain range* Argentina 30 D7
A Coruña *Town* Spain 58 E2
Açu *Town* Brazil 29 M3
Adamawa Highlands *Mountain range* Cameroon 42 D8
'Adan *see* Aden
Adana *Town* Turkey 76 G6
Adapazari *Town* Turkey 76 E4
Ad Dahnā' *Desert* Saudi Arabia 83 E9
Ad Dakhla *Town* Western Sahara 36 C7
Ad Dammām *Town* Saudi Arabia 83 E9
Ad Dawḥah *see* Doha
Addis Ababa *Capital* Ethiopia 39 F9
Adelaide *Town* South Australia, Australia 105 J7
Aden *Town* Yemen 83 D13
Aden, Gulf of *Indian Ocean* 83 E13
Adirondack Mountains New York, USA 8 H4
Ādīs Ābeba *see* Addis Ababa
Adiyaman *Town* Turkey 76 H6
Adrar *Town* Algeria 36 G6
Aegean Sea Greece 67 F9
Afghanistan *Country* 84 H7
Afmadow *Town* Somalia 39 G11
Afyon *Town* Turkey 76 E5
Agadez *Town* Niger 41 L4
Agadir *Town* Morocco 36 E5
Agen *Town* France 55 D10
Agialoúsa *Town* Cyprus 80 B7
Āgra *Town* India 87 I3
Ağri *Town* Turkey 77 K4
Agrigento *Town* Sicily, Italy 61 E13
Agropoli *Town* Italy 61 F10
Aguachica *Town* Colombia 26 C5
Agua Prieta *Town* Mexico 18 F3
Aguascalientes *Town* Mexico 19 I7
Aguaytía *Town* Peru 27 B10
Aguilas *Town* Spain 59 J8
Aguililla *Town* Mexico 19 I8
Ahaggar *Mountain range* Algeria 37 I7
Ahlen *Town* Germany 56 C7
Ahmadābād *Town* India 86 G4
Ahuachapán *Town* El Salvador 22 E5
Ahvāz *Town* Iran 82 E7
Aiken *Town* South Carolina, USA 11 J4
Ailigandí *Town* Panama 23 N7
'Aïn Ben Tili *Town* Mauritania 40 G2
Aiquile *Town* Bolivia 27 E12
Aïr, Massif de l' *Mountain range* Niger 41 L4
Aix-en-Provence *Town* France 55 G11
Aizu *Town* Japan 93 G9
Ajaccio *Town* France 55 I13
Ajo *Town* Arizona, USA 16 E5
Akchâr *Desert* Mauritania 40 E3
Akhalts'ikhe *Town* Georgia 77 K3
Akhisar *Town* Turkey 76 C5
Akhtubinsk *Town* Russian Federation 73 D11
Akita *Town* Japan 92 F8
Akjoujt *Town* Mauritania 40 E3
Akkeshi *Town* Japan 92 H5
Akron *Town* Ohio, USA 13 M6
Akrotírion *Town* Cyprus 80 A8
Aksai Chin *Administrative region* China 88 D6
Aksaray *Town* Turkey 76 F5
Akşehir *Town* Turkey 76 E5
Aktau *Town* Kazakhstan 78 D6
Aktobe *Town* Kazakhstan 78 E6
Aktsyabrski *Town* Belarus 71 F11
Akula *Town* Democratic Republic of Congo 43 F9
Akune *Town* Japan 93 B14
Alabama *State* USA 10 G5
Alabama River Alabama, USA 10 G6
Al 'Amārah *Town* Iraq 82 D7
Alamo *Town* Nevada, USA 14 H7
Alamogordo *Town* New Mexico, USA 16 H5
Åland *Island group* Finland 49 F9
Alanya *Town* Turkey 76 E7
Al 'Aqabah *Town* Jordan 81 D14
Alaşehir *Town* Turkey 76 D5
Alaska *Province* Canada 4 E5
Alaska, Gulf of Alaska, USA 4 E6
Alaska Range *Mountain Range* Alaska, USA 4 E5
Albacete *Town* Spain 59 J6
Alba Iulia *Town* Romania 68 E6
Albania *Country* 65 F12
Albany *River* Ontario, Canada 6 F5
Albany *Town* Western Australia, Australia 104 E7
Albany *Town* Georgia, USA 10 H6
Albany *Town* New York, USA 9 I5
Al Bāridah *Town* Syria 80 F8
Al Baṣrah *Town* Iraq 82 D7
Alberta *Province* Canada 4 H7
Albert, Lake Democratic Republic of Congo 43 I9
Albuquerque *Town* New Mexico, USA 16 H1
Alcañiz *Town* Spain 59 K5
Alcoy *Town* Spain 59 K7
Alderney *Island* Channel Islands, UK 51 G13
Aleksin *Town* Russian Federation 73 C9
Alençon *Town* France 54 D7
Alenquer *Town* Brazil 29 I2
Aleppo *Town* Syria 80 E6
Alessandria *Town* Italy 60 C5
Aleutian Islands *Island Group* Alaska, USA 4 B5
Alexander Archipelago *Island* British Colombia, Canada 4 E7
Alexandria *Town* Louisiana, USA 10 E6
Alexandria *Town* Egypt 38 D4
Alexandria *Town* Romania 68 F7
Alexandroúpoli *Town* Greece 66 G8
Alga *Town* Kazakhstan 78 E6
Algarve *Region* Spain 58 E8
Algeciras *Town* Spain 58 G9
Alger *see* Algiers
Algeria *Country* 36 H5
Al Ghābah *Town* Oman 83 G10
Algiers *Capital* Algeria 36 H3
Algona *Town* Iowa, USA 12 H5
Al Ḥasakah *Town* Syria 80 H5
Al Ḥillah *Town* Iraq 82 D7
Al Ḥudaydah *see* Hodeida
Al Ḥufūf *Town* Saudi Arabia 83 E9
Alíartos *Town* Greece 67 E11
Alicante *Town* Spain 59 J6
Alice Springs *Town* Northern Territory, Australia 105 I4
Aliquippa *Town* Pennsylvania, USA 8 E7
Al Ismā'īlīya *Town* Egypt 38 E4
Al Jafr *Town* Jordan 81 E12
Al Jaghbūb *Town* Libya 37 N5
Al Jahrā' *Town* Kuwait 82 D8
Al Jawf *Town* Saudi Arabia 82 B8
Al Jazīrah *Physical region* Syria/Iraq 80 I5
Al Karak *Town* Jordan 81 E12
Al Khums *Town* Libya 37 K4
Alkmaar *Town* Netherlands 52 E7
Al Kufrah *Town* Libya 37 N7
Al Kūt *Town* Iraq 82 D7
Al Kuwayt *see* Kuwait
Allāhābād *Town* India 87 I4
Allegheny Plateau Pennsylvania/New York, USA 8 F6
Allentown *Town* Pennsylvania, USA 9 H7
Al Līth *Town* Saudi Arabia 83 B11
Alma-Ata *see* Almaty
Al Madīnah *see* Medina
Al Mafraq *Town* Jordan 81 E10
Al Majma'ah *Town* Saudi Arabia 83 D9
Al Mālikīyah *Town* Syria 80 I4
Al Manāmah *see* Manama
Almansa *Town* Spain 59 K7
Al Marj *Town* Libya 37 M4
Almaty *Town* Kazakhstan 78 G8
Al Mawṣil *see* Mosul
Al Mayādīn *Town* Syria 80 H6
Almelo *Town* Netherlands 52 G8
Almere *Town* Netherlands 52 F8
Almería *Town* Spain 59 J8
Al'met'yevsk *Town* Russian Federation 73 F9
Al Minyā *Town* Egypt 38 D4
Almirante *Town* Panama 23 K8
Al Mukallā *Town* Yemen 83 E13
Alofi *Capital* Niue 103 K7
Alotip *Town* Indonesia 97 N8
Alpena *Town* Michigan, USA 13 L4
Alpine *Town* Texas, USA 17 I7
Alps *Mountain range* Central Europe 57 D12
Al Qāmishlī *Town* Syria 80 I4
Al Qunayṭirah *Town* Syria 81 D9
Altai Mountains *Mountain range* Mongolia/ Russian Federation 88 F4
Altamaha River Georgia, USA 11 I5
Altamira *Town* Brazil 29 J2
Altamura *Town* Italy 61 H10
Altar, Desierto de *Desert* Mexico 18 D2
Altay *Town* China 88 F3
Altay *Town* Mongolia 88 H3
Altin Köprü *Town* Iraq 82 C6
Altiplano *Physical region* Bolivia 27 E13
Altoona *Town* Pennsylvania, USA 9 F7
Altun Ha *Ancient site* Belize 22 F2
Altun Shan *Mountain range* China 88 G5
Al 'Umarī *Town* Jordan 81 F11
Al 'Uwaynāt *Town* Libya 37 J6
Alupka *Town* Ukraine 69 K7
Alva *Town* Okahoma, USA 17 L3
Al Wajh *Town* Saudi Arabia 83 A9
Alwar *Town* India 86 H3
Al Wari'ah *Town* Saudi Arabia 82 D8
Alytus *Town* Lithuania 70 D8
Amamapare *Town* Indonesia 97 N7
Amantea *Town* Italy 61 G12
Amarapura *Town* Myanmar 94 B6
Amarillo *Town* Texas, USA 17 J4
Amazon *River* Brazil 29 J2
Amazon Basin Brazil 28 G3
Ambanja *Town* Madagascar 45 M4
Ambarchik *Town* Russian Federation 78 L3
Ambato *Town* Ecuador 26 A8
Amboasary *Town* Madagascar 45 L7
Ambon *Town* Indonesia 97 K7
American Samoa *Dependent territory* USA, Pacific Ocean 103 K6
Amersfoort *Town* Netherlands 52 F8
Amfilochía *Town* Greece 67 C10
Amherst *Town* Nova Scotia, Canada 7 K7
Amiens *Town* France 54 E6
Amman *Capital* Jordan 81 E11
'Ammān *see* Amman
Ammóchostos *Town* Cyprus 80 B8
Āmol *Town* Iran 82 F5
Amos *Town* Québec, Canada 6 H6
Amritsar *Town* India 86 H2
Amstelveen *Town* Netherlands 52 F8
Amsterdam *Capital* Netherlands 52 E8
Am Timan *Town* Chad 42 F6
Amudu Gulf *see*
Amundsen Gulf Canada 4 H4
Amundsen-Scott *Research station* Antarctica 110 E6
Amundsen Sea Southern Ocean 110 B7
Amuntai *Town* Indonesia 96 H7
Amur *River* China 89 L2
Amyderýa *River* Uzbekistan 84 G4
Anadyr' *Town* Russian Federation 78 M2
Anamur *Town* Turkey 76 F7
Anápolis *Town* Brazil 29 K5
Anatolia *Plateau* Turkey 76 E6
Anchorage *Town* Alaska, Canada 4 E5
Ancona *Town* Italy 60 F7
Andalucía *Region* Spain 58 H8
Andaman Islands *Island group* India 87 M8
Andaman Sea Indian Ocean 87 M8
Anderson *Town* Indiana, USA 13 K6
Andes *Mountain range* South America 26–27, 30–31
Andijon *Town* Uzbekistan 85 K4
Andkhvoy *Town* Afghanistan 84 H5
Andorra *Country* 55 D12
Andorra la Vella *Capital* Andorra 55 D12
Andreanof Islands *Island Group* Alaska, USA 4 A4
Andrews *Town* Texas, USA 17 J5
Andria *Town* Italy 61 H10
Andros Island Bahamas 24 F2
Andros Town *Town* Bahamas 24 F2
Angarsk *Town* Russian Federation 79 I7
Angeles *Town* Philippines 97 I2
Angel Falls *Waterfall* Venezuela 26 F6
Ångermanälven *River* Sweden 48 E7
Angers *Town* France 54 C7
Angkor Wat *Ancient site* Cambodia 95 F10
Anglesey *Island* Wales, UK 51 E9
Angola *Country* 44 E3
Angola Basin *Undersea feature* Atlantic Ocean 33 M6
Angoulême *Town* France 55 D9
Angren *Town* Uzbekistan 85 J3
Anguilla *Dependent territory* UK, Atlantic Ocean 25 N5
Anhui *Administrative region* China 91 J5
Ankara *Capital* Turkey 76 F4
Annaba *Town* Algeria 37 I3
An Nafūd *Desert* Saudi Arabia 82 B8
'Annah *Town* Iraq 82 C6
An Najaf *Town* Iraq 82 C7
Annamitique, Chaîne *Mountain range* Laos 94 F8
Annapolis *Town* Maryland, USA 8 G8
Ann Arbor *Town* Michigan, USA 13 L5

An Nāṣirīyah *Town* Iraq 82 D7
Annecy *Town* France 55 G9
Anniston *Town* Alabama, USA 10 H4
Anqing *Town* China 91 J6
Anshan *Town* China 91 L2
Anshun *Town* China 90 G7
Antakya *Town* Turkey 76 H7
Antalya *Town* Turkey 76 E6
Antananarivo *Capital* Madagascar 45 M5
Antarctica 110
Antarctic Peninsula Antarctica 110 B4
Antibes *Town* France 55 H11
Anticosti, Île d' *Island* Québec, Canada 7 K5
Antigua *Island* Antigua & Barbuda 25 N6
Antigua & Barbuda *Country* 25 N5
Anti-Lebanon *Mountain range* Syria 81 E9
Antofagasta *Town* Chile 30 D5
Antony *Town* France 54 E7
Antsiranana *Town* Madagascar 45 M3
Antwerp *Town* Belgium 53 E10
Antwerpen *see* Antwerp
Anyang *Town* China 91 J4
Anzio *Town* Italy 61 E9
Aomen *see* Macao
Aomori *Town* Japan 92 F7
Aoraki *Mountain* New Zealand 107 C11
Aosta *Town* Italy 60 B4
Aozou *Town* Chad 42 E3
Apatity *Town* Russian Federation 72 D5
Apeldoorn *Town* Netherlands 52 F8
Apennines *Mountain range* Italy 60 C8
Āpia *Capital* Samoa I03 K7
Apoera *Town* Suriname 26 G6
Appalachian Mountains USA 8 H4
Appingedam *Town* Netherlands 52 G6
Appleton *Town* Wisconsin, USA 13 J4
Apuseni, Munpii *Mountain range* Romania 68 E5
Āqchah *Town* Afghanisatan 85 I5
Aquidauana *Town* Brazil 29 I6
Arabian Peninsula Saudi Arabia 82 B8
Arabian Sea Indian Ocean 83 H10
Aracaju *Town* Brazil 29 N4
Araçuai *Town* Brazil 29 L6
'Arad *Town* Israel 81 D12
Arad *Town* Romania 68 D6
Arafura Sea Australia 105 I1
Araguaia, Rio *River* Brazil 29 J5
Araguaína *Town* Brazil 29 K3
Araguari *Town* Brazil 29 K6
Arāk *Town* Iran 82 E6
Arakan Yoma *Mountain range* Myanmar 94 B7
Aral Sea Uzbekistan/Kazakhstan 84 G1
Aral'sk *Town* Kazakhstan 78 E7
Aranda de Duero *Town* Spain 59 I4
'Ar'ar *Town* Saudi Arabia 82 C7
Ararat, Mount *Town* Turkey 77 L4
Arbīl *Town* Iraq 82 D6
Archangel *Town* Russian Federation 72 E6
Arco *Town* Italy 60 D5
Arctic Ocean 111 M5
Ardabīl *Town* Iran 82 E5
Ardakān *Town* Iran 82 F7
Ardennes *Physical region* Belgium 53 F13
Arequipa *Town* Peru 27 D12
Arezzo *Town* Italy 60 E7
Argalastí *Town* Greece 67 E10
Argenteuil *Town* France 54 E6
Argentina *Country* 31 E9
Argentine Basin *Undersea feature* Atlantic Ocean 33 J8
Argo *Town* Sudan 38 D6
Århus *Town* Denmark 49 C12
Arica *Town* Chile 30 D7
Arizona *State* USA 16 E4
Arkansas *State* USA 10 E3
Arkansas City *Town* Kansas, USA 12 G8
Arkhangel'sk *see* Archangel
Arklow *Town* Ireland 51 D9
Arles *Town* France 55 F11
Arlington *Town* Texas, USA 17 M5
Arlington *Town* Virginia, USA 11 K2
Arlon *Town* Belgium 53 F13
Armenia *Country* 77 L4
Armenia *Town* Colombia 26 B6
Armstrong *Town* Ontario, Canada 6 E5

Arnaía *Town* Greece 67 E9
Arnhem *Town* Netherlands 53 F9
Arnhem Land *Region* Australia 105 I2
Ar Ramādī *Town* Iraq 82 C6
Arran, Isle of *Island* Scotland, UK 50 E7
Ar Raqqah *Town* Syria 80 G6
Arras *Town* France 54 F5
Ar Rawḍatayn *Town* Kuwait 82 D8
Arriaga *Town* Mexico 19 M9
Ar Riyāḍ, *see* Riyadh
Ar Rub' al Khālī *Desert* Saudi Arabia 83 E11
Ar Rustāq *Town* Oman 83 G9
Ar Rut'bah *Town* Iraq 82 B6
Artashat *Town* Armenia 77 L4
Artemisa *Town* Cuba 24 D3
Artvin *Town* Turkey 77 J3
Arua *Town* Uganda 39 E10
Aruba *Dependent territory* Netherlands, Atlantic Ocean 25 J8
Arusha *Town* Tanzania 39 F12
Arvidsjaur *Town* Sweden 48 E6
Arys' *Town* Kazakhstan 78 F7
Asadābād *Town* Afghanisatan 85 K7
Asahikawa *Town* Japan 92 G5
Asamankese *Town* Ghana 41 I8
Āsānsol *Town* India 87 K4
Ascension Island *Dependent territory* St Helena, Atlantic Ocean 33 K5
Ascoli Piceno *Town* Italy 60 F8
Aseb *Town* Eritrea 38 G8
Ashdod *Town* Israel 81 C11
Asheville *Town* North Carolina, USA 11 I4
Ashgabat *Capital* Turkmenistan 84 F5
Ashkelon *Town* Israel 81 C11
Ashmyany *Town* Belarus 70 E8
Ash Shadādah *Town* Syria 80 H5
Ash Shāriqah *Town* United Arab Emirates 83 G9
Ash Shiḥr *Town* Yemen 83 E13
Asipovichy *Town* Belarus 71 F10
Asmara *Capital* Eritrea 38 F7
As Sabkhah *Town* Syria 80 G6
Assad, Lake Syria 80 F6
Aş Şafāwī *Town* Jordan 81 F10
As Salv *Town* Jordan 81 D11
Assam *Region* India 87 L3
Assamakka *Town* Niger 41 K4
As Samāwah *Town* Iraq 82 D7
Assen *Town* Netherlands 52 G6
As Sukhnah *Town* Syria 80 G7
As Sulaymānīyah *Town* Iran 82 D6
As Sulayyil *Town* Saudi Arabia 83 D11
Aş Şuwār *Town* Syria 80 H6
As Suwaydā' *Town* Syria 81 E10
Astana *Capital* Kazakhstan 78 F6
Asti *Town* Italy 60 C5
Astrakhan' *Town* Russian Federation 73 D12
Asunción *Capital* Paraguay 30 G4
Aswān *Town* Egypt 38 E5
Asyūṭ *Town* Egypt 38 E5
Atacama Desert Chile 30 D6
Atbara *Town* Sudan 38 E7
Atbasar *Town* Kazakhstan 78 F6
Ath *Town* Belgium 53 D11
Athabasca, Lake Saskatchewan, Canada 5 I7
Athens *Capital* Greece 67 E11
Athens *Town* Georgia, USA 11 I4
Athína *see* Athens
Athlone *Town* Ireland 51 C9
Ati *Town* Chad 42 E6
Atka *Town* Russian Federation 78 L4
Atka *Town* Alaska, USA 4 B5
Atlanta *Town* Georgia, USA 10 H4
Atlantic City *Town* New Jersey, USA 9 I8
Atlantic Ocean 32–33
Atlas Mountains *Mountain range* Morocco/Algeria 36 F4
Atsumi *Town* Japan 92 F8
Aṭ Ṭā'if *Town* Saudi Arabia 83 B10
Aṭ Ṭalfilah *Town* Jordan 81 E12
At Tall al Abyaḍ *Town* Syria 80 F5
Aṭ Ṭanf *Town* Syria 81 G9
Attawapiskat *Town* Ontario, Canada 6 G5
Atyrau *Town* Kazakhstan 78 E6
Auch *Town* France 55 D11
Auckland *Town* New Zealand 106 F5
Augsburg *Town* Germany 57 E10

Augusta *Town* Georgia, USA 11 I5
Augusta *Town* Maine, USA 9 K3
Aurangābād *Town* India 86 H5
Aurillac *Town* France 55 E10
Aurora *Town* Colorado, USA 15 L6
Aurora *Town* Illinois, USA 13 J6
Austin *Town* Texas, USA 17 L7
Australes, Îles *Island chain* French Polynesia 103 N8
Australia *Country* 105 L5
Australian Capital Territory *Territory* Australia 105 L8
Austria *Country* 57 G11
Ausuituq *see* Grise Fiord
Auxerre *Town* France 54 F7
Avarua *Capital* Cook Islands 103 M8
Aveiro *Town* Portugal 58 E5
Avellino *Town* Italy 61 F10
Avezzano *Town* Italy 61 F9
Aviemore *Town* Scotland, UK 50 E5
Avignon *Town* France 55 F11
Ávila *Town* Spain 58 H5
Avilés *Town* Spain 58 G2
Avon *Town* New York, USA 8 F5
Āwash *Town* Ethiopia 39 G9
Awbārī *Town* Libya 37 K6
Axel Heiberg Island Nunavut, Canada 5 I2
Ayacucho *Town* Peru 27 C11
Ayaguz *Town* Kazakhstan 78 G7
Ayaviri *Town* Peru 27 D11
Aydin *Town* Turkey 76 C6
Ayers Rock *see* Uluru
Ayorou *Town* Niger 41 J5
Ayutthaya *Town* Thailand 95 D10
Ayvalik *Town* Turkey 76 C5
Azaouâd *Desert* Mali 41 I4
A'zāz *Town* Syria 80 E5
Azerbaijan *Country* 77 M4
Azores *Island group* Portugal 32 H5
Azov, Sea of Black Sea 69 L6
Azuaga *Town* Spain 58 G7
Azul *Town* Argentina 31 G9
Az Zaqazig *Town* Egypt 38 E4
Az Zarqā' *Town* Jordan 81 E11
Az Zāwiyah *Town* Libya 37 K4

B

Baalbek *Town* Lebanon 80 E8
Baardheere *Town* Somalia 39 G11
Baarn *Town* Netherlands 52 E8
Babayevo *Town* Russian Federation 72 C7
Babruysk *Town* Belarus 71 F10
Babuyan Channel *Strait* Philippines 97 J1
Bacabal *Town* Brazil 29 L3
Bacău *Town* Romania 68 G6
Bačka Palanka *Town* Serbia 64 G7
Bac Liêu *Town* Vietnam 95 G12
Bacolod City *Town* Philippines 97 J3
Badajoz *Town* Spain 58 F6
Baden-Baden *Town* Germany 57 C9
Bad Hersfeld *Town* Germany 56 D7
Badlands *Region* North Dakota, USA 12 E3
Bafatá *Town* Guinea-Bissau 40 E6
Baffin Bay Nunavut, Canada 5 K3
Baffin Island Nunavut, Canada 5 K4
Bafoussam *Town* Cameroon 42 C8
Bafra *Town* Turkey 76 G3
Bagé *Town* Brazil 29 J9
Baghdad *Capital* Iraq 82 D6
Baghlān *Town* Afghanistan 85 J6
Bago *Town* Myanmar 94 B8
Bagrationovsk *Town* Kaliningrad 70 B7
Baguio *Town* Philippines 97 I2
Bahamas *Country* 24 G3
Baharly *Town* Turkmenistan 84 F4
Bahāwalpur *Town* Pakistan 86 G3
Bahía Blanca *Town* Argentina 31 F9
Bahir Dar *Town* Ethiopia 38 F8
Bahrain *Country* 83 F9
Bahushewsk *Town* Belarus 71 G9
Baia Mare *Town* Romania 68 E5
Baikal, Lake Russian Federation 79 J6
Bailén *Town* Spain 59 I7
Ba Illi *Town* Chad 42 E6

Bairiki *Capital* Kiribati 103 I4
Baishan *Town* China 89 M4
Baja *Town* Hungary 63 E12
Baja California *Peninsula* Mexico 18 D4
Bajram Curri *Town* Albania 65 F10
Baker *Town* Oregon, USA 14 H3
Baker & Howland Islands *Dependent territory* USA, Pacific Ocean 103 J4
Baker Lake *Town* Nunavut, Canada 5 J6
Bakersfield *Town* California, USA 14 G7
Bākhtarān *Town* Iran 82 D6
Baki *see* Baku
Baku *Capital* Azerbaijan 77 N3
Balakovo *Town* Russian Federation 73 E10
Balashov *Town* Russian Federation 73 D10
Balaton *Lake* Hungary 63 D12
Balclutha *Town* New Zealand 107 C13
Baleares, Islas *see* Balearic Islands
Balearic Islands *Island group* Spain 59 M5
Bāleshwar *Town* India 87 K5
Bali *Island* Indonesia 96 H8
Balikesir *Town* Turkey 76 C4
Balikpapan *Town* Indonesia 96 H6
Balkanabat *Town* Turkmenistan 84 D4
Balkan Mountains *Mountain range* Bulgaria 66 D6
Balkh *Town* Afghanisatan 85 I6
Balkhash *Town* Kazakhstan 78 G7
Balkhash, Lake Kazakhstan 78 G7
Ballarat *Town* Victoria, Australia 105 K8
Balsas *Town* Brazil 29 L3
Balsas, Río *River* Mexico 19 J8
Bălpi *Town* Moldova 68 H5
Baltic Sea Northern Europe 49 D12
Baltimore *Town* Maryland, USA 9 G8
Balykchy *Town* Kyrgyzstan 85 M3
Bam *Town* Iran 82 G8
Bamako *Capital* Mali 40 G6
Bambari *Town* Central African Republic 42 F8
Bamberg *Town* Germany 56 E8
Bamenda *Town* Cameroon 42 C8
Banda Aceh *Town* Indonesia 96 C4
Bandarbeyla *Town* Somalia 39 I9
Bandar-e 'Abbās *Town* Iran 82 G8
Bandar-e Būshehr *Town* Iran 82 E8
Bandar-e Khamīr *Town* Iran 82 G8
Bandar Lampung *Town* Indonesia 96 E7
Bandar Seri Begawan *Capital* Brunei 96 H5
Banda Sea Indonesia 97 K7
Bandirma *Town* Turkey 76 C4
Bandundu *Town* Democratic Republic of Congo 43 E11
Bandung *Town* Indonesia 96 F8
Bangalore *Town* India 86 H7
Banghāzī *see* Benghazi
Bangkok *Capital* Thailand 95 D10
Bangladesh *Country* 87 K4
Bangor *Town* Maine, USA 9 L3
Bangor *Town* Wales, UK 51 E9
Bangui *Capital* Central African Republic 42 E8
Ban Hua Hin *Town* Thailand 95 D10
Bāniyās *Town* Syria 80 D7
Banja Luka *Town* Bosnia & Herzegovina 64 D7
Banjarmasin *Town* Indonesia 96 H7
Banjul *Capital* Gambia 40 E5
Banks Peninsula New Zealand 107 E11
Banská Bystrica *Town* Slovakia 63 E10
Bantry *Town* Ireland 51 B11
Baoji *Town* China 90 H5
Baoshan *Town* China 90 E7
Baotou *Town* China 89 J5
Ba'qūbah *Town* Iraq 82 D6
Bar *Town* Montenegro 65 E11
Bārāmati *Town* India 86 H6
Baranavichy *Town* Belarus 71 D10
Barbados *Country* 25 P7
Barbuda *Island* Antigua & Barbuda 25 N5
Barcelona *Town* Venezuela 26 E5
Barcelona *Town* Spain 59 M4
Bareilly *Town* India 87 I3
Barents Sea Arctic Ocean 111 N8
Bar Harbor *Town* Maine, USA 9 L3
Bari *Town* Italy 61 H10
Barillas *Town* Guatemala 22 D3
Barinas *Town* Venezuela 26 D5

Bremerhaven *Town* Germany 56 D5
Brenner Pass *Italy/Austria* 60 E4
Brescia *Town* Italy 60 D5
Brest *Town* Belarus 71 B10
Brest *Town* France 54 A6
Brezovo *Town* Bulgaria 66 F6
Bria *Town* Central African Republic 42 F8
Briançon *Town* France 55 G10
Bridgeport *Town* Connecticut, USA 9 I6
Bridgetown *Capital* Barbados 25 P7
Bridlington *Town* England, UK 50 H8
Brig *Town* Switzerland 57 C12
Brighton *Town* England, UK 51 H11
Brindisi *Town* Italy 61 I10
Brisbane *Town* Queensland, Australia 105 M6
Bristol *Town* England, UK 51 F11
Bristol Channel *Wales/England, UK* 51 E11
British Columbia *Province* Canada 4 G7
British Indian Ocean Territory *Dependent territory* UK, Indian Ocean 99 J5
British Virgin Islands *Dependent territory* UK, Atlantic Ocean 25 M5
Brittany *Region* France 54 B6
Brive-la-Gaillarde *Town* France 55 D10
Brno *Town* Czech Republic 63 D9
Broken Arrow *Town* Okahoma, USA 17 M3
Brookhaven *Town* Mississippi, USA 10 F6
Brooks Range *Mountain Range* Alaska, USA 4 F4
Broome *Town* Western Australia, Australia 104 F3
Brownfield *Town* Texas, USA 17 J5
Brownwood *Town* Texas, USA 17 L6
Brownsville *Town* Texas, USA 17 M9
Bruges *Town* Belgium 53 C10
Brugge *see* Bruges
Brunei *Country* 96 H5
Brussel *see* Brussels
Brussels *Capital* Belgium 53 D11
Bruxelles *see* Brussels
Bryan *Town* Texas, USA 17 M6
Bryansk *Town* Russian Federation 73 B9
Bucaramanga *Town* Colombia 26 C5
Bucharest *Capital* Romania 68 F7
Bucureşti *see* Bucharest
Budapest *Capital* Hungary 63 E11
Buenaventura *Town* Colombia 26 B6
Buena Vista *Town* Bolivia 27 E12
Buenos Aires *Capital* Argentina 30 G8
Buffalo *Town* New York, USA 8 F5
Buffalo *Town* South Dakota, USA 12 E3
Bug *River* Poland 62 G6
Buguruslan *Town* Russian Federation 73 F10
Buḩayrat al Asad *see* Lake Assad
Bujanovac *Town* Serbia 65 G10
Bujumbura *Capital* Burundi 39 D12
Bukavu *Town* Democratic Republic of Congo 43 H10
Bukoba *Town* Tanzania 39 E11
Bulawayo *Town* Zimbabwe 44 H5
Bulgaria *Country* 66 F6
Bumba *Town* Democratic Republic of Congo 43 G9
Bungo-suidō *Strait* Japan 93 D13
Bünyan *Town* Turkey 76 G5
Buraydah *Town* Saudi Arabia 83 C9
Burdur *Town* Turkey 76 D6
Burgas *Town* Bulgaria 66 H6
Burgos *Town* Spain 59 I3
Burgundy *Region* France 54 F8
Buriram *Town* Thailand 95 E9
Burketown *Town* Queensland, Australia 105 J3
Burkina Faso *Country* 41 I6
Burlington *Town* New York, USA 9 I4
Burma *see* Myanmar
Burns *Town* Oregon, USA 14 G4
Burnsville *Town* Minnesota, USA 12 H4
Bursa *Town* Turkey 76 D4
Burundi *Country* 39 D12
Buta *Town* Democratic Republic of Congo 43 G9
Butterworth *Town* Malaysia 96 D4
Butuan *Town* Philippines 97 K4
Buxoro *Town* Uzbekistan 84 H4
Buynaksk *Town* Russian Federation 73 D14

Büyükağri Daği *see* Ararat, Mount
Buzău *Town* Romania 68 G7
Buzuluk *Town* Russian Federation 73 F10
Byahoml' *Town* Belarus 71 F9
Byalynichy *Town* Belarus 71 G10
Bydgoszcz *Town* Poland 62 E6
Byelaruskaya Hrada *Ridge* Belarus 71 D9
Bytom *Town* Poland 62 E8
Bytča *Town* Slovakia 63 E9

C

Cabanatuan *Town* Philippines 97 J2
Cabimas *Town* Venezuela 26 D5
Cabinda *Town* Angola 44 D1
Cabinda *Province* Angola 44 D1
Caborca *Town* Mexico 18 E3
Cabot Strait *Canada* 7 L6
Cáceres *Town* Spain 58 G6
Cachimbo *Town* Brazil 29 I4
Cachimbo, Serra do *Mountain range* Brazil 29 I4
Cadiz *Town* Philippines 97 J3
Cádiz *Town* Spain 58 G9
Cadiz, Gulf of *Spain* 58 F8
Caen *Town* France 54 D6
Cagayan de Oro *Town* Philippines 97 K4
Cagliari *Town* Sardinia, Italy 61 B11
Caguas *Town* Puerto Rico 25 L5
Caicos Passage *Strait* Bahamas 25 I3
Cairns *Town* Queensland, Australia 105 L3
Cairo *Capital* Egypt 38 E4
Cajamarca *Town* Peru 27 B9
Čakovec *Town* Croatia 64 D5
Calabar *Town* Nigeria 41 L8
Calafat *Town* Romania 68 E7
Calais *Town* France 54 E5
Calais *Town* Maine, USA 9 L2
Calama *Town* Chile 30 D4
Calaraşi *Town* Romania 68 G7
Calatayud *Town* Spain 59 J4
Calbayog *Town* Philippines 97 J3
Calcutta *see* Kolkata
Calgary *Town* Alberta, Canada 4 H8
Cali *Town* Colombia 26 B6
Calicut *Town* India 86 H8 *see also* Kozhikode
California *State* USA 14 H7
California, Gulf of *Mexico* 18 E4
Callao *Town* Peru 27 B11
Caltanissetta *Town* Sicily, Italy 61 E13
Caluula *Town* Somalia 38 I8
Camacupa *Town* Angola 44 E3
Camagüey *Town* Cuba 24 F4
Camaná *Town* Peru 27 C12
Ca Mau *Town* Vietnam 95 F12
Cambodia *Country* 95 F10
Cambrai *Town* France 54 F5
Cambrian Mountains *Wales, UK* 51 F10
Cambridge *Town* England, UK 51 H10
Cambridge *Town* Maryland, USA 8 H9
Cambridge *Town* Ohio, USA 13 M6
Cambridge Bay *Town* Nunavut, Canada 5 I5
Camden *Town* Maine, USA 9 K4
Cameroon *Country* 42 C8
Camopi *Town* French Guiana 26 I7
Campeche *Town* Mexico 19 N7
Campeche, Bay of *Mexico* 19 M7
Câm Pha *Town* Vietnam 94 G6
Câmpina *Town* Romania 68 F7
Campina Grande *Town* Brazil 29 N4
Campinas *Town* Brazil 29 K7
Campobasso *Town* Italy 61 F9
Campo Grande *Town* Brazil 29 I6
Campos *Town* Brazil 29 L7
Câmpulung *Town* Romania 68 E6
Cam Ranh *Town* Vietnam 95 H11
Çanakkale *Town* Turkey 76 C4
Çanakkale Boğazi *see* Dardanelles
Canada *Country* 4 G8
Canary Islands *Island group* Spain, Atlantic Ocean 33 K3
Canaveral, Cape *Coastal feature* Florida, USA 11 J7
Canavieiras *Town* Brazil 29 M5
Canberra *Capital* Australia 105 L8

Cancún *Town* Mexico 19 P6
Cangzhou *Town* China 91 J3
Caniapiscau, Réservoir de *Reservoir* Québec, Canada 7 I4
Çankiri *Town* Turkey 76 F4
Cannanore *Town* India 86 H8 *see also* Kannur
Cannes *Town* France 55 H12
Canoas *Town* Brazil 29 J8
Canon City *Town* Colorado, USA 15 K6
Cantábrica, Cordillera *Mountain range* Spain 58 G3
Canterbury *Town* England, UK 51 I11
Cân Thơ *Town* Vietnam 95 G12
Canton *Town* Ohio, USA 13 M6
Canyon *Town* Texas, USA 17 J4
Cape Basin *Undersea feature* Atlantic Ocean 33 M7
Cape Breton Island *Nova Scotia, Canada* 7 L7
Cape Charles *Town* Virginia, USA 11 L2
Cape Coast *Town* Ghana 41 I8
Cape Horn *Coastal feature* Chile 31 E15
Cape Town *Capital* South Africa 44 F9
Cape Verde *Country* 33 K4
Cape Verde Basin *Undersea feature* Atlantic Ocean 33 J4
Cape York Peninsula *Queensland, Australia* 105 K2
Cap-Haïtien *Town* Haiti 25 I5
Capitán Arturo Prat *Research station* Antarctica 110 B4
Caprivi Strip *Physical region* Namibia 44 G4
Caracaraí *Town* Brazil 28 H1
Caracas *Capital* Venezuela 26 E4
Caravelas *Town* Brazil 29 M6
Carbonia *Town* Sardinia, Italy 61 B11
Cárdenas *Town* Cuba 24 E3
Cardiff *Town* Wales, UK 51 F11
Carei *Town* Romania 68 E5
Caribbean Sea *Atlantic Ocean* 32 H4
Carlisle *Town* England, UK 50 F7
Carlisle *Town* Pennsylvania, USA 8 G7
Carlow *Town* Ireland 51 D9
Carlsbad *Town* New Mexico, USA 17 I5
Carmarthen *Town* Wales, UK 51 E10
Carmelita *Town* Guatemala 22 E2
Carmen *Town* Mexico 19 N7
Carnarvon *Town* Western Australia, Australia 104 D5
Carolina *Town* Brazil 29 K3
Caroline Islands *Island group* Micronesia 102 F3
Carpathian Mountains *Mountain range* Poland/Slovakia/Romania 68 F5
Carpentaria, Gulf of *Australia* 105 J2
Carpi *Town* Italy 60 D6
Carrara *Town* Italy 60 D6
Carson City *Town* Nevada, USA 14 G6
Cartagena *Town* Colombia 26 B5
Cartagena *Town* Spain 59 K8
Carthage *Ancient site* Tunisia 37 J3
Cartwright *Town* Newfoundland & Labrador, Canada 7 L4
Carúpano *Town* Venezuela 26 F4
Caruthersville *Town* Missouri, USA 13 J8
Cary *Town* North Carolina, USA 11 K3
Casablanca *Town* Morocco 36 G4
Cascade Range *Mountain Range* Oregon/Washington, USA 14 F4
Caserta *Town* Italy 61 F10
Casey *Research station* Antarctica 110 G7
Casper *Town* Wyoming, USA 15 K4
Caspian Depression *Lowland* Russian Federation 73 D12
Caspian Sea *Asia* 73 D13
Casteggio *Town* Italy 60 C5
Castellon de la Plana *Town* Spain 59 K5
Castelvetrano *Town* Sicily, Italy 61 D13
Castlebar *Town* Ireland 50 B8
Castricum *Town* Netherlands 52 E7
Castries *Capital* St. Lucia 25 O7
Castrovillari *Town* Italy 61 G11
Catacamas *Town* Honduras 22 H4
Catalonia *Region* Spain 59 L4
Cataluña *see* Catalonia
Catania *Town* Sicily, Italy 61 G13
Catanzaro *Town* Italy 61 H12

Catskill Mountains *New York, USA* 8 H5
Caucasia *Town* Colombia 26 B5
Caucasus *Mountain range* Asia/Europe 77 J2
Caviana de Fora, Ilha *Island* Brazil 29 K2
Cayenne *Capital* French Guiana 26 I6
Cayes *Town* Haiti 24 H5
Cayman Islands *Dependent territory* UK, Atlantic Ocean 24 E5
Cebu *Town* Philippines 97 J3
Cecina *Town* Italy 60 D7
Cedar City *Town* Utah, USA 15 I6
Cedar Falls *Town* Iowa, USA 12 H5
Cedar Rapids *Town* Iowa, USA 13 I5
Cefalù *Town* Sicily, Italy 61 E12
Celebes *Island* Indonesia 97 J7
Celebes Sea *Pacific Ocean* 97 I5
Celje *Town* Slovenia 57 H12
Celldömölk *Town* Hungary 63 D11
Celle *Town* Germany 56 E6
Celtic Sea *Atlantic Ocean* 51 C11
Cenderawasih, Teluk *Bay* Indonesia 97 M6
Central African Republic *Country* 42 G8
Central, Cordillera *Mountain range* Colombia 26 B7
Central, Cordillera *Mountain range* Dominican Republic 25 J5
Central, Cordillera *Mountain range* Panama 23 K8
Central Pacific Basin *Undersea feature* Pacific Ocean 109 J5
Central, Planalto *Physical region* Brazil 29 K5
Central Range *Mountain range* Papua New Guinea 102 E5
Central Siberian Uplands *Plateau* Russian Federation 79 I5
Central, Sistema *Mountain range* Spain 58 H5
Central Valley *California, USA* 14 G5
Ceram Sea *Pacific Ocean* 97 K7
Cerignola *Town* Italy 61 G10
Cerro de Pasco *Town* Peru 27 B10
Cesena *Town* Italy 60 E6
České Budějovice *Town* Czech Republic 63 B9
Český Krumlov *Town* Czech Republic 63 B10
Ceuta *Town* Spain 58 H9
Cévennes *Mountain range* France 55 F11
Ceyhan *Town* Turkey 76 G6
Ceylanpinar *Town* Turkey 77 J6
Chachapoyas *Town* Peru 27 B9
Chad *Country* 42 E5
Chad, Lake *Chad* 42 D5
Chāgai Hills *Mountain range* Pakistan 86 E2
Chaillu, Massif du *Mountain range* Gabon 43 C10
Chakhānsūr *Town* Afghanisatan 84 G8
Chalatenango *Town* El Salvador 22 F4
Chalkidikí *Peninsula* Greece 67 E9
Challans *Town* France 54 C8
Challenger Deep *Undersea feature* Pacific Ocean 108 H4
Châlons-en-Champagne *Town* France 54 G6
Chalon-sur-Saône *Town* France 54 G8
Chaman *Town* Pakistan 86 F2
Chambéry *Town* France 55 G10
Champagne *Region* France 54 F7
Champaign *Town* Illinois, USA 13 J6
Champlain, Lake *New York, USA* 9 I4
Champotón *Town* Mexico 19 N7
Chañaral *Town* Chile 30 C5
Chandīgarh *Town* India 86 H2
Chandrapur *Town* India 87 I5
Changchun *Town* China 89 M3
Changde *Town* China 91 I6
Chang Jiang *see* Yangtze
Changsha *Town* China 91 I6
Changzhi *Town* China 91 I4
Channel Islands *Dependent territory* UK 51 G13
Channel Tunnel *UK/France* 51 I11
Chantada *Town* Spain 58 F3
Chanthaburi *Town* Thailand 95 E10
Chaoyang *Town* China 91 K2
Chaozhou *Town* China 91 J8
Chapayevsk *Town* Russian Federation 73 E10
Chārīkār *Town* Afghanistan 85 J6
Charity *Town* Guyana 26 G5
Charleroi *Town* Belgium 53 E12

D

DALAIN HOB – ERENHOT

Dalain Hob *Town* China 89 I5
Dalandzadgad *Town* Mongolia 89 I4
Đa Lat *Town* Vietnam 95 H11
Dalby *Town* Queensland, Australia 105 M5
Dali *Town* China 90 F7
Dalian *Town* China 91 K3
Dallas *Town* Texas, USA 17 M5
Dalmatia *Cultural Region* Croatia 64 C8
Damascus *Capital* Syria 81 E9
Dampier *Town* Western Australia, Australia 104 E4
Dampier, Selat *Strait* Indonesia 97 L6
Damqawt *Town* Yemen 83 F12
Danakil Desert Ethiopia 38 G8
Đă Năng *Town* Vietnam 95 H9
Dandong *Town* China 91 L3
Danube *River* Germany 57 D10
Danville *Town* Virginia, USA 11 J3
Danzhou *Town* Hainan, China 90 H9
Danzig, Gulf of Poland 62 E4
Dar'ā *Town* Syria 81 E10
Dardanelles *Strait* Turkey 76 B4
Dar es Salaam *Capital* Tanzania 39 G13
Darfur *Cultural region* Sudan 38 C8
Darhan *Town* Mongolia 89 I3
Darien, Gulf of Panama 23 O7
Darjiling *Town* India 87 K3
Darling River New South Wales, Australia 105 K7
Darlington *Town* England, UK 50 F8
Darmstadt *Town* Germany 56 D8
Darnah *Town* Libya 37 M4
Dartmoor *Physical region* England, UK 51 E11
Dartmouth *Town* Nova Scotia, Canada 7 L7
Darwin *Town* Northern Territory, Australia 104 H1
Daşoguz *Town* Turkmenistan 84 F3
Datong *Town* China 91 I3
Daugavpils *Town* Latvia 70 F7
Dāvangere *Town* India 86 H7
Davao *Town* Philippines 97 K4
Davao Gulf Philippines 97 K4
Davenport *Town* Iowa, USA 13 I6
David *Town* Panama 23 K8
Davis *Research station* Antarctica 110 G5
Dawei *Town* Myanmar 95 C10
Dayr az Zawr *Town* Syria 80 H6
Dayton *Town* Ohio, USA 13 L7
Daytona Beach *Town* Florida, USA 11 J7
Dead Sea Jordan 81 D11
Deán Funes *Town* Argentina 30 E7
Death Valley California, USA 14 H7
Debar *Town* Macedonia 65 F11
Dębica *Town* Poland 63 G9
Debrecen *Town* Hungary 63 G11
Decatur *Town* Illinois, USA 13 J7
Deccan *Plateau* India 87 I5
Děčín *Town* Czech Republic 62 B8
Deggendorf *Town* Germany 57 F9
Deh Bīd *see* Şafāshahr
Deh Shū *Town* Afghanisatan 84 G9
Dekéleia *Town* Cyprus 80 B8
Delārām *Town* Afghanistan 84 G8
Delaware *State* USA 8 H8
Delft *Town* Netherlands 53 D9
Delhi *Town* India 86 H3
Delicias *Town* Mexico 18 H4
Delmenhorst *Town* Germany 56 D5
Del Rio *Town* Texas, USA 17 K7
Deltona *Town* Florida, USA 11 J7
Dembia *Town* Central African Republic 42 G8
Demopolis *Town* Alabama, USA 10 G5
Denekamp *Town* Netherlands 52 G8
Den Helder *Town* Netherlands 52 E7
Denizli *Town* Turkey 76 D6
Denmark *Country* 49 B12
Denov *Town* Uzbekistan 85 I5
Denpasar *Town* Indonesia 96 H8
Denton *Town* Texas, USA 17 M5
Denver *Town* Colorado, USA 15 L5
Dera Ghāzi Khān *Town* Pakistan 86 G2
Derbent *Town* Russian Federation 73 D14
Derby *Town* England, UK 51 G9
De Ridder *Town* Louisiana, USA 10 E6
Derweza *Town* Turkmenistan 84 F4
Desē *Town* Ethiopia 38 G8
Des Moines *Town* Iowa, USA 12 H6
Dessau *Town* Germany 56 F7
Detroit *Town* Michigan, USA 13 L5
Deva *Town* Romania 68 E6
Deventer *Town* Netherlands 52 F8
Devon Island Nunavut, Canada 5 J3
Dezfūl *Town* Iran 82 E7
Dezhou *Town* China 91 J4
Dhaka *Capital* Bangladesh 87 L4
Dhanbād *Town* India 87 K4
Diamantina, Chapada *Mountain range* Brazil 29 L4
Dibrugarh *Town* India 87 M3
Điên Biên *Town* Vietnam 94 E6
Dieppe *Town* France 54 E5
Digos *Town* Philippines 97 K4
Dijon *Town* France 54 G8
Dikhil *Town* Djibouti 38 G8
Dikson *Town* Russian Federation 78 H4
Dili *Capital* East Timor 97 K8
Di Linh *Town* Vietnam 95 H11
Dilolo *Town* Democratic Republic of Congo 43 G13
Dimashq *see* Damascus
Dimitrovgrad *Town* Russian Federation 73 E10
Dimitrovgrad *Town* Bulgaria 66 G7
Dinajpur *Town* Bangladesh 87 K4
Dinar *Town* Turkey 76 D6
Dinaric Alps *Mountain range* Bosnia & Herzegovina/Montenegro 64 C8
Dinguiraye *Town* Guinea 40 F6
Diourbel *Town* Senegal 40 E5
Dirē Dawa *Town* Ethiopia 39 G9
Divinópolis *Town* Brazil 29 L6
Divo *Town* Côte d'Ivoire 40 H8
Diyarbakir *Town* Turkey 77 J6
Djanet *Town* Algeria 37 J7
Djelfa *Town* Algeria 36 H4
Djibouti *Country* 38 G8
Djibouti City *Capital* Djibouti 38 G8
Dnieper *River* Ukraine 69 J6
Dnieper Lowland Ukraine 69 J3
Dniester *River* Ukraine 68 H4
Dniprodzerzhyns'k *Town* Ukraine 69 K4
Dnipropetrovs'k *Town* Ukraine 69 K4
Doba *Town* Chad 42 E7
Doboj *Town* Bosnia & Herzegovina 64 E7
Dobrich *Town* Bulgaria 66 H5
Dodecanese *Island group* Greece 67 G12
Dodekánisa *see* Dodecanese
Dodge City *Town* Kansas, USA 12 F7
Dodoma *Capital* Tanzania 39 F13
Doğubayazit *Town* Turkey 77 L4
Doha *Capital* Qatar 83 F9
Dokkum *Town* Netherlands 52 F6
Dôle *Town* France 54 G8
Dolisie *Town* Congo 43 D11
Dolni Chiflik *Town* Bulgaria 66 H6
Dolomites *Mountain range* Italy 60 E4
Dolores *Town* Uruguay 30 G8
Dolores *Town* Guatemala 22 E3
Dolores *Town* Argentina 31 G9
Dolores Hidalgo *Town* Mexico 19 J7
Dominica *Country* 25 O6
Dominican Republic *Country* 25 J4
Don *River* Russian Federation 73 D11
Doncaster *Town* England, UK 51 G9
Donegal *Town* Ireland 50 C7
Donets *River* Ukraine 69 L4
Donets'k *Town* Ukraine 69 M5
Dongguan *Town* China 91 J8
Đông Ho'i *Town* Vietnam 94 G8
Donostia-San Sebastián *Town* Spain 59 J2
Doolow *Town* Ethiopia 39 G10
Dordogne *River* France 55 D10
Dordrecht *Town* Netherlands 53 E9
Dortmund *Town* Germany 56 C7
Dos Hermanas *Town* Spain 58 G8
Douala *Town* Cameroon 42 C8
Douglas *Capital* Isle of Man 50 E8
Douglas *Town* Arizona, USA 16 F6
Dover *Town* Delaware, USA 8 H8
Dover *Town* England, UK 51 I11
Dovrefjell *Plateau* Norway 48 C8
Dra, Hamada du *Plateau* Algeria 36 E5
Drahichyn *Town* Belarus 71 C10
Drakensberg *Mountain range* South Africa 44 H8
Drake Passage Southern Ocean 110 A4
Dralfa *Town* Bulgaria 66 G5
Dráma *Town* Greece 66 E8
Drammen Norway 49 B10
Drava *River* Croatia 64 E6
Dresden *Town* Germany 56 G7
Drina *River* Bosnia & Herzegovina 65 E9
Drobeta-Turnu Severin *Town* Romania 68 D7
Drogheda *Town* Ireland 50 D8
Drummondville *Town* Québec, Canada 7 I7
Dryden *Town* Ontario, Canada 6 D5
Dubai *Town* United Arab Emirates 83 G9
Dubăsari *Town* Moldova 68 H5
Dubayy *see* Dubai
Dublin *Capital* Ireland 51 D9
Du Bois *Town* Pennsylvania, USA 8 F7
Dubrovnik *Town* Croatia 65 D10
Dubuque *Town* Iowa, USA 13 I5
Dudelange *Town* Luxembourg 53 F14
Duisburg *Town* Germany 56 C7
Duk Faiwil *Town* Sudan 39 E9
Dulan *Town* China 88 H6
Dulovo *Town* Bulgaria 66 H5
Duluth *Town* Minnesota, USA 13 I3
Dūmā *Town* Syria 81 E9
Dumont d'Urville *Research station* Antarctica 110 F7
Dumyāt *Town* Egypt 38 E4
Dunaújváros *Town* Hungary 63 E11
Dunav *River* Bulgaria 66 G5
Dunav *see* Danube
Dunavska Ravnina *Plain* Bulgaria 66 E5
Dundee *Town* South Africa 45 I7
Dundee *Town* Scotland, UK 50 F6
Dunedin *Town* New Zealand 107 C13
Dunfermline *Town* Scotland, UK 50 E6
Dunkerque *Town* France 54 F4
Dunkirk *Town* New York, USA 8 E6
Dún Laoghaire *Town* Ireland 51 D9
Duqm *Town* Oman 83 H11
Durango *Town* Mexico 18 H6
Durango *Town* Colorado, USA 15 K7
Durban *Town* South Africa 45 I8
Durham *Town* England, UK 50 G7
Durham *Town* North Carolina, USA 11 K3
Durrës *Town* Albania 65 E11
Dushan *Town* China 90 H7
Dushanbe *Capital* Tajikistan 85 J5
Düsseldorf *Town* Germany 56 C7
Dutch Harbor *Town* Alaska, USA 4 B5
Duyun *Town* China 90 H7
Dzerzhinsk *Town* Russian Federation 73 D9
Dzhalal-Abad *Town* Kyrgyzstan 85 L4
Dzhelandy *Town* Tajikistan 85 K5
Dzhergalan *Town* Kyrgyzstan 85 N3
Dzhusaly *Town* Kazakhstan 78 E7
Dzuunmod *Town* Mongolia 89 J3

E

East Antarctica *Region* Antarctica 110 F5
Eastbourne *Town* England, UK 51 H12
East Cape *Coastal feature* New Zealand 106 I6
East China Sea Pacific Ocean 91 L6
Easter Island Chile, Pacific Ocean 109 M7
Eastern Ghats *Mountain range* India 87 J6
Eastern Sayans *Mountain range* Russian Federation 79 I7
East Kilbride *Town* Scotland, UK 50 E6
East Korea Bay North Korea/South Korea 91 M3
Eastleigh *Town* England, UK 51 G11
East London *Town* South Africa 44 H8
East Pacific Rise *Undersea feature* Pacific Ocean 109 L7
East Sea Pacific Ocean 93 D10 *see also* Japan, Sea of
East Siberian Sea Arctic Ocean 111 N3
East Timor *Country* 97 K8
Eau Claire *Town* Wisconsin, USA 13 I4
Eberswalde-Finow *Town* Germany 56 G5
Ebetsu *Town* Japan 92 F5
Ebolowa *Town* Cameroon 43 C9
Ebro *River* Spain 59 J4
Ecuador *Country* 26 A8
Ed Damer *Town* Sudan 38 E7
Ed Debba *Town* Sudan 38 D7
Ede *Town* Nigeria 41 K7
Ede *Town* Netherlands 52 F8
Edéa *Town* Cameroon 42 C8
Edinburgh *Town* Scotland, UK 50 F6
Edirne *Town* Turkey 76 C3
Edmonton *Town* Alberta, Canada 4 H8
Edmundston *Town* New Brunswick, Canada 7 J6
Edna *Town* Texas, USA 17 M7
Edolo *Town* Italy 60 D4
Edremit *Town* Turkey 76 C4
Edward, Lake Democratic Republic of Congo 43 I10
Edwards Plateau Texas, USA 17 K7
Eemshaven *Town* Netherlands 52 G6
Effingham *Town* Illinois, USA 13 J7
Eger *Town* Hungary 63 F11
Egypt *Country* 38 D5
Eidfjord *Town* Norway 49 B9
Eindhoven *Town* Netherlands 53 F10
Eivissa *see* Ibiza
Elat *Town* Israel 81 D14
Elâziğ *Town* Turkey 76 H5
Elbasan *Town* Albania 65 F12
Elbe *River* Germany/Czech Republic 56 E5
Elbląg *Town* Poland 62 E5
El'brus *Mountain* Russian Federation 73 C13
El Cajon *Town* California, USA 14 H8
El Callao *Town* Venezuela 26 F5
Elche *Town* Spain 59 K7
Elda *Town* Spain 59 K7
El Dorado *Town* Venezuela 26 F6
Eldoret *Town* Kenya 39 F11
Elektrostal' *Town* Russian Federation 72 C8
El Fasher *Town* Sudan 38 C8
El Geneina *Town* Sudan 38 C8
Elgin *Town* Illinois, USA 13 J5
El Goléa *Town* Algeria 36 H5
Elista *Town* Russian Federation 73 C11
El-Jadida *Town* Morocco 36 E4
Ełk *Town* Poland 62 G5
El Khârga *Town* Egypt 38 D5
Ellesmere Island Nunavut, Canada 5 J2
Ellsworth Land *Region* Antarctica 110 C6
El Mahbas *Town* Western Sahara 36 E6
El Mina *Town* Lebanon 80 D8
Elmira *Town* New York, USA 8 G6
El Mreyyé *Desert* Mauritania 40 G3
Elmshorn *Town* Germany 56 D5
El Muglad *Town* Sudan 38 D8
El Obeid *Town* Sudan 38 D8
El Oued *Town* Algeria 37 I4
Eloy *Town* Arizona, USA 16 E5
El Paso *Town* Texas, USA 16 H6
El Porvenir *Town* Panama 23 M7
El Progreso *Town* Honduras 22 G3
El Salvador *Country* 22 E5
El Sáuz *Town* Mexico 18 G4
El Tigre *Town* Venezuela 26 E5
Emba *Town* Kazakhstan 78 E6
Emden *Town* Germany 56 C5
Emerald *Town* Queensland, Australia 105 L4
Emmen *Town* Netherlands 52 G7
Empalme *Town* Mexico 18 F4
Empty Quarter *see* Ar Rub' al Khālī
Encarnación *Town* Paraguay 30 H6
Encs *Town* Hungary 63 G10
Endeh *Town* Indonesia 97 J8
England *National Region* UK 51 G9
English Channel UK/France 51 H12
Enid *Town* Oklahoma, USA 17 L3
En Nâqoûra *Town* Lebanon 81 D10
Enschede *Town* Netherlands 52 G8
Ensenada *Town* Mexico 18 C3
Entebbe *Town* Uganda 39 E11
Enugu *Town* Nigeria 41 L7
Eolie, Isole *Island* Italy 61 F12
Épinal *Town* France 54 H7
Equatorial Guinea *Country* 43 C9
Erdenet *Town* Mongolia 89 I3
Ereğli *Town* Turkey 76 F6
Erenhot *Town* China 89 K4

GŁOGÓW – HOLON

Głogów *Town* Poland 62 D7
Gloucester *Town* England, UK 51 F10
Gniezno *Town* Poland 62 D6
Gobi *Desert* Mongolia 89 I4
Godāvari *River* India 86 H5
Godhra *Town* India 86 G4
Godoy Cruz *Town* Argentina 30 D8
Goes *Town* Netherlands 53 D10
Goiânia *Town* Brazil 29 K6
Göksun *Town* Turkey 76 H6
Golan Heights *Mountain range* Syria 81 D10
Goldsboro *Town* North Carolina, USA 11 K3
Goleniów *Town* Poland 62 C5
Golmud *Town* China 88 G6
Goma *Town* Democratic Republic of Congo 43 H10
Gombi *Town* Nigeria 41 M6
Gómez Palacio *Town* Mexico 18 H5
Gonaïves *Town* Haiti 25 I5
Gonder *Town* Ethiopia 38 F8
Gondia *Town* India 87 I5
Good Hope, Cape of *Coastal feature* South Africa 44 F9
Goor *Town* Netherlands 52 G8
Göppingen *Town* Germany 57 D9
Gorakhpur *Town* Pakistan 87 J3
Goraãde *Town* Bosnia & Herzegovina 65 E9
Gorē *Town* Ethiopia 39 F9
Gorgān *Town* Iran 82 F5
Gori *Town* Georgia 77 L3
Görlitz *Town* Germany 56 G7
Gorontalo *Town* Indonesia 97 J6
Gorzów Wielkopolski *Town* Poland 62 C6
Gosford *Town* New South Wales, Australia 105 M7
Goshogawara *Town* Japan 92 F7
Göteborg *see* Gothenburg
Gotel Mountains Nigeria 41 M7
Gotha *Town* Germany 56 E7
Gothenburg *Town* Sweden 49 C11
Gotland *Island* Sweden 49 E11
Gōtsu *Town* Japan 93 C12
Göttingen *Town* Germany 56 D7
Gouda *Town* Netherlands 53 E9
Governador Valadares *Town* Brazil 29 L6
Gradaús, Serra dos *Mountain range* Brazil 29 J4
Grafton *Town* New South Wales, Australia 105 N6
Grafton *Town* North Dakota, USA 12 G2
Grampian Mountains Scotland, UK 50 E5
Granada *Town* Spain 59 I8
Granada *Town* Nicaragua 22 H6
Gran Chaco *Plain* Paraguay 30 G4
Grand Bahama Island Bahamas 24 F1
Grand Canyon Arizona, USA 16 E3
Grand Cayman *Island* West Indies 24 E5
Grande, Bahía *Bay* Argentina 31 E13
Grand Erg Occidental *Desert* Algeria 36 G5
Grand Erg Oriental *Desert* Algeria 37 I5
Grande, Rio *River* Mexico/USA 16 G5
Grand Forks *Town* North Dakota, USA 12 G2
Grand Rapids *Town* Minnesota, USA 12 H3
Grand Rapids *Town* Michigan, USA 13 K5
Grand-Santi *Town* French Guiana 26 H6
Grants Pass *Town* Oregon, USA 14 F4
Grayling *Town* Alaska, USA 4 D4
Graz *Town* Austria 57 H11
Great Australian Bight *Sea feature* Australia 104 G7
Great Barrier Island New Zealand 106 G4
Great Barrier Reef *Coral reef* Australia 105 L3
Great Basin Nevada, USA 14 H6
Great Bear Lake Northwest Territories, Canada 4 H5
Great Dividing Range *Mountain range* Queensland/New South Wales, Australia 105 L4
Greater Antilles *Island group* Caribbean Sea 24 G5
Greater Caucasus *Mountain range* Asia/Europe 77 M3
Great Falls *Town* Montana, USA 15 J2
Great Hungarian Plain Hungary 63 F12
Great Inagua *Island* Bahamas 25 I4
Great Karoo *Plateau* South Africa 44 F8
Great Khingan Range *Mountain range* China 89 L3
Great Rift Valley Africa 39 F12
Great Sand Sea *Desert* Egypt 38 C4
Great Sandy Desert Western Australia, Australia 104 G4
Great Slave Lake Northwest Territories, Canada 4 H6
Great Victoria Desert Western Australia/ South Australia, Australia 104 G6
Great Wall of China *Ancient monument* China 89 J5
Great Yarmouth *Town* England, UK 51 I9
Greece *Country* 67 D11
Greeley *Town* Colorado, USA 15 L5
Green Bay *Town* Wisconsin, USA 13 J4
Greenfield *Town* Massachusetts, USA 9 J5
Greeneville *Town* Tennessee, USA 11 I3
Greenland *Dependent territory* Denmark, Atlantic Ocean 111 C8
Greenland Sea Arctic Ocean 111 M7
Green Mountains Vermont, USA 9 I5
Greenock *Town* Scotland, UK 50 E6
Greensboro *Town* North Carolina, USA 11 J3
Greenville *Town* Mississippi, USA 10 F5
Greenville *Town* South Carolina, USA 11 I4
Greifswald *Town* Germany 56 F4
Grenada *Country* 25 O8
Grenadines, The *Island group* St Vincent & The Grenadines 25 O8
Grenoble *Town* France 55 G10
Gresham *Town* Oregon, USA 14 F3
Grevenmacher *Town* Luxembourg 53 G13
Greymouth *Town* New Zealand 107 D10
Grey Range *Mountain range* New South Wales/Queensland, Australia 105 K6
Griffin *Town* Georgia, USA 10 H5
Grimsby *Town* England, UK 51 H9
Grise Fiord *Town* Nunavut, Canada 5 J3
Grójec *Town* Poland 62 F7
Groningen *Town* Netherlands 52 G6
Grootfontein *Town* Namibia 44 F5
Grosseto *Town* Italy 60 D8
Groznyy *Town* Russian Federation 73 D14
Gubkin *Town* Russian Federation 73 C10
Grudziądz *Town* Poland 62 E5
Gryazi *Town* Russian Federation 73 C10
Guadalajara *Town* Spain 59 I5
Guadalajara *Town* Mexico 19 I7
Guadalcanal *Island* Solomon Islands 102 G6
Guadalupe *Town* Mexico 19 I6
Guadeloupe *Dependent territory* France, Atlantic Ocean 25 O6
Guaimaca *Town* Honduras 22 G4
Gualeguaychú *Town* Argentina 30 G8
Guam *Dependent territory* USA, Pacific Ocean 102 D2
Guamúchil *Town* Mexico 18 G5
Guanabacoa *Town* Cuba 24 D3
Guanajuato *Town* Mexico 19 J7
Guanare *Town* Venezuela 26 D5
Guangdong *Administrative region* China 91 J8
Guangxi *Administrative region* China 90 H8
Guangyuan *Town* China 90 H5
Guangzhou *Town* China 91 I8
Guantánamo *Town* Cuba 24 H4
Guantánamo Bay *Territory* USA, Cuba 24 H5
Guasave *Town* Mexico 18 G5
Guatemala *Country* 22 D3
Guatemala City *Capital* Guatemala 22 D4
Guayaquil *Town* Ecuador 26 A8
Guaymas *Town* Mexico 18 E4
Guéret *Town* France 55 E9
Guernsey *Island* Channel Islands, UK 51 F13
Guerrero Negro *Town* Mexico 18 D4
Guiana Highlands *Mountain range* Colombia/Venezuela/Brazil26 F7
Guider *Town* Cameroon 42 D7
Guildford *Town* England, UK 51 G11
Guilin *Town* China 91 I7
Guinea *Country* 40 F6
Guinea Bissau *Country* 40 E6
Guinea, Gulf of Atlantic Ocean 33 M5
Guiyang *Town* China 90 H7
Guizhou *Administrative region* China 90 G7
Gujrānwāla *Town* Pakistan 86 H2
Gujrāt *Town* Pakistan 86 H2
Gulbarga *Town* India 86 H6
Gulbene *Town* Latvia 70 G6
Gulf, The Middle East 82 E6
see also Persian Gulf
Guliston *Town* Uzbekistan 85 J4
Gulu *Town* Uganda 39 E10
Gümüşhane *Town* Turkey 76 H4
Güney Doğu Toroslar *Mountain range* Turkey 76 H6
Gusau *Town* Nigeria 41 K6
Güstrow *Town* Germany 56 F5
Gütersloh *Town* Germany 56 D6
Guwāhāti *Town* India 87 L3
Guyana *Country* 26 G6
Gwādar *Town* Pakistan 86 D3
Gwalior *Town* India 87 I3
Gyomaendrőd *Town* Hungary 63 G11
Gyöngyös *Town* Hungary 63 F11
Győr *Town* Hungary 63 D11
Gyumri *Town* Armenia 77 K

H

Haarlem *Town* Netherlands 52 E8
Haast *Town* New Zealand 107 B11
Hachinohe *Town* Japan 92 G7
Hadera *Town* Israel 81 D10
Ha Đông *Town* Vietnam 94 G7
Haeju *Town* North Korea 91 L3
Hagåtña *Capital* Guam 102 E2
Hagerstown *Town* Maryland, USA 8 F8
Ha Giang *Town* Vietnam 94 G6
Hague, The *Capital* Netherlands 52 D8
Haicheng *Town* China 91 L2
Haifa *Town* Israel 81 D10
Haikou *Town* China 91 I9
Ḥā'il *Town* Saudi Arabia 82 C8
Hainan *Administrative region* China 90 H9
Hainan Dao *Island* China 91 I9
Hai Phong *Town* Vietnam 94 G7
Haiti *Country* 25 I5
Hajdúhadház *Town* Hungary 63 G11
Hakodate *Town* Japan 92 F6
Ḥalab *see* Aleppo
Halifax *Town* Nova Scotia, Canada 7 L7
Halle *Town* Germany 56 F7
Halle *Town* Belgium 53 D11
Halle-Neustadt *Town* Germany 56 F7
Halley *Research station* Antarctica 110 D4
Halmstad *Town* Sweden 49 C11
Hamadān *Town* Iran 82 E6
Ḥamāh *Town* Syria 80 E7
Hamamatsu *Town* Japan 93 F11
Hamar *Town* Norway 49 C9
Hamburg *Town* Germany 56 E5
Hamburg *Town* New York, USA 9 F5
Hamersley Range *Mountain range* Western Australia, Australia 104 F4
Hamhŭng *Town* North Korea 91 M3
Hami *Town* China 88 G4
Hamilton *Town* Scotland, UK 50 E6
Hamilton *Town* New Zealand 106 G6
Hamilton *Town* Ontario, Canada 6 G8
Hamm *Town* Germany 56 C7
Hanamaki *Town* Japan 92 G8
Handan *Town* China 91 J4
Ha Negev *see* Negev
Hangzhou *Town* China 91 K6
Hannover *Town* Germany 56 D6
Ha Nôi *Capital* Vietnam 94 F7
Hantsavichy *Town* Belarus 71 D10
Hanzhong *Town* China 90 H5
Haradok *Town* Belarus 70 H8
Harare *Capital* Zimbabwe 45 I4
Harbel *Town* Liberia 40 F8
Harbin *Town* China 89 M3
Hardangervidda *Plateau* Norway 49 B9
Hardenberg *Town* Netherlands 52 G7
Hārer *Town* Ethiopia 39 G9
Hargeysa *Town* Somalia 39 H9
Ḥārim *Town* Syria 80 D6
Harlingen *Town* Texas, USA 17 M9
Harlow *Town* England, UK 51 H10
Harper *Town* Liberia 40 G8
Harrisburg *Town* Pennsylvania, USA 9 G7
Harrogate *Town* England, UK 50 G6
Hârşova *Town* Romania 68 G7
Hartford *Town* Connecticut, USA 9 J6
Hartlepool *Town* England, UK 50 G7
Hasselt *Town* Belgium 53 E11
Hastings *Town* New Zealand 106 H8
Hastings *Town* England, UK 50 H11
Hapeg *Town* Romania 68 E6
Hatteras, Cape *Coastal feature* North Carolina, USA 11 L3
Hat Yai *Town* Thailand 95 D13
Haugesund *Town* Norway 49 A10
Havana *Capital* Cuba 24 D3
Havant *Town* England, UK 51 G11
Havelock *Town* North Carolina, USA 11 L4
Hawaiian Ridge *Undersea feature* Pacific Ocean 109 J4
Hawera *Town* New Zealand 106 F8
Haysyn *Town* Ukraine 68 H4
Hazar *Town* Turkmenistan 84 D4
Heard & McDonald Islands *Dependent territory* Australia, Indian Ocean 99 I8
Hearst *Town* Ontario, Canada 6 F6
Hebei *Administrative region* China 91 J3
Hebron *Town* Israel 81 D11
Heerlen *Town* Netherlands 53 F11
Hefa *see* Haifa
Hefei *Town* China 91 J5
Hegang *Town* China 89 M2
Heidelberg *Town* Germany 57 D9
Heidenheim an der Brenz *Town* Germany 57 E10
Heilbronn *Town* Germany 57 D9
Heilong Jiang *see* Amur
Heilongjiang *Administrative region* China 89 M2
Heimdal Sweden 48 D7
Hekimhan *Town* Turkey 76 H5
Helena *Town* Montana, USA 15 I3
Helmond *Town* Netherlands 53 F10
Helsingborg *Town* Sweden 49 C12
Helsinki *Capital* Finland 49 G9
Henan *Administrative region* China 91 I5
Henan *Town* Qinghai, China 89 I6
Hengduan Shan *Mountain range* China 90 E7
Hengelo *Town* Netherlands 52 G8
Hengyang *Town* China 91 I7
Henzada *Town* Myanmar 94 B8
Herāt *Town* Afghanisatan 84 G7
Herford *Town* Germany 56 D6
Hermosillo *Town* Mexico 18 E4
Hexian *Town* China 91 I8
Hidalgo del Parral *Town* Mexico 18 H5
Hida-sanmyaku *Mountain range* Japan 93 E10
High Point *Town* North Carolina, USA 11 J3
Hikurangi *Town* New Zealand 106 F4
Hildesheim *Town* Germany 56 D6
Hillsboro *Town* New Hampshire, USA 9 J5
Hilversum *Town* Netherlands 52 E8
Himalayas *Mountain range* Asia 87 I2
Himeji *Town* Japan 93 D12
Ḥimş *Town* Syria 80 E8
Hînceşti *Town* Moldova 68 H5
Hindu Kush *Mountain range* Afghanisatan/ Pakistan 85 J6
Hinthada *Town* Myanmar 94 B8
Hirosaki *Town* Japan 92 F7
Hiroshima *Town* Japan 93 C12
Hitachi *Town* Japan 93 G9
Hitoyoshi *Town* Japan 93 C14
Hjørring *Town* Denmark 49 B11
Hlobyne *Town* Ukraine 69 J4
Hlybokaye *Town* Belarus 70 F8
Hobart *Town* Tasmania, Australia 105 K10
Hobro *Town* Denmark 49 B11
Hô Chi Minh *Town* Vietnam 95 G11
Hodeida *Town* Yemen 83 C12
Hódmezővásárhely *Town* Hungary 63 F12
Hodonín *Town* Czech Republic 63 D10
Hof *Town* Germany 56 F8
Hōfu *Town* Japan 93 C13
Hohhot *Town* China 89 K5
Hokkaidō *Island* Japan 92 G5
Holguín *Town* Cuba 24 G4
Hollabrunn *Town* Austria 57 H10
Holmsund *Town* Sweden 48 F7
Holon *Town* Israel 81 D11

Myitkyina *Town* Myanmar 94 C5
Mykolayiv *Town* Ukraine 69 J5
Myrhorod *Town* Ukraine 69 K3
Mýrina *Town* Greece 67 F9
Myrtle Beach *Town* South Carolina, USA 11 K4
Mysore *Town* India 86 H8
My Tho *Town* Vietnam 95 G11
Mzuzu *Town* Malawi 45 J3

N

Naberezhnyye Chelny *Town* Russian Federation 73 F9
Nãblus *Town* Israel 81 D11
Nacala *Town* Mozambique 45 K4
Nadi *Town* Fiji 103 I7
Nadvirna *Town* Ukraine 68 F4
Nadym *Town* Russian Federation 78 G5
Naga *Town* Philippines 97 J2
Nagano *Town* Japan 93 F10
Nagaoka *Town* Japan 93 F9
Nagasaki *Town* Japan 93 B14
Nagato *Town* Japan 93 C12
Nãgercoil *Town* India 86 H9
Nagornyy Karabakh *Region* Azerbaijan 77 M4
Nagoya *Town* Japan 93 F11
Nãgpur *Town* India 87 I5
Nagqu *Town* China 88 G7
Nagykanizsa *Town* Hungary 63 D12
Nagykőrös *Town* Hungary 63 F11
Naha *Town* Ryukyu Islands 93 A16
Nã'ïn *Town* Iran 82 F7
Nain *Town* Newfoundland & Labrador, Canada 7 K3
Nairobi *Capital* Kenya 39 F11
Najin *Town* North Korea 91 M2
Najrãn *Town* Saudi Arabia 83 C12
Nakagawa *Town* Japan 92 F1
Nakamura *Town* Japan 93 D13
Nakatsugawa *Town* Japan 93 F11
Nakhodka *Town* Russian Federation 79 M7
Nakhon Ratchasima *Town* Thailand 95 E9
Nakhon Sawan *Town* Thailand 95 D9
Nakhon Si Thammarat *Town* Thailand 95 D12
Nakuru *Town* Kenya 39 F11
Nal'chik *Town* Russian Federation 73 C13
Nãlut *Town* Libya 37 J5
Namangan *Town* Uzbekistan 85 K3
Nam Đinh *Town* Vietnam 94 G7
Namib Desert Namibia 44 E5
Namibe *Town* Angola 44 D4
Namibia *Country* 44 E5
Nampa *Town* Idaho, USA 14 H4
Nampula *Town* Mozambique 45 K4
Namur *Town* Belgium 53 E12
Nanaimo *Town* British Colombia, Canada 4 G9
Nancha *Town* China 89 M2
Nanchang *Town* China 91 J6
Nanchong *Town* China 90 H6
Nancy *Town* France 54 H7
Nãnded *Town* India 86 H6
Nanfeng *Town* China 91 J7
Nanjing *Town* China 91 K5
Nanning *Town* China 90 H8
Nanping *Town* China 91 K7
Nanterre *Town* France 54 E6
Nantes *Town* France 54 C8
Nantucket *Town* Massachusetts, USA 9 K6
Nantucket Island Massachusetts, USA 9 K6
Nanyang *Town* China 91 I5
Napa *Town* California, USA 14 F6
Napier *Town* New Zealand 106 H7
Naples *Town* Italy 61 F10
Napoli *see* Naples
Napo, Río *River* Peru 26 C8
Narathiwat *Town* Thailand 95 E13
Narita *Town* Japan 93 G10
Närpes *Town* Finland 48 F8
Närpiö *see* Närpes
Narva *Town* Estonia 70 H4
Narvik *Town* Norway 48 E4

Nãsãud *Town* Romania 68 F5
Nãshik *Town* India 86 G5
Nashua *Town* New Hampshire, USA 9 J5
Nashville *Town* Tennessee, USA 10 G3
Nassau *Capital* Bahamas 24 G2
Nasser *Lake* Egypt 38 E6
Nata *Town* Botswana 44 H5
Natal *Town* Brazil 29 N3
Natitingou *Town* Benin 41 J6
Natzrat *see* Nazareth
Nauru *Country* 102 H4
Nauta *Town* Peru 27 C9
Navapolatsk *Town* Belarus 70 G8
Navassa Island *Dependent territory* USA, Atlantic Ocean 24 H5
Navoiy *Town* Uzbekistan 85 I4
Navojoa *Town* Mexico 18 F5
Nawãbshãh *Town* Pakistan 86 F3
Nayoro *Town* Japan 92 F4
Nay Pyi Taw *Capital* Myanmar 94 C7
Nazareth *Town* Israel 81 D10
Nazca *Town* Peru 27 C11
Nazilli *Town* Turkey 76 D6
Nazrēt *Town* Ethiopia 39 G9
N'Dalatando *Town* Angola 44 E2
Ndélé *Town* Central African Republic 42 F7
Ndjamena *Capital* Chad 42 D6
Neagh, Lough *Lake* Northern Ireland, UK 50 D8
Neápoli *Town* Greece 67 G14
Neápoli *Town* Greece 67 C9
Near Islands *Island Group* Alaska, USA 4 A3
Nebraska *State* USA 12 F5
Necochea *Town* Argentina 31 G10
Neftekamsk *Town* Russian Federation 73 F9
Negēlē *Town* Ethiopia 39 G10
Negev *Desert* Israel 81 D12
Negombo *Town* Sri Lanka 87 I9
Negotin *Town* Serbia 64 H8
Negro, Rio *River* Brazil 28 G2
Neijiang *Town* China 90 G6
Nei Mongol Zizhiqu *see* Inner Mongolia
Neiva *Town* Colombia 26 B7
Nellore *Town* India 87 I7
Nelson *Town* New Zealand 107 E9
Nemuro *Town* Japan 92 H4
Nepal *Country* 87 J3
Neryungri *Town* Russian Federation 79 K6
Netanya *Town* Israel 81 D11
Netherlands *Country* 52 E7
Neubrandenburg *Town* Germany 56 F5
Neuchâtel *Town* Switzerland 57 C11
Neufchâteau *Town* Belgium 53 F13
Neumünster *Town* Germany 56 D4
Neunkirchen *Town* Germany 57 C9
Neuquén *Town* Argentina 31 D10
Neustadt an der Weinstrasse *Town* Germany 57 C9
Neu-Ulm *Town* Germany 57 E10
Neuwied *Town* Germany 56 C8
Nevada *State* USA 14 H6
Nevinnomyssk *Town* Russian Federation 73 C11
Nevşehir *Town* Turkey 76 G5
New Amsterdam *Town* Guyana 26 G6
Newark *Town* New Jersey, USA 9 I7
Newark *Town* New York, USA 8 G5
New Bedford *Town* Massachusetts, USA 9 K6
Newberg *Town* Oregon, USA 14 F3
New Britain *Island* Papua New Guinea 102 F5
New Caledonia *Island* New Caledonia 102 G8
New Caledonia *Dependent territory* France, Pacific Ocean 102 G7
Newcastle *Town* New South Wales, Australia 105 M7
Newcastle upon Tyne *Town* England, UK 50 F7
New Delhi *Capital* India 86 H3
Newfoundland *Island* Ontario, Canada 7 M5
Newfoundland & Labrador *Province* Canada 7 L4
Newfoundland Basin *Undersea feature* Atlantic Ocean 33 J2
New Glasgow *Town* Nova Scotia, Canada 7 L7

New Guinea *Island* Indonesia/ Papua New Guinea 102 D5
New Hampshire *State* USA 9 J4
New Haven *Town* Connecticut, USA 8 I6
New Iberia *Town* Louisiana, USA 10 E6
New Jersey *State* USA 9 I7
Newman *Town* Western Australia, Australia 104 E4
New Mexico *State* USA 17 I4
New Orleans *Town* Louisiana, USA 10 F6
New Plymouth *Town* New Zealand 106 F7
Newport *Town* Vermont, USA 9 I3
Newport *Town* Wales, UK 51 F11
Newport News *Town* Virginia, USA 11 L3
New Providence *Island* Bahamas 24 G2
Newquay *Town* England, UK 51 E12
Newry *Town* Northern Ireland, UK 50 D8
New Siberian Islands *Island group* Russian Federation 79 K3
New South Wales *State* Australia 105 L7
Newtownabbey *Town* Northern Ireland, UK 50 D7
New York *State* USA 8 G5
New York *Town* New York, USA 9 I7
New Zealand *Country* 107 E9
Ngaoundéré *Town* Cameroon 42 D7
Ngo *Town* Congo 43 D10
Nguigmi *Town* Niger 41 M5
Nha Trang *Town* Vietnam 95 H10
Niagara Falls *Town* Ontario, Canada 6 G8
Niagara Falls *Town* New York, USA 8 E5
Niagara Falls *Waterfall* Canada/USA 8 E6
Niamey *Capital* Niger 41 J5
Nia-Nia *Town* Democratic Republic of Congo 43 H9
Nicaragua *Country* 22 H5
Nicaragua, Lago de *Lake* Nicaragua 23 I6
Nice *Town* France 55 H11
Nicholls Town *Town* Bahamas 24 F2
Nicobar Islands *Island group* India 87 M8
Nicosia *Capital* Cyprus 80 B8
Nicoya *Town* Costa Rica 22 H7
Nicoya, Golfo de *Gulf* Costa Rica 23 I7
Nida *Town* Lithuania 70 C6
Nieuw-Bergen *Town* Netherlands 53 F9
Niğde *Town* Turkey 76 G6
Niger *Country* 41 K5
Niger *River* Niger/Nigeria 41 J6
Nigeria *Country* 41 M7
Niger, Mouths of the *Coastal feature* Nigeria 41 K8
Niigata *Town* Japan 93 F9
Nïhama *Town* Japan 93 D12
Niitsu *Town* Japan 93 F9
Nijmegen *Town* Netherlands 53 F9
Nikiniki *Town* Indonesia 97 J8
Nikopol' *Town* Ukraine 69 K5
Nikšić *Town* Montenegro 65 E10
Nile *River* East Africa 38 E5
Nile Delta Egypt 38 E4
Nîmes *Town* France 55 F11
Ninetyeast Ridge *Undersea feature* Indian Ocean 99 K4
Ninety Mile Beach *Coastal feature* New Zealand 106 E3
Ningbo *Town* China 91 L6
Ningxia *Administrative region* China 89 J6
Niort *Town* France 54 D8
Nipipon, Lake *Québec, Canada 6 E6
Niš *Town* Serbia 65 H9
Nişab *Town* Saudi Arabia 82 D8
Nitra *Town* Slovakia 63 E10
Niue *Dependent territory* New Zealand, Pacific Ocean 103 K7
Nizãmãbãd *Town* India 87 I6
Nizhnekamsk *Town* Russian Federation 73 F9
Nizhnevartovsk *Town* Russian Federation 78 G5
Nizhniy Novgorod *Town* Russian Federation 73 E9
Nizhniy Odes *Town* Russian Federation 72 G7
Nizhyn *Town* Ukraine 69 J2
Nkayi *Town* Congo 43 D11
Nkongsamba *Town* Cameroon 42 C8
Nobeoka *Town* Japan 93 C14

Noboribetsu *Town* Japan 92 F6
Nogales *Town* Arizona, USA 16 F6
Nogales *Town* Mexico 18 E3
Nokia *Town* Finland 48 G8
Nokou *Town* Chad 42 D5
Nong Khai *Town* Thailand 94 E8
Noordwijk aan Zee *Town* Netherlands 52 D8
Norak *Town* Tajikistan 85 J5
Norderstedt *Town* Germany 56 E5
Nordhorn *Town* Germany 56 C6
Nordkapp *see* North Cape
Norfolk *Town* Nebraska, USA 12 G5
Norfolk *Town* Virginia, USA 11 L3
Norfolk Island *Dependent territory* Australia, Pacific Ocean 109 I7
Noril'sk *Town* Russian Federation 78 H4
Norman *Town* Oklahoma, USA 17 L4
Normandy *Region* France 54 D6
Norrköping *Town* Sweden 49 E10
Norrtälje *Town* Sweden 49 E10
North Albanian Alps *Mountain range* Serbia/ Montenegro 65 F10
Northampton *Town* England, UK 51 G10
North Bay *Town* Ontario, Canada 6 G7
North Cape *Coastal feature* New Zealand 106 E3
North Cape *Coastal feature* Norway 48 G2
North Carolina *State* USA 11 K4
North Charleston *Town* South Carolina, USA 11 J5
North Dakota *State* USA 12 F3
Northern Cook Islands *Island group* Cook Islands 103 M6
Northern Dvina *River* Russian Federation 72 E7
Northern Ireland *Political region* UK 50 D7
Northern Mariana Islands *Dependent territory* USA, Pacific Ocean 102 D1
Northern Sporades *Island group* Greece 67 E10
Northern Territory *State* Australia 104 H4
North Island New Zealand 106 G7
North Korea *Country* 91 M3
North Little Rock *Town* Arkansas, USA 10 E4
North Sea Europe 50 G4
North West Highlands *Mountain range* Scotland, UK 50 E4
Northwest Pacific Basin *Undersea feature* Pacific Ocean 109 I3
Northwest Territories *Province* Canada 4 H6
Norway *Country* 48 B8
Norwegian Sea Arctic Ocean 111 M8
Norwich *Town* England, UK 51 H9
Noshiro *Town* Japan 92 F7
Noşratãbãd *Town* Iran 82 H7
Nottingham *Town* England, UK 51 G9
Nouâdhibou *Town* Mauritania 40 E3
Nouakchott *Capital* Mauritania 40 E4
Nouméa *Capital* New Caledonia 102 H8
Nova Iguaçu *Town* Brazil 29 L7
Novara *Town* Italy 60 C5
Novaya Zemlya *Island* Russian Federation 72 G4
Novi Sad *Town* Serbia 64 F7
Novocheboksarsk *Town* Russian Federation 73 E9
Novocherkassk *Town* Russian Federation 73 C11
Novodvinsk *Town* Russian Federation 72 E6
Novokuznetsk *Town* Russian Federation 78 H7
Novolazarevskaya *Research station* Antarctica 110 E3
Novomoskovs'k *Town* Ukraine 69 K4
Novomoskovsk *Town* Russian Federation 73 C9
Novorossiysk *Town* Russian Federation 73 B12
Novoshakhtinsk *Town* Russian Federation 73 C11
Novosibirsk *Town* Russian Federation 78 H6
Novotroyits'ke *Town* Ukraine 69 K6
Nowy Sącz *Town* Poland 63 F9
Noyon *Town* France 54 F6
Nsawam *Town* Ghana 41 I8

PENNINES – QUZHOU

Pennines *Hills* England, UK 50 F8
Pennsylvania *State* USA 8 F7
Penonomé *Town* Panama 23 L8
Penrith *Town* England,UK 50 F7
Pensacola *Town* Florida, USA 10 G6
Penza *Town* Russian Federation 73 D10
Penzance *Town* England, UK 51 D12
Peoria *Town* Illinois, USA 13 J6
Perchtoldsdorf *Town* Austria 57 H10
Pereira *Town* Colombia 26 B6
Pergamino *Town* Argentina 30 F8
Perm' *Town* Russian Federation 73 G9
Pernik *Town* Bulgaria 66 D6
Perote *Town* Mexico 19 K7
Perpignan *Town* France 55 E12
Persian Gulf Middle East 82 E6
see also Gulf, The
Perth *Town* Western Australia, Australia 104 E7
Perth *Town* Scotland,UK 50 F6
Peru *Country* 27 C10
Perugia *Town* Italy 60 E8
Pervomays'k *Town* Ukraine 69 I5
Pesaro *Town* Italy 60 F7
Pescara *Town* Italy 60 F8
Peshāwar *Town* Pakistan 86 G1
Pessac *Town* France 55 C10
Petah Tikva *Town* Israel 81 D11
Peterborough *Town* South Australia, Australia 105 J7
Peterborough *Town* Ontario, Canada 6 H8
Peterborough *Town* England, UK 51 H10
Peterborough *Town* South Australia, Australia 105 J7
Peterhead *Town* Scotland, UK 50 F5
Peter I Island *Dependent Territory* Norway, Southern Ocean 110 B6
Petersburg *Town* Virginia, USA 11 K2
Peters Mine *Town* Guyana 26 G6
Petra *Town* Jordan 81 E13
Petrinja *Town* Croatia 64 C6
Petrodvorets *Town* Russian Federation 72 C6
Petropavlovsk *Town* Kazakhstan 78 G6
Petropavlovsk-Kamchatskiy *Town* Russian Federation 79 M5
Petrozavodsk *Town* Russian Federation 72 D6
Pevek *Town* Russian Federation 78 L2
Pforzheim *Town* Germany 57 D9
Phan Thiêt *Town* Vietnam 95 H11
Phetchaburi *Town* Thailand 95 D10
Philadelphia *Town* Pennsylvania, USA 8 H7
Philippines *Country* 97 J2
Phitsanulok *Town* Thailand 94 D8
Phnom Penh *Capital* Cambodia 95 F11
Phoenix *Town* Arizona, USA 16 E5
Phoenix Islands *Island group* Kiribati 103 J5
Phuket *Town* Thailand 95 C13
Phuket, Ko *Island* Thailand 95 C12
Piacenza *Town* Italy 60 D5
Piatra-Neamp *Town* Romania 68 G5
Picos *Town* Brazil 29 L3
Picton *Town* New Zealand 107 F9
Piedras Negras *Town* Mexico 19 J4
Pielinen *Lake* Finland 48 H7
Pierre *Town* South Dakota, USA 12 F4
Pietermaritzburg *Town* South Africa 45 I8
Pietersburg *see* Polokwane
Pikeville *Town* Kentucky, USA 11 I2
Piła *Town* Poland 62 D6
Pinar del Río *Town* Cuba 24 D3
Píndos *see* Pindus Mountains
Pindus Mountains *Mountain range* Greece 67 C10
Pine Bluff *Town* Arkansas, USA 10 E4
Pingdingshan *Town* China 91 I5
Pinsk *Town* Belarus 71 D11
Piotrków Trybunalski *Town* Poland 62 F7
Piraeus *Town* Greece 67 E11
Pirot *Town* Serbia 65 H10
Pisa *Town* Italy 60 D7
Pisco *Town* Peru 27 B11
Písek *Town* Czech Republic 63 B9
Pistoia *Town* Italy 60 D6
Pitcairn Islands *Dependent Territory* UK, Pacific Ocean 109 L6
Pitești *Town* Romania 68 F7
Pittsburgh *Town* Pennsylvania, USA 8 E7
Pittsfield *Town* Massachusetts, USA 8 J5
Piura *Town* Peru 27 A9
Placetas *Town* Cuba 24 E3
Plano *Town* Texas, USA 17 M5
Plata, Río de la *River* Argentina 31 H9
Platinum *Town* Alaska, USA 4 D5
Platte River Nebraska, USA 12 G6
Plattsburgh *Town* New York, USA 9 I3
Plauen *Town* Germany 56 F8
Plenty, Bay of New Zealand 106 I16
Plesetsk *Town* Russian Federation 72 E7
Pleven *Town* Bulgaria 66 F5
Płock *Town* Poland 62 F6
Ploiești *Town* Romania 68 F7
Plovdiv *Town* Bulgaria 66 F7
Plungė *Town* Lithuania 70 C6
Plymouth *Capital* Montserrat 25 N6
Plymouth *Town* England, UK 51 E12
Plzeň *Town* Czech Republic 63 B9
Po *River* Italy 60 E6
Pobedy, Pik *Mountain* China 88 E4
Pocahontas *Town* Arkansas, USA 10 F3
Podgorica *Capital* Montenegro 65 E10
Podil's'ka Vysochyna *Mountain range* Ukraine 68 H4
Podol'sk *Town* Russian Federation 72 C8
Pointe-à-Pitre *Town* Guadeloupe 25 O6
Pointe-Noire *Town* Congo 43 C11
Poitiers *Town* France 54 D8
Pokharā *Town* Nepal 87 J3
Poland *Country* 62 E7
Polatli *Town* Turkey 76 F5
Polatsk *Town* Belarus 70 G8
Pólis *Town* Cyprus 80 A8
Polokwane *Town* South Africa 45 H7
Poltava *Town* Ukraine 69 K3
Polýkastro *Town* Greece 66 D8
Polynesia *Region* Pacific Ocean 103 N6
Pomeranian Bay Poland 62 C5
Pompano Beach *Town* Florida, USA 11 J8
Ponce *Town* Puerto Rico 25 L5
Pondicherry *Town* India 87 I8
Ponferrada *Town* Spain 58 G3
Ponta Grossa *Town* Brazil 29 J7
Pontevedra *Town* Spain 58 E3
Pontiac *Town* Michigan, USA 13 L5
Pontianak *Town* Indonesia 96 F6
Poole *Town* England, UK 51 G12
Popayán *Town* Colombia 26 B7
Popocatépetl *Mountain* Mexico 19 K8
Porbandar *Town* India 86 F5
Pordenone *Town* Italy 60 F5
Poreč *Town* Croatia 64 A6
Pori *Town* Finland 49 F9
Porirua *Town* New Zealand 107 F9
Póros *Town* Greece 67 E12
Port Alfred *Town* South Africa 44 H9
Port Arthur *Town* Texas, USA 17 N7
Port Augusta *Town* South Australia, Australia 105 J7
Port-au-Prince *Capital* Haiti 25 J5
Port Blair *Town* India 87 M7
Port Elizabeth *Town* South Africa 44 H9
Port-Gentil *Town* Gabon 43 B10
Port Harcourt *Town* Nigeria 41 L8
Portland *Town* Oregon, USA 14 F3
Portland *Town* Maine, USA 8 K4
Portland *Town* Victoria, Australia 105 J8
Port Laoise *Town* Ireland 51 C9
Port Louis *Capital* Mauritius 45 O6
Port Macquarie *Town* New South Wales, Australia 105 N7
Port Moresby *Capital* Papua New Guinea 102 E6
Porto *Town* Portugal 58 E4
Porto Alegre *Town* Brazil 29 J9
Portobelo *Town* Panama 23 M7
Port-of-Spain *Capital* Trinidad & Tobago 25 O9
Porto-Novo *Capital* Benin 41 J7
Porto Torres *Town* Sardinia, Italy 61 B9
Porto Velho *Town* Brazil 28 G4
Portoviejo *Town* Ecuador 26 A8
Port Said *Town* Egypt 38 E4
Portsmouth *Town* England, UK 51 G12
Portsmouth *Town* New Hampshire, USA 9 K5
Portsmouth *Town* Virginia, USA 11 L3
Port Sudan *Town* Sudan 38 F6
Portugal *Country* 58 F5
Port-Vila *Capital* Vanuatu 102 H7
Porvoo *Town* Finland 49 G9
Posadas *Town* Argentina 30 H6
Poso *Town* Indonesia 97 J6
Potenza *Town* Italy 61 G10
P'ot'i *Town* Georgia 77 J3
Potiskum *Town* Nigeria 41 M6
Potomac River Virginia, USA 11 K2
Potosí *Town* Bolivia 27 E13
Potsdam *Town* Germany 56 F6
Po Valley Italy 60 D5
Poza Rica *Town* Mexico 19 K7
Požega *Town* Serbia 65 F9
Poznań *Town* Poland 62 D6
Pozzallo *Town* Sicily, Italy 61 F14
Prague *Capital* Czech Republic 62 B8
Praha *see* Prague
Praia *Capital* Cape Verde 33 K4
Prato *Town* Italy 60 D7
Prenzlau *Town* Germany 56 G5
Přerov *Town* Czech Republic 63 D9
Presidente Epitácio *Town* Brazil 29 J7
Prešov *Town* Slovakia 63 G9
Prespa, Lake Macedonia 65 G12
Presque Isle *Town* Maine, USA 9 L1
Preston *Town* England, UK 50 F8
Prestwick *Town* Scotland, UK 50 E7
Pretoria *Capital* South Africa 44 H6
see also Tshwane
Préveza *Town* Greece 67 C10
Price *Town* Utah, USA 15 J6
Prichard *Town* Alabama, USA 10 G6
Prienai *Town* Lithuania 70 D8
Prieska *Town* South Africa 44 G8
Prilep *Town* Macedonia 65 G12
Primorsk *Town* Kaliningrad 70 B6
Primorsko *Town* Bulgaria 66 H7
Prince Edward Islands *Island group* South Africa 98 H7
Prince George *Town* British Colombia, Canada 4 G8
Prinzapolka *Town* Nicaragua 23 J5
Pripet *River* Belarus 71 E11
Pripet Marshes *Wetland* Belarus/ Ukraine 71 D11
Priština *Capital* Kosovo 65 G10
Prizren *Town* Kosovo 65 G10
Probolinggo *Town* Indonesia 96 H8
Progreso *Town* Mexico 19 O6
Prokhladnyy *Town* Russian Federation 73 C13
Prokuplje *Town* Serbia 65 G9
Prostějov *Town* Czech Republic 63 D9
Providence *Town* Rhode Island, USA 8 J6
Provincetown *Town* Massachusetts, USA 9 K5
Provo *Town* Utah, USA 15 J5
Prudhoe Bay *Town* Alaska, USA 4 F4
Pruszków *Town* Poland 62 F7
Pryluky *Town* Ukraine 69 J3
Przemyśl *Town* Poland 63 G9
Pskov *Town* Russian Federation 72 B7
Pucallpa *Town* Peru 27 C10
Pudasjärvi *Town* Finland 48 G6
Puebla *Town* Mexico 19 K8
Pueblo *Town* Colorado, USA 15 L6
Puerto Angel *Town* Mexico 19 L9
Puerto Ayacucho *Town* Venezuela 26 E6
Puerto Barrios *Town* Guatemala 22 F3
Puerto Cortés *Town* Honduras 22 F3
Puerto Deseado *Town* Argentina 31 E12
Puerto Escondido *Town* Mexico 19 L9
Puerto La Cruz *Town* Venezuela 26 E5
Puerto Lempira *Town* Honduras 23 I3
Puertollano *Town* Spain 58 H7
Puerto López *Town* Colombia 26 D4
Puerto Maldonado *Town* Peru 27 D11
Puerto Montt *Town* Chile 31 C10
Puerto Plata *Town* Dominican Republic 25 J5
Puerto Princesa *Town* Philippines 97 I4
Puerto Rico *Dependent territory* USA, Atlantic Ocean 25 L6
Puerto Suárez *Town* Bolivia 27 G12
Puerto Vallarta *Town* Mexico 18 H7
Puerto Varas *Town* Chile 31 C10
Puget Sound *Bay* Washington, USA 14 F2
Pula *Town* Croatia 64 A6
Puławy *Town* Poland 62 G7
Pune *Town* India 86 G6
Punjab *Region* Pakistan/India 86 H2
Puno *Town* Peru 27 D12
Punta Alta *Town* Argentina 31 F10
Punta Arenas *Town* Chile 31 D14
Puntarenas *Town* Costa Rica 23 I7
Puntland *Cultural region* Somalia 39 H9
Puri *Town* India 87 K5
Purmerend *Town* Netherlands 52 E8
Purus, Rio *River* Brazil 28 F4
Pusan *Town* South Korea 91 M4
Putrajaya *Capital* Malaysia 96 E5
Putumayo, Río *River* Colombia 26 C8
Puurmani *Town* Estonia 70 G5
Pyatigorsk *Town* Russian Federation 73 C11
Pyay *Town* Myanmar 94 B8
Pyechin *Town* Myanmar 94 A7
Pýlos *Town* Greece 67 C12
Pyn-Oo-Lwin *Town* Myanmar 94 C6
P'yŏngyang *Capital* North Korea 91 L3
Pyrenees *Mountain range* France/ Spain 55 C12
Pyryatyn *Town* Ukraine 69 J3

Q

Qaidam Pendi *Basin* China 88 H6
Qalāt *Town* Afghanistan 85 I8
Qal 'at Bīshah *Town* Saudi Arabia 83 C11
Qamdo *Town* China 88 H7
Qarokŭl *Town* Tajikistan 85 L4
Qarshi *Town* Uzbekistan 85 I5
Qasr Farâfra *Town* Egypt 38 D5
Qavanā *Town* Syria 81 D9
Qatar *Country* 83 F9
Qattara Depression *Desert basin* Egypt 38 D4
Qazimämmäd *Town* Azerbaijan 77 N4
Qazvīn *Town* Iran 82 E6
Qilian Shan *Mountain range* China 88 H5
Qinā *Town* Egypt 38 E5
Qingdao *Town* China 91 K4
Qinghai *Administrative region* China 88 H6
Qingzang Gaoyuan *see* Tibet, Plateau of
Qinhuangdao *Town* China 91 K3
Qinzhou *Town* China 90 I18
Qiqihar *Town* China 89 L2
Qira *Town* China 88 D6
Qitai *Town* China 88 F4
Qizilrabot *Town* Tajikistan 85 L5
Qom *Town* Iran 82 E6
Qo'qon *Town* Uzbekistan 85 K4
Qorveh *Town* Iran 82 D6
Quang Ngai *Town* Vietnam 95 H9
Quanzhou *Town* China 91 K7
Quartu Sant' Elena *Town* Sardinia, Italy 61 B11
Quba *Town* Azerbaijan 77 N3
Québec *Province* Canada 7 I5
Québec *Town* Québec, Canada 7 I7
Queen Elizabeth Islands *Island Group* Northern Canada 5 I3
Queensland *State* Australia 105 K4
Queenstown *Town* New Zealand 107 B12
Quelimane *Town* Mozambique 45 J5
Querétaro *Town* Mexico 19 J7
Quesada *Town* Costa Rica 23 I7
Quetta *Town* Pakistan 86 F2
Quezaltenango *Town* Guatemala 22 D4
Quibdó *Town* Colombia 26 B6
Quillabamba *Town* Peru 27 D11
Quilon *Town* India 86 H9 *see also Kollam*
Quimper *Town* France 54 B7
Quincy *Town* Missouri, USA 13 I7
Quito *Capital* Ecuador 26 B7
Qŭrghonteppa *Town* Tajikistan 85 J5
Quy Nhơn *Town* Vietnam 95 H10
Quzhou *Town* China 91 K6

R

Rabat *Capital* Morocco 36 E4
Rabinal *Town* Guatemala 22 E4
Rabyānah, Ramlat *Desert* Libya 37 M6
Race, Cape *Coastal feature* Newfoundland & Labrador, Canada 7 N6
Rach Gia *Town* Vietnam 95 F12
Racine *Town* Wisconsin, USA 13 J5
Radom *Town* Poland 62 G7
Rafaela *Town* Argentina 30 F7
Rafah *Town* Israel 81 C12
Ragusa *Town* Sicily, Italy 61 F14
Rahīmyār Khān *Town* Pakistan 86 G3
Rāichūr *Town* India 86 H6
Raipur *Town* India 87 J5
Rājahmundry *Town* India 87 J6
Rājkot *Town* India 86 G4
Rajshahi *Town* Bangladesh 87 K4
Raleigh *Town* North Carolina, USA 11 K3
Ralik Chain *Island chain* Marshall Islands 102 H2
Râmnicu Vâlcea *Town* Romania 68 E7
Rancagua *Town* Chile 30 D8
Rānchi *Town* India 87 J4
Randers *Denmark* 49 B12
Rangoon *Town* Myanmar 94 B8
Rangpur *Town* Pakistan 87 L3
Rankin Inlet *Town* Nunavut, Canada 5 J6
Rapid City *Town* South Dakota, USA 12 E4
Ra's al 'Ayn *Town* Syria 80 G4
Rasht *Town* Iran 82 E5
Ratak Chain *Island chain* Marshall Islands 102 H2
Rathkeale *Town* Ireland 51 B10
Rat Islands *Island Group* Alaska, USA 4 A4
Ratlām *Town* India 86 H4
Raton *Town* New Mexico, USA 17 I3
Rättvik *Town* Sweden 49 D9
Raukumara Range *Mountain range* New Zealand 106 I7
Rāulakela *Town* India 87 J5
Rauma *Town* Finland 49 F9
Ravenna *Town* Italy 60 E6
Rāwalpindi *Town* Pakistan 86 G1
Rawicz *Town* Poland 62 D7
Rawlins *Town* Wyoming, USA 15 K5
Rawson *Town* Argentina 31 F11
Razgrad *Town* Bulgaria 66 G5
Reading *Town* Pennsylvania, USA 9 H7
Reading *Town* England, UK 51 G11
Realicó *Town* Argentina 30 E8
Rechytsa *Town* Belarus 71 F11
Recife *Town* Brazil 29 N4
Recklinghausen *Town* Germany 56 C7
Recogne *Town* Belgium 53 E13
Reconquista *Town* Argentina 30 G6
Red Deer *Town* Alberta, Canada 4 H8
Redding *Town* California, USA 14 F5
Red River USA 17 K4
Red Sea *Africa/Asia* 83 B9
Reefton *Town* New Zealand 107 D10
Regensburg *Town* Germany 57 F9
Reggane *Town* Algeria 36 G6
Reggio di Calabria *Town* Italy 61 G13
Reggio nell' Emilia *Town* Italy 60 D6
Regina *Town* Saskatchewan, Canada 5 I9
Rehovot *Town* Israel 81 D11
Reims *Town* France 54 F6
Rengat *Town* Indonesia 96 E6
Rennes *Town* France 54 C7
Reno *Town* Nevada, USA 14 G5
Renqiu *Town* Hebei, China 91 J3
Republika Srpska *Administrative region* Bosnia & Herzegovina 64 D7
Repulse Bay *Town* Nunavut, Canada 5 K5
Resistencia *Town* Argentina 30 G6
Reşiţa *Town* Romania 68 D6
Resolute *Town* Nunavut, Canada 5 J3
Réunion *Dependent territory* France, Indian Ocean 45 O6
Reus *Town* Spain 59 L4
Reutlingen *Town* Germany 57 D10
Rijau *Town* Belgium 37 E11
Reykjavík *Capital* Iceland 111 D9

Reynosa *Town* Mexico 19 K5
Rēzekne *Town* Latvia 70 G7
Rheine *Town* Germany 56 C6
Rhine *River* Europe 56 C8
Rho *Town* Italy 60 C5
Rhode Island *State* USA 9 J6
Rhodes *Town* Greece 67 I13
Rhodope Mountains *Mountain range* Bulgaria 66 G7
Rhône *River* France 55 F11
Ribeirão Preto *Town* Brazil 29 K7
Rîbniţa *Town* Moldova 68 H5
Richmond *Town* Kentucky, USA 10 H2
Richmond *Town* Virginia, USA 11 K2
Ried im Innkreis *Town* Austria 57 G10
Rīga *Capital* Latvia 70 E5
Riga, Gulf of *Latvia* 70 E5
Rijeka *Town* Croatia 64 B6
Rimini *Town* Italy 60 E7
Rimouski *Town* Québec, Canada 7 J6
Riobamba *Town* Ecuador 26 A8
Río Bravo *Town* Mexico 19 K5
Río Cuarto *Town* Argentina 30 E8
Rio de Janeiro *Town* Brazil 29 L7
Río Gallegos *Town* Argentina 31 E14
Rio Grande *Town* Brazil 29 J9
Ríohacha *Town* Colombia 26 C4
Rio Lagartos *Town* Mexico 19 O6
Río Verde *Town* Mexico 19 J7
Rivera *Town* Uruguay 30 H7
River Falls *Town* Wisconsin, USA 13 I4
Riverside *Town* California, USA 14 G8
Riverton *Town* Wyoming, USA 15 K4
Rivne *Town* Ukraine 68 G2
Rivoli *Town* Italy 60 B5
Riyadh *Capital* Saudi Arabia 83 D9
Road Town *Capital* British Virgin Islands 25 M5
Rize *Town* Turkey 77 J3
Roanoke *Town* Virginia, USA 11 J3
Roatán *Town* Honduras 22 G3
Robinson Range *Mountain range* Western Australia, Australia 104 F5
Robstown *Town* Texas, USA 17 L8
Rochefort *Town* Belgium 53 E12
Rochefort *Town* France 55 D9
Rochester *Town* New York, USA 8 F5
Rochester *Town* Minnesota, USA 13 I4
Rockford *Town* Illinois, USA 13 J5
Rockhampton *Town* Queensland, Australia 105 M4
Rock Hill *Town* South Carolina, USA 11 J4
Rock Sound *Town* Bahamas 24 G2
Rocky Mountains *Canada/USA* 4, 14
Ródos *see* Rhodes
Roeselare *Town* Belgium 53 C11
Rogatica *Town* Bosnia & Herzegovina 64 E8
Rogers *Town* Arkansas, USA 10 D3
Roi Et *Town* Thailand 95 F9
Rokycany *Town* Czech Republic 63 B9
Roma *Town* Queensland, Australia 105 M5
Roma *see* Rome
Roman *Town* Romania 68 G5
Romania *Country* 68 E6
Rome *Capital* Italy 61 E9
Romny *Town* Ukraine 69 J2
Rondonópolis *Town* Brazil 29 I6
Ronne Ice Shelf *Ice feature* Antarctica 110 C5
Roosendaal *Town* Netherlands 53 D10
Røros *Town* Norway 48 C8
Rosario *Town* Argentina 30 F8
Rosario *Town* Paraguay 30 H5
Rosarito *Town* Mexico 18 C2
Roseau *Capital* Dominica 25 O6
Rosenheim *Town* Germany 57 F10
Roslavl' *Town* Russian Federation 73 B9
Ross *Town* New Zealand 107 D10
Ross Ice Shelf *Ice feature* Antarctica 110 D7
Rosso *Town* Mauritania 40 E4
Rossosh' *Town* Russian Federation 73 C10
Ross Sea Antarctica 110 D7
Rostock *Town* Germany 56 F4
Rostov-na-Donu *Town* Russian Federation 73 C11
Roswell *Town* New Mexico, USA 17 I5
Rothera *Research station* Antarctica 110 B5

Rotorua *Town* New Zealand 106 G6
Rotorua, Lake New Zealand 106 G6
Rotterdam *Town* Netherlands 53 E9
Roubaix *Town* France 54 F5
Rouen *Town* France 54 E6
Round Rock *Town* Texas, USA 17 L6
Rovigo *Town* Italy 60 E6
Roxas City *Town* Philippines 97 J3
Rozdol'ne *Town* Ukraine 69 J6
Rožňava *Town* Slovakia 63 F10
Ruatoria *Town* New Zealand 106 I6
Rubizhne *Town* Ukraine 69 M4
Rudnyy *Town* Kazakhstan 78 E6
Rudzyensk *Town* Belarus 71 E10
Rufino *Town* Argentina 30 F8
Rukwa, Lake Tanzania 39 E13
Ruoqiang *Town* China 88 F5
Ruse *Town* Bulgaria 66 G5
Rushmore, Mount *Mountain* South Dakota, USA 12 E4
Russellville *Town* Arkansas, USA 10 E3
Russian Federation *Country* 78 G6
Rust'avi *Town* Georgia 77 L3
Ruston *Town* Louisiana, USA 10 E5
Rutland *Town* Vermont, USA 9 I4
Rwanda *Country* 39 D12
Ryazan' *Town* Russian Federation 73 D9
Rybinsk *Town* Russian Federation 72 D8
Rybnik *Town* Poland 62 E8
Ryki *Town* Poland 62 G7
Ryukyu Islands *Island chain* Japan 93 A16
Rzeszów *Town* Poland 63 G9
Rzhev *Town* Russian Federation 72 C8

S

Saalfeld *Town* Germany 56 E8
Saarbrücken *Town* Germany 57 C9
Sab' Ābār *Town* Syria 80 F8
Šabac *Town* Serbia 64 F7
Sabadell *Town* Spain 59 M4
Sabah *Cultural region* Malaysia 96 H5
Sabaya *Town* Bolivia 27 D12
Sabhā *Town* Libya 37 K6
Sabinas *Town* Mexico 19 I4
Sabinas Hidalgo *Town* Mexico 19 J4
Sable Island *Québec, Canada* 7 M7
Sabzevār *Town* Iran 82 G8
Sacramento *Town* California, USA 14 F6
Sacramento Mountains New Mexico/ Texas, USA 16 H5
Sacramento Valley California, USA 14 F5
Şa'dah *Town* Yemen 83 C12
Şafāshahr *Town* Iran 82 F7
Safi *Town* Morocco 36 E4
Sagaing *Town* Myanmar 94 B6
Sāgar *Town* India 87 I4
Saginaw *Town* Michigan, USA 13 L5
Sagua la Grande *Town* Cuba 24 E3
Sagunto *Town* Spain 59 K6
Sahara *Desert* North Africa 36–37, 40–41
Sahel *Desert* North Africa 41 K5
Saïda *Town* Lebanon 81 D9
Saiki *Town* Japan 93 C13
Saimaa *Lake* Finland 48 H8
St Albans *Town* England, UK 51 H10
Saint Albans *Town* West Virginia, USA 11 I2
St Andrews *Town* Scotland, UK 51 F10
St. Anthony *Town* Newfoundland & Labrador, Canada 7 M4
Saint Augustine *Town* Florida, USA 11 J6
St-Brieuc *Town* France 54 B6
St. Catharines *Town* Ontario, Canada 6 G8
St-Chamond *Town* France 55 F10
St-Claude *Town* France 55 G9
St Croix *Island* Virgin Islands 25 M5
St-Denis *Capital* Réunion 45 O6
St-Étienne *Town* France 55 F10
St-Gaudens *Town* France 55 D11
St-Georges *Town* French Guiana 26 I6
St. George's *Capital* Grenada 25 O8
St George's Channel Europe 51 D10
St Helena *Dependent Territory* UK Atlantic Ocean 33 L6

St Helier *Capital* Jersey, Channel Islands 51 G13
St-Jean, Lac *Lake* Canada 7 I6
Saint John *Town* New Brunswick, Canada 7 K7
St John's *Capital* Antigua & Barbuda 25 N5
St. John's *Town* Newfoundland & Labrador, Canada 7 N5
Saint Joseph *Town* Missouri, USA 12 H7
Saint Kitts & Nevis *Country* 25 N6
St-Laurent-du-Maroni *Town* French Guiana 26 H6
St. Lawrence *River* Canada/USA 7 J6
St. Lawrence, Gulf of Canada 7 L6
Saint Lawrence Island Alaska, USA 4 D4
Saint Louis *Town* Senegal 40 E5
Saint Louis *Town* Illinois, USA 13 J7
St. Lucia *Country* 25 O7
St Lucia Channel *Martinique* 25 O7
St-Malo *Town* France 54 C6
St. Moritz *Town* Switzerland 57 D12
St-Nazaire *Town* France 54 B8
St-Omer *Town* France 54 E5
Saint Paul *Town* Minnesota, USA 13 I4
St Peter Port *Capital* Guernsey, Channel Islands 51 F13
Saint Petersburg *Town* Russian Federation 72 C7
Saint Petersburg *Town* Florida, USA 11 I8
St Pierre & Miquelon *Dependent Territory* France, Atlantic Ocean 7 M6
St-Quentin *Town* France 54 F6
Saint Vincent *Island* St Vincent and the Grenadines 25 O7
Saint Vincent & The Grenadines *Country* 25 O7
Saint Vincent Passage *Strait* St. Lucia 25 O7
Sakai *Town* Japan 93 E12
Sakata *Town* Japan 92 F8
Sakhalin, Ostrov *Island* Russian Federation 79 M6
Şäki *Town* Azerbaijan 77 M3
Salado, Río *River* Argentina 30 F6
Salamanca *Town* Chile 30 C7
Salamanca *Town* Spain 58 G5
Salamiyah *Town* Syria 80 E7
Salavat *Town* Russian Federation 73 G10
Saldus *Town* Latvia 70 D5
Salé *Town* Morocco 36 F4
Salem *Town* Nepal 87 I8
Salem *Town* Oregon, USA 14 F3
Salerno *Town* Italy 61 F10
Salihorsk *Town* Belarus 71 E10
Salima *Town* Malawi 45 J3
Salina *Town* Kansas, USA 12 G7
Salina Cruz *Town* Mexico 19 M9
Salinas *Town* California, USA 14 F7
Salisbury *Town* Maryland, USA 9 H9
Salonica *Town* Greece 66 E8
Salonta *Town* Romania 68 D5
Sal'sk *Town* Russian Federation 73 C11
Salta *Town* Argentina 30 E5
Saltillo *Town* Mexico 19 J5
Salt Lake City *Town* Utah, USA 15 I5
Salto *Town* Uruguay 30 G7
Salvador *Town* Brazil 29 M5
Salween *River* Myanmar 94 C7
Salyān *Town* Nepal 87 J3
Salzburg *Town* Austria 57 F10
Salzgitter *Town* Germany 56 E6
Samalayuca *Town* Mexico 18 G3
Samar *Island* Philippines 97 K3
Samara *Town* Russian Federation 73 E10
Samarinda *Town* Indonesia 97 I6
Samarqand *Town* Uzbekistan 85 I4
Şamaxi *Town* Azerbaijan 77 N3
Sambalpur *Town* India 87 J5
Samoa *Country* 103 K6
Sampit *Town* Indonesia 96 G7
Samsun *Town* Turkey 76 H3
Samtredia *Town* Georgia 77 K3
Samui, Ko *Thailand* 95 D12
Samut Prakan *Town* Thailand 95 E10
San *Town* Mali 40 H6
Şan'ā' *see* Sanaa
Sanaa *Capital* Yemen 83 C12
Sanae *Research station* Antarctica 110 D3

Tanganyika, Lake *Democratic Republic of Congo* 43 I12
Tanggula Shan *Mountain range China* 88 G7
Tangier *Town Morocco* 36 F3
Tangshan *Town China* 91 K3
Tan-Tan *Town Morocco* 36 D5
Tanzania *Country* 39 E12
Taoudenni *Town Mali* 40 H3
Tapa *Town Estonia* 70 G4
Tapachula *Town Mexico* 19 N9
Tapajós, Rio *River Brazil* 29 I3
Tarābulus *see* Tripoli
Tarancón *Town Spain* 59 I6
Taranto *Town Italy* 61 H10
Taranto, Gulf *Italy* 61 H11
Tarapoto *Town Peru* 27 B9
Taraz *Town Kazakhstan* 78 F8
Tarbes *Town France* 55 D11
Târgovişte *Town Romania* 68 F7
Târgu Jiu *Town Romania* 68 E7
Târgu Mureş *Town Romania* 68 F5
Tarija *Town Bolivia* 27 E13
Tarim Basin *China* 88 F5
Tarnobrzeg *Town Poland* 62 G8
Tarnów *Town Poland* 63 F9
Tarragona *Town Spain* 59 L4
Tarsus *Town Turkey* 76 G6
Tartu *Town Estonia* 70 G5
Ţarţūs *Town Syria* 80 D7
Tarvisio *Town Italy* 60 F4
Tashkent *Capital Uzbekistan* 85 J3
Tash-Kumyr *Town Kyrgyzstan* 85 K3
Tasikmalaya *Town Indonesia* 96 F8
Tasmania *State Australia* 105 K9
Tasman Sea *Pacific Ocean* 105 M8
Tassili-n-Ajjer *Plateau Algeria* 37 I6
Tatabánya *Town Hungary* 63 E11
Tathlith *Town Saudi Arabia* 83 C11
Tatra Mountains *Slovakia* 63 F9
Tatvan *Town Turkey* 77 K5
Taungdwingyi *Town Myanmar* 94 B7
Taunggyi *Town Myanmar* 94 C7
Taunton *Town England, UK* 51 F11
Taupo *Town New Zealand* 106 G7
Taupo, Lake *New Zealand* 106 G7
Tauranga *Town New Zealand* 106 G6
Taurus Mountains *Mountain range Turkey* 76 E6
Tawau *Town Malaysia* 97 I5
Taxco *Town Mexico* 19 K8
Taxiatosh *Town Uzbekistan* 84 F2
Taymā' *Town Saudi Arabia* 82 B8
Taymyr Peninsula *Russian Federation* 79 I3
T'bilisi *Capital Georgia* 77 L3
Tczew *Town Poland* 62 E5
Teapa *Town Mexico* 19 N8
Tebingtinggi *Town Indonesia* 96 D5
Tecomán *Town Mexico* 19 I8
Tecpan *Town Mexico* 19 J9
Tecuci *Town Romania* 68 G6
Tegal *Town Indonesia* 96 F7
Tegucigalpa *Capital Honduras* 22 G4
Tehrān *Capital Iran* 82 E6
Tehuacán *Town Mexico* 19 L8
Tehuantepec *Town Mexico* 19 M9
Tehuantepec, Gulf of *Mexico* 19 M9
Tehuantepec, Istmo de *Isthmus Mexico* 19 M8
Tejen *Town Turkmenistan* 84 F5
Te Kao *Town New Zealand* 106 E3
Tekeli *Town Kazakhstan* 78 G8
Tekirdağ *Town Turkey* 76 C3
Tel Aviv-Yafo *Town Israel* 81 C11
Temirtau *Town Kazakhstan* 78 F7
Temple *Town Texas, USA* 17 M6
Temuco *Town Chile* 31 C10
Ténéré *Physical region Niger* 41 M4
Tennessee *State USA* 10 G3
Tennessee River *Alabama/Tennessee, USA* 10 G4
Tepic *Town Mexico* 18 H7
Teplice *Town Czech Republic* 62 B8
Tequila *Town Mexico* 19 I7
Teramo *Town Italy* 60 F8
Teresina *Town Brazil* 29 M3

Termiz *Town Uzbekistan* 85 I5
Ternate *Town Indonesia* 97 K6
Terni *Town Italy* 60 E8
Ternopil' *Town Ukraine* 68 G3
Terrassa *Town Spain* 59 M4
Terre Haute *Town Indiana, USA* 13 K7
Teruel *Town Spain* 59 K5
Teseney *Town Eritrea* 38 F8
Tessalit *Town Mali* 41 J3
Tete *Town Mozambique* 45 I4
Tetouan *Town Morocco* 36 F3
Tevere *River Italy* 60 E8
Texarkana *Town Texas, USA* 17 N5
Texas *State USA* 17 L6
Teziutlán *Town Mexico* 19 K7
Thai Binh *Town Vietnam* 94 G7
Thailand *Country* 95 D9
Thailand, Gulf of *Pacific Ocean* 95 E11
Thai Nguyên *Town Vietnam* 94 G6
Thakhèk *Town Laos* 94 F8
Thamarit *Town Oman* 83 G11
Thandwe *Town Myanmar* 94 B8
Thanh Hoa *Town Vietnam* 94 F7
Thar Desert *Pakistan/India* 86 F3
Thaton *Town Myanmar* 94 C8
Thayetmyo *Town Myanmar* 94 B7
The Fens *Physical region England, UK* 51 H9
Thessaloníki *see* Salonica
The Valley *Capital Anguilla* 25 N5
Thimphu *Capital Bhutan* 87 L3
Thiruvananthapuram *Town India* 86 H9 *see also* Trivandrum
Thracian Sea *Greece* 66 F8
Thun *Town Switzerland* 57 C11
Thunder Bay *Town Ontario, Canada* 6 E6
Thurso *Town Scotland,UK* 50 E3
Tianjin *Town China* 91 J3
Tianjin Shu *Administrative region China* 91 J3
Tianshui *Town China* 89 J6
Tiberias, Lake *Israel* 81 D10
Tibesti *Mountain range Chad* 42 E3
Tibet *Administrative region China* 88 F7
Tibet, Plateau of *China* 88 F6
Tîchît *Town Mauritania/China* 40 G4
Ticul *Town Mexico* 19 O6
Tien Shan *Mountain range Kyrgyzstan* 85 L3
Tierra del Fuego *Region Argentina/Chile* 31 D14
Tifu *Town Indonesia* 97 K7
Tighina *Town Moldova* 68 H6
Tigris *River Iraq* 82 C6
Tiguentourine *Town Algeria* 37 J6
Tijuana *Town Mexico* 18 C2
Tikal *Ancient site Guatemala* 22 E2
Tikhoretsk *Town Russian Federation* 73 C12
Tikhvin *Town Russian Federation* 72 C7
Tiksi *Town Russian Federation* 78 J4
Tilburg *Town Netherlands* 53 E10
Timaru *Town New Zealand* 107 D12
Timbedgha *Town Mauritania* 40 G5
Timbuktu *Town Mali* 41 I4
Timişoara *Town Romania* 68 D6
Timor Sea *Asia/Australasia* 97 J9
Tindouf *Town Algeria* 36 E6
Tirana *Capital Albania* 65 F11
Tiranë *see* Tirana
Tiraspol *Town Moldova* 68 H6
Tirol *Region Austria* 57 F11
Tiruchchirāppalli *Town India* 87 I8
Tisa *River Hungary* 63 F11
Tivoli *Town Italy* 61 E9
Tizi Ouzou *Town Algeria* 36 H3
Tiznit *Town Morocco* 36 E5
Tlaquepaque *Town Mexico* 19 I7
Tlaxcala *Town Mexico* 19 K8
Tlemcen *Town Algeria* 36 G4
Toamasina *Town Madagascar* 45 M5
Tobago *Island Trinidad & Tobago* 25 O8
Tobol'sk *Town Russian Federation* 78 G5

Tocantins, Rio *River Brazil* 29 K4
Tocopilla *Town Chile* 30 D4
Todi *Town Italy* 60 E8
Togo *Country* 41 J7
Tokar *Town Sudan* 38 F7
Tokat *Town Turkey* 76 H4
Tokelau *Dependent territory New Zealand, Pacific Ocean* 103 K6
Tokmak *Town Kyrgyzstan* 85 L3
Tokmak *Town Ukraine* 69 L5
Tokoroa *Town New Zealand* 106 G6
Tokushima *Town Japan* 93 D12
Tōkyō *Capital Japan* 93 G10
Toledo *Town Spain* 59 I6
Toledo *Town Ohio, USA* 13 L6
Toliara *Town Madagascar* 45 L6
Tolitoli *Town Indonesia* 97 J6
Tolmin *Town Slovenia* 57 G12
Toluca *Town Mexico* 19 J8
Tol'yatti *Town Russian Federation* 73 E10
Tomakomai *Town Japan* 92 F5
Tomaszów Mazowiecki *Town Poland* 62 F7
Tombouctou *see* Timbuktu
Tomini, Gulf of *Indonesia* 97 J6
Tomsk *Town Russian Federation* 78 H6
Tonga *Country* 103 K7
Tongatapu Group *Island group Tonga* 103 J8
Tongchuan *Town China* 90 H4
Tonghe *Town China* 89 M2
Tongzi *Town China* 90 H6
Tongking, Gulf of *South China Sea* 90 H9
Tongliao *Town China* 89 L3
Tongxin *Town China* 89 J6
Tongzi *Town China* 90 H6
Tônlé Sap *Lake Cambodia* 95 F10
Tonopah *Town Nevada, USA* 14 H6
Tooele *Town Utah, USA* 15 I5
Toowoomba *Town Queensland, Australia* 105 M6
Topeka *Town Kansas, USA* 12 G7
Torez *Town Ukraine* 69 M5
Torgau *Town Germany* 56 F7
Torino *see* Turin
Torkestan Mountains *Mountain range Afghanistan* 84 H6
Toro *Town Spain* 58 H4
Toronto *Town Ontario, Canada* 6 G8
Toros Dağlari *see* Taurus Mountains
Torquay *Town England, UK* 51 F12
Torre del Greco *Town Italy* 61 F10
Torrejón de Ardoz *Town Spain* 59 I5
Torrelavega *Town Spain* 59 I2
Torrente *Town Spain* 59 K6
Torreón *Town Mexico* 19 I5
Torres Strait *Australia/Papua New Guinea* 105 K1
Torres Vedras *Town Portugal* 58 E6
Torrington *Town Wyoming, USA* 15 L5
Toruń *Town Poland* 62 E6
Torzhok *Town Russian Federation* 72 C8
Toscana *see* Tuscany
Toscano, Archipelago *Coastal feature Italy* 60 D8
Toshkent *see* Tashkent
Totness *Town Suriname* 26 H6
Tottori *Town Japan* 93 D11
Touggourt *Town Algeria* 37 I4
Toukoto *Town Mali* 40 G5
Toul *Town France* 54 G7
Toulon *Town France* 55 G12
Toulouse *Town France* 55 D11
Tourcoing *Town France* 54 F5
Tournai *Town Belgium* 53 C11
Tours *Town France* 54 D8
Tovarkovskiy *Town Russian Federation* 73 C9
Towada *Town Japan* 92 G7
Tương Đương *Town Vietnam* 94 G7
Townsville *Town Queensland, Australia* 105 L3
Towson *Town Maryland, USA* 8 G8
Toyama *Town Japan* 93 F10
Toyota *Town Japan* 93 F11
Tozeur *Town Tunisia* 37 I4
Trabzon *Town Turkey* 76 H3
Trang *Town Thailand* 95 D13
Transantarctic Mountains *Mountain range Antarctica* 110 D6

Transnistria *Cultural region Moldova* 68 H5
Transylvania *Cultural region Romania* 68 E5
Transylvanian Alps *Mountain range Romania* 68 E5
Trapani *Town Sicily, Italy* 61 D12
Trâpeăng Vêng *Town Cambodia* 95 F10
Trasimeno, Lago *Italy* 60 E7
Tra Vinh *Town Vietnam* 95 G12
Tremelo *Town Belgium* 53 E11
Trenčín *Town Slovakia* 63 E10
Trenque Lauquen *Town Argentina* 31 F9
Trent *River England, UK* 51 G9
Trento *Town Italy* 60 E4
Trenton *Town Pennsylvania, USA* 8 G7
Tres Arroyos *Town Argentina* 31 F9
Treviso *Town Italy* 60 E5
Trier *Town Germany* 56 B8
Trieste *Town Italy* 60 F5
Trincomalee *Town Sri Lanka* 87 I9
Trinidad *Island Trinidad & Tobago* 25 O9
Trinidad *Town Uruguay* 30 G3
Trinidad *Town Bolivia* 27 E11
Trinidad & Tobago *Country* 25 O9
Tripoli *Town Lebanon* 80 D8
Tripoli *Capital Libya* 37 K4
Tripolitania *Cultural region Libya* 37 K5
Tristan de Cunha *Dependent Territory St Helena, Atlantic Ocean* 33 L7
Trivandrum *Town India* 86 H9 *see also* Thiruvananthapuram
Trnava *Town Slovakia* 63 D10
Trois-Rivières *Town Québec, Canada* 7 I7
Trollhättan *Town Sweden* 49 C10
Tromsø *Town Norway* 48 E4
Trondheim *Town Norway* 48 C7
Troy *Town New York, USA* 8 I5
Troyes *Town France* 54 F7
Trujillo *Town Spain* 58 G6
Trujillo *Town Peru* 27 A10
Trzcianka *Town Poland* 62 D6
Tshela *Town Democratic Republic of Congo* 43 D11
Tshikapa *Town Democratic Republic of Congo* 43 F12
Tshwane *Capital South Africa* 44 H6 *see also* Pretoria
Tsu *Town Japan* 93 E11
Tsugaru-kaikyo *Strait Japan* 92 F7
Tsuruga *Town Japan* 93 E11
Tsuruoka *Town Japan* 92 F8
Tuamotu Islands *Island group French Polynesia* 103 O7
Tuapse *Town Russian Federation* 73 B12
Tuba City *Town Arizona, USA* 16 E3
Tubmanburg *Town Liberia* 40 F7
Ţubruq *Town Libya* 37 N4
Tucson *Town Arizona, USA* 16 E5
Tucumcari *Town New Mexico, USA* 17 I4
Tudmur *Town Syria* 80 F7
Tuguegarao *Town Philippines* 97 J1
Tukums *Town Latvia* 70 E5
Tula *Town Russian Federation* 73 C9
Tulancingo *Town Mexico* 19 K7
Tulcán *Town Ecuador* 26 B7
Tulcea *Town Romania* 68 H7
Tulsa *Town Oklahoma, USA* 17 M3
Tuluá *Town Colombia* 26 B6
Tumbes *Town Peru* 26 A8
Tumuc-Humac Mountains *Mountain range Brazil* 29 I1
Tungaru *Island chain Kiribati* 103 I4
Tungsten *Town Northwest Territories, Canada* 4 G6
Tunis *Capital Tunisia* 37 J3
Tunisia *Country* 37 J4
Tunja *Town Colombia* 26 C6
Tupelo *Town Mississippi, USA* 10 G4
Turan Lowland *Plain Central Asia* 84 F2
Ţurayf *Town Saudi Arabia* 82 B7
Turbat *Town Pakistan* 86 E3
Turda *Town Romania* 68 F5
Turin *Town Italy* 60 B5
Turkana, Lake *Kenya* 39 F10
Turkestan *Town Kazakhstan* 78 F7
Turkey *Country* 76 F5
Türkmenabat *Town Turkmenistan* 84 H4

Index

Acknowledgements

For the 2011 edition, Dorling Kindersley would like to thank:

Natalie Godwin for jacket design, Niki Foreman for proofreading, Matilda Gollon for editorial help, and Carron Brown for the index and for editorial help.

CD production team:

Senior digital graphic designer Nain Singh Rawat
Producer Lakshmi Rao
Technical manager Jay Prakash Pandey
Producer and data architect Archna Sharma
Technical coordinator Amit Verma
Assistant editor Suchi Smita
Assistant graphic designer Vikas Sachdeva
Assistant DTP designers Abhishek Verma, Rohit Rojal
Senior producer, digital content Briar Towers

The publisher would like to thank the following for their kind permission to reproduce their photographs: (Key: a-above; b-below/bottom; c-centre; f-far; l-left; r-right; t-top)

i Corbis: B.S.P.I. (bl); Steve Rayner (fbr). **Photoshot:** World Pictures (fbl, br). **ii Corbis:** Stephanie Maze (br). **Getty Images:** Jim Cummins / Stone (cra). **Science Photo Library:** 1995 Worldsat International, and J. Knighton (l). **iii Corbis:** Sergio Pitamitz (br). **Robert Harding Picture Library:** Robert Frerck (cl); Frans Lemmens (cra). **v Corbis:** Frans Lanting (clb); Ludovic Maisant (bl); Werner H. Mueller (cla/dunes). **vi Corbis:** Howard Davies (br). **viii Corbis:** Jacky Naegelen / Reuters (cra). **2 Corbis:** Alan Schein Photography (bl). **Robert Harding Picture Library:** John Miller (cra). **3 Corbis:** Peter M. Wilson (clb). **Science Photo Library:** 1995 Worldsat International, and J. Knighton (globe). **4 Alaska Stock:** (clb). **Corbis:** Gunter Marx Photography (bl); Charles O'Rear (tr). **Photoshot:** World Pictures (bc). **5 Corbis:** Staffan Widstrand (tc); Peter M. Wilson (br/mountain background). **NHPA / Photoshot:** T. Kitchin and V. Hurst (cra); Andy Rouse (fbr/bear). **6 Cephas Picture Library:** Fred R. Palmer (tr). **Corbis:** Benjamin Rondel (bl/Toronto). Press Association Images: Tony Marshall / EMPICS Sport; (bc). **7 Corbis:** William A. Bake (br); Richard J. Nowitz (cra). **Photoshot:** Egmont Strigl / imagebroker; (tr); World Pictures (tl). **8 Pictures Colour Library:** (ca). **Robert Harding Picture Library:** Stuart Pearce / Age Fotostock (bl). **9 Corbis:** Alan Schein Photography (br); Paul Barton (crb); Ralf-Finn Hestoft (tl); Farrell Grehan (c). **Robert Harding Picture Library:** Andy Caulfield / Panoramic Images (tr). **10 Corbis:** Owen Franken (crb). **Getty Images:** Andy Sacks (cla). **Redferns:** (bc). **Robert Harding Picture Library:** Peter Lilja / Age Fotostock (br). **11 Corbis:** Tony Arruza (br); Flip Schulke (cb). **Getty Images:** Matthew Stockman (tc). **12 Corbis:** Blaine Harrington III (cl/buffalo). **Dorling Kindersley:** American Museum of Natural History, London (fcl). **Rex Features:** Sipa Press (bc). **Robert Harding Picture Library:** Sergio Pitamitz (br). **13 Corbis:** Philip Gould (br); Julie Habel (tl). **Getty Images:** Jim Cummins / Stone (crb). **14 Robert Harding Picture Library:** Liane Cary / age fotostock (bl); Melissa Farlow / National Geographic (tc). **15 Corbis:** Dean Conger (ca); Jong Beom Kim / TongRo (clb); Lester Lefkowitz (br). **Rex Features:** Sipa Press (bc). **Robert Harding Picture Library:** Louise Murray (tr). **Science Photo Library:** George Bernard (bl). **16 Corbis:** B.S.P.I. (br); Richard Ransier (ftr). **Dorling Kindersley:** Hopi Learning Centre (br/doll). **Getty Images:** Eric Schnakenberg / Photographer's Choice (tr). **Robert Harding Picture Library:** Tony Gervis (bl). **17 NASA:** (tr). **Robert Harding Picture Library:** Walter Rawlings (bl). **18 Corbis:** Keith Dannemiller (tr); Danny Lehman (br). **Robert Harding Picture Library:** Robert Frerck / Odyssey / Chicago (cl). **Still Pictures:** Julio Etchart (bl). **19 Corbis:** Macduff Everton (tr); Tim Thompson (tc). **Getty Images:** Bruce Stoddard / Stone (ftl). 20 Corbis: Stephen Frink (cl); Sergio Pitamitz (crb). **Eye Ubiquitous / Hutchison:** Robert Francis (br). Photoshot: World Pictures (bl). **21 Corbis:** Poisson d'avril / Photocuisine (ca); Arvind Garg (tl). **Eye Ubiquitous / Hutchison:** Robert Francis (clb). **Photoshot:** World Pictures / Intervision (tr). **Robert Harding Picture Library:** Jose Enrique Molina / age fotostock (crb). **22 Corbis:** Bill Gentile (cl). **Photoshot:** Martin Engelmann (bl). **23 Corbis:** Wolfgang Kaehler (cb); Peter Turnley (clb). **Eye Ubiquitous / Hutchison:** John Fuller (tl). **Photoshot:** World Pictures (ca). **Robert Harding Picture Library:** John Miller (tr). **24 Robert Harding Picture Library:** P. Narayan / Age Fotostock (cra). **South American Pictures:** Jason Howe (b). **25 Photoshot:** World Pictures (clb). **Science Photo Library:** 1995, Worldsat International and J. Knighton (globe). **26 Corbis:** Pablo Corral V (cla). **Photoshot:** World Pictures (cr). **South American Pictures:** (tl). **27 Dorling Kindersley:** British Museum (br). **Eye Ubiquitous / Hutchison:** H. Jelliffee (tr); Paul Seheult (tl); Eric Lawrie (cra). **Photoshot:** World Pictures (bl). **Robert Harding Picture Library:** Gavin Hellier (cr). **28 Corbis:** Yann Arthus-Bertrand (crb). **Eye Ubiquitous / Hutchison:** Dr Nigel Smith (br). **Robert Harding Picture Library:** (clb). **South American Pictures:** Jason Howe (bl). **29 Corbis:** Stephanie Maze (ca). **Photoshot:** (br). **Tomek Sierek:** (tr). **30 Corbis:** Tony Arruza (br). **Photoshot:** World Pictures (bc). **Robert Harding Picture Library:** Bildagentur Schuster / Gluske (cla); Ken Welsh / Age Fotostock (tl). **31 Corbis:** Fulvio Roiter (tr). **Photoshot:** World Pictures (cla). **Robert Harding Picture Library:** Victor Englebert (bl); P. Narayan / Age Fotostock (tl). **South American Pictures:** (b). **32 Corbis:** Carlos Dominguez (crb); Wolfgang Kaehler (br). **NHPA / Photoshot:** B. & C. Alexander (bl). **Robert Harding Picture Library:** (tr); Roy Rainford (cra); Adam Woolfitt (clb). **33 Corbis:** George D. Lepp (br); Hans Strand (tr). **35 Science Photo Library:** Tom Van Sant, Geosphere Project / Planetary Visions (t). **36 Eye Ubiquitous / Hutchison:** Mary Jelliffee (br). **Photoshot:** World Pictures (tr, cl). **37 Corbis:** Benjamin Lowy (b). **Dorling Kindersley:** British Museum (tc). **Getty Images:** Frans Lemmens / The Image Bank (crb). **Photoshot:** World Pictures (tr). **Robert Harding Picture Library:** T.D. Winter (tl). **38 Corbis:** Michael Hanson / National Geographic Society (tr). **Photoshot:** World Pictures (br). **Robert Harding Picture Library:** Nakamura (ca). **39 Corbis:** Karl Ammann (br). **Eye Ubiquitous / Hutchison:** (tr); Jeremy Horner (bl); Sarah Errington (bc). **40 Dorling Kindersley:** Barnabas Kindersley (bl). **Panos Pictures:** Teun Voeten; (br/diamond). **Robert Harding Picture Library:** J. Lightfoot (cla). **41 Corbis:** Charles & Josette Lenars (bl). **Eye Ubiquitous / Hutchison:** Crispin Hughes (cr, br). **Panos Pictures:** Clive Shirley (tl). **42 Corbis:** Skip Brown / National Geographic Society (tl). **Dorling Kindersley:** Powell Cotton Museum (bc). **Eye Ubiquitous / Hutchison:** Sarah Errington (br). **Photoshot:** World Pictures (tc). **43 Dorling Kindersley:** Natural History Museum, London (cra/copper). **Eye Ubiquitous / Hutchison:** (c); Trevor Page (br). **Getty Images:** Nicolas Cotto / AFP (tr); Per-Anders Pettersson / The Image Bank (bl). **44 Corbis:** Anthony Bannister (cla). **Photoshot:** (bl). **Robert Harding Picture Library:** Alain Evrard (bc). **45 Alamy Images:** AfriPics.com (br/buffalo background). **Corbis:** Peter Turnley (bl). **Dreamstime.com:** Eric Isselée (fbr/lion). **Eye Ubiquitous / Hutchison:** Sarah Errington (tl); Liba Taylor (tr); Crispin Hughes (tc). **Robert Harding Picture Library:** Chris Mattison / age fotostock (crb/lemur). **47 Photoshot:** World Pictures (cr). **Science Photo Library:** Tom Van Sant, Geosphere Project / Planetary Visions (t). **48 Corbis:** Charles & Josette Lenars (tl). **Photoshot:** Paul Thompson / World Pictures (br). **Robert Harding Picture Library:** Kim Hart (ftl). **49 Corbis:** Jean-Pierre Amet / Sygma (tl); Dave Bartruff (tr); Stephanie Maze (cla). **TopFoto.co.uk:** Francis Dean / Imageworks (crb). **50 Corbis:** David Paterson / WildCountry (tr); Michael St. Maur Sheil (br). **Pictures Colour Library:** (bc). **Robert Harding Picture Library:** Eye Ubiquitous (tc). **51 Corbis:** Tommy Hindley / NewSport (bc). **Eye Ubiquitous / Hutchison:** Philp Wolmouth (br). **Pictures Colour Library:** Charles Bowman (cr). **Robert Harding Picture Library:** Mark Mawson / Robert Harding World Imagery (tr). **52 Corbis:** Owen Franken (br). **Photoshot:** World Pictures (bc). **Robert Harding Picture Library:** Adam Woolfitt (tl). **53 Corbis:** Dave Bartruff (bl); Ray Juno (br); Owen Franken (tr, tl). **54 Corbis:** G. Bowater (cb); Roger Ressmeyer (ftl). **Photoshot:** (tl). **55 Corbis:** Pierre Perrin / Sygma (bl); Kim Sayer (br); Mike Powell (cra). **Photoshot:** Carol Pucci / Seattle Times / MCT (tl). **56 Corbis:** Arnd Wiegmann / akw / Reuters (tl). **Getty Images:** Michael Rosenfeld (bc). **Masterfile:** Didier Dorval (tr). **Rex Features:** Sipa Press (br). **57 Corbis:** Dominic Ebenbichler / Reuters (cr). **Getty Images:** Sylvain Grandadam (tr); Jess Stock (br). **58 Corbis:** Morton Beebe (bl). **Dreamstime.com:** Photooiasson (Álvaro Germán Vilela) (clb). **Robert Harding Picture Library:** Jesus Nicolas Sanchez / age fotostock (cla). **59 Corbis:** Patrick Ward (br). **Getty Images:** AFP (tr). **Panos Pictures:** David Constantine (cr). **Pictures Colour Library:** © FMGB Guggenheim Bilbao Museoa. Photo by Charles Bowman. All rights reserved. Total or partial reproduction is prohibited. (tl). **Robert Harding Picture Library:** Robert Frerck (bl). **60 Corbis:** Jörg Carstensen / DPA (cl). **Rex Features:** Enrica Scalfari (tr). **Robert Harding Picture Library:** R. Richardson (br). **61 Art Directors & TRIP:** (cra). **Eye Ubiquitous / Hutchison:** Trevor Page (bc). **Photoshot:** World Pictures (r). **Pictures Colour Library:** (clb). **62 Dreamstime.com:** Taratorki (Ewa Rejmer) (tr). **Panos Pictures:** David Constantine (cla). **Robert Harding Picture Library:** (tl). **63 Eye Ubiquitous / Hutchison:** Liba Taylor (cb). **Photoshot:** Rick Strange / World Pictures (tl); World Pictures (tr, br). **64 Eye Ubiquitous / Hutchison:** (ca). **Press Association Images:** Tony Marshall (bc). **Photoshot:** World Pictures (tl). **65 Corbis:** John Heseltine (cb). **Eye Ubiquitous / Hutchison:** David Watson (br). **Robert Harding Picture Library:** G. R. Richardson (tr); Phil Robinson (bl). **66 Corbis:** Marco Cristofori / Robert Harding World Imagery (tl). **Eye Ubiquitous / Hutchison:** Melanie Friend (crb, br). **Robert Harding Picture Library:** (tr). **67 Corbis:** Dallas & John Heaton / Free Agents Limited (cb); Clay Perry (tl). **Photoshot:** Lorraine Nicol / World Pictures (bl); World Pictures (tr); World Pictures / Mauritius Images (br). **68 Art Directors & TRIP:** P. Mercea (br). **Eye Ubiquitous / Hutchison:** Nick Haslam (clb). **Photoshot:** World Pictures (bl). **Pictures Colour Library:** (cla). **69 Art Directors & TRIP:** D. Mossienko (tr); N.& J. Wiseman (cr). **Corbis:** Barry Lewis (bl). **Eye Ubiquitous / Hutchison:** Liba Taylor (br). **70 Art Directors & TRIP:** T. Noorits (tl). **Robert Harding Picture Library:** Angelo Cavalli (bc). **71 Corbis:** Serge Attal / Sygma (bl); Dimitri Iundt / TempSport (tr); Niall Benvie (fcra); Nik Wheeler (tl); Staffan Widstrand (bc). **Photoshot:** Paul Thompson / World Pictures (br). **72 Corbis:** Robbie Jack (bc); Steve Rayner (tr). **Photoshot:** World Pictures (cla). **73 Art Directors & TRIP:** D. Iusupov (ca). **Corbis:** Gavin Hellier / Robert Harding World Imagery (br). **Dorling Kindersley:** Pitt Rivers Museum (tc). **Eye Ubiquitous / Hutchison:** Victoria Ivleva-Yorke (tr); Liba Taylor (bl, tl). **75 Science Photo Library:** Tom Van Sant / Geosphere Project / Planetary Visions (t). **76 Corbis:** Dave G. Houser (br); Lawrence Manning (cl); Adam Woolfitt (tr). **Photoshot:** Adina Amsel / World Pictures (bl). **77 Corbis:** Arne Hodalic (bl); David Turnley (tr); Nik Wheeler (br). **78 Corbis:** Peter Turnley (bc). **Eye Ubiquitous / Hutchison:** Sarah Errington (bl). **79 Alamy Images:** Arcticphoto (tr). **Corbis:** Wolfgang Kaehler (bl); Gregor Schmid (crb). **Pictures Colour Library:** (cr). **Robert Harding Picture Library:** Morales (br). **80 Corbis:** David Turnley (cla). **Photoshot:** José Nicolas / Hemis.fr / World Pictures (cb); Rick Strange / World Pictures (br); World Pictures (fcla). **81 Corbis:** Christine Osborne (fcrb/police officer). **Eye Ubiquitous / Hutchison:** Bernard Gerard (bl); James Henderson (tr). **Photoshot:** Jonathan Carlile / Imagebrokers (tl). **Robert Harding Picture Library:** Michael Short (br/landscape). **82 Dorling Kindersley:** British Library (c). **Eye Ubiquitous / Hutchison:** Bernard Gerard (b). **Getty Images:** Bruno Morandi (tc). **Rex Features:** Stuart Clarke (tl). **83 Dorling Kindersley:** Barnabas Kindersley (br). **Eye Ubiquitous / Hutchison:** John Nowell (crb). **Robert Harding Picture Library:** Mohamed Amin (bl); Walter Bibikow (tl). **84 Corbis:** S. Sabawoon (bl). **Getty Images:** Shah Marai / AFP (cb). **85 Corbis:** David Turnley (cr); Nevada Wier (cb, tr/mountains, tr). **Robert Harding Picture Library:** Ivan Vdovin (br). **86 Corbis:** Keren Su (br). **Eye Ubiquitous / Hutchison:** Sarah Errington (clb). **Getty Images:** Martin Puddy (cl). **87 Alamy Images:** Tibor Bognar (tr). **Eye Ubiquitous / Hutchison:** Horner (bl). **Pictorial Press Ltd:** (crb). **Robert Harding Picture Library:** David Beatty (tl); Frans Lemmens (clb). **88 Eye Ubiquitous / Hutchison:** Sarah Murray (b); Stephen Pem (cla). **88-89 Robert Harding Picture Library:** Philippe Michel (tc). **89 Eye Ubiquitous / Hutchison:** Melanie Friend (bl); Stephen Pern (tr). **Photoshot:** Rudi Pigneter (clb). **Robert Harding Picture Library:** G. Hellier (br); Doug Traverso (cr). **90 Corbis:** Douglas Peebles (tr). **Eye Ubiquitous / Hutchison:** Melanie Friend (cb); Jeremy Horner (bl). **Photoshot:** World Pictures (cla). **91 Corbis:** Michael S. Yamashita (bc). **Eye Ubiquitous / Hutchison:** Trevor Page (tl); Christine Pemberton (br). **Getty Images:** Kim Jae-Hwan / AFP (cra). **Photoshot:** World Pictures (crb). **92 Corbis:** Robert Holmes (tl). **Getty Images:** Paul Chesley / Stone (cl). **Photoshot:** World Pictures (br). **Pictures Colour Library:** (tr). **93 Corbis:** Michael S. Yamashita (bl). **Eye Ubiquitous / Hutchison:** Jon Burbank (tl); N. Haslam (clb). **Getty Images:** Panoramic Images (tr). **Robert Harding Picture Library:** Gavin Hellier (ca). **94 Corbis:** (cla). **Eye Ubiquitous / Hutchison:** Rene Giudicelli (tl). **Photoshot:** (tc); World Pictures (tr). **95 Eye Ubiquitous / Hutchison:** Norman Froggatt (cr). **Photoshot:** Stuart Pearce / World Pictures (br). **Robert Harding Picture Library:** (clb) Alain Evrard (tr). **96 Corbis:** (cl); Tom Brakefield (tr). **Eye Ubiquitous / Hutchison:** John Halt (br); Juliet Highet (bl). **Rex Features:** Tim Rooke (cra). **97 Corbis:** Dean Conger (br). **Eye Ubiquitous / Hutchison:** Michael Macintyre (ca); Dr Nigel Smith (cr). **Rex Features:** Sipa Press (tr). **98 Eye Ubiquitous / Hutchison:** Isabella Tree (tr). **Photoshot:** Josef Beck (cla); Hartmut Röder (cr); World Pictures (bl). **Still Pictures:** Roland Seitre (cb). **99 Corbis:** Theo Allofs (cra). **Photoshot:** Eye Ubiquitous / Hutchison (tr). **Rex Features:** Wilhemsen (br). **100 Corbis:** Sergio Pitamitz (bl); Keren Su (cra). **101 Corbis:** Wolfgang Kaehler (cl). **Getty Images:** Travel Pix (br). **Science Photo Library:** 1995, Worldsat International and J. Knighton (globe). **102 Corbis:** B.S.P.I. (tr). **Dorling Kindersley:** Mark O'Shea (bl). **Eye Ubiquitous / Hutchison:** Michael Macintyre (bc). **103 Corbis:** Wolfgang Kaehler (bl). Eye Ubiquitous / Hutchison: Nick Haslam (cra); Michael MacIntyre (tr). **Robert Harding Picture Library:** Upperhall Ltd (tl). **104 Corbis:** Penny Tweedie (cla). **Eye Ubiquitous / Hutchison:** N. Durrell McKenna (clb). **Getty Images:** Panoramic Images (cla/landscape background). **Press Association Images:** Phil Walter / EMPICS Sport (bc). **Robert Harding Picture Library:** Ken Gillham (tr). **105 Corbis:** Sergio Pitamitz (br). **Eye Ubiquitous / Hutchison:** Robert Francis (bl). **Getty Images:** Jeff Hunter / Photographer's Choice (cra). **Robert Harding Picture Library:** Neale Clark (crb). **106 Photoshot:** Rick Strange / World Pictures (crb); Paul Thompson / World Pictures (tl); World Pictures (br). **107 Photoshot:** Jeny McMillan (tr). **Rex Features:** Simon Runting (bl). **Robert Harding Picture Library:** Jeremy Bright (cb); Julia Thorne (tl). **108 Getty Images:** Andy Hall / Australian Defense Force (clb); Jeremy Woodhouse / Photodisc (cra). **Photolibrary:** Seiden Allan / Pacific Stock; ; (tr). **Robert Harding Picture Library:** Andoni Canela (bl). **Verena Tunnicliffe:** (crb). **109 Corbis:** Wolfgang Kaehler (tr); Stephanie Maze (br). **Robert Harding Picture Library:** Warren Finlay / International Stock (cra). **110 Eye Ubiquitous / Hutchison:** Isabella Tree (bl). **NASA:** (cla). **Robert Harding Picture Library:** Thorsten Milse (br); Geoff Renner (tr). **Still Pictures:** Marc Steinmetz / VISUM; (clb). **111 Corbis:** Composite Image / Alaska Stock LLC (tr); Tim Davis (br); Vince Streano (cla); Torleif Svensson (crb).

Jacket: *Front:* **Getty Images:** Thomas Jackson (tr) (giraffe on CD), Eric Meola / The Image Bank (fbl); **naturepl.com:** Brandon Cole bl, Pete Oxford (br, tr) (monks on CD); **Science Photo Library:** Simon Fraser (tc) (geyser on CD), David R. Frazier (cra) (rainbow on CD), Planetary Visions Ltd. (globe); *Back:* **Alamy Images:** Dallas & John Heaton / Stock Connection Blue (fbr) **Getty Images:** V. Giannella / De Agostini Picture Library (cb) Thomas Jackson (fbl) Christopher Roberts / Axiom Photographic Agency (clb) (church); **naturepl.com:** John Cancalosi (clb) Pete Oxford (cb) (monks); **Science Photo Library:** Simon Fraser (bl) (geyser), Planetary Visions Ltd (globe); *Spine:* **Dorling Kindersley:** Jamie Marshall (t); **naturepl.com:** John Cancalosi (boy), Brandon Cole (bottom image).

All other images © Dorling Kindersley

For further information see: www.dkimages.com

Limit of summer pack ice

Greenland Sea

Spitsbergen

Franz Josef Land

Severnaya Zemlya

New Sib Islands

Limit of winter pack ice

Laptev Sea

Denmark Strait

Iceland

Norwegian Sea

Scandinavia

Barents Sea

Novaya Zemlya

Kara Sea

Lena

Khrebet Chersky

North Sea

Baltic Sea

Yenisey

Yenisey

Central Siberian Plateau

West Siberian Plain

Ob'

S i b e r i a

British Isles

North European Plain

Volga

Lake Baikal

Ok

E U R O P E

Carpathian Mts

U r a l   M o u n t a i n s

A S I A

Bay of Biscay

Alps

Danube

Altai Mountains

Manchurian Plain

Amur

Iberian Peninsula

Balkans Mts

Black Sea

Caucasus

Caspian Sea

Aral Sea

Lake Balkhash

Tien Shan

G o b i

Sea of Japan (East Sea)

S

Azores

Mediterranean

Anatolia

Iranian Plateau

Pamirs

Kunlun Mountains

Yellow River

Yellow Sea

Japan

Madeira

Atlas Mountains

Sea

Zagros Mountains

Hindu Kush

△ K2 8611m

Plateau of Tibet

Kyushu

Canary Islands

S a h a r a

Libyan Desert

Syrian Desert

Indus

H i m a l a y a s

△ Mount Everest 8850m

Yangtze

East China Sea

Ryukyu Islands

Ahaggar

Nile

Red Sea

Persian Gulf

Ganges

Thar Desert

Taiwan

Tibesti

Arabian Peninsula

Deccan

Philippine Sea

A F R I C A

S a h e l

Niger

Ethiopian Highlands

Gulf of Aden

Arabian Sea

Western Ghats

Eastern Ghats

Bay of Bengal

Mekong

South China Sea

Philippine Islands

Philippine Trench

Mariana Islands

M Caro

Cape Verde Islands

Adamawa Highlands

Horn of Africa

Sri Lanka

Andaman Islands

Gulf of Guinea

Great Rift Valley

Lake Victoria

Maldive Islands

Nicobar Islands

Malay Peninsula

Borneo

Celebes

Congo

Congo Basin

Great Rift Valley

△ Kilimanjaro 5895m

Somali

Seychelles

Sumatra

E a s t   I n d i e s

New Guinea

A T L A N T I C

Ascension Island

Lake Tanganyika

Basin

Arabian Basin

Java Trench

Java Sea

Java

St Helena

Great Rift Valley

Lake Nyasa

I N D I A N

Timor Sea

Arafura Sea

O C E A N

Angola Basin

Zambezi

Mozambique Channel

Madagascar

Ninetyeast Ridge

Mauritius Réunion

Great Sandy Desert

G

Namib Desert

Kalahari Desert

O C E A N

AUSTRALIA

Cape Basin

Drakensberg

Great Victoria Desert

Mid-Atlantic Ridge

Cape of Good Hope

Southwest Indian Ridge

Nullarbor Plain

Tristan da Cunha Gough Island

Southeast Indian Ridge

Darlin

Kerguelen

Tasmani

Bas

Limit of winter pack ice

South Indian Basin

S O U T H E R N   O C E A N

A N T A R C T I C A

Limit of summer pack ice